SOMETHING ABOUT THE AUTHOR®

Something about
the Author *was named
an* **"Outstanding
Reference Source,"**
*the highest honor given
by the American
Library Association
Reference and Adult
Services Division.*

ISSN 0276-816X

something ABOUT THE AUTHOR®

Facts and Pictures about Authors
and Illustrators of Books for Young People

volume 121

GALE GROUP

Detroit
New York
San Francisco
London
Boston
Woodbridge, CT

STAFF

Scot Peacock, *Managing Editor, Literature Product*
Mark W. Scott, *Publisher, Literature Product*

iccrz

ty Balcer, Sara L. Constantakis, Kristen A. Dorsch, Lisa Kumar, Thomas M
, Motoko Fujishiro Huthwaite, Arlene M. Johnson, Michelle Poole, Thoma:
Harris, Jennifer Kilian, Maikue Vang, *Assistant Editors,* Anna Marie Dahr
Administrative Support, Joshua Kondek, Mary Ruby, *Technical Training Specialists*

Alan Hedblad, Joyce Nakamura, *Managing Editors*
Susan M. Trosky, *Literature Content Coordinator*

Victoria B. Cariappa, *Research Manager;* Tracie A. Richardson, *Project Coordinator;* Maureen Emeric, Barbara McNeil, Gary J. Oudersluys, Cheryl L. Warnock, *Research Specialists;* Sarah Genik, Ron Morelli, Tamara C. Nott, *Research Associates;* Nicodemus Ford, *Research Assistant;* Michelle Campbell, *Administrative Assistant*

Maria L. Franklin, *Permissions Manager;* Julie Juengling, *Permissions Associate*

Mary Beth Trimper, *Manager, Composition and Prepress;* Dorothy Maki, *Manufacturing Manager;* Stacy Melson, *Buyer*

Babara J. Yarrow, *Manager, Imaging and Multimedia Content;* Randy Bassett, *Imaging Supervisor;* Robert Duncan, Dan Newell, *Imaging Specialists;* Pamela A. Reed, *Imaging Coordinator;* Dean Dauphinais, *Senior Editor;* Robyn V. Young, *Project Manager;* Kelly A. Quin, *Editor*

Library of Congress Catalog Card Number 72-27107

ISBN 0-7876-4709-8
ISSN 0276-816X

Printed in the United States of America

10 9 8 7 6 5 4 3 2 1

Contents

Authors in Forthcoming Volumes

Below are some of the authors and illustrators that will be featured in upcoming volumes of *SATA*. These include new entries on the swiftly rising stars of the field, as well as completely revised and updated entries (indicated with *) on some of the most notable and best-loved creators of books for children.

Virginia Aronson: After graduating from college, Aronson began a writing career based on two of her interests: long-distance running and vegetarianism. Today, in addition to her general health titles, Aronson has written a number of young adult nonfiction books, including *The History of Motown* and a biography of tennis stars Venus and Serena Williams.

Ehud Ben-Ezer: For over forty years, Israeli author Ben-Ezer has written novels, plays, short stories, and works for children. In 1997, his book *Hosni the Dreamer: An Arabian Tale* was released to great critical acclaim. The story tells of a young shepherd boy whose faith in both himself and poetry is ultimately rewarded.

James P. Delgado: In addition to his career as a writer, Delgado serves as executive director of the Vancouver Maritime Museum and co-host of *The Sea Hunters,* a National Geographic weekly television series. Delgado has used his expertise as a maritime archaeologist to write several acclaimed books, including *Shipwrecks from the Westward Movement* and *Native American Shipwrecks.*

David Elliot: Elliot's career as an illustrator began when he sketched pencil drawings of animals at the Edinburgh Zoo in Scotland. After returning to his native New Zealand, Elliot became a full-time children's author and illustrator. His popular books include *Arthur's Star* and *Sydney and the Seamonster.*

*Rosa Guy: Guy is a prolific and acclaimed Caribbean American author whose writing career began more than fifty years ago. She is best known for her novels that depict both the struggles and triumphs of inner-city black American youth. Among Guy's numerous writing honors are the Coretta Scott King Award, which she won in 1982 for *Mother Crocodile*, and a 1983 Parents' Choice Award for *New Guys Around the Block.*

Jonathan Langley: English artist and writer Langley has provided illustrations for such classic children's books as *The Wind in the Willows* and *The Wizard of Oz.* Langley also illustrates his own books for young readers. In 1998, he received the *Parents* magazine Best Illustrated Book Award for his work in Michael Rosen's *SNORE!*

Amy Littlesugar: Littlesugar is a writer who has found success with her unique style of creating fictionalized accounts of actual people and events. Her writings include *Marie in Fourth Position*, a fictional rendering of the chorus girl immortalized in Degas's sculpture, *The Little Dancer*, and *Freedom School, Yes!*, the story of a black child in Mississippi who attends school for the first time during the turbulent 1960s civil rights movement.

*Kyoko Mori: An award-winning poet and novelist, Mori is a Japanese American author whose writing has been strongly influenced by her mother's suicide when Mori was just twelve years old. Mori's 1993 book *Shizuko's Daughter* is a fictional account of her mother's death, and received numerous awards and commendations, including a *Publishers Weekly* Editor's Choice citation and a *New York Times* Notable Book award.

Rodman Philbrick: A screenwriter as well as a novelist, Philbrick started his career as an author of adult thrillers before shifting his interest to young adult fiction. Philbrick's novels for adolescents include *The Fire Pony*, *The Last Book in the Universe*, and the incredibly popular *Freak the Mighty*, which was produced as a motion picture in 1998.

*Ellen Wittlinger: Wittlinger is a novelist, poet, and playwright best known for her coming-of-age books for young adults. Most of Wittlinger's protagonists are sensitive and lovable misfits who experience romantic love for the first time. Wittlinger received a Printz honor book citation for her 1999 work *Hard Love.*

*Ed Young: Young is an acclaimed illustrator who often finds inspiration in the folklore of his native China. He has received many honors for his work, including the Caldecott Medal in 1990 for his picture book, *Lon Po Po.* In 2000, Young illustrated *The Hunter: A Chinese Folktale* by Mary Casanova.

Introduction

Something about the Author (SATA) is an ongoing reference series that examines the lives and works of authors and illustrators of books for children. *SATA* includes not only well-known writers and artists but also less prominent individuals whose works are just coming to be recognized. This series is often the only readily available information source on emerging authors and illustrators. You'll find *SATA* informative and entertaining, whether you are a student, a librarian, an English teacher, a parent, or simply an adult who enjoys children's literature.

What's Inside SATA

SATA provides detailed information about authors and illustrators who span the full time range of children's literature, from early figures like John Newbery and L. Frank Baum to contemporary figures like Judy Blume and Richard Peck. Authors in the series represent primarily English-speaking countries, particularly the United States, Canada, and the United Kingdom. Also included, however, are authors from around the world whose works are available in English translation. The writings represented in *SATA* include those created intentionally for children and young adults as well as those written for a general audience and known to interest younger readers. These writings cover the entire spectrum of children's literature, including picture books, humor, folk and fairy tales, animal stories, mystery and adventure, science fiction and fantasy, historical fiction, poetry and nonsense verse, drama, biography, and nonfiction.

Obituaries are also included in *SATA* and are intended not only as death notices but also as concise overviews of people's lives and work. Additionally, each edition features newly revised and updated entries for a selection of *SATA* listees who remain of interest to today's readers and who have been active enough to require extensive revisions of their earlier biographies.

New Autobiography Feature

Beginning with Volume 103, *SATA* features three or more specially commissioned autobiographical essays in each volume. These unique essays, averaging about ten thousand words in length and illustrated with an abundance of personal photos, present an entertaining and informative first-person perspective on the lives and careers of prominent authors and illustrators profiled in *SATA*.

Two Convenient Indexes

In response to suggestions from librarians, *SATA* indexes no longer appear in every volume but are included in alternate (odd-numbered) volumes of the series, beginning with Volume 57.

SATA continues to include two indexes that cumulate with each alternate volume: the Illustrations Index, arranged by the name of the illustrator, gives the number of the volume and page where the illustrator's work appears in the current volume as well as all preceding volumes in the series; the Author Index gives the number of the volume in which a person's biographical sketch, autobiographical essay, or obituary appears in the current volume as well as all preceding volumes in the series.

These indexes also include references to authors and illustrators who appear in Gale's *Yesterday's Authors of Books for Children, Children's Literature Review,* and *Something about the Author Autobiography Series.*

Easy-to-Use Entry Format

Whether you're already familiar with the *SATA* series or just getting acquainted, you will want to be aware of the kind of information that an entry provides. In every *SATA* entry the editors attempt to give as complete a picture of the person's life and work as possible. A typical entry in *SATA* includes the following clearly labeled information sections:

• *PERSONAL:* date and place of birth and death, parents' names and occupations, name of spouse, date of marriage, names of children, educational institutions attended, degrees received, religious and political affiliations, hobbies and other interests.

• *ADDRESSES:* complete home, office, electronic mail, and agent addresses, whenever available.

• *CAREER:* name of employer, position, and dates for each career post; art exhibitions; military service; memberships and offices held in professional and civic organizations.

• *AWARDS, HONORS:* literary and professional awards received.

• *WRITINGS:* title-by-title chronological bibliography of books written and/or illustrated, listed by genre when known; lists of other notable publications, such as plays, screenplays, and periodical contributions.

• *ADAPTATIONS:* a list of films, television programs, plays, CD-ROMs, recordings, and other media presentations that have been adapted from the author's work.

• *WORK IN PROGRESS:* description of projects in progress.

• *SIDELIGHTS:* a biographical portrait of the author or illustrator's development, either directly from the biographee—and often written specifically for the *SATA* entry—or gathered from diaries, letters, interviews, or other published sources.

• *BIOGRAPHICAL AND CRITICAL SOURCES:* cites sources quoted in "Sidelights" along with references for further reading.

• *EXTENSIVE ILLUSTRATIONS:* photographs, movie stills, book illustrations, and other interesting visual materials supplement the text.

How a SATA Entry Is Compiled

A *SATA* entry progresses through a series of steps. If the biographee is living, the *SATA* editors try to secure information directly from him or her through a questionnaire. From the information that the biographee supplies, the editors prepare an entry, filling in any essential missing details with research and/or telephone interviews. If possible, the author or illustrator is sent a copy of the entry to check for accuracy and completeness.

If the biographee is deceased or cannot be reached by questionnaire, the *SATA* editors examine a wide variety of published sources to gather information for an entry. Biographical and bibliographic sources are consulted, as are book reviews, feature articles, published interviews, and material sometimes obtained from the biographee's family, publishers, agent, or other associates.

Entries that have not been verified by the biographees or their representatives are marked with an asterisk (*).

Contact the Editor

We encourage our readers to examine the entire *SATA* series. Please write and tell us if we can make *SATA* even more helpful to you. Give your comments and suggestions to the editor:

BY MAIL: Editor, *Something about the Author,* The Gale Group, 27500 Drake Rd., Farmington Hills, MI 48331-3535.

BY TELEPHONE: (800) 877-GALE

BY FAX: (248) 699-8054

Something about the Author Product Advisory Board

The editors of *Something about the Author* are dedicated to maintaining a high standard of excellence by publishing comprehensive, accurate, and highly readable entries on a wide array of writers for children and young adults. In addition to the quality of the content, the editors take pride in the graphic design of the series, which is intended to be orderly yet inviting, allowing readers to utilize the pages of *SATA* easily and with efficiency. Despite the longevity of the *SATA* print series, and the success of its format, we are mindful that the vitality of a literary reference product is dependent on its ability to serve its users over time. As literature, and attitudes about literature, constantly evolve, so do the reference needs of students, teachers, scholars, journalists, researchers, and book club members. To be certain that we continue to keep pace with the expectations of our customers, the editors of *SATA* listen carefully to their comments regarding the value, utility, and quality of the series. Librarians, who have firsthand knowledge of the needs of library users, are a valuable resource for us. The *Something about the Author* Product Advisory Board, made up of school, public, and academic librarians, is a forum to promote focused feedback about *SATA* on a regular basis. The five-member advisory board includes the following individuals, whom the editors wish to thank for sharing their expertise:

- **Eva M. Davis,** Teen Services Librarian, Plymouth District Library, Plymouth, Michigan

- **Joan B. Eisenberg,** Lower School Librarian, Milton Academy, Milton, Massachusetts

- **Francisca Goldsmith,** Teen Services Librarian, Berkeley Public Library, Berkeley, California

- **Monica F. Irlbacher,** Young Adult Librarian, Middletown Thrall Library, Middletown, New York

- **Caryn Sipos,** Librarian--Young Adult Services, King County Library System, Washington

Acknowledgments

Grateful acknowledgment is made to the following publishers, authors, and artists whose works appear in this volume.

ARDLEY, NEIL (RICHARD). Streeter, Clive, illustrator. From a cover of *The Science Book of Air* by Neil Ardley. Harcourt, Brace & Company, 1991. Illustrations copyright © 1991 by Dorling Kindersley Limited. Reproduced by permission of publisher.

ASHBY, YVONNE. Ashby, Yvonne, photograph. Reproduced by permission of Yvonne Ashby.

AYER, ELEANOR H. Cover of *Parallel Journeys* by Eleanor H. Ayer. Atheneum, 1995. Copyright © 1995 by Helen H. Ayer. Reproduced by permission of Atheneum an imprint of Simon & Schuster Macmillan.

BARBOUR, KAREN. From an illustration in *A Sip of Aesop* by Jane Yolen. Scholastic, 1995. Illustrations copyright © 1995 Karen Barbour. All rights reserved. Reproduced by permission of the publisher.

BERGUM, CONSTANCE R. Bergum, Constance R., photograph. Reproduced by permission./ From an illustration in *Seya's Song* by Ron Hirschi. Sasquatch Books, 1992. Illustrations copyright © 1992 by Constance R. Bergum. Reproduced by permission./ From an illustration in *Grandma Buffalo, May and Me* by Carol Curtis Stilz. Sasquatch Books, 1995. Illustrations copyright © 1995 by Constance R. Bergum. Reproduced by permission.

BOERST, WILLIAM J. Boerst, William J., photograph. Timeless Studios. Reproduced by permission of William J. Boerst.

BONNER, MIKE. Bonner, Mike, photograph. Reproduced by permission of Mike Bonner.

BOTTNER, BARBARA. All photographs reproduced by permission.

BRACKETT, VIRGINIA (ROBERTS MEREDITH). Brackett, Virginia, photograph. Reproduced by permission of Virginia Brackett.

BROOKS, MARTHA. Pederson, Judy, illustrator. From a cover of *Two Moons in August* by Martha Brooks. Ground Wood Books, 1991. Reproduced by permission of Douglas & McIntyre Ltd./ Brooks, Martha, photograph. Groundwood/ Douglas & McIntyre Books Ltd. Reproduced by permission of Martha Brooks.

BRUST, STEVEN K. (ZOLTAN). Brust, Steven K., photograph by David Dyer-Bennett. Reproduced by permission of Steven K. Brust./ A cover of *Freedom & Necessity* by Emma Bull and Steven K. Brust. Reproduced by permission of Steven K. Brust.

BUTLER, CHARLES (CADMAN). Benioff, Carol, illustrator. From a cover of *The Darkling* by Charles Butler. Margaret K. McElderry Books, 1998. Copyright © 1998 by Charles Butler. Reproduced by permission of Margaret K. McElderry Books an imprint of Simon & Schuster Macmillan.

CADNUM, MICHAEL. Cadnum, Michael, photograph. Copyright © by Robert Mewton. Reproduced by the permission of the author./ Steadman, Broek, illustrator. From a cover of *Breaking the Fall* by Michael Cadnum. Puffin Books, 1994. Cover illustration © Broek Steadman, 1994. Reproduced by permission of Penguin Books Ltd./ Binger, Bill, illustrator. From a cover of *Ghostwright* by Bill Binger. Carroll & Graf, 1993. Reproduced by permission.

CLEARY, BEVERLY (ATLEE BUNN). Cleary, Beverly, photograph by Patricia Clap. Reproduced by permission of Patricia Clap./ Illustration by Louis Darling. From *Ramona the Pest,* by Beverly Cleary. William Morrow, 1968. Copyright © 1968 by Beverly Cleary. All rights reserved. Reproduced by permission of William Morrow and Company./ Tiegreen, Alan, illustrator. From a cover of *Ramona and Her Father* by Beverly Cleary. Avon Camelot, 1990. Copyright © 1975, 1977 by Beverly Cleary. Reproduced by permission of HarperCollins Publishers./Tiegreen, Alan, illustrator. From a cover of *Ramona Quimby, Age 8* by Beverly Cleary. Avon Books, 1981. Copyright © 1981 by Beverly Cleary. Reproduced by permission of HarperCollins Publishers.

COLLINS, DAVID R(AYMOND). Collins, David R., photograph. Reproduced by permission of David R. Collins./ A cover of *Write a Book For Me: The Story of Marguerite Henry* by David R. Collins. Morgan Reynolds, Inc., 1999. Copyright © 1999 by David R. Collins. Reproduced by permission./ From *Tales For Hard Times* by David R. Collins. Copyright 1990 by David R. Collins. Illustrations by David Mataya. Published by Carolrhoda Books, Inc. A division of The Lerner Publishing Group. Reproduced by the permission of the publisher. All Rights Reserved./ Nolte, Larry, illustrator. From a cover of *Tiger Woods: Golfing Champion* by David R. Collins. Pelican Publishing, 1999. Illustrations copyright © 1999 by Larry Nolte. Reproduced by permission/ Nolte, Larry, illustrator. From an illustration in *Casimir Pulaski: Soldier on Horseback* by David R. Collins. Pelican, 1997. Illustrations copyright © 1997 by Larry Nolte. Reproduced by permission.

something about the author

ARDLEY, Neil (Richard) 1937-

Personal

Born May 26, 1937, in Wallington, Surrey, England; son of Sydney Vivian (a clerk) and Alma Mary (Rutty) Ardley; married Bridget Mary Gantley (a researcher), September 3, 1960; children: Jane Catherine. *Education:* University of Bristol, B.Sc., 1959. *Hobbies and other interests:* Musical composition.

Addresses

Home—Lathkill House, Youlgrave, Derbyshire DE4 1WL, England. *Office*—13a Priory Ave., London W4, England.

Career

World Book Encyclopedia, London, England, editor, 1962-66; Hamlyn Publishing Group, London, editor, 1967-68; full-time writer. *Member:* Royal Society of Arts (fellow).

Awards, Honors

Science Book Prize and Times Educational Senior Information Book Award, both 1989, both for *The Way Things Work.*

Writings

FOR CHILDREN

(Editor and adapter) *How Birds Behave* (adapted from John Sparks's *Bird Behavior*), Hamlyn Publishing Group, 1969, Grosset, 1971.

Atlas of Space, Macdonald Educational, 1970.

Experiments with Heat, Wolfe Publishing, 1970.

What Do You Know?, Hamlyn Publishing Group, 1972.

(Editor) Elizabeth S. Austin and Oliver L. Austin, *The Look-It-Up Book of Birds,* revised edition, Collins, 1973.

The Earth and Beyond, Macmillan, 1974.

Countries and Homes, Macmillan, 1974.

Birds, Sampson Low, 1975, Warwick Press, 1976, revised edition, 1982.

Atoms and Energy, Sampson Low, 1975, Warwick Press, 1976, revised edition, 1982.

Purnell's Find Out about Wonders of the World, Purnell Books, 1976.

(Editor) Vaclav Kvapil, *Exploring the Universe,* Hamlyn Publishing Group, 1976.

The Amazing World of Machines, Angus & Robertson, 1977.

Let's Look at Birds, Ward Lock, 1977, Derrydale, 1979.

Man and Space, Macdonald Educational, 1978.

The Scientific World, Pan Books, 1978.

Know Your Underwater Exploration, Rand McNally, 1978, published in England as *Underwater Exploration,* Purnell Books, 1978.

Musical Instruments, Macmillan, 1978, Silver Burdett, 1980.

People and Homes, Macmillan, 1978.

Neil Ardley teaches basic principles of air and flight with simple experiments. (Cover photo by Clive Streeter.)

Guide to Birds, Pan Books, 1979.
Purnell's Find Out about Birds, Purnell Books, 1979.
Stars, Macdonald Educational, 1980, Silver Burdett, 1981.
Our World of Nature: A First Picture Encyclopedia, Purnell Books, 1981.
(With wife Bridget Ardley) *One Thousand One Questions and Answers,* Kingfisher Books, 1981.
Nature, illustrated by Chris Shields, Pan Books, 1981.
Transport on Earth, F. Watts, 1981.
Out into Space, F. Watts, 1981.
Tomorrow's Home, F. Watts, 1981.
At School, Work, and Play, F. Watts, 1981.
Our Future Needs, F. Watts, 1982.
Health and Medicine, F. Watts, 1982.
Future War and Weapons, F. Watts, 1982.
Fact or Fantasy, F. Watts, 1982.
Computers, Warwick Press, 1983.
Working with Water, F. Watts, 1983.
Using the Computer, F. Watts, 1983.
My Favourite Encyclopedia of Science, Hamlyn Publishing Group, 1983.
Hot and Cold, F. Watts, 1983.
Sun and Light, F. Watts, 1983.
First Look at Computers, F. Watts, 1983.
Making Metric Measurements, F. Watts, 1984, published in England as *Making Measurements,* F. Watts, 1984.
Exploring Magnetism, F. Watts, 1984.
Making Things Move, F. Watts, 1984.
Discovering Electricity, F. Watts, 1984.

Air and Flight, F. Watts, 1984.
Sound and Music, F. Watts, 1984.
Simple Chemistry, F. Watts, 1984.
Force and Strength, F. Watts, 1984.
How Things Work, Silver Burdett, 1984.
ZX Spectrum and User Guide, Dorling Kindersley, 1984.
The Science of Energy, Macmillan, 1985.
Music: An Illustrated Encyclopedia, Hamlyn Publishing Group, 1987.
My Own Science Encyclopedia, Hamlyn Publishing Group, 1987.
Exploring the Universe, Macmillan, 1987.
The Inner Planets, Macmillan, 1987.
The Outer Planets, Macmillan, 1987.
(With David Macaulay) *The Way Things Work,* Houghton, 1988.
(With wife Bridget Ardley) *Skin, Hair and Teeth,* Macmillan, 1988.
The World of the Atom, F. Watts, 1989.
Music, Knopf, 1989.
(With wife Bridget Ardley) *India,* Macmillan, 1989.
(With wife Bridget Ardley) *Greece,* Macmillan, 1989.
Twentieth-Century Science, Wayland, 1989.
(With David West) *The Giant Book of the Human Body,* Hamlyn Publishing Group, 1989.
Bridges, Macmillan, 1989.
Dams, Macmillan, 1989.
Oil Rigs, Macmillan, 1989.
Language and Communications, F. Watts, 1989.
Sound Waves to Music, Gloucester Press, 1990.
Wings and Things, Puffin Books, 1990.
Snap Happy, Puffin Books, 1990.
Tune In, Puffin Books, 1991.
Bits and Chips, Puffin Books, 1991.
Light, Heinemann, 1991, Macmillan, 1992.
The Science Book of Light, Harcourt, 1991.
The Science Book of Water, Harcourt, 1991.
The Science Book of Colour, Harcourt, 1991.
The Science Book of Air, Harcourt, 1991.
The Science Book of Things That Grow, Harcourt, 1991.
The Science Book of Magnets, Harcourt, 1991.
The Science Book of Sound, Harcourt, 1991.
The Science Book of Electricity, Harcourt, 1991.
The Science Book of the Senses, Harcourt, 1992.
The Science Book of Machines, Harcourt, 1992.
The Science Book of Hot and Cold, Harcourt, 1992.
The Science Book of Energy, Harcourt, 1992.
The Science Book of Weather, Harcourt, 1992.
The Science Book of Numbers, Harcourt, 1992.
The Science Book of Motion, Harcourt, 1992.
The Science Book of Gravity, Harcourt, 1992.
Heat, Simon & Schuster, 1992.
101 Great Science Experiments, Dorling Kindersley, 1993.
Dictionary of Science: 2,000 Key Words Arranged Thematically, DK Publishing, 1995.
A Young Person's Guide to Music: A Listener's Guide, DK Publishing, 1995.
How Things Work: 100 Ways Parents and Kids Can Share the Secrets of Technology, Reader's Digest Association, 1995.
Jets, DK Publishing, 1997.

(With David Macaulay) *The New Way Things Work,* Houghton, 1998.

Electricity, Simon & Schuster, 1999.

Music, DK Publishing, 2000.

Science, DK Publishing, 2000.

FOR ADULTS

(Editor) Arrigo Polillo, *Jazz: A Guide to the History and Development of Jazz and Jazz Musicians,* Hamlyn/American, 1969.

Birds of Towns, Almark Publishing, 1975.

Birds of the Country, Almark Publishing, 1975.

Birds of Coasts, Lakes, and Rivers, Almark Publishing, 1976.

(With Brian Hawkes) *Bird-Watching,* Macdonald Educational, 1978.

Bird Life, Sackett & Marshall, 1978.

Birds of Britain and Europe, Ward Lock, 1978.

(With Ian Ridpath) *The Universe,* Silver Burdett, 1978.

Illustrated Guide to Birds and Birdwatching, Kingfisher Books, 1980.

(With Robin Kerrod) *The World of Science,* Macdonald & Co., 1982.

Contributor to *Our World Encyclopedia, Joy of Knowledge Encyclopedia, Collins Music Encyclopedia, Caxton Yearbook, Children's Britannica, The Biographical Dictionary of Scientists (Physicists),* and *The Children's Illustrated Encyclopedia.*

Sidelights

Neil Ardley is a British writer with over one hundred books to his credit. His far-ranging interests have taken him from nonfiction titles on birding and jazz to all aspects of science. Though he has written titles for an adult audience, the vast majority of his work is aimed at juvenile readers, with numerous titles in Watts's "Action Science" series as well as in Harcourt's "The Science Book of ..." series. Recognized for his clear and concise informational approach, Ardley generally focuses on a hands-on technique, employing simple experiments in his books to demonstrate larger scientific truths.

Born in Surrey, England, in 1937, Ardley grew up during World War II and attended the University of Bristol, where he earned a bachelor's degree in science in 1959. From 1962 to 1966 he was an editor of the *World Book Encyclopedia;* then he worked as an editor for a time at a British publishing house before turning to writing full time in 1969. Ardley once commented, "My experience with the *World Book Encyclopedia* gave me an appreciation of the necessity to express ideas clearly and concisely. In my information books, I've tried to link this to a sense of wonder at the marvels of the world."

Ardley has spent over three decades doing precisely that, and his books on topics from building bridges to computers to the why's of weather attest to his own curiosity vis-a-vis the natural world. Sylvia S. Marantz,

writing in *School Library Journal,* described as "mind-boggling" the broad range of questions Ardley answers in his 1984 title, *How Things Work.* In this book, Ardley tackles the mechanics of everything from a refrigerator to the human body. "Students can look up a machine, manufacturing operation or even body part in the index," Marantz explained, "and be referred to a clear picture and explanation." In his *Computers,* Ardley took on that complex topic in a "detailed approach to the subject," according to John Brown in a *School Librarian* review. Ardley looks at the history of computers, their applications, and their internal architecture and processes in a "clearly written text with broader scope than most books on the subject written for children," according to Zena Sutherland in the *Bulletin of the Center for Children's Books.* In *The World of the Atom* Ardley turned his nonfiction lens on the building blocks of matter, dealing with concepts such as elements, compounds, crystals, radioactivity, and nuclear energy. Godfrey Hall, writing in *School Librarian,* noted in particular a "fascinating section on solutions" and "an excellent glossary." Hall concluded, "This is the kind of book which would be useful on its own, or as part of the series."

Ardley has written for several series, most prominently in the "Action Science" and "The Science Book of ..." collections. The former series is aimed at primary school students and provides simple experiments to accompany science facts. In *Working with Water,* for example, students can float an egg, make a siphon, or show how water has a skin to it. "Each experiment is described and illustrated very carefully," observed a reviewer for *Junior Bookshelf,* "and the last paragraph in each case gives the scientific explanation for the results." The same reviewer pointed out that such experiments entail a "minimum of equipment, are not messy and yet are fascinating with practical applications." In *Hot and Cold* and *Sun and Light,* Ardley continues this winning combination of fact and hands-on projects. "The experiments are, for the most part, written in a clear, easy-to-follow style," noted Gale P. Jackson in a *School Library Journal* review of both volumes. Ardley's *Exploring Magnetism* and *Making Metric Measurements* "will motivate curious students to further investigation," noted Andrea Antico in *School Library Journal,* and *Booklist* contributor Karen Stars Hanley felt that *Making Metric Measurements* would be "a handy source of project ideas and inspiration" for students in the middle grades. Hanley concluded, "As with other titles in the Action Science series, the scientific explanation underlying each experiment is highlighted, and emphasis is placed on sound methodology." A reviewer for *Junior Bookshelf* thought that Ardley's *Making Things Move* for the same series "is a book to interest all children, not just those who are forever experimenting." Denise M. Wilms, reviewing Ardley's *Making Things Move* and *Discovering Electricity* in *Booklist,* wrote that the "strength of these experiments and activities lies in their simplicity: they can be done easily by a child alone or in a group." In *Air and Flight* and *Sound and Music* Ardley provides the same hands-on approach to these subjects. Antico wrote in a *School Library Journal* review that "these readable, colorful books will motivate young scientists." Reviewing several volumes in the series, including *Air and Flight,* Robert H. Cordella noted in *Science Books and Films* that each book "is well written, well illustrated, and well bound."

Another popular effort from Ardley is "The Science Book of . . . " series. These books are similar in format and in projected audience to the "Action Science" series, but they substitute color photographs for the drawings found in the earlier titles. Each title in "The Science Book of . . . " series includes from ten to fourteen experiments on the subject at hand and employ common household items in most cases. Numbered, step-by-step instructions take the young scientist through each experiment or activity, with each step carefully photographed. "All of the volumes begin with appropriate cautions about safety measures, and include special warning symbols for any steps that require caution and/or adult help," noted Susan L. Rogers in a *School Library Journal* review of *The Science Book of Air* and several other titles in the series. Rogers also praised the multi-ethnic mix of youngsters portrayed in the illustrations as well as the fact that the books "demonstrate a useful balance of action and knowledge." A reviewer for *Science Books and Films* also noted the "hands-on" approach to the books in the series, calling the experiments "exciting." Such experiments will, the reviewer concluded, "produce satisfying, tangible results that will spark continuing interest in science." *Booklist* critic Carolyn Phelan, reviewing several titles in the series, including *The Science Book of Air,* felt that "this is one of the more attractive series of science experiment books to appear lately." Phelan also noted that most of the equipment for the experiments in the books would be "readily available in the average household."

Yet another popular series for which Ardley has contributed titles is "The Way It Works" books from Macmillan. These books introduce middle graders to scientific topics from electricity to heat and light. Combining color photos with simple, clear text, the series attempts to make technology comprehensible to young readers. Small boxes on each page also highlight information and provide interesting facts. Leigh Riesenfeld, reviewing Ardley's *Light* in *Appraisal: Science Books for Young People,* felt that it "provided clear answers to some questions that I am frequently asked, for example, What is a Hologram? How does a laser work? What is radar?" Engineering and construction practices are introduced in the "How We Build Series" to which Ardley contributed several volumes, including *Bridges, Dams,* and *Oil Rigs.* Reviewing the entire group of books, Susan Penny wrote in *School Library Journal* that the series was "well-conceived" and the "information is well organized and is presented concisely in nontechnical language." A historical overview introduces each topic, and then the building process itself is described along with science experiments that relate to each step in the construction.

Ardley has also taken his experimental approach to science as a whole with his 1993 *101 Great Science Experiments.* This book includes activities grouped in eleven topical divisions, such as air and gasses, light, color, senses, electricity, and others. "School and public libraries will do parents and children a great favor by adding *101 Great Science Experiments* to their collections," commented James Rettla in *Wilson Library Bulletin.* Denia Hester, reviewing the same title in *Booklist,* declared, "What makes this book special is the clean, simple format with equally simple instructions." Gary A. Griess, reviewing *101 Great Science Experiments* in *Science Books and Films,* felt that "[a]mong several books of this type, [Ardley's] ranks high because of the simplicity of the materials it requires, as well as its ease of execution, quality of illustrations, and accuracy of information." Other general reference science and fact books from Ardley include *Dictionary of Science,* which defines over two thousand chemistry and physics terms, and the award-winning *The Way Things Work* and *The New Way Things Work,* both in collaboration with David Macaulay, the latter being "a sure bet for both adult and juvenile collections," according to *Booklist*'s Stephanie Zvirin.

Ardley is also a musician, both composing music and playing the synthesizer. One of his earliest books for adults was a jazz history and directory. For juveniles, he has also demonstrated his love for music in the 1987 title *Music: An Illustrated Encyclopedia,* as well as in the 1995 book *A Young Person's Guide to Music.* The former title is "an excellent addition to any music shelf and a great gift for any music lover," according to Barbara Jo McKee in *Voice of Youth Advocates.* In *A Young Person's Guide to Music* Ardley focuses on classical music and uses an accompanying CD to illustrate the music discussed. *Booklist*'s Phelan opined that "this book offers music students a wide range of options," from a study of musical instruments to a survey of classical music from ancient through baroque and on to modern. Phelan further commented that the book is a "rich resource for young people who want to understand orchestral music." Tim Moses, reviewing the same title for *Boston Book Review* online, concluded that "this book is an excellent guide to understanding one of mankind's oldest and greatest art forms."

Ardley, in the decades he has been writing children's books, has tackled a wide range of topics. Whether explicating the make-up of the atom, or describing how to build a bridge, or explaining how to play a French horn, he has continually demonstrated that concision and clarity are the best tools in the nonfiction writer's workshop.

Biographical and Critical Sources

BOOKS

The New Grove Dictionary of Jazz, St. Martin's Press, 1994.

PERIODICALS

Appraisal: Science Books for Young People, winter, 1992, p. 79; winter, 1993, Leigh Riesenfeld, review of *Light,* pp. 87-88; winter-spring, 1996, pp. 8-9.

Booklist, June 1, 1984, Karen Stars Hanley, review of *Making Metric Measurements,* p. 1395; October 1, 1984, Denise M. Wilms, review of *Making Things Move* and *Discovering Electricity,* p. 214; September 1, 1985, p. 637; May 15, 1989, p. 1642; March 1, 1991, Carolyn Phelan, review of *The Science Book of Air* and others, p. 1381; February 1, 1994, Denia Hester, review of *101 Great Science Experiments,* p. 1003; October 15, 1995, p. 414; December 15, 1995, Carolyn Phelan, review of *A Young Person's Guide to Music,* p. 694; December 1, 1998, Stephanie Zvirin, review of *The New Way Things Work,* p. 674.

Bulletin of the Center for Children's Books, June, 1984, Zena Sutherland, review of *Computers,* p. 101.

Chicago Tribune Book World, March 18, 1984, p. 30.

Horn Book Guide, fall, 1991, p. 294; spring, 1992, p. 98; spring, 1993, p. 103; spring, 1994, p. 116; spring, 1996, p. 328; fall, 1996, p. 125.

Junior Bookshelf, December, 1983, review of *Working with Water,* p. 240; March, 1984, review of *Making Things Move,* p. 123; June, 1988, p. 133; June, 1990, p. 139.

New Scientist, November 21, 1992, p. 45C.

Publishers Weekly, October 23, 1995, p. 70.

RQ, summer, 1996, p. 567.

School Librarian, March, 1984, John Brown, review of *Computers,* pp. 267-268; March, 1989, Godfrey Hall, review of *The World of the Atom,* p. 107.

School Library Journal, March, 1984, Gale P. Jackson, review of *Sun and Light* and *Hot and Cold,* p. 153; June, 1984, p. 79; September, 1984, Sylvia S. Marantz, review of *How Things Work,* pp. 75-76; September, 1984, Andrea Antico, review of *Making Measurements* and *Exploring Magnetism,* p. 112; April, 1985, Andrea Antico, review of *Sound and Music* and *Air and Flight,* p. 84; July, 1985, p. 173; March, 1991, Susan Penny, review of *Bridges* and others, p. 198; May, 1991, Susan L. Rogers, review of *The Science Book of Air* and others, pp. 96, 98; August, 1992, p. 150; March, 1993, p. 203; August, 1996, p. 112.

Science Books and Films, March-April, 1986, p. 226; January-February, 1986, Robert H. Cordella, review of *Air and Flight* and others, pp. 162-163; March, 1992, p. 50; April, 1994, Gary A. Griess, review of *101 Great Science Experiments,* p. 79; June-July, 1995, review of "The Science Book of ..." series, pp. 129-130.

Times Educational Supplement, November 19, 1989, p. 34; November 8, 1991, p. 32; February 7, 1992, p. 34; November 24, 1995, p. 15.

Voice of Youth Advocates, June, 1987, Barbara Jo McKee, review of *Music: An Illustrated Encyclopedia,* p. 95.

Washington Post Book World, May 14, 1989, p. 20.

Wilson Library Bulletin, March, 1994, James Rettla, review of *101 Great Science Experiments,* p. 94.

ON-LINE

Boston Book Review, http://bookwire.bowker.com/ (March 3, 2000).*

—*Sketch by J. Sydney Jones*

* * *

ASHBY, Yvonne 1955-

Personal

Born December 6, 1955, in Adelaide, South Australia; daughter of Laszlo George (a building contractor) and Charlotte Elizabeth (Schmidt) Ory; married Mark Leonard Ashby (a teacher), December 13, 1980; children: Lisel May Ashby, Alice Hope Ashby. *Education:* Loreto College, Advanced Certificate in Interior Design, 1976, Diploma of Graphic Design, 1980. *Religion:* Roman Catholic. *Hobbies and other interests:* Social justice issues.

Addresses

Home and office—17 Ayrbank Ave., Stonyfell, Adelaide, South Australia 5066. *Agent*—Omnibus Books, 52

Yvonne Ashby

Fullarton Rd., Norwood, South Australia, 5067. *E-mail*—yashby@hotmail.com.

Career

Self-employed artist, designer, illustrator, 1980—. Color consultant. Active in the Sovereign Military Hospitaller Order of St. John of Jerusalem of Rhodes and of Malta (DONAT).

Awards, Honors

"My Vision of Australia" Competition, winner (painting section), and National Winner, Order of Australia Association.

Writings

ILLUSTRATOR

Rodney Martin, *The Monster Alphabet,* ERA Publications, 1984, Ideals Publications, 1988.

Mary Diestel-Feddersen, *Try Again, Sally Jane,* ERA Publications, 1986.

Nadia Dwyer, *Matthew's Lemon Fish,* Lutheran Publishing House, 1992.

Helen Manthorpe, *Solo Bush Babies, Kangaroo,* Omnibus, 2000.

Helen Manthorpe, *Solo Bush Babies, Possum,* Omnibus, 2000.

Sidelights

Yvonne Ashby told *SATA:* "I have always loved drawing. As a child I was encouraged by my parents and grandparents and throughout my school career to realize I had a gift. I studied Interior Design but found the mechanical drawing procedures stifling. Through a love of children's books I studied graphic design where illustrating became my strongest and most favoured subject. Early in my career, I worked for publishing companies doing simple line illustrations and front covers ranging from cooking books to geographical publications. I have always loved the watercolour medium for books; however, my fine art paintings are usually executed in acrylic and gouache mediums. I believe I am on a journey of self-discovery and try not to let too many influences dictate my style; however, my favourite artists are from the Impressionist School. I love spontaneity and the *Solo Bush Babies* books fit into this category. My advice to new illustrators would be to maintain your integrity."

Biographical and Critical Sources

PERIODICALS

School Library Journal, October, 1987, Barbara Hutcheson, review of *Try Again, Sally Jane,* p. 110.

AYER, Eleanor H. 1947-

Personal

Born September 6, 1947, in Burlington, VT; daughter of William H. (a plumbing and heating contractor) and Shirley T. (an elementary school teacher; maiden name, Thomas) Hubbard; married John Ayer (a publisher); children: Madison, William. *Education:* Newhouse School of Journalism, Syracuse University, B.S., 1969, M.S., 1970.

Addresses

Home—Frederick, CO.

Career

Editor and freelance writer. Laubach Literacy Foundation, Syracuse, NY, associate editor for *News for You,* 1967-69, associate editor of New Readers Press, 1969-70; *Jackson Hole Guide,* Jackson, WY, assistant editor, 1971; Jende-Hagan (book distribution and publishing company), Frederick, CO, co-founder, editor, and marketing manager, 1972—; Pruett Publishing Company, Boulder, CO, production/promotion coordinator, 1972; Shields Publishing Company, Fort Collins, CO, production/promotion coordinator, 1973-74; Renaissance House Publishing Company, Frederick, editor and marketing manager, 1984—. Founder and writer for *The American Traveller* (travel guides), 1987—. *Member:* Society of Children's Book Writers and Illustrators, Rocky Mountain Book Publishers Association, Mountain and Plains Booksellers Association, Colorado Authors' League.

Awards, Honors

Top Hand Awards for young adult nonfiction, Colorado Authors' League, 1991, for *Teen Marriage,* and 1992, for *The Value of Determination;* Notable Children's Trade Book in the Field of Social Studies designation, Children's Book Council/National Council for the Social Studies, 1992, for *Margaret Bourke-White: Photographing the World;* Top Hand Award for specialty writing, Colorado Authors' League, 1992, for *Southwest Traveler: A Guide to the Anasazi and Other Ancient Southwest Indians.*

Writings

FOR YOUNG ADULTS; NONFICTION

Teen Marriage, Rosen (New York City), 1978.

Germany, Rourke, 1990.

The Value of Determination, Rosen (New York City), 1991.

Berlin ("Cities at War" series), Simon & Schuster (New York City), 1992.

Boris Yeltsin: Man of the People, Dillon (New York City), 1992.

Margaret Bourke-White: Photographing the World, Dillon, 1992.

Our Flag ("I Know America" series), Millbrook, 1992.

Our National Monuments ("I Know America" series), Millbrook, 1992.

The Anasazi, Walker, 1993.

Everything You Need to Know about Teen Fatherhood, Rosen (New York City), 1993.

Teen Suicide: Is It Too Painful to Grow Up?, Twenty-first Century Books/Holt (New York City), 1993.

Our Great Rivers and Waterways ("I Know America" series), Millbrook, 1994.

Ruth Bader Ginsburg: Fire and Steel on the Supreme Court, Dillon, 1994.

The United States Holocaust Memorial Museum: America Keeps the Memory Alive, Dillon, 1994.

Everything You Need to Know about Stress, Rosen (New York City), 1994.

Everything You Need to Know about Depression, Rosen (New York City), 1994.

(With Helen Waterford and Alfons Heck) *Parallel Journeys,* Atheneum (New York City), 1995.

Germany: In the Heartland of Europe ("Exploring Cultures of the World" series), Benchmark (Tarrytown, NY), 1996.

Poland: A Troubled Past, a New Start ("Exploring Cultures of the World" series), Benchmark (Tarrytown, NY), 1996.

Adolf Hitler ("The Importance of ..." series), Lucent (San Diego, CA), 1996.

Homeless Children ("Overview" series), Lucent (San Diego, CA), 1997.

Colorado ("Celebrate the States" series), Benchmark (New York City), 1997.

It's Okay to Say No: Choosing Sexual Abstinence ("Teen Pregnancy Prevention" series), Rosen (New York City), 1997.

Lewis Latimer: Creating Bright Ideas, Raintree/Steck-Vaughn (Austin, TX), 1997.

The Survivors ("Holocaust Library"), Lucent (San Diego, CA), 1998.

Charles Dickens ("The Importance of ..." series), Lucent (San Diego, CA), 1998.

Life as a Nazi Soldier ("The Way People Live" series), Lucent (San Diego, CA), 1998.

In the Ghettos: Teens Who Survived the Ghettos of the Holocaust, Rosen (New York City), 1999.

Teen Smoking ("Overview" series), Lucent (San Diego, CA), 1999.

NONFICTION; "COLORADO CHRONICLES" SERIES; ILLUSTRATED BY JANE KLINE

Famous Colorado Men, Renaissance House (Frederick, CO), 1980.

Famous Colorado Women, Renaissance House (Frederick, CO), 1981.

Indians of Colorado, Renaissance House (Frederick, CO), 1981.

Hispanic Colorado, Renaissance House (Frederick, CO), 1982.

Colorado Wildlife, Renaissance House (Frederick, CO), 1983.

(Editor) *Colorado Businesses,* Renaissance House (Frederick, CO), 1984.

(Editor) Suzanne Thumhart, *Colorado Wonders,* Renaissance House (Frederick, CO), 1986.

Colorado Chronicles Index, Renaissance House (Frederick, CO), 1986.

NONFICTION; "AMERICAN TRAVELER" SERIES

Colorado Traveler: Hall of Fame: A Gallery of the Rich and Famous, Renaissance House (Frederick, CO), 1987.

Colorado Traveler; Birds; A Guide to Colorado's Unique Varieties, Renaissance House (Frederick, CO), 1987.

Colorado Traveler: Parks and Monuments, Renaissance House (Frederick, CO), 1987.

Colorado Traveler: Colorado Wildflowers: A Guide to Colorado's Unique Varieties, Renaissance House (Frederick, CO), 1987.

Colorado Traveler: Colorado Wildlife: A Guide to Colorado's Unique Animals, Renaissance House (Frederick, CO), 1987.

Colorado Traveler: Skiing, Renaissance House (Frederick, CO), 1987.

Colorado Traveler: Discover Colorado, Renaissance House (Frederick, CO), 1988.

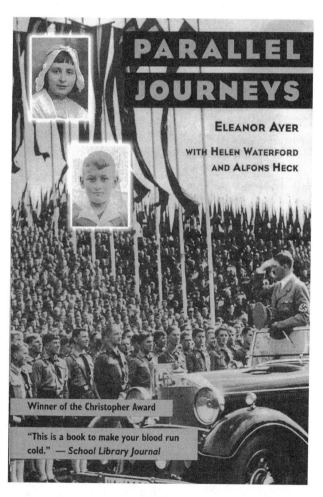

Eleanor H. Ayer parallels the true stories of Helen Waterford, a young German Jew who was sent to the Auschwitz death camp, and Alfons Heck, a teenage commander in the Hitler Youth.

Arizona Traveler: Birds of Arizona: A Guide to Unique Varieties, Renaissance House (Frederick, CO), 1988.

Arizona Traveler: Discover Arizona: The Grand Canyon State, Renaissance House (Frederick, CO), 1988.

Arizona Traveler: Arizona Wildflowers, Renaissance House (Frederick, CO), 1989.

Arizona Traveler: Indians of Arizona: A Guide to Arizona's Heritage, Renaissance House (Frederick, CO), 1990.

Southwest Traveler: A Guide to the Anasazi and Other Ancient Southwest Indians, Renaissance House (Frederick, CO), 1991.

Californian Traveler: Earthquake Country: Traveling California's Fault Lines, Renaissance House (Frederick, CO), 1992.

California Traveler: Parks and Monuments of California: A Scenic Guide, Renaissance House (Frederick, CO), 1992.

NONFICTION; "HOLOCAUST" SERIES

A Firestorm Unleashed: January 1942-June 1943, Blackbirch (Woodbridge, CT), 1998.

Inferno: July 1943-April 1945, Blackbirch (Woodbridge, CT), 1998.

(With Stephen D. Chicoine) *From the Ashes: May 1945 and After,* Blackbirch (Woodbridge, CT), 1998.

FICTION

Green Light on the Tipple, Platte 'N Press, 1978.

OTHER

Also author of revised editions of *Drug Abuse,* 1991, *Sexual Abuse,* 1992, and *Family Violence,* 1993, all published by Rosen; and editor of volumes in the "American Traveler" series, published by Renaissance House.

Sidelights

A woman with varied interests, Eleanor H. Ayer has spent much of her adult career making history come alive for students. From biographies such as *Ruth Bader Ginsberg: Fire and Steel on the Supreme Court* to self-help books for teens to guide books focusing on her home state of Colorado and other parts of the United States, Ayer brings a thorough understanding and the ability to provide food for thought to each of her subjects. Of special interest to the author is the Holocaust and the Nazi politics that precipitated it, having been the subject of several of Ayer's books. Among these is the critically praised 1998 work *The Survivors,* which discusses the emotional and physical aftereffects of the Holocaust on those who lived through the horror of Hitler's attempt to eliminate the Jews.

Born in Burlington, Vermont, in 1947, Ayer attended Syracuse University. Graduating with a degree in journalism in 1969, she went on to obtain her master's degree the following year before moving to the western United States to begin her career in writing and publishing. After working for several different publishers in both Wyoming and Colorado, Ayer joined Renaissance House Publishing Company in 1984, where she

worked on a series of books that included *Indians of Colorado* and *Colorado Businesses.* Three years later, in 1987, she decided to break out on her own as a freelance author of travel guides. *Our National Monuments,* one of her first efforts, discusses twenty-two monuments, parks, and other historic sites: the events they commemorate, the history of their construction, and efforts underway to preserve them. 1994's *Our Great Rivers and Waterways* continues in the same vein, with a geographical description of rivers in the United States and a discussion of the part each of these waterways has played in the nation's history. Both part of the "I Know America" series, Ayer's books were described as "concise summaries presented in an attractive format" by *School Library Journal* contributor Sylvia S. Marantz. Other books reflecting Ayer's fascination with the United States' historic landscape include *The Anasazi,* a report on the archeological evidence of the Pre-Columbian culture that once flourished in the American Southwest, and *Colorado,* a detailed description of the state that encompasses geography, history, government, and culture.

Ayer adopts a straightforward approach in her books directed at teen readers. In 1997's *It's Okay to Say No: Choosing Sexual Abstinence* she "realistically addresses" the choice to abstain from sexual relationships, according to *Booklist* contributor Frances Bradburn. Commenting on Ayer's inclusion of practical advice from experts, parents, and other teens, Bradburn went on to note that the author "convincingly presents [abstinence's] sometimes less immediate benefits." *Everything You Need to Know about Teen Fatherhood* begins with the risks associated with sexual relations, one of which is pregnancy. Addressing herself to young men who are about to be fathers, Ayer explains the importance of commitment when deciding to be part of a child's life. The author "neither preaches or scolds as she considers the emotions and practical considerations associated with teen fatherhood," added Stephanie Zvirin in her favorable *Booklist* appraisal of the work. In *Everything You Need to Know about Stress* Ayer alerts young people to the many subtle and not-so-subtle sources of pressure and stress in their lives, while in *Teen Smoking* she adopts a less supportive attitude, encouraging young people to quit smoking through a discussion of peer pressure, a look at the way teens are manipulated by tobacco advertising, and a list of tips for breaking the habit. In his review of *Teen Smoking* in *Booklist,* reviewer Randy Meyer cited Ayer's work as "peppered with insightful quotes ... that humanize the issue."

Beginning with 1994's *The United States Holocaust Memorial Museum: America Keeps the Memory Alive,* Ayer has spent a great deal of time researching and writing about one of the most tragic eras in human history: German dictator Adolph Hitler's efforts to eliminate the Jewish race and others through imprisonment and mass executions. In *The Survivors,* published in 1998, she uses both primary and secondary source material to describe the efforts of those liberated from Nazi concentration camps in May of 1945 to start a new life: their move to Displaced Persons camps, their often futile efforts to return to home and find family members who had disappeared, and the anti-Semitism they encountered. Citing the book as "exemplary for both its quality of writing and its thorough treatment of the situation," critic Heidi Borton praised *The Survivors* as a "welcome addition" to books for teen readers in her *Voice of Youth Advocates* review. Other books focusing on the Holocaust and its aftermath include *In the Ghettos: Teens Who Survived the Ghettos of the Holocaust, Adolph Hitler,* and *From the Ashes: May 1945 and After.* Ayer also aided in the work of two people who lived to tell about life in Hitler's Germany. *Parallel Journeys* presents the accounts of both Helen Waterford, then a young Jewish woman living in Germany who was captured after fleeing to Holland and sent to Auschwitz, and Alfons Heck, a member of the Hitler Youth who joined the army and fought on the German Front. Praising Ayer's contribution of a historical background through which readers can more easily relate to the co-authors' memoirs, *Voice of Youth Advocates* contributor Judy Silverman added: "It's impossible to praise this book too highly."

Biographical and Critical Sources

PERIODICALS

Booklist, June 15, 1992, p. 1818; December 1, 1992; October 1, 1993, Stephanie Zvirin, review of *Everything You Need to Know about Teen Fatherhood,* p. 327; May 15, 1995, Hazel Rochman, review of *Parallel Journeys,* p. 1647; September 1, 1997, Frances Bradburn, review of *It's Okay to Say No,* p. 69; October 15, 1997, Hazel Rochman, review of *A Firestorm Unleashed,* p. 396; January 1, 1999, Randy Meyer, review of *Teen Smoking,* p. 884.

Bulletin of the Center for Children's Books, January, 1998, Betsy Hearne, review of *A Firestorm Unleashed,* pp. 162-163.

Kirkus Reviews, January 1, 1993, review of *The Anasazi,* p. 1.

Kliatt, November, 1999, Ann Kramer, review of *Homeless Children,* p. 4.

Publishers Weekly, June 26, 1995, review of *Parallel Journeys,* p. 109.

School Library Journal, October, 1992, p. 124; March, 1993, Pat Katka, review of *Boris Yeltsin,* p. 205; June, 1994, Sylvia S. Marantz, review of *Our Great Rivers and Waterways,* p. 136; April, 1995, Claudia Morrow, review of *Ruth Bader Ginsberg: Fire and Steel on the Supreme Court,* p. 158; September, 1995, Sharon Grover, review of *The United States Holocaust Memorial Museum: America Keeps the Memory Alive,* p. 204; January, 1996, Pat Katka, review of *Adolph Hitler,* pp. 128, 131; August, 1997, Allison Trent Bernstein, review of *Colorado,* pp. 160-161; January, 1998, Edward Sullivan, review of *It's Okay to Say No,* p. 118; February, 1998, Marcia Posner, review of *A Firestorm Unleashed,* p. 134; July, 1998, Marcia Posner, review of *The Survivors,* p. 102; August, 1999, Jack Forman, review of *In the Ghetto,* pp. 165-166.

Science Books and Films, May, 1993, James E. Ayers, review of *The Anasazi,* p. 110.

Voice of Youth Advocates, December, 1992, p. 298; August, 1993, Lana Voss, review of *Boris Yeltsin,* p. 173; August, 1995, Judy Silverman, review of *Parallel Journeys,* p. 178; December, 1998, Heidi Borton, review of *The Survivors,* p. 376; June, 1999, Beth E. Anderson, review of *The Importance of Charles Dickens,* p. 128.*

*   *   *

AZAR, Penny 1952-

Personal

Born July 1, 1952, in Forbes, New South Wales, Australia; daughter of Bruce Downey (a banker) and Pamela Dunlop (a homemaker); married Gideon Azar (a consulting engineer); children: Alon, Cissy. *Education:* Attended National Art School.

Addresses

Home and office—202 Ryde Rd., Pymble, 2073 Australia. *E-mail*—PennyAzar@hotmail.com.

Career

Author and illustrator. Former editor at the University of Technology in Israel; former art and primary grades teacher in private schools in Africa. *Member:* Australian Society of Authors, Children's Book Council, Society of Children's Book Writers and Illustrators.

Awards, Honors

Shortlisted for the Australian Multicultural Children's Book Award, 1994.

Writings

PICTURE BOOKS; SELF-ILLUSTRATED

Albert's Birthday, Harcourt (New York City), 1992.
Not Zackly, Harcourt, 1993.
Madeline's New Boots, Scholastic (New York City), 1999.
Encore! Encore!, Scholastic (New York City), 2001.
Vanilla, Chocolate and Caramel, Wright Group (Bothell, WA), 2001.
A Guessing Game, Wright Group, 2001.
Marcus the Mighty, Blake (London, England), 2001.

ILLUSTRATOR

Libby Gleeson, *Mum Goes to Work,* Ashton Scholastic (Sydney, Australia), 1992, published in the United States as *Mom Goes to Work,* Scholastic, 1992.

Sidelights

Picture book author and illustrator Penny Azar told *SATA:* "My aim is to entertain, teach, and to make it so unobtrusive that a child is unaware that they are gaining knowledge and new skills. My artwork: I try to keep it alive by using movement and colour. My characters are vibrant and active, sometimes a little naughty, but then who isn't? I like to write true-to-life, and I suppose, since I never feel grown up myself, my characters have a larger *essence-of-me* in them.

"There are always a couple of stories rattling around in my head, a couple of manuscripts waiting for the light of day, and a couple waiting for editing," Azar added. "I love doing books. I feel like a mini Spielberg, or a Hitchcock. But I am the writer, director, producer,

costumer, the actor. I fully recommend it. It's painful fun!"

Biographical and Critical Sources

BOOKS

Mallan, Kerry, *In the Picture: Perspectives on Picture Book Art and Artists,* Centre for Information Studies, Charles Stuart University, 1999.

PERIODICALS

Magpies, November, 1999, Barbara James, review of *Madeline's New Boots,* p. 26.

B

BARBOUR, Karen 1956-

Personal

Born October 29, 1956, in San Francisco, CA; daughter of Donald C. (a physician) and Nancy B. Barbour; married Hermann Lederle (an artist), 1981. *Education:* University of California, Davis, B.A., 1976; San Francisco Art Institute, M.F.A., 1980.

Addresses

Home and office—51 Warren St., 5th Floor, New York, NY 10007.

Career

Freelance illustrator, author, animator, and painter.

Awards, Honors

Certificate of Excellence, American Institute of Graphic Arts Book Show, and Parents' Choice Award, Parents' Choice Foundation, both 1987, both for *Little Nino's Pizzeria.*

Writings

FOR CHILDREN; SELF-ILLUSTRATED

Little Nino's Pizzeria, Harcourt (San Diego, CA), 1987.
Nancy, Harcourt (San Diego, CA), 1989.
Mister Bow Tie, Harcourt (San Diego, CA), 1991.

ILLUSTRATOR

Helen Barolini, *Festa: Recipes and Recollections of Italy,* Harcourt (San Diego, CA), 1988.
Arnold Adoff, *Flamboyan,* Harcourt (San Diego, CA), 1988.
James Berry, *When I Dance: Poems,* Harcourt (San Diego, CA), 1991.
Anna Kate Winsey, *Toby Is My Best Friend,* Silver Burdett (Morristown, NJ), 1992.

Adoff, *Street Music: City Poems,* HarperCollins (New York City), 1995.
Jane Yolen, *A Sip of Aesop,* Blue Sky Press (New York City), 1995.
Eric Metaxas, *Princess Scargo and the Birthday Pumpkin: The Native American Legend,* Rabbit Ears (New York City), 1996.

Karen Barbour illustrates thirteen fables in Jane Yolen's A Sip of Aesop.

Lee Bennett Hopkins, editor, *Marvelous Math: A Book of Poems*, Simon & Schuster (New York City), 1997.

Juan Felipe Herrere, *Laughing Out Loud, I Fly: Poems in English and Spanish*, HarperCollins (New York City), 1998.

Eve Bunting, *I Have an Olive Tree*, HarperCollins (New York City), 1999.

Sidelights

The work of artist Karen Barbour has graced the pages of a number of well-received children's books, including *I Have an Olive Tree* by Eve Bunting and *A Sip of Aesop* by Jane Yolen. In addition to working with other picture-book authors, Barbour has created several original works, including *Nancy* and *Mister Bow Tie*, the latter a story about a homeless man who is befriended by a young girl and her family. In *Nancy* a newcomer extends a hand of friendship as a way to break into an established clique of four best friends in her new neighborhood and finds that creativity is the key to acceptance. "Ms. Barbour has a real fix on what it is to be young," observed *New York Times Book Review* contributor Christina Olson in praise of *Nancy*. "While the story ... has its appeal, it is the raucous artwork that grabs readers' attention and holds it," added Ilene Cooper in her *Booklist* appraisal. Cooper also noted Barbour's uninhibited use of wavy lines, polka dots, and fun, vibrant colors.

Born in San Francisco in 1956, Barbour attended both the University of California and the San Francisco Art Institute, earning her master of fine arts degree in 1980. Her first picture-book effort, *Little Nino's Pizzeria*, proved to be a success, winning her both a commendation from the American Institute of Graphic Arts and a Parents' Choice Foundation award. Published in 1987, *Little Nino's Pizzeria* sparked the interest of book publishers looking for talented artists to enhance the work of established authors. Barbour's move to New York City put her in proximity to a number of these publishers, and she was quick to gain illustration assignments. Her first illustration job—an Italian cookbook titled *Festa*—was published in 1988; moving from there to picture books was a short step to a successful career.

When I Dance, a collection of poems by James Berry, meshes the sounds of English with those of Berry's native Caribbean, and critics remarked that Barbour's artwork adds to the overall effect with its use of folk-style motifs. Also praised by reviewers are Barbour's bright and fanciful paintings for Lee Bennett Hopkins' *Marvelous Math: A Book of Poems*. *School Library Journal* contributor Lee Bock called them "lively illustrations [that] dance and play around the poems." In yet another poetry collection, Arnold Adoff's *Street Music: City Poems*, Barbour's whimsical artwork brings to life the hustle and bustle of crowded city streets. "Graceful, stylized forms fill the pages with pattern and texture against vibrant background colors," noted *Horn Book* reviewer Nancy Vasilakis. Similarly, a *Publishers Weekly* critic said Barbour's pictures "vibrate a jazzy fluidity and rhythm."

Barbour's artwork for *I Have an Olive Tree*, a picture book by Eve Bunting, was praised for both its historical accuracy and its overall technique. Noting that the illustrations "have the flavor of Greek folk art," a *Horn Book* reviewer commended in particular Barbour's use of a "multi-hued palette and curving lines." A *Publishers Weekly* contributor called the book "visually arresting," while *Booklist* reviewer Hazel Rochman explained that the artist's flat, bright paintings, with their heavy, black lines, "combine folk art and magic realism to show the circles of connection that sweep across time and place."

Biographical and Critical Sources

PERIODICALS

Booklist, October 1, 1989, Ilene Cooper, review of *Nancy*, p. 343; February 1, 1995, Carolyn Phelan, review of *Street Music: City Poems*, p. 1005; May 15, 1999, Hazel Rochman, review of *I Have an Olive Tree*, p. 1702; March 15, 2000, review of *Laughing Out Loud, I Fly*, p. 1342.

Horn Book, July-August, 1991, Mary M. Burns, review of *When I Dance*, p. 469; May-June, 1995, Nancy Vasilakis, review of *Street Music: City Poems*, p. 337; July, 1999, review of *I Have an Olive Tree*, p. 452.

Kirkus Reviews, August 15, 1991, review of *Mister Bow Tie*, p. 1086.

New York Times Book Review, November 26, 1989, Christina Olson, review of *Nancy*, p. 23; November 10, 1991, Dinitia Smith, review of *Mister Bow Tie*, p. 52.

Publishers Weekly, September 6, 1991, review of *Mister Bow Tie*, p. 103; April 19, 1993, video review of *Princess Scargo and the Birthday Pumpkin*, p. 29; December 19, 1994, review of *Street Music: City Poems*, p. 54; August 7, 1995, review of *A Sip of Aesop*, p. 460; May 24, 1999, review of *I Have an Olive Tree*, p. 78.

School Library Journal, November, 1989, Karen Litton, review of *Nancy*, p. 74; September, 1995, JoAnn Rees, review of *A Sip of Aesop*, p. 198; October, 1997, Lee Bock, review of *Marvelous Math*, p. 118.*

*   *   *

BERGUM, Constance R. 1952-

Personal

Born June 23, 1952, in Helena, MT; daughter of Andrew J. (a draftsman) and Mary Eva (a secretary; maiden name, Stubblefield) Rummel; married Ron Bergum (a pharmacist), June 19, 1976; children: William, Elizabeth, Sophia. *Education:* Attended University of Montana, 1970-75; Marywood University, M.F.A. (illustration), 2000. *Politics:* Liberal. *Religion:* Roman Catholic. *Hobbies and other interests:* Gardening, walking.

Addresses

Home—812 Madison Ave., Helena, MT 59601. *E-mail*—conartist23@aol.com

Career

Freelance illustrator, 1981—; artist at schools, 1985—. President and member of board of directors, Holter Museum of Art, 1993-99. *Member:* Society of Children's Book Writers and Illustrators.

Awards, Honors

Ezra Jack Keats Fellowship to the Kerlan Collection at the University of Minnesota Library, 1993; Magazine Merit Award, Society of Children's Book Writers and Illustrators, for "Where Do the Ducks Go," 1996; Washington State Writer's Award, 1998, for *Seya's Song.*

Writings

ILLUSTRATOR

Gayle Shirley, *M Is for Montana,* Falcon Press, 1988.
Gayle Shirley, *C Is for Colorado,* Falcon Press, 1989.
Gayle Shirley, *A Is for Animals,* Falcon Press, 1991.
Ron Hirschi, *Seya's Song,* Sasquatch Books, 1992.
Carol Curtis Stilz, *Grandma Buffalo, May and Me,* Sasquatch Books, 1995.
Lester L. Laminack, *The Sunsets of Miss Olivia Wiggins,* Peachtree Press, 1998.

Sidelights

Constance Bergum told *SATA:* "As a child growing up in Helena, Montana, I had two sources of art and history to draw upon. The first was our only museum, the Montana Historical Society. Being the oldest girl among seven children, any of the younger ones who could walk were handed over to me on Sunday afternoons for a trip to the museum. For my mother, this was her only opportunity for an hour or two of comparative quiet; for me it was a mixed experience. I loved the museum, with the wonderful dioramas showing Montana history, the bison family gazing at me with those quiet brown eyes and a whole room of Charlie Russell paintings and sculpture. I wasn't crazy about the cowboy and Indian subject matter, but even I could tell that this guy could draw. But my quiet enjoyment was constantly interrupted by fussy little kids. And none of them were ever happy until we were at our last stop—the stuffed albino bison.

"My second visual resource was the Saint Helena Cathedral's stained glass windows. I still gaze at them in admiration. They were designed and executed by the F. X. Zettler Company of Munich, Germany, around 1912. The stained glass pieces are painted to form the figures. Some unnamed master or masters drew Pre-Raphaelite figures with the most exquisite modeling of hands and feet and faces. Mass is still for me a weekly drawing lesson.

Constance R. Bergum

"To succeed in life, all of us need adults who make us feel special as children. I had an abundance of such people in my life, aunts and great aunts, and a wonderful art teacher throughout junior high and high school, Larry Hayes. At the University of Montana I retreated to the only corner of the art school that felt safe—watercolor painting, where the head teacher painted realistically. In the 1970s this was radical. After college, I found an entry-level job with the University of Montana as a graphic artist. Those four years were the time of my real design training, when I clearly formed my desire to be an illustrator. After a year on the West Coast working as an exhibit designer for a zoo, I returned to my home town with my husband, began raising children (three), and worked towards getting published as a children's book illustrator. While pregnant with my third baby, I formed a partnership with a local writer and we published our own book—*M Is for Montana,* the first of three alphabet books. It was a blockbuster of sorts [and is] now in its eighth printing. In 1991 I had the opportunity to illustrate *Seya's Song,* a S'Klallam Indian story. In the process of researching the story, I had the pleasure of working with members of the tribe, using some as models. The book served to reintroduce the S'Klallam language to the tribe's children and to remind them of their own stories and heritage. It was very satisfying to be illustrating a book that made such a contribution.

"My most recent trade book, *The Sunsets of Miss Olivia Wiggins,* introduced me to a new world. I found my Miss Olivia, Valentine Mitchell, in a local nursing home. We've become friends and while she did not have Alzheimer's when we first met, she now does and the book and our friendship are all the more poignant. I have now illustrated six trade books and as many educational titles. Some of my favorite works are the short pieces I do for magazines. Illustrating for children has introduced me to wonderful people whom I would never have had the pleasure of meeting otherwise. It has allowed me to celebrate childhood and old age, and my own culture and others'."

Bergum's illustrations for Ron Hirschi's *Seya's Song* accompany a text characterized by Janice Del Negro in *Booklist* as "simple, poetic, and concrete." The book celebrates the way of life of a small tribe of Native Americans from northwestern Washington state by depicting the people's relationship to the salmon in the rivers, the seasons, and the cycle of life. "The watercolor

Grandmother Seya passes on the culture and language of the S'Klallam tribe to her granddaughter in Seya's Song, *written by Ron Hirschi and illustrated by Bergum.*

illustrations interlace elements of the girl's modern life with aspects of the natural world and with references to traditional stories and dance," noted Carolyn Polese in *School Library Journal.* The text interweaves thirty words from the nearly forgotten S'Klallam Indian language, which also appear in a glossary at the back of the book. "Because of the high quality of text and art, the book may speak eloquently to readers with a special affinity for ... Native American tribes," concluded a reviewer for *Publishers Weekly.*

In *Grandma Buffalo, May, and Me,* Bergum celebrates her native Montana with warmly colored illustrations to match the story of young Poppy, who is on a trip with her family to her grandmother's home in that state. Along the way, the girl studies a family photo album and asks questions about her ancestors; among the sights seen is a buffalo ranch where descendants of a buffalo Poppy's Grandma May once fed now live. "Bergum's illustrations are colorful and warm and a few—such as the double-page spread of Poppy touching the buffalo through a wire fence—are quite charming," averred Jennifer Fleming in *School Library Journal. Booklist* reviewer Leone McDermott dubbed this "a useful introduction to the concept of the family tree."

In *The Sunsets of Miss Olivia Wiggins* author Lester L. Laminack tells a poignant story of an elderly woman with Alzheimer's disease and a visit from her daughter, Angel, and great-grandson, Troy. Throughout the visit, Miss Wiggins appears not to recognize or even notice her visitors, but the things they say and do trigger strong

Poppy learns about her heritage on a trip to Montana, where her great-grandmother grew up. (Illustration from Grandma Buffalo, May, and Me, *written by Carol Curtis Stilz and illustrated by Bergum.)*

memories of earlier, joyful times. "Realistic watercolors flow gently between present and past in this tender depiction of a life well lived," remarked Susan Dove Lempke in *Booklist.* Although a reviewer for *Publishers Weekly* contended that Bergum's watercolor illustrations heighten the book's sentimental approach to aging, "Children perplexed or upset by their own visits to deteriorating elders may find this book helpful and even consoling," the reviewer concluded.

Biographical and Critical Sources

PERIODICALS

Booklist, January 1, 1993, Janice Del Negro, review of *Seya's Song,* p. 806; October 1, 1995, Leone McDermott, review of *Grandma Buffalo, May, and Me,* p. 327; May 1, 1998, Susan Dove Lempke, review of *The Sunsets of Miss Olivia Wiggins,* p. 1521.
Publishers Weekly, November 9, 1992, review of *Seya's Song,* p. 82; March 30, 1998, review of *The Sunsets of Miss Olivia Wiggins,* p. 82.
School Library Journal, May, 1993, Carolyn Polese, review of *Seya's Song,* p. 99; December, 1995, Jennifer Fleming, review of *Grandma Buffalo, May, and Me,* p. 92; July, 1998, Martha Topol, review of *The Sunsets of Miss Olivia Wiggins,* p. 78.

*   *   *

BLOOM, Freddy 1914-2000

OBITUARY NOTICE—See index for SATA sketch: Born February 6, 1914, in New York, NY; died May 20, 2000. Administrator, writer. Freddy Bloom was a freelance writer who served as founding chairperson of the National Deaf Children's Society in 1956. From 1939 to 1941 she was affiliated with the Malaya Tribune Group of newspapers in Singapore, which led to her subsequent five-month detainment and interrogation there regarding a suspected spy-ring. Following her release in 1945, Bloom reunited with her husband and gave birth to their first child one year later. Due to prolonged vitamin deficiencies both Bloom and her husband experienced in the prison camp, her daughter was born deaf. As there was very little help for parents of deaf children at that time, Bloom set out to create a network of people and information for the deaf community. A talented writer, she wrote and published a number of books that brought to light the ordeals and triumphs of deaf children; her first book, *Our Deaf Children,* was published in 1963, and her juvenile book *The Boy Who Couldn't Hear,* followed in 1979. In 1980 her diary account of her experience as a prisoner of the Japanese in Singapore was published as *Dear Philip.*

OBITUARIES AND OTHER SOURCES:

BOOKS

The Writers Directory 1988-1990, 8th Edition, St. James Press (Chicago), p. 92.

PERIODICALS

The Independent (London, England), June 30, 2000, p. 6.
London Times, June 19, 2000.

*   *   *

BOERST, William J. 1939-

Personal

Born February 17, 1939; married July 5, 1968; wife's name, Rachel M. (a guidance secretary); children: Robin K., Julie M. *Education:* State University of New York College at Fredonia, B.S.Ed.; also attended State University of New York College at Potsdam, Syracuse University, and College of Saint Rose. *Politics:* Democrat. *Religion:* Atheist. *Hobbies and other interests:* Kayaking, reading, gardening.

Addresses

Home—40 Meadow Lane, Jamestown, NY 14701. *E-mail*—bill2@alltel.net.

Career

English teacher at a public school in northern New York, 1962-63; U.S. Peace Corps, Washington, DC, elementary schoolteacher in Liberia, 1963-65; teacher of English and speech at a high school in Watertown, NY, 1965-67; Board of Education, Jamestown, NY, junior high school teacher, then high school English teacher, 1967-2000; writer, 2000—. Founding member, Chautauqua Area Writers and Chautauqua County Writing/Reading Process Teachers.

Writings

Isaac Asimov: Writer of the Future, Morgan Reynolds (Greensboro, NC), 1999.
Time Machine: The Story of H. G. Wells, Morgan Reynolds (Greensboro, NC), 2000.
Edgar Rice Burroughs: Creator of Tarzan, Morgan Reynolds (Greensboro, NC), 2000.
George Orwell, Morgan Reynolds (Greensboro, NC), in press.

Contributor of articles, poems, and short fiction to periodicals, including *English Journal, Language Arts, Iowa English Bulletin, Not Your Average Zine, Poet,* and *Artifacts.* Newsletter editor, Vegetarian Society of Chautauqua/Allegheny.

Biographical and Critical Sources

PERIODICALS

Booklist, December 1, 1998, Roger Leslie, review of *Isaac Asimov,* p. 657; January 1, 2000, Carolyn Phelan, review of *Time Machine,* p. 908; July, 2000, Phelan, review of *Edgar Rice Burroughs,* p. 2019.
Book Report, September-October, 1999, Jim Miller, review of *Isaac Asimov,* p. 67.
School Library Journal, January, 1999, Linda Wadleigh, review of *Isaac Asimov,* p. 135; December, 1999, Jennifer Ralston, review of *Time Machine,* p. 146.

ON-LINE

Amazon.com, www.amazon.com/ (August 26, 2000).

*   *   *

BONNER, Mike 1951-

Personal

Born September 15, 1951, in Vancouver, WA; son of James Joseph (a civil engineer) and Lois Mae (a homemaker; maiden name, Ling) Bonner; married Carol Kleinheksel (a college administrator), January 9, 1982; children: Karen Nicole. *Education:* Attended University of Oregon, 1971-1973, and Oregon State University, 1969-70. *Politics:* "Unclassifiable." *Religion:* Roman Catholic. *Avocational interests:* Books, sports, art, film, good food.

Addresses

E-mail—mavomike@netscape.net.

Career

Department of Justice, Eugene, OR, paralegal for ten years; Public Welfare Division, Florence, OR, assistance

William J. Boerst

worker for four years; Oregon Health Science University, Portland, record specialist for seven years.

Writings

Collecting Football Cards: A Complete Guide with Prices, Wallace-Homestead (Radnor, PA), 1995.
Basketball Legends: Shawn Kemp, Chelsea House (Philadelphia, PA), 1997.
Hockey Legends: Paul Kariya, Chelsea House (Philadelphia, PA), 1998.
Baseball Legends: Randy Johnson, Chelsea House (Philadelphia, PA), 1999.
Race Car Legends: Jeremy Mayfield, Chelsea House (Philadelphia, PA), 1999.
Collecting Basketball Cards: A Complete Guide with Prices, toExcel (San Jose, CA), 1999.
How to Become an Elected Official, Chelsea House (Philadelphia, PA), 2000.
How a Bill Is Passed, Chelsea House (Philadelphia, PA), 2000.
The Composite Guide to Strongman Competition, Chelsea House (Philadelphia, PA), 2000.

Contributor to periodicals, including *Sports Collectors Digest, Sports Map, Sports Cards Gazette, Old Oregon, Treasure Chest,* and *Delphi Collectibles Forum.*

Work in Progress

The Forever Girl, A Novel of Ancient Rome; Collecting Vintage Video Games: A Complete Guide with Prices, completion expected in 2001; research on sports memorabilia, as the basis for articles.

Sidelights

Mike Bonner told *SATA:* "Since my early teenage years, I have always wanted to be a writer. Although I knew from the start I had a lot of talent, it took many years for me to find an appropriate style and a lucrative outlet for my work. One of the problems I had in the beginning was that being a writer was never something that people in my experience ever thought of becoming. There was no mentor in my life. Far from it. In truth, I endured a considerable amount of ridicule for having a dream that was somewhat out of the ordinary. But I persisted. Now that I am older, I find that my verbal powers are in peak form. I can say things in ways others have never thought of saying them and literally can make the words dance whenever I feel like it. I am self-taught, but probably better off for it. In the next twenty years (if I should live so long) I expect to compose my finest work. In the meantime, I truly enjoy writing books for middle school students and expect to continue composing them for as long as assignments keep coming my way.

Mike Bonner

"At home, I love spending time with my wife Carol and daughter Karen. I like to waste idle moments reflecting on the days and years of my life. I get a kick out of sports, especially football. As a worker in a variety of social service occupations, I believe I have seen it all. When I read fiction, I prefer a rough, sardonic approach. I love such writers as Charles Bukowski, Raymond Chandler, Dashiell Hammett, and the 1950s 'phenom' Grace Metalious. One writer who amuses me currently is Steven Saylor. I like his mysteries set in ancient times. Most of the books I see for sale nowadays I dismiss. There is a basic dishonesty to much contemporary fiction that leaves me cold. Rarely do I find much to recommend among modern writers, and I absolutely detest romance novels as a genre. In my view, they demean men and, at bottom, are a form of feminine pornography. Give me one true love story instead of a thousand phony ones. Ah well. These are some of the things I think about as I pursue my literary career and meanwhile keep on going to the day job that pays our bills."

Biographical and Critical Sources

ON-LINE

Amazon.com, http://www.amazon.com/ (August 26, 2000).

Autobiography Feature

Barbara Bottner

1943-

TO BE OR NOT TO BE

I grew up in Great Neck, Long Island, aka East Egg in Fitzgerald's *The Great Gatsby,* in the early fifties, when moving to the suburbs was something almost every middle-class first-generation Jewish family aspired to. My parents wanted me to have a good education, but the future after that was never defined. I took the silence to mean I was meant to do what I saw most fifties women doing: raise a family, play a good golf game, have my nails done weekly, and order out for dinner; in other words, to be a Princess. The story that I will tell you here will explain why once I left the North Shore of Long Island, outside of having a great collection of take-out Chinese menus, the rest of these things never happened to me.

I was born near the Grand Concourse in the Bronx during World War II, the first child of a very ambitious man and a very good-looking, sometimes clothes model. They were in their early twenties, children by our standards. I imagine my mother was attracted to my father who was dynamic and fearless, and my father was attracted to my mother who was tall, thin, and elegant. Both middle children, they also shared a very strict parent; for my father, it was his father, for my mother, her mother.

My father didn't serve because he worked for the Lewyt Vacuum Corporation. Lewyt also manufactured airplane parts for the army, and he was thus deemed important to the war effort. The war, however, was threatening to everyone, and people tended to settle down young. And sometimes impetuously. Thus, my parents' marriage and, probably, thus me.

In their wedding picture my father looks you straight in the eye. He apparently knows what he is doing, but you can catch the pensiveness in my mother's face. She must have suspected it was not going to be easy, going from her mother's authoritarian home, where she was obedient and perfectionistic, to make a home with a man who had a large, commanding personality. Hindsight allows me to say that I can't see why they thought they were meant for each other, war or not. It took them eighteen years to find out they weren't. They split up acrimoniously during the fifties, when divorce was still uncommon, but within a few months divorce broke out like wildfire; our community was ablaze

in heartbreak, gossip, and broken families. Divorce began to seem like the perfect solution to those hasty marriages.

When I see pictures of myself as a young child, I am blond, brown-eyed, dressed fastidiously in hand-made clothes proudly tailored by my maternal grandparents. I was fashion itself. This put a crimp into some of my activities. I was a tomboy by nature, rebellious, physically active, a first baseman, a pitcher, a basketball forward.

In the Bronx, we lived in an apartment building off the Grand Concourse until I was seven. From those years, the outstanding memories are the smell of macaroons during Passover, cigars anytime my grandfathers were around, and the tall, salty pretzels from the corner store. I also remember the delicious aroma of strong coffee and strudel; those were the days when grandmothers cooked. I loved the snow, sledding, and collecting acorns in the park.

One night when I was about five or so, there was a terrible hullabaloo in my house. I picked up the fact that my father was in an airplane accident. My mother tried to keep her despair to herself, but I understood as the evening went on: he was dead. Two hours later he glided, all smiles, through the front door. At Dulles airport in Washington, D.C., he had characteristically refused to be bumped from his original flight even though it was overbooked. "Do you know who I am?" he had trumpeted. They let him make the earlier flight. Horribly, the later plane went down, killing all aboard. This explains why, in part, I thought my father was God Himself.

Going downstairs and out into the street was carefully monitored by my anxious mother. I received my first kiss from a boy when I took the more interesting route to school across a cemetery with my best friend, who later moved to Connecticut. I adored her and sobbed inconsolably when she left.

My brother's birth, when I was four, was an event I greeted with very mixed feelings. I was suddenly invisible to all the doting aunts and uncles and grandparents. I found this to be a terrible change, of course. My needs for affection were enormous. There wasn't a lot of physical touching coming from my mother even when I was young. The intense sibling rivalry that my all too adorable brother

Barbara Bottner

brought out in me fueled many of my picture books. Among them is *Big Boss, Little Boss,* an "I Can Read" book about the competition between sisters, and *Jungle Day,* where a pesty younger brother solves an impossible problem for his sibling.

Things have changed: I count my talented, good-natured brother Jeffrey as one of my best friends.

The Hungarians Are Coming

My mother came from a very opinionated Hungarian family, the one that invented the family feud. I was the youngest child and, when we visited my grandparents, I have a vivid memory of one aunt in one room, one of her sisters or brothers in another, each hurt and furious, and recounting their sibling's sins to anyone that would listen. I would patrol the hallways, spying. I thought the commotion was fascinating.

Eventually, they would forgive each other in a tearful reconciliation. This took place over scrumptious coffee and cakes. These were probably the first stories I ever heard and were very dramatic.

My grandmother's family had had money in Europe, owned farmland, wore expensive clothes, employed servants. To find themselves disenfranchised, working long, hard days on the Lower East side and then the Upper West side must have been very difficult. They always looked gorgeous, however; they all knew how to sew and how to buy fine clothes at a discount.

This Hungarian side of the family was strict and formal, except for the enormous family party they held once a year. As the oldest grandchild, I attended. It was an all-night affair at the Chardash Restaurant in New York City. They downed the cabbage soup, the chicken paprikash, the nukkla and stuffed derma along with sweet Hungarian wine. Then it would all break loose. The fiddlers would play their violins in the most florid styles until my relatives were all in tears. Then my uncles would throw themselves into dancing the Chardash to the hoots and hollers of everyone else until they fell down on the dance floor, exhausted. Eventually they'd return to their tables to be served a dubash tart with strong Hungarian coffee and liqueurs. And then it would begin again, the singing and the crying on into the night. I thought these nights were magical, even though I was little and fell asleep before they were over.

I was always disappointed the next day, however, when everyone would resume their strict attitudes. You could never guess these same people had it inside them to sing and dance, to squeeze each other with tremendous emotion, and laugh with gusto. By morning, you couldn't scrape a hug off anyone.

Bootsie Barker Is Born

Down the hall, my mother had a best friend. She and her daughter, Carole, came to see us almost every day. Carole was much bigger than I was and intimidated me to the point of torture, on the one hand. But on the other, I was always happy for company. I was half her size and probably a wimp. Carole's frequent visits and my feelings of intimidation became *Bootsie Barker Bites.* I wrote Bootsie at the behest of my students when I showed them a photo of Carole and me, and recounted the story.

Bootsie is a universal meanie that children recognize. She has become *Zaza, la Peste* in France, *Betti Becker beisst* in German, *La Temible Ninasaurio* in Spanish, and was also translated into Japanese.

The Austrians

My father's family had also fled the shtetls; those of Austria. My grandfather had a family-famous crooked finger from shooting himself to keep out of World War I. He was the Don of the family, having succeeded in bringing over his dozen brothers and sisters to this country and helping them all restart their lives here. He had once been handsome, but in his later years I remember him as an energetic, fun-loving gnome, long on personality, storytelling, and humor. We grandchildren gathered around his cigar-smelling living room, waiting for him to finish a round of pinochle with his numerous brothers, to hear his tales. He told us he was always respectful towards his father, never daring to contradict him. But once, the story goes, he was so angry, as he left the house he pulled the

The Hungarians, Bottner's maternal relatives, including Bottner's grandmother (standing right of the lamp) and grandfather (standing behind the lamp).

door off the jamb and walked through it! The only way he could impart how he felt and still be "respectful."

My father was one of three, the only boy, and bent on succeeding in this new world of New York. He grew up helping in his family's laundry business, delivering packages after school. To this day, he has trouble carrying anything but a briefcase.

My father was told by his mother, "You can be the president if you want." As the only boy of three children, he was the one expected to make it big. Now he claims that since he grew up in the Depression, he did anything to make a dollar, including a dive head first onto a rain-drenched beach. He also developed a competitive streak, which I inherited.

He made his way through high school, skipping a year, then on to college, playing basketball in college at five foot nine, the shortest guy on the team. He was to become legendary in later years, making it out of the ghetto to become president of an international company, have a limo, travel by the Concorde, be quoted in the *New York Times,* and meet many famous actors and politicians. His was a regular Horatio Alger story, achieving more than he or his parents ever dreamed possible. The whole family was proud of him, although some were also jealous.

I had lots of cousins, and we were close as kids, which was very wholesome. It is strange that now, my life as a writer is so full of solitude. I never designed it this way, but that's part of the job description. A writer is always processing things, reorganizing life, and, unless you pull back, the muses refuse to speak. Sometimes they are silent even when you *do* pull back. But that's another story.

Surrounded by Good Taste

I was treated to dance lessons when I was as young as four. My mother loved the ballet, but when she was a child on the lower East Side, she sustained eye damage from an accident while playing with her older brother. This meant she had to give up her coveted lessons to go to the ophthalmologist. Both my parents encouraged me to perform at family functions. Inevitably someone would drag out the wooden platform at almost every gathering and urge the young 'uns to strut their stuff. While my cousin Linda had to be coerced into doing her tap dancing routine, nothing could keep me from flying across the living room in my ballet slippers. So there I was, doing grande jetés, never imagining that one day I would write and draw about these moments, or that the passion for dance would stay with me for my whole life, not to mention a certain hunger for the spotlight.

We were surrounded by good taste. My mother loved handiwork and art. The whole family sewed or knitted and embroidered. They could fashion a suit for you while you waited for dessert, with the darts and pleats in all the right places. They knew fabrics and cuts. Their fingers were geniuses, their hands were never idle. There was a difficult side to living with these talents, however. My mother's house was for show; she was always after us not to be messy. I think that also meant not to have messy feelings. I had bushel loads of them and I was frustrated by needing to appear unemotional and fastidiously neat. My mother and I were completely different people. I think she probably dreamed of an adorable, beautiful, obedient daughter—a

"With my parents in the Bronx," about 1947.

model, an angel, like she'd been. Instead, she got a hurricane in the form of a child. We were temperamentally unsuited to each other. I couldn't be what she planned on, and she wasn't what I needed. It's sad to say we spent a lifetime inside this problem. I wrote *Messy* to, in a small way, relive those difficult moments and make them better for myself, and also to help other children who, like me, were less than perfect. And to hint that inside that messiness, there are gifts.

But I did inherit my mother's family's talent in the form of a love for art, especially painting and drawing. I always drew pictures and was praised for them. I'll always remember the day I moved to Great Neck and was shown around the second grade by a classmate, Susie, who I thought was beautiful. Later in class we had to draw. I began, unaware of my surroundings. The next thing I knew, a bunch of kids were peering over my shoulder. "Look at what the new girl is drawing. She's better than Susie!"

One of them went to check out Susie's paper. "Oh, no, Susie's better!" And so it went all afternoon. The scene found its way into my middle-grade novel, *The World's Greatest Expert on Absolutely Everything ... Is Crying.* That was the first novel I attempted. It took three years, off and on, to find the right plot. The main character, Katherine Ann Millicent Franklin, was fashioned from a friend who was the daughter and granddaughter of two famous

American writers. She was beautiful and had done everything, been everywhere, and never let anyone forget it. She succeeded in making me jealous. But once my friends read my book and pointed out that *I* had the same know-it-all qualities, I had to admit that this was true. And here was the strangest thing. I wrote a character who was the focus of two girls' attention. His name was Tucker T. Cobbwebber. He was a scientist not involved in the emotions flying around him. Years later, I met someone who was an older version of Tucker. I married him. Life comes in handily for art, and art comes in handily for life, as well.

"The original Bootsie, Carol Horowitz (right), her mother (left), my mother and me."

The emotional difficulties I had growing up in my family have informed my writing. I was a child who never felt safe with my mother, constantly thought I was adopted, cried in my room, wished I would die, wrote secret tomes of vengeance which I kept in my sock drawer, and lived through a twelve-year divorce when I was the most susceptible to losing my father. I was always in fear: when would trouble break out? When would I be hit? My brother retreated to his room. My relatives didn't pick up on the ongoing turmoil of my life. I could never live up to my mother's standards, and my father was busy with his own life. I became a kid who didn't feel seen, heard, understood, or validated. I was dangerously lonely, too.

Leaving home was the solution. I was never there if I could manage it. When I was thirteen I ran away. Ignorantly, I checked into the only hotel in town, right next to the Long Island railroad station. I had a nebulous plan to take a morning train to New York City. And then … ? The police found me the same night and ushered me home.

The external world was my solace, the family was the threat. I am lucky that I was outgoing and accepted by my peers. Besides the miserable transformation that is also known as the eighth grade, my social life was full. I'll never forget when a fifth grader marched up to me and said, "Teach me how to flirt. I'll pay you." I've used that line in a book.

Much of my writing for children has been to revisit childhood in order to transform it. I believe the reason I can hear the young voice I still carry inside of me is because that young person inside me stayed very much alive; she was never really integrated. So when she speaks, I listen.

Behind the Wheel

When I was able to drive, I gained a measure of control. Many a night I sped over to my best friend's house under the pretense we were going to study math. Off we went to the Village to listen to jazz. I believed we were extremely cool. Oddly enough, my mother never questioned my less than impressive math scores. Nor did my father. I never got caught. Although I cherished my liberty, I found having it tossed at me so nonchalantly both sad and disappointing.

My father's career was flourishing. He went to Revlon and, to my fifteen-year-old mind, this new job translated into thoughts of guaranteed glamour. The reality was that he became a company man. We hardly saw him. One night, he packed and left. When my mother and father split up, I was so shocked, I didn't speak to my father for six months. For the next several years, I shuttled between my parents' homes. A year later I attended my father's wedding with my new step-brother, Victor, who was a classmate. The sequence of events, the trauma around them, my mother's near nervous breakdown, all had a surreal quality to it. It would take years to sort out all that happened. I don't believe I was introspective by nature. I was forced to become that way through circumstances.

Questions Without Answers

I was becoming a bad kid, almost kicked out of summer camp and driving my parents crazy. I couldn't live with either one of them for long. I was snotty and disrespectful, zooming out of Princess territory, searching for answers, trying to find a way through my conflicts. If these difficulties hadn't occurred, I never would have been driven to creating in the demanding way a fine artist must. I imagine a parallel life sometimes, where I would have been a designer or a dancer.

I didn't have the luxury of dreams of the future. I was too angry, rebellious, and scornful of authority to listen to anyone except my girlfriends. My close friendships were crucial. The other ingredient for me to handle my life was looking to other artists. The arts became compelling. There you could be who you were.

I sensed that art transforms. Through art I entered an abstract universe which released me from the pain of life. In art everything and anything is the raw material. I sought out museums and films and plays and music and dance to give my experiences meaning, and in those places discovered myself over and over again. I resonated to what others before me said. It was a pathway.

My best friend's mother, Millie Klingman, herself a painter, someone whom I respected and admired, took me aside one day and said, "Listen to me. It's *not* you. You are fine." She saw my struggle. She knew I blamed myself, that I thought I was horribly flawed. Millie might have saved my life. No other adult saw and spoke to me with that kind of respect and concern.

I have always tried to do a similar service for my reader. That's why my work represents emotions as they are, treats them as important and mirrors them, so my readers can feel validated and liberated in my presence.

I was dealing with questions such as, "Am I innately flawed? Bad? Unworthy of love? Will I always be so angry? What can I do with these feelings?"

Even in my youngest picture books, I allow my characters anger. In *Zoo Song,* apples are tossed at annoying neighbors. In many of my stories, annoyance or anger or teasing or rebelliousness or intimidation are part of the makeup of the characters. In fact, they direct the story line.

And the value of being creative shows up, too, in every single book I've written. I can't shake it, it's such a strong part of me. *Zoo Song* is about three cantankerous animals in a zoo who eventually learn to play music together. *Messy* and *Dumb Old Casey Is a Fat Tree* are about dance. *Myra* is about the power of imagination. And in *The World's Greatest Expert on Absolutely Everything ... Is Crying,* the fifth grade teacher holds "We Are Wonderful Day," in which the main characters are involved in doing something uniquely creative. In *Doing the Toledo,* Genine is begged by her brother to do a dance. In *Hurricane Music,* Aunt Margaret plays the clarinet and says, "Gotta dance, gotta sing, gotta do my thing-a-ling."

Nana Hannah's Piano features a baseball-loving boy who allows his tango-dancing granny to inspire him to learn how to play the piano.

Boys Will Be Men ... Eventually

By the time I was in high school, the focus of my life was boys. Boys were required to tell me how much they loved me and couldn't live without me. Then, zap, they were gone. I was always dropping one for the other; I was a teenage trophy hunter. I needed them to feel validated.

"My mother and father with my maternal grandparents," 1950s.

I had no understanding of the male animal, of course, not to mention my own motives. Basically, I was deeply lonely. I was fortunate that back in those days we didn't do drugs. And lucky, too, that I was never drawn to alcohol. It was just pure attention that I craved.

It is these years that I drew on for my novel *Let Me Tell You Everything, Memoirs of a Lovesick Intellectual* and for one of the themes for *Nothing in Common. Let Me Tell You Everything* is about a girl who is lovesick for her teacher at the same time she is reading all kinds of feminist material exhorting her to be independent and free of needing men.

Was I like (Simone) de Beauvoir, really independent deep down inside no matter whom she longed for? Or was I like other women, ready to cave in to male society just to feel secure? How could I claim to be a feminist, when truly the most important thing to me was not how good my paper for class was, not what I would grow up to be, but how good I looked for Mr. Price?

This was my dilemma: how to integrate all that I'd learned and read about how important it is to become your own person with your own identity, with my deep desire for love. At the core, the love I really craved was motherlove. But that was, by my teenage years, an impossible hope.

In the book, there is an answer of sorts. A strong, older woman, who is an altruist, inspires the heroine to feel she can fulfill herself in working for world peace. She is a completely realized person, a mentor, but also flawed and human. Buddhism, the religion I practice, teaches that the component of doing for others is an ingredient to becoming whole and finding your true self. Still, I am not sure that, dramatically, the ending truly works.

I Was Ready for College

I had decided to study art and I plunged into the curriculum at Boston University's School of Fine Arts after passing up a chance to attend Pratt in much-too-close-for-comfort Brooklyn. I was crazy about painters like George Grosz, who gave graphic commentary and warning to what he believed to be the decline of decency in post-World War I Germany. He and others such as Emile Nolde, whose work condemned the debauchery of the Nazis, became known as the German Expressionists. On their canvases, I saw the representation of the rage and torment of *my* inner life. My turmoil had a picture. My art had a direction. I painted images my mother thought were grotesque and, of course, being a teenager, that in itself thrilled me.

I was in for serious art training in Boston. I had teachers who were very committed. Everyone in freshman class regularly received C's in drawing. I was horrified. It turned out, our teachers were grading us in comparison with Da Vinci. From that perspective, I calmed down. I loved art. I loved learning design, tolerated perspective,

"My brother, Jeffrey, and me onstage at summer camp. I liked it; he didn't."

assiduously drew nudes once I recovered from being so close to strangers' naked bodies, and longed for the day I would break into oils. The smells of art school, the collection of rebels and outsiders, put me into ecstasy. Never before had I felt so at home. I loved that people read Rimbaud, talked museums instead of popularity. I loved Boston. I loved, most of all, being on my own.

I worked my way over the Charles River to Brandeis University. My Brandeis boyfriend played the conga drums and smoked a pipe. We frequented jazz clubs, discussed Olitunji over beers, discovered Joan Baez and Bob Dylan, and rode on a motor scooter. I thought I was happy until I received mail from the Midwest. My best friend, Lynnzee Klingman, was at the University of Wisconsin, hanging out with kids from New York City. They were working for the Friends of the Student Nonviolent Coordinating Committee (SNCC) and going to classes in World Civilization and American History. Lynnzee convinced me this was the place for me. I had to ask myself, did I always want to be a spoiled kid from Great Neck, or did I really want to leave the mold behind?

Convinced that this was the next step for me, I applied to Wisconsin. Off to the freezing cold I went.

Being even farther away from home enthralled me. The level of discourse was intense. The Civil Rights movement had found one of its most dedicated homes at the Madison campus; there was always action. And in l962 students everywhere were involved in examining the values of their parents. These years were precursors to the sixties revolution. If you were at Madison, you saw Jesse Jackson give his earliest lectures, you heard Tracy Nelson sing the Blues, Boz Scaggs break out with his first performances. Professors Taylor and Mosse raised your appreciation of history. You went on marches, stayed up all night arguing the finer points of Marxism. You heard Ben Sidran play his jazz licks, and you certainly nearly froze to death.

The years at Madison helped me formulate into a thinking individual. Exposed to this kind of learning and these amazing people, I was never the same again.

The education I received at Wisconsin is reflected in the concerns of the main character of *Let Me Tell You Everything*. Brogan studies "The Greening of America." In this novel I set out to engage teenagers beyond their emotional life into a discussion about society. Teenagers are acutely aware of the world they are about to enter.

But Madison was so *cold!* My friend Susan Stern, a French major, had designs to study at the Louvre, in Paris. This sounded like a great idea to me, even though I'd received a D in high school French. For one thing, Paris *had* to be warmer than Wisconsin. And the art! We began a secretive campaign to study abroad.

Paris—My Life on the Left Bank

Without admittance to any institution, I brazenly told my father the university was sponsoring a junior year abroad. I told the university my father was insisting I spend a year in France. So the next fall, Susan and I set sail. I was to study in an *atelier* at the Ecole des Beaux Arts, living on a small allowance, the kind that students everywhere learn to stretch in imaginative ways. Once I'd been admitted to the Beaux Arts, I managed to write a letter to the dean of the art school. He assured me credits to cover my year abroad. A brilliant stroke on my part, because I only painted about half a dozen canvases in France. Good ones. I got my credits.

Susan, the scholar, had studied French and expected so much of herself that she became tongue-tied the minute we stepped foot on French soil. I, on the other hand, officially the French failure, was immune to embarrassment. We had to get a room, get a meal, and no verb conjugations would get in the way. We lived on the Left Bank in a small pensione. Our concierge made breakfasts of apricot jam, croissants, and great bowls of delicious coffee. And over these meals, we met wonderfully interesting people traveling through Europe. Eventually, Susan's French made a miraculous recovery and she became the more eloquent one. We were there the day Kennedy was assassinated, and it seemed that every Frenchmen thought we'd understand what was going on because we were American.

About halfway through the year, rushing through the Metro, I encountered an old friend, Matthew Robbins. A few months later, I moved in with Matthew and his college roommates. Between us we had four motorcycles and a slightly expanded food allowance. Walter Murch's father, Murch Sr., was a painter, and Matthew Robbins's brother Daniel was co-curator of the Guggenheim. Because of these art connections, we were invited to private collections of rare Impressionist paintings. We also went to all the gallery openings, and we broke bread often with the then eighty-year-old Madame Gleize in her apartment over the Bois de Boulogne. Madame was the widow of Albert Gleize, one of the chief architects of the Cubist movement. Madame Gleize was so charming, vibrant, brilliant, and coquettish with her lorgnettes, which she would snap open when she was especially interested in something someone said, I was convinced she was stealing my boyfriend away. To Andrew Feenberg, the philosopher amongst us, she demanded, "Explique moi de Sartres." (Explain Sartre to me.) She had known Sartres; this was just her way of inviting Andrew into conversation. *I* would like to be this charming at eighty-four.

Paris has always been a feast for student eyes and stomachs. Everything was cheap. Lunch was twenty-five cents, including wine. Of course, sometimes it was horsemeat.

I painted every single day, the light changing as it filtered through the enormous windows of the atelier while my French friends argued away the afternoons, posted at each other's canvases, smoking Gauloises, and sipping strong coffee. My English friend, Alisha Sufit, now a singer/songwriter in London, and I would snicker at their intensity and wonder when they'd get back to their own paintings.

We were always at the museums, at films at the Cinemeque Francais, or taking midnight spins around the Arc de Triomphe on motorcycles. I was the happiest I'd ever been in my life.

My father had suspicions that I was not living with girls, so he sent one of his employees to check on me in the apartment. We lived near Parc de Montsouris, in a working-class neighborhood, not in the center of town. Needless to say, the apartment was covered with motorcycle parts and helmets, bomber jackets, wrenches ... all kinds of masculine paraphernalia. One of my fondest images of that year is me standing on the balcony of the

As a ballet dancer in her college days.

apartment, floating down hair rollers, nylon stockings and blouses to make it look as if it was inhabited by females, "who weren't in" at the time. It worked.

While living in France, I traveled to Spain, Italy, and England. After a year, I felt at home in Europe. It was real culture shock when I returned to my mid-western University of Wisconsin. Susan and I were by then famous on our campus. But the courses that awaited me at school were all the ones I had postponed, thinking I never would graduate college. I just didn't think I had it in me. So I was stuck with Psych One, Biology, and Geology.

The Furthest Trip

Only a year later, living in the mountains of Santa Barbara, I would see geology students. But now they were perched on the ledges of the three-thousand-foot mountain I called home. I often thought of the determined geologists in the Midwest, doomed to their flat plains and rolling hills.

I was in Santa Barbara doing graduate work in painting. When I graduated Wisconsin, I realized that in the outside world there was nothing related to art that I could do to sustain myself except to go into advertising, which was a dirty word to me, a sixties person. Advertising was a rip-off of people's minds; I wanted to do something "pure," not to mention I was still rebelling. I didn't want to do anything my parents thought I should. In retrospect, I could have had many doors opened for me. But I was searching for truth, meaning, expression, so it really wasn't a choice. I decided to take my master's degree. I moved to the hills behind the University of Santa Barbara, to a small community called Painted Cave. I experimented with LSD during that period, which was, I guess, the furthest "trip" I could take; I had already taken so many. It gave me a glimpse into pure consciousness, the joy of simply being alive and completely in the moment. However, the road back was a long one; it seriously disoriented me for several years to come.

Still No Inkling

My career as a professional person began when I was back in New York City, ready to face earning a living. How would I pull myself together, now that I was in my early twenties? I have tremendous sympathy for young people, especially the ones who are unsure of their future and how they will fit into society. We are all so different, and our ways are unique. My husband, for instance, says he missed the sixties completely; he was in medical school.

I became fascinated by theater when I was painting sets for an Off Broadway production at the New Dramatists Guild down on Fourth Street. A couple of clues made me realize that *I* wanted to be onstage. The first came when my eight-foot-tall puppets completely dwarfed the actors and made them look like insignificant midgets. The second was when the lead actress could not pronounce the word of a composer and the infuriated director was about to fire her. I realized, "I could do this!" More importantly, I wanted to. It was a whim that came out of my past. I had old, cheerful memories of being onstage. And I was by nature dramatic; my mother used to call me Sarah Bernhardt. And I did have some of that Hungarian blood. (I've been called "over-dramatic" most of my life. But that's how it *seemed!*)

To sustain myself, I did the usual smorgasbord of jobs: waitress, elementary school teacher, office clerk, salesperson. In the long run I was utterly unsuited to them all, although I loved teaching kids. I taught kindergarten and first grade in Harlem. I found the children hungry for learning, and it was from the challenges of teaching them without the benefit of any training myself that my short films for children's television evolved.

I signed up for acting lessons. Luckily, I became a member of La Mama Plexus, the avant-garde theater group founded by Ellen Stewart, the genius who fostered the talents of Pulitzer-prize-winning playwright Sam Shepard, Leonard Melfi, and the brilliant Tom O'Horgan, creator of *Hair.* I was cast in a repertory show. Within a year, we were touring Europe and the USA. We mostly performed a very confrontational play, daring audiences to respond to our challenges and even insults. We prided ourselves on doing the work of Andreii Growtoski. His work is the subject of the film, *My Dinner With Andre.* We spent hours doing the *Cat,* and other preverbal workouts that had us groaning like various animals.

Being in repertory, I was strangely judgmental about the plays that we picked to perform; I didn't approve of the writing! I had absolutely *no* inkling why.

In England, we played on the West End. I had the part of a revolutionary. Singing was required. The musicians immediately adjusted my songs to a monotone. I was terrified on stage. I had to fight very hard to feel accepted. It wasn't in my nature to imagine I was approved of. This was a tremendous growing experience for me; I had to work with the darker side of my personality which was shouting in my ear, "You're no good," and get on with it, challenge myself to fulfill the role. I put everything I had into this battle every single night. I made some headway.

And it took me years to realize that when I was comfortable and knew the registers, I could sing adequately. In any case, in 1969, our little band was one of many in London. All the American acting troupes were in England that summer: the Living Theater, the Open Theater, and many others made every night lively. There was nothing else for me then except our little world of the theater. Sunrise was the signal that it was time to go to bed.

At the end of the summer, the Equinox, we all went down to Stonehenge together. The Living Theater enraged the Druids who, once a year, perform a sacred ceremony there. They climbed the ancient rock formations and struck incredible poses at dawn. We all thought it was funny when the Druids turned around and left in protest. We had no sense of robbing these people of their ritual. Now, I see it from the Druids's point of view.

Coming back to the States after Europe was once again a real letdown. New York in the summer is a cement jail sentence, and it was business as usual for the actors. I went up for some roles outside the troupe. This was before women's lib. I discovered, with the other women in the troupe, that the men at La Mama were misogynists. During one of our rehearsals for a play I did *not* want to be in, I broke my right leg in three places. As they carried me from the emergency room, I distinctly remember asking the doctor, hope resonating in my voice, "Does this mean I can't act for awhile?" The doctor laughed.

For several months, I was laid up in a cast up to my hip. I guess it took that much to keep me in one place with a lot of time to think. I slowly remembered the joy of painting, where you didn't have to wait for scores of others to be ready in order to be creative. I had an inspiration: I would go into children's books. That idea had never crossed my mind before, but I couldn't afford to be a painter. You need years of growing your reputation before you could expect to earn a living, and I had to support myself immediately. So, children's books were my solution. It was commercial but "pure." A way to make art that was both personal and had a mass audience; it made perfect sense.

I also believe on another level, instinctively, I knew I had to go back to childhood and heal some of my experiences. My books had loving, understanding mothers,

"I'm seated front row far right," Paris, 1965.

children who were understood even when they were testy. What seemed like a random choice was probably very well thought out by another quarter of my personality.

Questa Paradiso

I had no idea what being an illustrator meant or how to go about it. But at last my compass had a direction, one I'd stick to for the first time in my life.

Children's book art meant I had to relearn how to draw from my fine arts background. I discovered this the hard way. I had taken around a portfolio the size of a door, filled with my best college work. Art directors and editors suggested I scale down the size. They sometimes gave me directions, information, inspiration, and even books. I found I had the ear of several of the best editors at the time. Elizabeth Shub was one. Beatrice Schenk de Regniers, author of *May I Bring A Friend,* one of my favorite picture books, was another. When I finally assembled a book dummy, I raced back uptown. I had concocted a story that was probably more a flashback to my days in the mountains of Santa Barbara. I will spare the details although I'll admit it had a psychedelic feel. Let's just say I was kindly encouraged to keep going, which I did. I promptly returned with a more mundane story about lima beans. I was just reaching for something I *thought* children would like, working from the outside in. I was firmly advised *not* to write books about food.

I spent hours in the libraries and book stores. I began to find favorite illustrators and authors; Maurice Sendak, Arnold Lobel, Russell Hoban, Hilary Knight, William Steig, Marjorie Sharmat among others.

Around that time I was in Boston accompanying a friend who was photographing the marathon for a magazine. But I didn't fit in and wanted to go home. I hopped back on a train to New York City. I gazed out the window impatiently. The train was *crawling!* Maybe all the conversations with editors finally inspired me. My thought was, "I could get home so much *faster* if only I was a giant." When I got home, I wrote *What Would You Do With a Giant?* I showed it a friend who had a nine-year-old son. At the time, there was only one boy in the story. Tim looked at me incredulously and said, "You can't have just *one* boy. *Where's the other boy?*" I added another character, realizing he was correct. Children are excellent, if not always kind, critics.

I went uptown to Knopf. Fabio Cohen was a legend in his own time. He was a Daumier silhouette, a grand Italian presence right up there on Fifty-second Street. I eagerly showed him my book dummy. "This book is publishable," he declared. "But I've never seen you before in my life! I can't just publish you off the street like that." I felt as if I were Eliza in *My Fair Lady.* Only I wasn't to get that room somewhere.

I was heartbroken, but also encouraged. He had said that magic word—"publishable."

One day I received a call from Barbara Gordon, who was then running Putnam's. She liked the *What Would You Do With a Giant?* dummy. She was seriously considering buying it and wanted to meet with me. When our meeting came around, the powers that be had already voted to accept it. I was handed a contract. My heart thumped wildly. I had just climbed the Everest of my own self-doubt

Bottner during her actress days.

and long-standing lack of confidence. My life had really begun. And I was going to receive something like three thousand dollars. My God, I could go back to Europe on that kind of money.

I began to illustrate the book. I made my entire apartment into a studio. I was working days at a center for seniors in Bushwick, Brooklyn. I shlepped on the Carnarsie line and arrived into what seemed like a foreign country. I was an Arts and Crafts counselor, helping truculent retirees from the Old World sew dresses.

The center was split down the middle—half Irish, half German, tempered by a fair amount of Italians. Once a week, they had alternating bands of polka players and schmaltzy Italian music. One older man looked around at the grey cinder blocks and the balloons hanging from the ceiling, and his cronies on the dance floor, and said to me, "Questa Paradiso." (This is Paradise.)

Evenings, when I returned from Paradise, I drew. Eventually, I was pleased with the black-and-white drawings that would be the basis for the color separation sheets I had to hand in. But I was in for a horrible experience. I turned in percentages (these were the olden days of color separation) that made the giant appear as if he'd just broken out in a case of lethal hives. His skin was fire engine red. I cried when I saw the finished book, which was primitive by any standards, but would have really had charm if only the giant were different. I pleaded and begged to correct the problem, but I was told it was too expensive. So my giant looks as if he's eternally embarrassed.

To Make a Difference

Right around then, on the long trail I'd wandered, I met someone who told me I ought to teach. I took his word for it, and marched over to Parsons School of Design, which was part of the New School. As I trotted in to be interviewed, I passed a man rushing out. He'd just quit this very position I was to land. I had nothing to qualify myself as a teacher except enthusiasm and timing, some might call it Fate. I told my interviewer I could do the job. He said the brochure was going to print, and he had no one in sight but me. And so I was hired on the spot, innocent of training.

A few weeks later I looked out on a sea of expectant faces. If they were aware of how little I knew, they'd make haste to a coffee bar, but I was not about to do anything but inspire confidence. I gave an assignment. When they were handed in, we discussed them. I, the Great Author/Artist, with exactly one picture book under my belt, led the criticism.

I distinctly remember a moment when I looked at someone's work which was posted on the board. Everything in the drawing was static and forced. There was no life anywhere, except for the cat. The cat had all the aliveness, the people were dead. I remarked about how strange that was, look at that incredibly witty cat, isn't *that* where your eye wants to go, isn't *that* who you want to know more about? The woman confessed how terrified she was of people and how much she loved animals, especially her cat. Moments like those gave me the confidence I needed. I was able to read people's drawings and make interpretations.

I believed wholeheartedly that since we'd all gone through childhood we all had stories to tell. Even those who said, "My childhood? I don't remember it," couldn't squirm off the hook. I relished observing the process of creativity unfold. It was a joy for me to make a contribution in helping the development that occurred every week. I'd

spent my early life feeling like I didn't make any difference, and finally, I knew I was.

It wasn't easy. I had people in my class from rehab situations, who were just biding their time; I had schizophrenics who wandered around the classroom in a disruptive way; I had alcoholics; I had angry teenage artists who reminded me of myself. I had every kind of person. In nurturing them, I experienced nurturing myself. It was very healthy for me, and I flourished along with my students. Talent was easy to recognize. And as I fed people with my observations about what made a good story, what were good characters, how to create endings, I found I was teaching myself. I was forced to teach what *I* needed to learn! Meanwhile, uptown, editors were guiding me on my way to what I thought would be a lifelong career.

The first book to be published from class was *That Man Is Talking to His Toes,* written and illustrated by Jacquii Hann. Jacquii had spent all semester drawing and swearing she was not a storyteller. I kept persisting, nagging. She's a diminutive person, and I know she thought I was ganging up on her. So the very last class of the semester, Jacquii came in with her very first book dummy, and it was complete and very funny. I had an editor visiting the class, Marjorie Cuyler from Holiday House. Marjorie took one look and *wanted* it! In the end,

"Me in my loft," New York, 1970s.

another house published the book. So, this was what it felt to mentor a person. Pretty nice feeling!

Around that time, I had another student, Laura Numeroff. Out of class she published *Amy for Short.* Laura is the author of the contemporary classic, *If You Give a Mouse a Cookie.*

Filmmaking: Frame By Frame

Although I fell more and more in love with the emotional honesty, the playfulness, and magic of children's books, I also took the next step, which was to make these drawings move. I learned how to animate from some classes at the School of Visual Arts. I could sit and draw forever! I decided to find work in the field. When I took around my sparse portfolio, I was happily rejected from every company in the city. I begged, "Just let me make coffee." I wanted to learn. Mostly a male trade, nobody was dying to open any doors for me.

Then I heard that the writers and producers of "Sesame Street" and "The Electric Company" were looking for filmmakers. I created some storyboards and sold five. Now I had an entirely new problem—to produce them. I had to hire one of these same animation companies that had refused to hire me. I chose one.

This experience taught me so much. You don't have to be an apprentice. You have to work to the level you are capable of, and the market will want you.

The finished product was sent to the Journees Internationale du Cinema D'Animation who sponsor a competition held every other year. I was informed, on official French stationery, that my films had been chosen to compete and, if I showed up in Annecy in June, all my expenses would be paid!

That summer in Annecy, New York City animators cleaned up: Frank Morris for his autobiographical short which was seven years in the making and winner of an Academy Award, Eli Noyes for *Sandman,* a ground-breaking film done entirely in sand, and others. I won "Best Film for TV," for my three "Electric Company" shorts (and I mean *short,* under three minutes!). I will never forget sitting in the auditorium in that medieval town and hearing these words boom overhead: *"Ce soir, nous avons dans le chambre, Barbara Bottner."* A light swooped over me, and then, so much applause! It was thrilling to be recognized so early in a career by peers with so much experience and talent themselves. I was presented with a zootrope, which sits on my desk today.

Those years in New York a lot of us were interested in the short personal film. Animated film was seen as a way into the soul; it created a world that was utterly personal and without limits. And your work often went on the short film circuit and was shown at competitions around the world. I decided to make *my* personal film. It was three minutes long, which is long if you are directing, producing, designing, drawing every frame, shooting and cutting it yourself. It was called *Later That Night,* and it originated in a dream in which I was trying to solve the conflict over being a strong woman in a man's world. It received a Cine Golden Eagle and was picked up for distribution, even though it had generous technical flaws. I had bought an old Bolex and installed it at my partner, Jody Silver's loft. Eventually, however, I realized how little I could earn in this venue, and that I lacked the patience and technical interest. I still have no desire to expand into the commercial animation market.

My Late Twenties, Maybe Thirty

But teaching at Parson's, the New School, and taking a fiction course there had whetted my appetite for longer books, novels. I found myself writing one. At one end of my loft were my drawings. One idea, many, many drawings. At the other end was my typewriter. Many ideas in one sentence. I liked this equation much better. I returned money and decided that where I lived the most deeply, I wanted to write longer books.

This was a difficult decision. I had to face questions and doubts all over again. Who was I to think others would be interested in what I had to say? I had a million shouts and whispers inside me saying "You're not allowed. You're no good. How *dare* you?" I had to face all this self-doubt all over again. I began a convoluted novel for adults and was surprised how assiduously I worked on it.

I was in my late twenties, maybe around thirty. I had absolutely no desire to be married, and having children is a concept I didn't even think about. I was an artist. I was learning, teaching, studying. My friends were all like me. Some brilliant, all gifted, all struggling to carve out an artist/writer/musician's life that would sustain them.

One day, I was asked by Elaine Edelman of Harper and Row to illustrate a manuscript. Oddly, the author of that manuscript, Shirley Gordon of the wonderful Crystal series, subsequently became a friend of mine. But I turned it down, because I figured I should only be doing my own work. This was the height of conceit because I didn't have that much of my own work back then. But I did have a story based on my experience as a ballet student. It was called *Dumb Old Casey Is a Fat Tree.* Elaine wisely asked me to send it to her. The page count of that first draft was sparse: about nine. Elaine read it. In the margins she asked questions. *Many* questions! When she returned the manuscript to me, I systematically went about answering them. That manuscript lengthened into twenty-seven typed pages, a real story, with a beginning, middle, end; a plot, even. Harper and Row published it with my own drawings. I told them to make the cover red, which they did. This experience with Elaine was key. I've learned from my editors; they have ushered me into places I would never have believed I could go. They taught me whatever I know about writing. I was so grateful. Still am.

Sometime later, my confidence growing, I became a serious student of young adult fiction. I read M. E. Kerr, Paul Zindel, Katherine Paterson, Richard Peck, Robert Cormier. There is such wonderful work in that field, and all the key components of a novel are present, only whittled down. You are always aware of *story.* I always preferred first person fiction. I loved knowing the character from his voice, and I knew that was the kind of book I wanted to write. And given my teen years, I was sure I had material.

Out West

Around this time, I moved west. I left New York because it had become stale for me. I'd been there for twelve years, most of them struggling to keep body and soul together. On every street I could remember a door I'd knocked on, a job I had done or been rejected for. So I rented a small bungalow in Hollywood with a backyard full of fig and orange trees. California seemed like deliverance.

Los Angeles, it turned out, has ten thousand resident writers. Every hopeful screenwriter arrives there believing their script will make them rich. I squelched any thoughts of working in the movies, and heard of a class given by novelist John Rechy, the highly acclaimed author of *City of Night,* now in its twenty-fifth printing, *Numbers, The Amazing Day of Amalia Gomez,* and many other titles. John was my first and only writing teacher. A combination of Susan Sontag, Liberace, and Johnny Carson, he was brilliant, generous, and entertaining; self-mocking, teasing, a sort of one-man show. I joined a small bunch of John devotees.

One day, while unpacking, I found thirty-five pages that I had written in New York City. Sometimes I would put unfinished work away, and I often hid it so well, I'd forget I'd ever written it. This time, when I rediscovered the manuscript, I submitted it to Linda Zuckerman, formerly a senior editor at Viking. She was temporarily freelancing as an editor. She gave me wonderful comments, but warned me that there were too many themes in the book. Focus it more and use the left-over material for other novels, she suggested.

I thought about this. But I wanted this book to be powerful, complex. I wanted it to cover the pain I had in growing up. This was about two girls who each had to deal with losses around their mothers, and a sort of sibling rivalry. So I kept going for another seventy pages. Always worried about money, I decided to submit it to Linda again, who was now the West Coast editor to HarperCollins. She bought it!

I still had to finish the book. I was about forty, and my mother was dying of cancer. I was frequently traveling back and forth to Florida where she lived alone. All the feelings of all the years of our estrangement made me want to find some closure and healing. My mother fought for her

Bottner with her husband, Gerald, about the time of their marriage, 1988.

life for four years. Her death was devastating to me. I realized how hard her life had been, and how many dreams she'd never fulfilled. I realized that the blindness in her eye she'd sustained as a young girl and other circumstances had made her insecure and unable to express herself. When my brother and I closed up her house in Florida, I found myself incredibly weak.

A short time after returning to L.A., I consulted a doctor. Chronic Fatigue Immune Deficiency Syndrome was brand new back then, just being recognized as a disease, but I got a working diagnosis. For the next year I was very sick with night sweats, fevers, no energy, glassy eyes, loss of appetite, loss of memory, crying jags, loss of sleep, frequent sore throats, and swollen glands. I was convinced that I was slowly following my mother into the grave. Maybe all the unfinished business was too much for me, I thought. And I was in mourning—for the mother I lost and the mother I wished I had and never would. I could barely care for myself, and because the disease was so unknown, those of us that had it in the mid-eighties were thought to be whiners and complainers.

Inner Voices

But I had this book to finish. I set up my computer in bed. I kept food in the house and didn't leave, except for absolute necessities. One of them was John Rechy's Tuesday night class, when I could make it.

This is when Melissa learns that her beloved mother surrogate, Mrs. Gregori, has died:

> "You sound like the poor, neglected child," said Gigi, her tone sharpened as she put the pizza in the oven.
>
> "And you don't sound like anyone's mother."
>
> "You really know how to get on my good side."
>
> "I didn't know you had one," I murmured.
>
> She dabbed on some powder. "Now that was stupid. Because I'm grounding you." She didn't even look at me.
>
> *"I just wanted us to make dinner!"*

Through Sara, the other narrator, I wrote about my own defensivness, denial, and determination. I wanted to write a deep book, one that could speak to some of the troubled kids I saw and heard about on the evening news. I also wanted to make the point that coming from a family with money can have its own set of problems. Not getting emotional needs met is a serious violation of a child's needs. Sara and Melissa are on two sides of the coin, but they are both hurting, both damaged.

This is Sara, when her defenses finally crumble after her mother's death:

> Mourning. It vacuums up everything. Your backbone goes, your will, your sense of smell, your ability to move, your rhythm, your desire for chocolate, for comfort, nice weather, new shoes, good grades, it all goes. I didn't miss anyone. I wasn't hungry. I bought a sandwich, didn't eat it. Food smelled wrong, noxious. I lived on a box of Saltines.

Two days drifted by. I'm not sure how. Maybe I slept some. I read an old magazine. I suppose I showered because there was a towel with moisture on it. This heartache had awful power: it blotted everything out. I wept torrents, but there was always more to weep. I was exhausted.

I went to the window and watched people on the street walk, kids jump around. Why did they bother? There was nothing to fight about, talk about, laugh about. They were pretending. Lying. Lying because to live was a lie, there was only death and loss, endings, disappointments, hurt. Idiots. Life was a lie. Why must they go on acting as if it was true.

I cried, imagined, spoke to her, yelled, screamed at her, blasphemed God, buried her, dug her up, explained to her, questioned her, forgave her, punished her, hid from her, revealed myself, refused to believe, and believed. I let the downpour come.

I alternated voices because while I was inside each character, their voice told me the next chapter, like hitting a tennis ball across the net. The ball would be lobbed back and forth almost by itself. All I had to do was serve. I was scared of the adventure, but I knew I was lucky to be on it.

I worked and reworked from John's comments, writing in the back bedroom of the little Hollywood bungalow on Citrus Avenue. When I turned the novel in, I was slowly beginning to come back from the treacherous effects of my disease.

X rays Expose the Bride in Me

Prankster Fate had a new adventure lined up. I had a test to take after being hospitalized for an undiagnosed problem. The doctors let me out after starving me for six days, leaving me uncharacteristically svelte. I ended up in a radiology office in Beverly Hills. For some reason, I decided to put on makeup the morning of the appointment.

The exam room was cold, as were the busy techs. I hadn't eaten for days. But there was one place of warmth; the radiologist's voice. It was like "butta." He had a gap tooth, and large, pleasant Russian features, which I always favored. He and I struck up a conversation we are still having; we married in 1988, a Jewish Buddhist wedding.

My husband, Gerald, has decidedly influenced my work. My recent picture book, *Nana Hannah's Piano,* is about a granny who loves the piano and the Pittsburgh Pirates, and her grandson, a Yankees fan. They are able to reach each other both through the love of music and sports. Gerald was the inspiration for this story, even furnishing the facts about the 1960 Yankees-Pirates World Series. He is Mr. Sports, after all. He's also a fastidious editor, a wonderful writer; an author-to-be, I believe. Each of us resides on different sides of our brains. We are extremely different people, and our life with each other is never dull.

During this time period, I was also writing for television. I wrote several episodes of "Winnie the Pooh," for Disney cable. Becoming A. A. Milne—what better training could you ask for? What an education that was! Milne created stories and conflict between the gentlest of characters. I also wrote for a sit-com, children's TV, tried

my hand at screenwriting, and sold two full-length (unproduced) features. This form is so demanding, so structured. I love the idea of writing the characters until they come to an inevitable confrontation. I admire how drama must work. And I've come to respect how hard it is to do. The demands of the form have added to my understanding of storytelling and also forced me to confront my own weaknesses as a writer.

Sometimes I will write fifty pages of intense, convincing, forward-moving story thick with possibilities, and then I start to think, what happens next? And I realize *I do not know!* Sometimes I put the manuscript away at this point. Sometimes I read it to friends. Sometimes I do an outline. And always I think, if I could write endings with as much zest as beginnings, I'd have a lot more work out there.

I believe our strengths and weaknesses on paper exactly mirror those we have in real life. Since I'm a very upfront, confrontational person, so are most of my characters. And my characters are complex like me, too. Often, too complex, as if my own unconscious has leapt out onto the page, helter skelter. It's the writer's job to control this. I'm still at it. I have problems when I try to force my characters to solve emotional issues I, myself, have not been able to solve in my own life—yet.

Writing never gets easier: for every tree you climb, there are acres of forest surrounding you.

There have been two steady anchors in my career, writing books for children and teaching. Passing through my classes were superstars-to-be, like Lane Smith, Joe Ranff, one of the creators of *Toy Story,* Barney Saltzburg, Diane Greenseid, Nancy Hayashi, Bruce Degen, Diana Blumenthal, illustrator of *Nana Hanna's Piano,* and many others who have careers as writers or writer/illustrators.

One day, someone came into my class, along with her mother, and she had the most terrific intensity. She also had been classically trained as an artist. She said she was lost, except for her desire to write and illustrate books for children. In order to get to class, she had to travel an hour each way from her home in Ventura County.

She was quiet and self-effacing, but her drawings were nervy, wry, and stunning. She amazed the class week after week with her work. From a class assignment, she created *Ruby, the Copycat,* which was published by one of my editors at Scholastic. By then, I was convinced I wanted to work with Peggy Rathmann. When I asked her to draw Bootsie, she was horrified. "I could never draw anyone as mean and horrible as this girl!"

I challenged her to try, to see how far she could push herself. A few classes later, she brought in the first sketches of Bootsie, which were hilarious. Peggy poured over the dummy, and so did her mother, Joy, and we faxed each other various versions. Even my husband got into the act by suggesting the "game" the girls play be "paleontologist." It was as if Bootsie had a life of her own, and heaven forbid that anyone get in her way.

Peggy won the Caldecott in 1996 for her fourth and hilarious book, *Officer Buckle and Gloria,* which she created in class from an assignment. We were all proud of her. We all knew it was only a matter of time until she'd nab it.

Bootsie Barker Ballerina came out in the spring of 1997. *Bootsie Barker Frankenstein* will follow. Another funny character, this one very needy and demanding, was published by Golden Books Entertainment; the first book is called *Marsha Makes Me Sick.*

I find myself chopped up into pieces; so many things interest me. I'm always coming up with picture book ideas. And they are so satisfying, so much story, so few words. I enjoy the working over them until they are perfect, like a poem. It suits my sense of *finishing* something to work on a picture book. Novels and screenplays are something that never seem to cease needing attention. Ever. I am working on a novel about Skinheads that tells the story of a young boy drawn against his better judgement into that movement. I am also working on a book about a girl in a mental hospital.

Here's an idea of how stories come to me. I was down in Fort Lauderdale on a glass bottom boat. The goal was to observe marine life. As it happened, this particular day was overcast and the sea was not calm. Minutes after we left the dock, I became extremely uncomfortable. I could not bear to look down into the glass bottom of the boat, because then I would lose control. But, finally, I forced myself, and what did I see? Not a dolphin, not incredible fish, but Bootsie Barker. I imagined her terrorizing Lisa, half fish, half girl. Lisa couldn't get away from her, even at sea. So that day was a present to me. *Bootsie Barker Overboard* was born.

Restructuring a Life

My husband and I moved to Hollywood, Florida, for his career as a physician. I am facing restructuring a life. I live in this quiet town by the sea, which sometimes seems as if I was given a chance to balance my former intense lifestyle. Luckily, this is an area that loves books and has a strong book community, headed by the beloved Mitch Kaplan of Books N' Books of Miami Beach. There are many writers hidden in them thar marshes. But still, I am considering what is important to spend my time on.

The answer I come up with is drama. Conflict, confrontation, pacing, character arcs, earned shifts in character, are most enticing. They force a writer to think like an architect. This is my exact area of weakness. On other days, I want to stick with my strengths. Voice, dialogue, humor. The battle goes on. And always which story to tell?

To Be Continued

For twelve years I have been a student of Japanese Buddhism. This religion has infused me with the understanding that the potential for good and evil exists in all of life: that we each have karma which is the result of causes we make by thought, word, and deed. Buddhism is a life-affirming philosophy that teaches us to take the obstacles and transform them into learning experiences. We call this turning "poison into medicine." I have learned that we all have tremendous power to root out negative tendencies and to win in our daily life. My own personal goal is to become as conscious as possible. I intend to write about characters who are forced by themselves or by circumstances to face who they are and what they're motivated by. This means that I aspire to honesty, clarity, and courage. There are always places where I am cloudy or running away. My

work is to keep running towards the hard spots. To make them funny, truthful, entertaining, and universal.

Thank you for reading! To those of you who are making the quest, keep writing! Keep going! You are on the journey that will eventually clarify, illuminate, and sanctify your life.

Writings

FOR CHILDREN; SELF-ILLUSTRATED

What Would You Do with a Giant?, Putnam, 1972.
Fun House, Prentice Hall, 1974.
Doing the Toledo, Four Winds Press, 1977.
There Was Nobody There, Macmillan, 1978.
Jungle Day, Delacorte, 1978.
Big Boss, Little Boss, Pantheon, 1978.
Myra, Macmillan, 1979.
Messy, Macmillan, 1979.
Mean Maxine, Pantheon, 1980.
Dumb Old Casey Is a Fat Tree, Harper & Row, 1984.
Two Messy Friends, Cartwheel, 1998.

FOR CHILDREN

Eek, a Monster, Macmillan, 1975.
The Box, Macmillan, 1975.
What Grandma Did on Her Birthday, Macmillan, 1975.
Horrible Hannah, illustrated by Joan Drescher, Crown, 1980.
The World's Greatest Expert on Everything Is Crying, Harper, 1984.
Zoo Song, illustrated by Lynn Munsinger, Scholastic, 1987.
Hurricane Music, illustrated by Paul Yalowitz, Putnam, 1995.
Nana Hanna's Piano, illustrated by Diana Cain, Putnam, 1997.
Bootsie Barker Bites, illustrated by Peggy Rathmann, Putnam, 1997.
Bootsie Barker Ballerina, illustrated by G. Brian Karas, HarperCollins, 1997.
Marsha Makes Me Sick, illustrated by Denise Brunkus, Golden Books, 1998.
Marsha Is Only a Flower, illustrated by Denise Brunkus, Golden Books, 2000.
It's Not Marsha's Birthday, illustrated by Denise Brunkus, Golden Books, 2001.
The Scaredy Cats, illustrated by Victoria Chess, Simon and Schuster, 2002.

YOUNG ADULT NOVELS

Nothing in Common: A Novel, Harper, 1986.
Let Me Tell You Everything: Memoirs of a Lovesick Intellectual, Harper, 1989.

ILLUSTRATOR

Sid Fleischmann, *Kate's Secret Riddle Book,* Watts, 1977.

OTHER

Also author of humor pieces for adults in various periodicals, including *LA Weekly* and *The Miami Herald.*

Contributor of short stories to *Cosmopolitan* and *Playgirl* and criticism of children's books for *New York Times Book Review* and *Los Angeles Times Book Review*. Has also written for television, for educational reading series, and designed, directed, and produced three short films for *The Electric Company*.

BRACKETT, Virginia (Roberts Meredith) 1950-

Personal

Born April 7, 1950, in Fort Riley, KS; daughter of Edmund Condon Roberts (in the military) and Helen Kost Roberts Ferranti (a teacher); married William R. Meredith, (a physician; divorced); married Edmund Charles Brackett (an educational administrator), July 26, 1991; children: Lisa Paige Meredith, Shandra Renee Meredith, William Wade Meredith, Marcus A. Brackett (stepson). *Education:* University of Arkansas Medical Center, B.S.M.T. (medical technology), 1973; Missouri Southern State College, B.S. (marketing and management), 1989; Pittsburgh State University, M.A. (English), 1991; University of Kansas, Ph.D. (English), 1998. *Politics:* Democrat. *Religion:* Protestant. *Hobbies and other interests:* Gardening, research on women writers, puzzles.

Virginia Brackett

Addresses

E-mail—gingerbrackett@hotmail.com.

Career

Medical technologist in Little Rock, AR, and Denver, CO, 1973-78; manager and co-owner of ophthalmology practice, Joplin, MO, 1978-89. Institute of Children's Literature, West Redding, CT, correspondence instructor, 1993-99; East Central University, Ada, OK, English instructor and professor, 1994-99; Triton College, River Grove, IL, English instructor, 1999—. *Member:* Society of Children's Book Writers and Illustrators, Modern Language Association, International Shakespeare Association, National Council of Teachers of English.

Awards, Honors

University of Kansas Merrill Research Award, 1994; included in catalog of recommended reading for teens, New York Public Library, 1996, for *Elizabeth Cary: Writer of Conscience;* East Central University research grants, 1997, 1998, for *Early Women Writers: Voices from the Margins;* Oklahoma Humanities Foundation research grant and East Central University grant, both 1999, both for "Angie Debo: American Indian Champion."

Writings

Elizabeth Cary: Writer of Conscience (juvenile biography), Morgan Reynolds (Greensboro, NC), 1996.

Charles Dickens's David Copperfield, Edcon Publishing, 1998.

Classic Love and Romance Literature: An Encyclopedia of Works, Characters, Authors and Themes (nonfiction), ABC-Clio (Santa Barbara, CA), 1999.

Jeff Bezos (juvenile biography), Chelsea House (Philadelphia, PA), 2000.

John Brown (juvenile biography), Chelsea House (Philadelphia, PA), 2001.

F. Scott Fitzgerald: A Biography, Morgan Reynolds (Greensboro, NC), 2001.

The Contingent Self: An Ideology of the Personal (adult nonfiction), Purdue University Press (West Lafayette, IN), 2001.

Contributor of more than one hundred stories and articles, juvenile and adult, to periodicals, including *Children's Writer, Byline, Write Now, Children's Digest, Turtle, Today's Family,* and *Today's Christian Woman.* Contributor of articles to academic journals, including *Notes & Queries, Mosaic,* and *Women and Language.*

Work in Progress

A biography of Angie Debo, Oklahoma American Indian rights activist, and research on Debo's childhood correspondence; a biography of F. Scott Fitzgerald for young adults; research on early women writers.

Sidelights

Virginia Brackett told *SATA:* "I did not begin writing for publication until I was almost forty years old. The article that jumpstarted my career featured my mother and my father, who was killed in Korea, and I overcame my hesitance to write through a creative writing course at a local university. Although I had enjoyed writing in high school (I wrote most of the scripts for our high school assemblies during my senior year), I ended up pursuing a career in medical technology, then business, and also helped to raise three children. I used all of these activities as an excuse not to write. Following a critical life change, I rediscovered the great nurturing effect of writing, and I returned to college in 1989 to obtain a graduate degree in English, believing that a serious study of literature would help my writing abilities. It certainly did that, but it also did more. Along the way, I discovered a love for teaching, which became my third vocation. I also decided that I wanted to mold what many readers might consider the 'esoteric' subject matter of academia for popular readers, including a young audience.

"My academic studies of early women writers (1500s-1800s) ignited a tremendous excitement over a group of courageous individuals about whom little was known. This led to the writing and publication of two of my books, *Elizabeth Cary: Writer of Conscience* and *Early Women Writers: Voices from the Margins.* All of the women discussed in these books wrote, and some even published, during an extremely difficult time for women to be heard. Their pursuit of creative goals I found astounding, and I wanted to share that with an audience [that seems] to most need that motivation and inspiration: young readers. No one can read of Elizabeth Cary, writing while separated from her children and rejected by her husband due to her religious beliefs, and fail to think 'Wow—if she can do it, so can I,' whatever that 'it' happens to be. As a writer, I've discovered the power to bring to life a brilliant woman whose story remained untold for literally centuries. Nothing intoxicates me as that act does. I would say to aspiring writers that the particular date on which you begin writing remains unimportant. What is important is the fact that you may, indeed, incorporate your personal passions into your writing. You simply must share those things you love the best with others."

Biographical and Critical Sources

PERIODICALS

Booklist, September 15, 1999, J. E. Sheets, review of *Classic Love and Romance Literature,* p. 301.
Choice, January, 2000, review of *Classic Love and Romance Literature,* p. 894.
Library Journal, August, 1999, Peter A. Dollard, review of *Classic Love and Romance Literature,* p. 74.
School Library Journal, Maru H. Cole, review of *Classic Love and Romance Literature,* p. 77.

*   *   *

BRIDE, Nadja
See NOBISSO, Josephine

*   *   *

BROOKS, Martha 1944-

Personal

Born July 15, 1944, in Ninette, Manitoba, Canada; daughter of Alfred Leroy (a thoracic surgeon) and Theodis (a nurse; maiden name, Marteinsson) Paine; married Brian Brooks (an owner and operator of an advertising and public relations firm), August 26, 1967; children: Kirsten. *Education:* St. Michael's Academy, Brandon, Manitoba, 1962.

Addresses

Home—58-361 Westwood Dr., Winnipeg, Manitoba, Canada R3K 1G4.

Career

Writer, 1972—; creative writing teacher in junior and senior high schools, through the Artist in the Schools program of the Manitoba Arts Council, beginning in early 1980s. Has also worked as a model, secretary, mentor to young writers, and a jazz singer.

Awards, Honors

Shortlisting for Governor General's Award for Children's Literature, 1988, and *Boston Globe/Horn Book* Honor Book Award, 1991, all for *Paradise Cafe and Other Stories;* Vicky Metcalf Award, Canadian Authors Association, 1989, for "A Boy and His Dog"; Chalmers Canadian Children's Play Award, 1991, for *Andrew's Tree;* Best Book for Young Adults selection, American Library Association, for *Two Moons in August;* Best Book for Young Adults selection and Best Books for Reluctant Readers selection, American Library Association, both for *Traveling on into the Light and Other Stories;* Best Book of the Year selection, American Library Association, 1997, Ruth Schwartz Award, and CLA Young Adult Canadian Book of the Year, 1998, all for *Bone Dance;* Mr. Christie's Book Award, 1999, for *Being with Henry.*

Writings

FOR YOUNG ADULTS

Paradise Cafe and Other Stories, Thistledown Press, 1988, Little, Brown, 1990.

Martha Brooks

Two Moons in August, Groundwood Books, 1991, Little, Brown, 1992.
Traveling on into the Light and Other Stories, Orchard, 1994.
Bone Dance, Orchard, 1997.
Being with Henry, DK Inc., 2000.

OTHER

A Hill for Looking, Queenston House, 1982.
Moonlight Sonata (play), produced at Prairie Theater Exchange, Winnipeg, Manitoba, Canada, 1994.
(With Maureen Hunter) *I Met a Bully on a Hill* (play; produced across Canada), Scirocco Drama, 1995.
Andrew's Tree (play; produced across Canada), Scirocco Drama, 1995.

Also author, with Sandra Birdsell and David Gillies, of the play *A Prairie Boy's Winter.*

Work in Progress

"Another book which, at the moment of this writing, is gathering power at the edge of dreamtime."

Sidelights

Canadian author Martha Brooks has penned award-winning short stories and several powerful novels for young readers, as well as several plays, all of which deal with the universal themes of love and loss. Her finely drawn characters learn to deal with the trials life sends their way and grow because of such trials. Brooks's first collection of short stories, *Paradise Cafe and Other Stories,* was nominated for the prestigious Governor

General's Award for Children's Literature in Canada, and "is a significant title in Canadian Young Adult literature for its 1988 publication signaled a rebirth of the short story collection as a legitimate vehicle for adolescents' recreational reading," according to Dave Jenkinson writing in *St. James Guide to Young Adult Writers.*

Brooks is known for tautly drawn stories and novels in which "each word is carefully chosen" to build "quietly eloquent sentences weaving a richly textured story that will appeal to introspective readers," as Judy Sasges described Brooks's fiction in *Voice of Youth Advocates.* In an interview for *Authors and Artists for Young Adults,* Brooks described her work as "cross-generational fiction." The author went on to note, "I have to say that I dislike the defining description, Young Adult Author. Right away, that has the propensity for limiting my readership. I'm really at a cross-roads with my writing. It would be so easy to tip over to the other side, in other words to write for a (much larger) adult audience. But I still feel that what I am doing is important in recording young adult experience, and in sharing with that audience. As well, there are some of us who dare to redefine the borders of our chosen art form and I think that's what I'm doing, along with other good people who refuse to stay put and do the same thing over and over again."

Brooks once explained that her fiction "is about that particular time in life when the senses are sharp and life is bewildering and pain and love have very blurry borders. What is important is that I try to be true to the characters I invent—listening to them, letting them tell their stories, and respecting the lives they live on the page as they face the realities of love, death, family turmoil, exploitation, addiction. I always keep in mind, though, the aspects of healing and hope because life is full of possibilities." Such instances of healing and hope are sprinkled throughout the stories in the collections *Paradise Cafe* and *Traveling on into the Light,* as well as in Brooks's three novels, *Two Moons in August, Bone Dance,* and *Being with Henry.*

Born in a rural community in Manitoba, Canada, Brooks grew up in a medical household. Her parents both worked at a tuberculosis (TB) sanatorium in southern Manitoba, and she came of age "on the lyrically beautiful grounds" of the sanatorium, living in "the sprawling red-roofed superintendent's residence. Hills rose above our house, and hills rolled away below to the shores of long green Pelican Lake. That was long ago, but my husband and I now spend most summer weekends at our cottage on that lake. The landscape of my youth still guides me spiritually, appearing as forceful entity in all of my fiction, but most specially in *Bone Dance.* Its latest incarnation is Heron Lake country in the final chapters of *Being with Henry.*"

When her older sister left for college, Brooks, only nine at the time and was left with few playmates. As a result, she turned to the patients at the sanatorium and to the staff, becoming a classically precocious child. "Children who grow up to be artists very often have unusual beginnings," Brooks once noted, "so these were mine—surrounded by people who were fighting to cure, or be cured of, a life-threatening disease. I, too, was not well. I suffered from recurring bouts with pneumonia as a child. All of these things made me an early and keen observer of human behavior; I had an 'old' way of looking at the world before I reached adulthood."

Brooks married an advertising and public relations professional in 1967, and moved to Winnipeg, Manitoba. With the birth of her daughter, Kirsten, she turned her hand to a long-time dream: becoming an author. However, for the first ten years that she was writing, editors were uninterested in her work. Finally in 1982 came her first publication, *A Hill for Looking,* but it was another six years before her next publication, the award-winning *Paradise Cafe.* This collection of fourteen stories deals with all varieties of love, from that of a boy

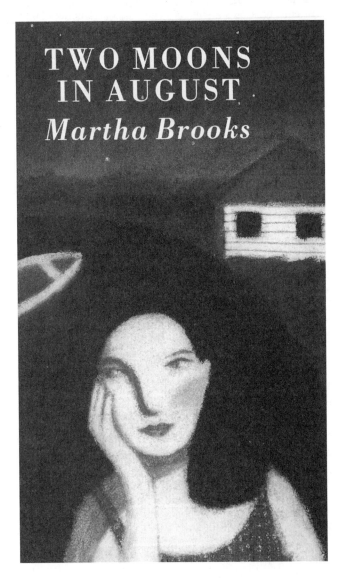

Friendship and romance with her sixteen-year-old neighbor help Sidonie and her family deal with the death of her mother. (Cover illustration by Judy Pederson.)

for his dying pet in "A Boy and His Dog," to first love in "Dying for Love," in which Ardis feels humiliated when her love is not returned by the best looking boy in class. In another tale, "The Crystal Stars Have Just Begun to Shine," teenage Deirdre plays matchmaker between her lonely father and the checkout woman at the local grocery. In "Like Lauren Bacall," Donalda relives the crush she once felt for her cousin and discovers that it was pure fantasy on her part. A retarded boy becomes part of a farm family in "The Way Things Are," and a girl is jilted because she is from the wrong side of the tracks in "King of the Roller Rink." Brooks used her own background to powerful effect in this first collection: many of the stories are set at a tuberculosis sanatorium, while others find their settings at an abandoned house, a roller rink, or the Paradise Cafe of the title.

Each of the stories in *Paradise Cafe* "packs an emotional wallop," according to Jenkinson, and none are longer than ten or eleven pages, making them a perfect fit for classroom reading. One of the most powerful is "A Boy and His Dog," which in 1988 won the Vicky Metcalf Short Story Award from the Canadian Authors Association. Buddy's dog Alphonse has been a beloved pet and companion since the boy was an infant, and now he learns that his dog is dying of cancer. "I'm fourteen going on fifteen and he's thirteen going on ninety-four," Buddy muses as he analyzes the unfairness of his pet's imminent death. Cynthia L. Beatty, writing in *Voice of Youth Advocates,* found this story "Especially touching." Beatty also commented, "There is enough variety in the stories for almost anyone to find several of interest." "The cast is diverse," noted Betsy Hearne in the *Bulletin of the Center for Children's Books,* "including French, Indian, and black characters. All share the pain and triumph of maturation with which young adult readers can identify." Reviewing the title in *Canadian Materials,* Gail Lennon felt that the stories could prove useful in a creative writing program because of their "excellent diction and use of figurative speech." Lennon went on to conclude, "It is among the best short story collections I have read in a long time!"

Brooks once recalled that the inspiration she had for her award-winning story in the collection. "How a story, for instance, like 'A Boy and His Dog' begins to be born is usually with a first line. 'My dog is old and he farts a lot.' I woke up one night with that line running through my head. It was a pretty funny line. It also contained a conflict, a necessary ingredient. It was sad, suggesting the theme, again, of love and loss. Within the first paragraph I had the voice of Buddy telling about his dog, Alphonse. The end result is of a boy's despairing over the unfairness of the death of Alphonse."

With her next work, *Two Moons in August,* Brooks turned to the novel format to tell the story of two girls in rural Manitoba in the summer of 1959 dealing with their grief over the loss of their mother. Sidonie's sixteenth birthday is approaching, as is the first anniversary of her mother's death. Sidonie's older sister Bobbi, back from college, escapes her sadness by taking on the role of boss, while her father has largely abandoned his daughters, throwing himself into his work at the local TB hospital. Sidonie is longing for the comfort of someone, anyone. Enter Kieran McMorran, the next door neighbor's son, who forms an attachment with Sidonie, helping her to work through her own grief. In the process, Kieran's problems also surface, and the two help each other toward a healing.

Ellen Ramsay, reviewing the novel in *School Library Journal,* felt that all the characters "are realistic individuals who develop credible insight and self-understanding over the course of the story." Ramsay concluded that *Two Moons in August* was a book that "belongs on the shelf with the few but essential novels that are both intelligently written and appealing to YA audiences." *Horn Book* reviewer Nancy Vasilakis commented that Brooks once again "explores the minute nuances" of love in a story which has the "sultry dog-day atmosphere of late summer." Vasilakis praised Brooks for the "leisurely" manner in which she let her story develop, "investing a wealth of meaning in the most trivial actions." Vasilakis added, "By the end of the novel, all the members of this sad family have acknowledged the need to exorcise the ghosts of the past.... An introspective, multidimensional narrative 'mixing memory with desire'—to quote Eliot's famous lines—with resounding effect." Peter Carver, reviewing *Two Moons in August* for *Quill and Quire,* felt that Brooks took up the challenge to chart the emotional territory of teens "with artfulness and insight." Carver further noted, "Martha Brooks conveys, with great skill, the cross-currents of feeling and behaviour that swirl around teenagers as they come of age.... Taken with her much admired *Paradise Cafe,* this new book confirms Martha Brooks is an eloquent writer of young-adult fiction."

Brooks credits her love of reading in part for her abilities as a writer. "I recently spoke in a telephone interview with grades nine to twelve students who were reading at a grade one to two level," Brooks once noted. "They had, in groups, with the help of their dedicated teacher, read some of my short stories. Their questions were thoughtful, as were my answers. They liked my writing because it is realistic. None of them had ever read an entire novel. I am re-reading *Anna Karenina.* Books open the world for us in a way that nothing else can. My experience with reading flows into my art, my life, my relationships with people. Reading allows me to intimately engage in the living experience of history, in the heartbeat and profound humanity of others whose experiences are vastly different from my own, in the exploration of landscapes where I have never been and may never have the opportunity to go, in the flowering of thought that may transform me and thus allow me to offer that gift of transformation to the life of someone else."

Brooks next found such possibilities for transformation in short stories. Annette Goldsmith of *Quill and Quire,* found *Traveling on into the Light and Other Stories,* Brooks's 1994 book of stories, a "memorable collection ... snapshots of young people yearning for love,

acceptance, and explanations." The collection consists of ten stories and a novella, "Moonlight Sonata," later adapted for a play. The adolescents here deal with more complex issues than those in Brooks's initial collection, and thus the stories themselves are also longer. Sidonie, from *Two Moons in August,* makes an appearance here, in "Sunday at Sidonie's," narrated from her boyfriend Kieran's point of view, and in "All the Stars in the Universe" and "A Wedding," both narrated by Sidonie. Told in the first person, the stories in this collection variously explore sexuality, deal with the death of a parent, or focus on survival. Lindsay looks for real love in the midst of artificiality in "Where Has Romance Gone"; Donald is accused of drug trafficking when an artistic creation is mistaken for a joint in "The Tiniest Guitar in the World"; runaway Laker is not wanted by his pregnant mother and stepfather in "The Kindness of Strangers"; a babysitter comes close to having an affair with the father of the child she is taking care of in "You've Always Been So Good to Me"; and, in the title story, Sam has difficulties dealing with his father's male lover.

"Martha Brooks balances ... sadness with hope," commented reviewer Annette Goldsmith, while *Booklist*'s Hazel Rochman noted, "It's the honesty about conflicting emotions and viewpoints that give this collection its power." Rochman also observed that, as with Brooks's first collection of stories, *Traveling on into the Light* also has an assortment of narrative voices which "show a remarkable range or young men and women across class and setting." "The young-adult protagonists in this taut, carefully crafted collection ... are struggling to make connections to keep their bearings under the strains of rejection, betrayal, or death," commented *Horn Book*'s Vasilakis. While Vasilakis felt the inclusion of three stories dealing with Sidonie and Kieran was "somewhat incongruously placed here," she observed that the collection as a whole "is piercingly direct in its depiction of young people struggling to find their way into adulthood." *Publishers Weekly* also found the collection "[m]oving and memorable," and noted that it demonstrated "a profound understanding of sorrow and joy."

Brooks has written two further novels, *Bone Dance,* published in 1997, and *Being with Henry,* published in 2000. In the former title, Alexandra meets a young man who shares her Native Canadian heritage when she inherits a cabin on a lake from her father. Together, the two deal with the spirits that haunt them both. Jenkinson, writing in *St. James Guide to Young Adult Writers,* remarked that *Bone Dance* "possesses a remarkable and engaging Yin-Yang quality." The reviewer was referring to the two halves of the story: seventeen-year-old Alexandra, or Alex, of Dene heritage, and eighteen-year-old Lonny, of Metis heritage. What brings the two together is a piece of property Alex inherits from her absent and undependable father. The property is a piece of unspoiled lakefront that had been in Lonny's family for generations, but which was sold to finance Lonny's education. The two meet at this disputed bit of property, both carrying emotional baggage, both needing to work through the spirits haunting their earlier lives. Alex must put to rest her resentment for the white father she never knew; Lonny attempts to deal with fears that he caused his mother's death as a child when he dug up sacred bones at an Indian burial site.

"Each character in *Bone Dance* is beautifully drawn, intelligent, and completely believable," commented Judy Sasges in *Voice of Youth Advocates*. *Quill and Quire* reviewer Teresa Toten noted, "This novel beautifully captures the drift and dance of two teenagers whose lives are embraced by spirits of the dead.... Read it and weep. But read it." Cheryl Archer described the novel in *Canadian Materials* as the "enchanting and spiritual journey of two [teenagers] who must confront their ghosts of memory and mysterious visions." Archer concluded, "This is a fine novel that will leave readers embracing nature and honouring the spirits of the ancestors. Another splendid book by award-winning Manitoba author Martha Brooks."

Brooks's novel *Being with Henry* is an adaptation of her earlier short story, "The Kindness of Strangers," which deals with Laker's adventures when he is forced out of his home by a bullying stepfather. "The story was one which my readers, both young and old, most fretted over," Brooks said. "The final scene upset them. Runaway Laker Wyatt makes his fateful wrenching phone call home, then he and his newfound friend, the elderly Henry Olsen, are left sitting silently together at Henry's kitchen table. A frequently asked question was 'Why would Laker Wyatt's mother reject him so cruelly—how could any mother do that to her son?' A twelve-year-old reader, who had found, mirrored back, his own sad relationship with his mother, asked me with direct poignancy, 'What will happen to him?'"

Being with Henry is an answer to the question. In the novel, Laker's earlier life is detailed, and then out on his own, he strikes up an unexpected friendship with a frail but determined old man. Brooks once said that the novel follows Laker's journey "to redefine his notion of family, loyalty and acceptance." Such a theme of love lost and love found fits neatly into the arc of Brooks's works.

"I see love and loss so much more clearly than I did when I was twenty, or thirty, or even forty," Brooks concluded for *Authors and Artists for Young Adults*. "And since that is the subject I write about, along with those other great themes such as forgiveness and regret and redemption, I bring a lifetime of observation to my subject. Old truths were never truer, like the adage about history repeating itself. Give me any seventeen-year-old, now, or in the past, or in the future, and I will tell you that this is a person who carries a burning terrible secret that no one will ever understand or forgive. So they think."

Biographical and Critical Sources

BOOKS

Authors and Artists for Young Adults, Volume 37, Gale, 2001.

Jenkinson, Dave, "Brooks, Martha," *St. James Guide to Young Writers,* 2nd edition, St. James Press, 1999.

PERIODICALS

Booklist, August, 1994, Hazel Rochman, review of *Traveling on into the Light and Other Stories,* p. 2039; September 15, 1997, p. 330; September 15, 1998, Sally Estes, review of *Bone Dance,* p. 220; April 1, 2000, Randy Meyer, review of *Being with Henry,* p. 1450.

Bulletin of the Center for Children's Books, December, 1990, Betsy Hearne, review of *Paradise Cafe and Other Stories,* pp. 79-80.

Canadian Materials, March, 1989, Gail Lennon, review of *Paradise Cafe and Other Stories;* October 17, 1997, Cheryl Archer, review of *Bone People.*

English Journal, November, 1995, p. 98.

Horn Book, March-April, 1992, Nancy Vasilakis, review of *Two Moons in August,* p. 208, January-February, 1995, N. Vasilakis, review of *Traveling on into the Light,* p. 62; November-December, 1997, Jennifer M. Brabander, review of *Bone Dance,* p. 677; May, 2000, review of *Being with Henry,* p. 309.

Maclean's, November 10, 1997, John Bemrose, "Deft Handling of Thorny Issues," p. 70.

Publishers Weekly, October 31, 1994, Teresa Toten, review of *Traveling on into the Light and Other Stories,* p. 64; September 15, 1997, p. 78; June 6, 1998, review of *Two Moons in August,* p. 63; August 2, 1999, review of *Bone Dance,* p. 87; April 3, 2000, review of *Being with Henry,* p. 82.

Quill and Quire, November, 1991, Peter Carver, review of *Two Moons in August,* pp. 24-25; October, 1994, Annette Goldsmith, review of *Traveling on into the Light,* p. 38; November, 1997, T. Toten, review of *Bone Dance,* p. 44.

School Library Journal, December, 1990, p. 20; March, 1992, Ellen Ramsay, review of *Two Moons in August,* p. 256; August, 1994, p. 168; November, 1997, p. 330; May, 2000, Janet Hilbun, review of *Being with Henry,* p. 170.

Voice of Youth Advocates, February, 1991, Cynthia L. Beatty, review of *Paradise Cafe and Other Stories,* p. 350; December, 1997, Judy Sasges, review of *Bone Dance.*

Wilson Library Bulletin, February, 1995, p. 98.

—*Sketch by J. Sydney Jones*

*   *   *

BRUST, Steven K. (Zoltan) 1955-

Personal

Born November 23, 1955, in St. Paul, MN; son of William Z. (a professor) and Jean (Tilsen) Brust; married (separated); children: Corwin Edward, Aliera

Jean and Carolyn Rocza (twins), Antonia Eileen. *Education:* Attended University of Minnesota—Twin Cities. *Politics:* "Trotskyist." *Religion:* "Materialist." *Hobbies and other interests:* Cooking, poker, Middle-Eastern drumming.

Addresses

Home—3248 Portland Avenue S., Minneapolis, MN 55407. *E-mail*—kzb@dreamcafe.com. *Agent*—Valerie Smith, Route 44-55, RD Box 160, Modena, NY 12548.

Career

Employed as systems programmer, 1976-86, for various companies, including Network Systems, New Brighton, MN, 1983-86; full-time writer, 1986—. Former actor for local community theater; rock 'n' roll drummer; drummer for Middle-Eastern and Oriental dancers; folk guitarist, banjoist, singer, and songwriter. *Member:* Science Fiction Writers of America, Interstate Writers Workshop, Minnesota Science Fiction Society (executive vice-president), Pre-Joycean Fellowship.

Writings

SCIENCE FICTION AND FANTASY NOVELS

To Reign in Hell, Steel Dragon, 1984.
Brokedown Palace, Ace Books, 1985.
The Sun, the Moon, and the Stars, Armadillo Press, 1987.
Cowboy Feng's Space Bar and Grille, Ace Books, 1990.
The Phoenix Guards, Tor Books, 1991.
(With Megan Lindholm) *The Gypsy,* Tor Books, 1992.
Agyar, Tor Books, 1992.
Athyra, Ace Books, 1993.
Five Hundred Years After (sequel to *The Phoenix Guards*), Tor Books, 1994.

Steven K. Brust

ORCA, Ace Books, 1996.
(With Emma Bull) *Freedom and Necessity,* Tor Books, 1997.

"VLAD TALTOS" SERIES

Jhereg, Ace Books, 1983.
Yendi, Ace Books, 1984.
Teckla, Ace Books, 1986.
Taltos, Ace Books, 1988.
Phoenix, Ace Books, 1990.
Dragon, Tor Books, 1998.
The Book of Jhereg (contains *Jhereg, Yendi,* and *Teckla*), Ace Books, 1999.

OTHER

Work represented in anthologies, including *Liavek Anthology,* 1985.

Sidelights

In the realms of science fiction and fantasy, Steven K. Brust's fans have become accustomed to discovering exciting and strange, yet believable new worlds. "It is very easy to cheat when writing fantasy—to say, 'This is magic, it just works,' " Brust once commented. "But if one is able to avoid this trap, one has the power to work real magic with the story. For me, magic must be either an alternate set of physical laws, used to express something about how we view our tools, or else a metaphor for Mystery, or the Unknown, or whatever."

Brust's own Hungarian ancestry is evident in many of his books, especially his popular five-book series that chronicles the adventures of Vlad Taltos, a warlock and hired assassin educated by a swordsman and a sorceress, who carries out assignments on behalf of the Dragonlords of the Dragaeran Empire. In *Jhereg* (1983), the first book in the series, young Vlad is left to fend for himself when his father dies. The young man quickly discovers that his early education comes in handy when he has to rely on his own cunning and wit to survive among the powerful Dragaerans. In his *Booklist* review, Roland Green notes that "the book features intelligent world building" and "good handling of the assassin character."

Brust uses flashbacks to establish the chronology and setting of *Yendi* (1984), the second book in the series, which is actually a prequel. Here, readers discover how Vlad has risen through the ranks from his start as a small-time mobster to his current status as a major criminal. *Yendi* also chronicles the romance and courtship of Vlad and Cawti, the Dagger of the Jhereq, who would become his wife. Roland Green, again writing in *Booklist,* says that *Yendi* "is as intelligent, witty, and generally well written as its predecessor."

The third book in the series, *Teckla* (1986), picks up where the first, *Jhereg,* left off. This time, Vlad becomes involved in a revolution against the Dragaeran Empire along with the Teckla, the Empire's lowest class of citizens. During the rebellion, Vlad finds himself in the role of Cawti's protector, which only exacerbates their rocky relationship. The chronology of the series shifts again as the fourth novel, *Taltos* (1988), goes back to Vlad's early life. Writing about *Taltos* in *Voice of Youth Advocates,* Carolyn Caywood states, "This is one of the four novels of *Taltos* which will be of interest to the fantasy fan who discovers any one of them."

Phoenix, the fifth book in the series, finds Vlad embroiled once again in revolution and upheaval. This novel, which *Voice of Youth Advocates* reviewer Caywood describes as "more somber and more straightforward" than Brust's previous efforts, finds Vlad questioning his life-long beliefs and occupation. Caywood adds that some fans may be disappointed by the introspective nature of this book, but that "readers who are willing to follow the author's lead will discover that his conclusion has added depth to the entire series."

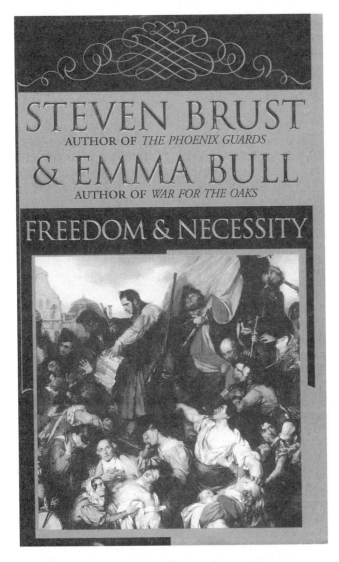

Amateur detective Susan Voight tries to discover why someone attempted to kill her revolutionary cousin and deprived him of his memory in this Victorian fantasy-mystery which unfolds through letters, diaries, and real documents. (Cover painting by G. Wappers.)

The Dragaeran Empire is not the only fantasy world that Brust envisions in rebellion and turmoil. *To Reign in Hell,* published just after *Jhereg* in 1984, takes place in Heaven where some of the angels are in the midst of their own revolution. "There are many fantasy novels that are thinly disguised Christian metaphors," Brust once stated. "So I wrote *To Reign in Hell,* which is a Christian metaphor that is really a thinly disguised fantasy novel." *Voice of Youth Advocates* reviewer Janet R. Mura applauds *To Reign in Hell* and declares that Brust "has created an engaging story with consummate skill and ability."

Another of Brust's tales derived from Hungarian folklore is *Brokedown Palace* (1985), a story of magic and determination set in a crumbling palace on the banks of the river of Faerie. The plot deals with four brothers who share power in the land of Fenario. Writing in *Voice of Youth Advocates,* Jean Kaufman remarks, "The author creates a land where magic is expected if not really loved." Kaufman goes on to refer to the book as "a sophisticated and rewarding fantasy."

In *The Sun, the Moon, and the Stars* (1987), a retelling of a Hungarian folktale in the idiom of modern fantasy, Brust again writes about brothers. This time, there are three, and they are on a quest to return the sun, moon, and stars to the sky, thereby bringing light to the world. Interestingly, Brust uses the folktale in this case as the framework for a novel depicting the struggle of five young artists to achieve the impossible. A reviewer for *Library Journal* explains how the author utilized his "Fantasist" conventions and generated a book that is "recommended for general fiction and fantasy collections."

With *Cowboy Feng's Space Bar and Grille* (1990), in which a fiendish paranoiac named the Physician decides to destroy his native planet in order to stop the spread of a deadly illness called Hags Disease, Brust proves that he can write science fiction as well as fantasy. The setting is Feng's, a bar and grille that features Jewish cooking, a dance floor, and the ability to travel through time and space. A contributor in *Publishers Weekly* notes that "Brust's fantasy landscape seems truer than the backdrops of many realistic novels" and, in *Voice of Youth Advocates,* Mary R. Voors calls the work "a compelling and humorous science fiction novel."

The Phoenix Guards (1991) is set in Dragaera, the same world that was home to Vlad Taltos in Brust's earlier books. Though a *Publishers Weekly* reviewer notes that this book "shares the wit and exuberance of the *Taltos* books," don't expect to find Vlad here; it is a thousand years earlier. Even its sequel, *Five Hundred Years After* (1994), is set too early for Vlad to make an appearance. "Full of flamboyant action and arch dialogue, this latest adventure in Brust's popular 'Dragaeran' novels pits sword against sorcery in classic swashbuckling style," according to a critic for *Library Journal.*

In *The Gypsy* (1992) a collaborative effort between Brust and Megan Lindholm, a sinister being called Fair Lady reaches out from a parallel universe seeking to extend her shadowy dominion through magic, corruption, and murder. Opposing her is a cast of magical archetypes fronted by the Gypsy. A reviewer in *Publishers Weekly* calls the book "a powerful and memorable fantasy" and Scott Winnett, writing in *Locus,* notes that it is "an exciting fantasy/mystery crossover," referring to Brust's and Lindholm's work as "one of the best jobs yet combining these contrasting genres. The marriage of the two genres is near-perfect."

Brust created something of a puzzle in *Agyar* (1992), an impressively wrought modern vampire/redemption yarn. The novel is presented as a bunch of bits and pieces, like a diary, written by John Agyar, an amateur with time on his hands and an old Royal typewriter, in the abandoned house where he is staying. The pieces of the puzzle are shaped by the author's first-person point of view; the clues lie more in what he doesn't say than what he does. Agyar's secret is pretty obvious, but Brust tantalizes, holding off on a firm confirmation for much of the novel. Eventually the puzzle pieces fall together, as events come to a head. *Locus* reviewer Carolyn Cushman considers *Agyar* "a different vampire novel, a striking contemporary dark fantasy." *Kirkus Reviews* notes that the work is "compact, understated, and highly persuasive. Brust accomplishes with a wry turn of phrase or a small flourish what others never achieve despite hundreds of gory spatters." *Washington Post Book World* reviewer Robert K. J. Killheffer refers to *Agyar* as "good, fast-moving, intelligent fun."

Brust collaborated with Emma Bull for his next book, *Freedom and Necessity* (1997). The story, which a *Publishers Weekly* critic describes as a "romantic mystery-adventure," unfolds in nineteenth-century England after a young man gets a letter from his cousin two months after his supposed death. Writing in *Booklist,* reviewer Roland Green calls *Freedom and Necessity* "an exceptional page-turner" that "deserves a place in every self-respecting fantasy collection."

In his next book, *Dragon* (1998), Brust brings back Vlad Taltos, his most popular protagonist. A prequel to *Yendi* and a sequel to *Jhereg, Dragon* recounts Vlad's early career as an assassin. When Vlad accepts an assignment to search for a stolen sword, his actions start a war between two dragonlords, and Vlad becomes a soldier in one of the dragonlord's armies. *Booklist*'s Green complains that in *Dragon,* "Brust's writing style has changed noticeably," but he concedes that "Vlad's devotees will not be put off by anything so petty as stylistic dissonance." Writing for *Library Journal,* reviewer Jackie Cassada states that *Dragon* "belongs in libraries" where the Vlad Taltos series is popular. A *Publishers Weekly* reviewer praises *Dragon* and the skill with which Brust incorporates his literary influences into the story: "As always, Brust invests Vlad with the panache of a Dumas musketeer and the colloquial voice of one of Roger Zelazny's Amber heroes. This is a rousing adventure with enough humor, action, and sneaky plot twists to please newcomers as well as longtime fans."

"There appears to be a split in literature between work with strong story values and nothing else, and work that has depth and power but no story values," Brust has said. "The stuff I enjoy reading most can be read as simple entertainment, but rewards more intense reading as well. Since I try to write the sort of stories I like to read, that is what I attempt to do in my own work. Science fiction is a category that allows and even encourages this, WHICH IS ONE OF THE REASONS I WRITE IT."

Biographical and Critical Sources

PERIODICALS

Analog: Science Fiction/Science Fact, September, 1987, p. 159; December, 1992, p. 161; June, 1993, p. 160.

Booklist, July, 1983, Roland Green, review of *Jhereg,* p. 1387; September 15, 1984, R. Green, review of *Yendi,* p. 108; February 15, 1986, p. 851; April 1, 1987, p. 1180; March, 1988, p. 1098; November 1, 1990, p. 504; August, 1991, pp. 2108, 2110; June 15, 1992, p. 1811; March 1, 1994, pp. 1185, 1188; March 15, 1997, R. Green, review of *Freedom and Necessity,* p. 1231; September 15, 1998, R. Green, review of *Dragon,* p. 205.

Bookwatch, June, 1993, p. 2.

Kirkus Reviews, March 1, 1987, p. 338; September 1, 1991, p. 1121; May 15, 1992, p. 641; December 15, 1992, review of *Agyar,* p. 1517; February 15, 1994, p. 179.

Kliatt, April, 1990, p. 22; November, 1993, p. 14; July, 1994, p. 13.

Library Journal, March 15, 1987, review of *The Sun, the Moon, and the Stars,* p. 93; September 15, 1991, p. 117; February 15, 1993, p. 196; March 15, 1994, review of *Five Hundred Years After,* p. 104. November 15, 1998, Jackie Cassada, review of *Dragon,* p. 95; August, 1999, Jackie Cassada, review of *Jhereg,* p. 148.

Locus, July, 1991, p. 33; October, 1991, p. 44; July, 1992, p. 47; September, 1992, Scott Winnett, review of *The Gypsy,* p. 37; April, 1993, p. 46; August, 1993, p. 44; February, 1994, Carolyn Cushman, review of *Agyar,* p. 75; March, 1994, p. 35; April, 1994, p. 47; May, 1994, p. 47.

Magazine of Fantasy and Science Fiction, December, 1987, p. 35; April, 1999, Michelle West, review of *Dragon,* p. 36.

Publishers Weekly, March 4, 1983, p. 97; June 1, 1984, p. 63; November 22, 1985, p. 50; March 27, 1987, p. 36; December 8, 1989, review of *Cowboy Feng's Space Bar and Grille,* p. 50; August 2, 1991, review of *The Phoenix Guards,* p. 66; May 25, 1992, review of *The Gypsy,* p. 43; February 14, 1994, p. 83; January 27, 1997, review of *Freedom and Necessity,* p. 77; October 19, 1998, review of *Dragon,* p. 60.

Science Fiction Chronicle, December, 1987, p. 46; July, 1990, p. 37; June, 1992, p. 33; December, 1992, p. 38; February, 1994, p. 28; June, 1994, p. 39.

Voice of Youth Advocates, June, 1986, Jean Kaufman, review of *Brokedown Palace,* p. 86; February, 1986, Janet R. Mura, *To Reign in Hell,* p. 393; August, 1988, Carolyn Caywood, review of *Taltos,* p. 137; June, 1990, Mary R. Voors, review of *Cowboy Feng's Space Bar and Grille,* p. 113; December, 1990, p. 269; February, 1991, C. Caywood, review of *Phoenix,* p. 361; April, 1991, p. 10; April, 1992, p. 40; December, 1992, p. 320; February, 1993, p. 345; August, 1994, p. 154; April, 1999, Nancy K. Wallace, review of *Dragon,* p. 45.

Washington Post Book World, May 2, 1993, Robert K. J. Killheffer, review of *Agyar,* p. 8.

ON-LINE

The Dream Cafe, www.dreamcafe.com/.

* * *

BUTLER, Charles (Cadman) 1963-

Personal

Born January 25, 1963, in Romsey, Hampshire, England; son of Thomas Crawford (a teacher) and Isobel (a teacher; maiden name, Bowman) Butler; married Nathalie Isabelle Blondel (a lecturer), September 10, 1994; children: Cecily, Nathaniel, Charlotte. *Education:* University of London, B.A., 1984; University of York, M.Sc., 1988, D.Phil., 1989. *Religion:* "Quaker (if anything)." *Hobbies and other interests:* Science, soccer, the supernatural.

Addresses

Home—Bristol, England. *Agent*—Caroline Sheldon, Thorley Manor Farm, Thorley, Yarmouth PO41 0SJ, England. *E-mail*—hannibal@thegates.fsbusiness.co.uk.

Career

University of the West of England, Bristol, senior lecturer in English literature, 1990—.

Writings

The Darkling (young adult novel), Orion, 1997, Margaret K. McElderry Books (New York City), 1998.
Timon's Tide (young adult novel), Orion, 1998, Margaret K. McElderry Books (New York City), 2000.

Work in Progress

A supernatural novel, *Calypso Dreaming;* a story about a doppelganger.

Sidelights

Charles Butler told *SATA:* "I was born in the market town of Romsey, in Hampshire. My family background is mixed: Welsh, seafaring, and Methodist on my mother's side; Quaker, vegetarian, and mildly eccentric on my father's. But they all loved words, and I grew up

A shadow named the Darkling on fifteen-year-old Petra's bedroom ceiling becomes more threatening after an unexpected meeting with old Mr. Century in Charles Butler's mystical novel. (Cover illustration by Carol Benioff.)

in an atmosphere where books were read and discussed as a matter of course. Even when my parents separated, it was into houses with adjoining gardens, and across the fence the conversations seemed to go on much as before. At that time I was more interested in soccer, having become a Manchester United fan at the age of seven (because I liked their strip—it still seems as good a reason as any).

"So, despite everything, I came to reading late. I was about ten by the time I discovered C. S. Lewis. Ever since, I've been drawn to books involving magic, ghosts, and the supernatural: what's generally called 'fantasy' (a term I dislike). Later I became a fan of Susan Cooper's 'The Dark Is Rising' series, Philippa Pearce's *Tom's Midnight Garden,* and Edith Nesbit's books (though only the magical ones). Alan Garner, Margaret Mahy, and Diana Wynne Jones have all been strong influences. In general I like my magic to have its source in our own world, rather than some fantasy alternative. As Alan Garner remarked long ago, if you dig up a screaming mandrake root in El Dorado, no one will bat an eyelid. Things like that happen in El Dorado every day. But dig it up in Acacia Avenue, and not only will the mandrake root scream—the reader may, too. That's an insight I've tried to use in my own work.

"One of the ways that fiction justifies itself—other than by giving pleasure—is by providing a means of *seeing*. I put a lot of effort into what's loosely called 'atmosphere' but is really a way of allowing the reader to perceive an aspect of reality that doesn't normally show itself. The back of the mind, the corner of the eye, the tip of the tongue: these are the tantalizing places. With *Timon's Tide* I tried to write a story in which the supernatural and 'ordinary' aspects of life both have a strong presence, but where the border between them is often blurred, so that the reader (and the main character) sometimes seem to see double. If I have succeeded, the result will be a new kind of experience."

Biographical and Critical Sources

PERIODICALS

Booklist, April, 1998, Anne O'Malley, review of *The Darkling,* p. 1312; June 1, 2000, Roger Leslie, review of *Timon's Tide,* p. 1880.

Book Report, January-February, 1999, Patsy Launspach, review of *The Darkling,* p. 59.

Horn Book, July-August, 1998, Terri Schmitz, review of *The Darkling,* p. 483.

Publishers Weekly, April 13, 1998, review of *The Darkling,* p. 76; July 3, 2000, review of *Timon's Tide,* p. 73.

School Library Journal, May, 1998, Susan L. Rogers, review of *The Darkling,* p. 138; June, 2000, Vicki Reutter, review of *Timon's Tide,* p. 142.

ON-LINE

Amazon.com, www.amazon.com/ (August 26, 2000).

C

CADNUM, Michael 1949-

Personal

Born May 3, 1949, in Orange, CA; married; wife's name, Sherina.

Addresses

Home—Albany, CA. *Agent*—Katharine Kidde, Kidde, Hoyt and Picard, 335 East 51st St., New York, NY 10022.

Career

Writer.

Awards, Honors

Creative Writing fellowship, National Endowment for the Arts; Helen Bullis Prize, *Poetry Northwest;* Owl Creek Book Award; finalist, *Los Angeles Times* Book Award; finalist, National Book Award.

Writings

Nightlight, St. Martin's (New York City), 1990.
Sleepwalker, St. Martin's (New York City), 1991.
Saint Peter's Wolf (for young adults), Carroll and Graf (New York City), 1991.
Calling Home (for young adults), Viking (New York City), 1991.
Ghostwright, Carroll and Graf (New York City), 1992.
Breaking the Fall (for young adults), Viking (New York City), 1992.
The Horses of the Night, Carroll and Graf (New York City), 1993.
Skyscape, Carroll and Graf (New York City), 1994.
Taking It (for young adults), Viking (New York City), 1995.
The Judas Glass, Carroll and Graf (New York City), 1996.
Zero at the Bone, Viking (New York City), 1996.
Edge (for young adults), Viking (New York City), 1997.

Michael Cadnum

In a Dark Wood (for young adults), Orchard, 1998.
Heat (for young adults), Viking (New York City), 1998.
Rundown, Viking (New York City), 1999.
The Book of the Lion, Viking (New York City), 2000.
Redhanded, Viking (New York City), 2000.
Raven of the Waves, Orchard, 2000.

PICTURE BOOKS

The Lost and Found House, illustrated by Steve Johnson and Lou Fancher, Viking (New York City), 1997.

POETRY

The Morning of the Massacre (chapbook), Bieler Press, 1982.

Wrecking the Cactus (chapbook), Salt Lick Press, 1985.

Invisible Mirror (chapbook), Ommation Press, 1986.

Foreign Springs (chapbook), Amelia Press (Bakersfield, CA), 1987.

By Evening, Owl Creek Press (Seattle, WA), 1992.

The Cities We Will Never See, Singular Speech Press (Canton, CT), 1993.

OTHER

Ella and the Canary Prince (fiction chapbook), Subterranean Press, 1999.

Together Again: The True Story of Humpty Dumpty (fiction chapbook), Subterranean Press, 2001.

Author of short essays, including "The Ghost and the Panda," in *Mystery Writer's Annual;* "Dreams with Teeth," in *Mystery Scene;* and a commentary to his poem "Sunbathing in Winter," in *Poet and Critic.* Contributor of a story to *Second Sight: Stories for a New Millennium,* Putnam, 1999. Contributor to numerous periodicals, including *America, Antioch Review, Beloit Fiction Journal, Beloit Poetry Journal, Commonweal,* and *Rolling Stone.* Writes occasional reviews for the "Read This" column in *New York Review of Science Fiction.*

Sidelights

During the 1980s Michael Cadnum was a nationally recognized poet, publishing his work in prestigious literary journals. By 1990 he was also gaining wide acclaim for his suspense novels. On first consideration, Cadnum's transition from serious poetry to popular fiction would seem to be have been an unlikely leap. To the contrary, however, his experience as a poet was an asset to his work as a novelist, and within a few years he rose to his current status as one of the foremost writers of horror novels and psychological thrillers. Although Cadnum began writing for an adult audience and only later specialized in novels for young adults, his books have consistently appealed to teenagers who enjoy a scary story. Many of his horror novels are variations on standard tales about ghosts, werewolves, and vampires, with a difference: he portrays complex characters and employs a literary writing style. Critics particularly admire Cadnum's psychological thrillers, which address serious problems experienced by young adults. According to Patrick Jones, a reviewer for *Horn Book,* "Cadnum isn't offering simple tales of good and evil but complex stories written in simple yet tense prose about 'good kids' doing evil things."

The author of some of the most terrifying novels being published today also has a whimsical side, which was revealed during an interview with *Authors and Artists for Young Adults* contributor Peggy Saari. Asked if he had any pets, Cadnum replied, "My current pet is a green and yellow parrot named Luke, who sometimes sits on my shoulder as I write and is one of my closest advisors." Cadnum grew up in Southern California. In the interview with Saari he recalled exploring the California shore: "My family spent a lot of time at the beach, the flat, sandy shore of Huntington Beach and Newport Beach.... Sometimes jellyfish washed up on shore, gigantic fried eggs with purple yolks. Sometimes there were sharks, cruising hammerheads the police tried to shoot from the pier. Late one afternoon everyone retreated from the water to watch a majestic dorsal fin slip majestically just beyond the breaking waves."

Cadnum had an early fascination with words. "The first word I learned to read was *We,*" he told Saari. "I was sitting in the garage of my family home on Monrovia Street in Costa Mesa, California. A book was open in my lap, and my father pointed out the word. I liked the capital W, but I probably thought, as I think now, that a word with such a handsome beginning should be a little longer. *We* is such a short word, but it shows that in a small space a word can stand for so much." Like most teenagers, Cadnum watched television; nevertheless, he derived greater pleasure from reading. "I have always felt our lives are too small, too thin and insubstantial. When we watch television—and I have always watched a lot of television—we are powerfully distracted from our routines, but only through reading are we really nourished."

The future poet and novelist was a voracious reader—"I always used to read everything I could get my hands on, from the steamiest trash to very difficult philosophy books I sometimes struggled to understand"—and through books he discovered the world. "By reading I was decoding the secrets the world around me did not want me to have," he explained, "parting the curtain and seeing the other, full-color existence that did not try to sell me beer or a new car." For Cadnum the key to these secrets is the library. "To this day I love libraries, much more than bookstores," he continued, "because libraries are welcoming, the same way novels are welcoming. Books, like so much in the real world, give, and ask nothing in return."

Cadnum has also unlocked the secrets of the world through personal experience. "At one time in my career I ran a Suicide Prevention Center in Southern Alameda County," he said in the interview. "I listened to many unhappy people on the telephone, and I learned that everyone has a story to tell, confessions and insights no one wanted to listen to. Young and old, there are people out there who struggle to articulate their hopes." He added, "I feel that these people on the margins of life, young people, people just out of jail, extremely talented people estranged from their families, are not on the margins at all. They are where life really is." In fact, Cadnum concluded, "It is the so-called mainstream men and women, so-called normal people, who are in danger of living empty lives."

In nearly all of his novels Cadnum portrays people who exist on the margins of life, such as successful professionals harboring unfulfilled desires or hidden demons and troubled teenagers coping with dysfunctional families. *Nightlight,* Cadnum's fiction debut, features Paul Wright, a restaurant reviewer who is bored with his job and has been haunted by a recurring nightmare. Paul is asked by his Aunt Mary to locate her missing son Len, an eccentric photographer who takes pictures of ghosts in cemeteries near his isolated cabin in northern California. When Paul invites his girlfriend Lise to go along on the trip he does not realize both Lise and Mary are having the same nightmare that torments him. Arriving at the cabin, Paul and Lise discover Len has disappeared, leaving behind all of his belongings as well as his tape-recorded conversations with a mysterious presence. Soon Paul and Lise are caught up in a series of unsettling events before they finally encounter Len's "companion." The plot builds to a frightening conclu-

sion that leaves the reader wondering whether Len was insane or had actually been haunted by ghosts.

Nightlight was greeted with unanimous praise from critics. *Locus* reviewer Scott Winnett termed the novel "a remarkable debut," citing the ambiguous ending as evidence that the "worst ghosts of all are the ones inside yourself." Another *Locus* contributor, Edward Bryant, judged *Nightlight* to be "literary horror at a high level" because of "the author's use of a poet's precision to pick just the right words and images." Bryant urged other horror fiction writers to "[p]ay attention to Michael Cadnum." In a review for *Voice of Youth Advocates,* Mary Lee Tiernan gave the first-time novelist a similar accolade, comparing him with Stephen King.

Cadnum delved into the supernatural again with his second novel, *Sleepwalker,* which features Davis Lowry, a famous archaeologist on a dig at an eighth-century bog in Yorkshire, England. Dreams of his dead wife compel Lowry to sleepwalk, and his work is interrupted by several accidents at the excavation site. Eventually he and his team unearth a 1,200-year-old Norse king, and when they see the corpse roaming the bog at night they suspect the mishaps and disasters were caused by supernatural forces. The story unfolds as Lowry and his colleagues try to solve the mystery. Eric W. Johnson recommended the book in *Library Journal* as "a richly textured and suitable mood study of revenge and terror" that is a "delicious blend" of reality and the paranormal.

Although Cadnum wrote *Saint Peter's Wolf* for adults, the book was placed on young adult reading lists. A retelling of the werewolf myth, it is the story of Benjamin Byrd, a proper San Francisco psychologist and art collector who is having marital problems. During a search for art treasures he finds a set of silver fangs. He then becomes obsessed with werewolves and is ultimately transformed into a beast that commits extremely violent acts. As Byrd changes back and forth from man to werewolf, he begins to appreciate the freedom and power he has as a creature of nature. He falls in love with Johanna, a woman who has also been transformed into a werewolf, and together they try to liberate themselves from their stifling human shapes.

During the interview with Saari, Cadnum discussed his purpose in writing the novel: "When I create a character like the psychologist in *Saint Peter's Wolf,* who finds himself able to change from an intelligent but constrained human to a werewolf, I am trying to celebrate our enormous potential for life. I think we are all deliciously complex, full of potential, part Sheriff of Nottingham and part Robin Hood." Don G. Campbell, a *Los Angeles Times Book Review* contributor, called *Saint Peter's Wolf* an "engrossing approach to a durable myth." Writing in *Voice of Youth Advocates,* Delia A. Culberson was even more laudatory. She found the novel to be "a spellbinding *tour de force* in a rare blend of fantasy, horror, adventure, suspense, and passionate love .... A superb, fascinating book that subtly evokes that ancient, primal yearning in all living, breathing things for total, exhilarating freedom."

A successful playwright is haunted by his former writing partner, who claims his manuscripts were stolen and wants the playwright's possessions and life, in this psychological thriller. (Cover illustration by Bill Binger.)

Calling Home was Cadnum's first book published specifically for young adults. "I wrote *Calling Home* thinking of it as a literary novel to be read by someone like myself," he told Saari. "When it was accepted for publication as a young adult novel I was very surprised, because I had never heard of a young adult market." *Calling Home* is the story of Peter, a teenage alcoholic who accidentally kills his best friend, Mead. The boys are sharing a bottle of cognac in the basement of an abandoned house next to Peter's home, and in a moment of drunken anger Peter punches Mead. When he realizes his friend is dead he begins impersonating Mead in calls to Mead's parents, telling himself throughout the novel, "Impersonating the dead is easy." In the meantime he tries to lead a normal life through an alcoholic haze, keeping up the ruse that Mead has run away. Finally the pressure becomes unbearable and he confesses to another friend, Lani, whose lawyer father gets Peter the help he needs. Running through the main action are subplots about Peter's estranged parents and his girl-friend Angela, who contributes to his alcohol problem.

Calling Home was widely reviewed, gaining Cadnum recognition as one of the foremost authors for young adults. In *Wilson Library Journal,* Cathi Dunn MacRae noted that Cadnum "skillfully shapes suspense through masterful control of language," taking readers "so completely inside this disconnected boy, ... they will never forget the experience." *Horn Book* reviewer Patty Campbell stated that *Calling Home* was an "exquisitely crafted work, a prose poem of devastating impact," adding that "Not since the debut of Robert Cormier with *The Chocolate War* ... has such a major talent emerged in adolescent literature...." Roger Sutton observed in *Bulletin of the Children's Center for Books* that *Calling Home* offers "probably the truest portrait of a teenaged alcoholic we've had in YA fiction."

Cadnum's next novel, *Ghostwright,* is a psychological thriller about Hamilton Speke, a successful playwright. Speke's life begins to unravel after the appearance of serial killer Timothy Asquith, who had been his writing partner long ago. Claiming Speke stole his manuscripts, Asquith demands a share of the playwright's property. During a struggle Speke kills Asquith, then he buries the body, only to see the "corpse" lurking around the estate a few days later. When Speke digs up the grave and finds a rotting deer carcass, he learns Asquith had staged the murder. Determined to kill Speke, Asquith sets fire to the estate in a bloody climactic scene. As Marylaine Block stated in *Library Journal, Ghostwright* is a "fine novel of psychological horror" that "keeps readers as uncertain as Speke about what is real, what is only imagined...." A *Publishers Weekly* critic wrote, "From start to astonishing finish, this good old-fashioned thriller delivers."

Like *Calling Home,* Cadnum's next novel for young adults, *Breaking the Fall,* depicts a troubled teenager as the main character. Stanley North, a sophomore in high school, has difficulty coping with his parents' crumbling marriage and is doing poorly at school. He is torn between the worlds of his emotionally balanced girl-friend Sky, who urges him to return to sports, and his self-destructive friend Jared, who tantalizes him with the dangerous game of breaking into houses. Stanley becomes increasingly caught up in the thrill of stealing small items from homes while the occupants are sleeping. At the same time he attempts to free himself from crime by perfecting his burgling skills, but in the process he loses the respect of his parents and Sky.

Once again critics praised Cadnum's engrossing, suspenseful plot and his ability to create sympathetic characters. In reviews for *Horn Book* Maeve Visser Knoth and Patty Campbell judged *Breaking the Fall* to be superior YA literature. According to Knoth, "The author writes truthfully about the seductive nature of power and friendships, recognizing the lengths to which young people will go in order to prove themselves." Campbell wrote that Cadnum upheld the promising talent he exhibited in *Calling Home.* Susan L. Rogers noted in *School Library Journal* that "Some readers may be disturbed by this story, although mature teens may find it a more realistic reflection of a troubled world...."

Breaking the Fall was followed by two psychological thrillers for adults, *The Horses of the Night* and *Skyscape.* In *The Horses of the Night* Cadnum gives a twist to the Faust legend in which a man sells his soul to the devil in return for power. Stratton Fields, a socially prominent San Francisco architect who "has it all," enters a contest to redesign Golden Gate Park. Plot complications multiply when he is accused of murdering the contest head. A *Kirkus Reviews* contributor noted that "Stratton wrestles with the questions of his sanity, while all along he grows in worldly and personal power—power that he can turn to good ... or evil." *Locus* reviewer Winnett stated that Cadnum communicates a compelling message in *The Horses of the Night:* "Dreams are never worth the price we pay for them. And you won't see the price tag until it's far too late."

Skyscape examines celebrity and media hype in the story of Curtis Newns, a world-renowned painter whose masterpiece, *Skyscape,* is mysteriously burned. Seeking help for a creative block from television psychiatrist Red Patterson, Newns becomes enmeshed in a spiraling descent into violence and death. A commentator for *Publishers Weekly* identified Patterson's "slowly reveal-ed character" as "the novel's center," adding that "although the revelations threaten to oversimplify Cad-num's argument about fame and genius, they make for an arresting climax." *Library Journal* reviewer Robert C. Moore observed that Cadnum addresses "some weighty questions: Does the media create our stars or simply magnify their qualities? Does art belong to its creator or to society?"

Cadnum again turned to young adult fiction with *Taking It, Zero at the Bone,* and *Edge.* In *Taking It,* the author sensitively traces the psychological deterioration of Anna Charles, a seventeen-year-old kleptomaniac who is the daughter of wealthy, divorced parents. The story opens as Anna plays a game of wits with department

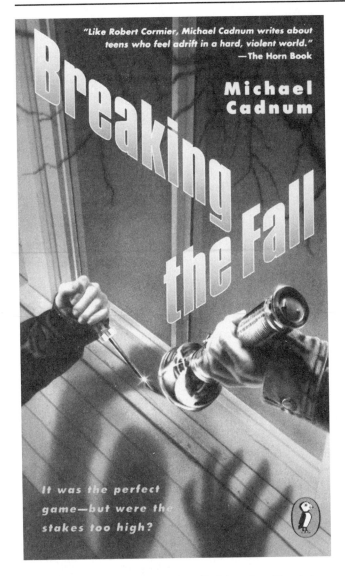

A high school sophomore is talked into breaking into houses while the owners are home and stealing something as proof. (Cover illustration by Broek Steadman.)

store detectives while trying to resist the temptation to shoplift items she does not need. This compulsion reflects her low self-esteem and growing alienation from family and friends, which are caused by her mother's remarriage and her father's remoteness. Eventually losing control, Anna steals her best friend's dog then drives 500 miles to see her brother Ted, who was her childhood idol. When she realizes she can no longer communicate with Ted, she steals his savings and sets out for Las Vegas. The spree culminates in the desert with a car wreck and Anna's emotional collapse. The novel ends on a hopeful note, however, as Anna's father finally gives her a chance to express her feelings.

Becky Kornman stated in a *Voice of Youth Advocates* review, "Cadnum realistically portrays an emotionally troubled teenager," noting that the reader "is drawn into Anna's mind and is able to experience her struggle . . . ." Praising Cadnum's "tight, beautiful prose" and his

"finesse" in handling Anna's problems, *Booklist* reviewer Merri Monks concluded that *Taking It* "should not be missed." A *Publishers Weekly* commentator was similarly impressed, declaring that Cadnum writes with "subtlety and tremendous insight" and "keeps readers on the edge of their seats with this taut psychological portrait."

Zero at the Bone is narrated by Cray Buchanan, a high-school senior whose sister, Anita, has disappeared. The novel examines the impact of this devastating event on Cray and his parents, who had all been productive, stable people. As they help the police search for Anita, their lives begin to unravel: they change as individuals, and they gradually question whether they really know one another. Upon discovering Anita's journal they realize they may not even have known her. A particularly compelling scene takes place in the morgue, as Cray and his parents wait to identify a body that turns out not to be Anita. Eventually the family pulls together again, although the mystery of Anita's disappearance is never solved.

The emotional anchor of *Zero at the Bone* is Cray, who has insight into the behavior of the people around him—in fact, he thinks he understands why Anita may have run away. As Carla A. Tripp notes in *Voice of Youth Advocates,* "Cray possesses an uncanny sense about people . . . . So, even though he feels pain and emptiness (i.e., zero at the bone) left by his sister's disappearance, he *will* survive." She termed it a "taut, psychological thriller," and a *Publishers Weekly* critic warned that "Fans of intense psychological dramas can expect to be emotionally drained by the time they reach the last chapter."

Family tragedy is also the subject of *Edge,* which *Bulletin of the Center for Children's Books* reviewer Deborah Stevenson called "a psychologically intense tale of inner struggle." Zachary Madison has dropped out of high school and works at a delivery job, yet he lacks direction. His life instantly becomes focused when his father, a successful science writer, is shot in a carjacking and left paralyzed. At first helpless and disbelieving, Zach decides to seek justice after the man accused of attacking his father is set free. *Horn Book* reviewer Amy E. Chamberlain claimed that "it's worth the read to find out if he's capable of avenging his father's death." Although the novel "treads in the shadows," she wrote, "[it] breaks through the murk with a satisfying conclusion." Stevenson also noted Cadnum's "dark narrative," but stressed that "measured, overdetermined prose suits the shadowy and searching mood."

Prior to *Edge,* Cadnum had published *The Judas Glass,* an adult novel based on the vampire legend. The complex plot revolves around Richard Stirling, an unhappily married attorney who falls in love with blind pianist Rebecca Pennant. He is shattered when Rebecca is found brutally murdered. After pricking his finger on an antique mirror and unwittingly taking the first step toward becoming a vampire, Richard himself dies when he crashes through a restaurant window. Clawing his way out of his coffin nine months later, he has the embalming fluid in his body replaced with human blood. Now a vampire, he resurrects Rebecca with his own blood and they revel in their superhuman existence. They soon realize their lives are unnatural, however, and Richard tries to become a human again. Critics remarked on Cadnum's continued virtuosity in giving a fresh perspective to old myths. Rachelle M. Blitz observed in *Voice of Youth Advocates* that "this unique, sometimes puzzling novel offers horror fans a fresh approach to the vampire tale." A *Publishers Weekly* critic asserted that "Cadnum brings an intensity of vision to this novel found in few other vampire stories," and she predicted that *The Judas Glass* was "bound to be one of the more provocative novels of 1996."

In 1997 Cadnum published *The Lost and Found House,* a picture book for children about the exciting, and unsettling, adventure of moving to a new home. His poetic, evocative text is complemented with paintings by Steven Johnson and Lou Fancher that portray the experience through the eyes of an unnamed small boy. In his interview with Saari, Cadnum commented about the autobiographical connection in the book: "My family moved several times during my childhood, much like the family in *The Lost and Found House.* I found the back gardens and new secret hideaways of the new houses fascinating. There were odd, lost treasures to be discovered—a discarded plastic soldier, a cat's eye marble— among the geraniums." Cadnum added that he wants to continue writing for children: "I enjoyed writing *The Lost and Found House*—and when I was a teacher I especially enjoyed working with very young children. I would very much like creating more such books."

Throughout his career as a novelist, Cadnum has continued publishing poetry and fiction in literary magazines, and several of his stories based on fairy tales have been published in anthologies. His novel *In a Dark Wood* is a retelling of the Robin Hood legend from the perspective of the Sheriff of Nottingham. "I did a tremendous amount of research for *In a Dark Wood,*" Cadnum recalled, "but I didn't know I was doing research. I thought I was reading about Robin Hood and traveling to Crusader castles in the Middle East and monasteries in France. I was just doing what I loved, and I turned out to know enough after a while to write a novel." Summarizing the story, Cadnum explained: "It takes place as the Sheriff of Nottingham struggles to come to grips with the chaos caused by an uncatchable, mischievous robber some people are calling Robin Hood," he said. Since his version of the Robin Hood tale offers "a gritty, naturalistic view of the Middle Ages," he stressed that *In a Dark Wood* will appeal to sophisticated young adult readers. "The assistant to the Sheriff, Hugh, is a young man, in his early teens," Cadnum stated, "but the novel is best considered a 'cross-over' book, not fitting into a typical YA category. It features torture, a boar hunt, a rampaging bear, archery, and bloodshed."

Another recent novel, *Heat,* features a platform diver who has been injured in an accident. Cadnum told *Saari*

how he developed the character of the swimmer: "As I wrote *Heat,* . . . I kept a Speedo swimsuit pinned to my bulletin board, the exact size and color my character wore," he said. "It was like having the character in the room with me." Further elaborating on his approach, Cadnum explained, "When I write a novel I live in the world of that story . . . . I want to become that character as I write, to smell the chlorine and feel the blood in my scalp."

Later he described his wider purpose in creating fiction: "I want to give a voice to characters who ordinarily never have one. So few people tell the story of a family that never discovers the truth about a missing child, as in *Zero at the Bone,*" Cadnum asserted. "Few people have seen the Robin Hood story through the eyes of the Sheriff of Nottingham, as I do in *In a Dark Wood.* I want to tell the secrets that are not told, and to see the world through new eyes." Finally, Cadnum is motivated by the ultimate challenge to a writer: "I want to experience the joys and fears of people whom I never really meet."

Biographical and Critical Sources

BOOKS

Authors and Artists for Young Adults, Volume 23, Peggy Saari interview with Cadnum, Gale, 1998.
St. James Guide to Young Adult Writers, second edition, St. James, 1999.

PERIODICALS

America, October 28, 1995, p. 27.
Booklist, July, 1991; November 15, 1992; July, 1995, Merri Monks, review of *Taking It,* p. 1879; August, 1996, p. 1094; December 1, 1997, p. 639; March 1, 1998, p. 1124; September 15, 1999, p. 252.
Bulletin of the Center for Children's Books, May, 1991, Roger Sutton, review of *Calling Home,* p. 212; July-August, 1997, Deborah Stevenson, review of *Edge.*
Georgia Review, fall, 1990, pp. 503-505.
Horn Book, November-December, 1992, Maeve Visser Knoth, review of *Breaking the Fall,* p. 726; March-April, 1994, Patrick Jones, "People Are Talking about . . . Michael Cadnum," pp. 177-180; May-June, 1994, Patty Campbell, review of *Calling Home;* January-February, 1996, p. 77; September-October, 1996, p. 602; July-August, 1997, Amy E. Chamberlain, review of *Edge,* p. 452; March-April, 1998, p. 219; March, 2000, p. 192.
Kirkus Reviews, May 1, 1991; May 15, 1992; June 1, 1993, review of *Horses of the Night,* p. 674.
Kliatt, March, 1994, Larry W. Prater, review of *Ghostwright,* p. 14.
Library Journal, February 15, 1991, Eric W. Johnson, review of *Sleepwalker,* p. 219; July, 1992, Marylaine Block, review of *Ghostwright,* pp. 119-120; July, 1993; September 1, 1994, Robert C. Moore, review of *Skyscape,* p. 213.
Locus, June, 1990, Edward Bryant, review of *Nightlight,* p. 23; June, 1990, Scott Winnett, review of *Nightlight,* p. 31; December, 1990, pp. 23-24; July, 1993, Scott Winnett, review of *Horses of the Night,* p. 33.

Los Angeles Times Book Review, July 21, 1991, Don G. Campbell, review of *Saint Peter's Wolf,* p. 6.

New York Times Book Review, March 31, 1991, Ed Weiner, review of *Sleepwalker,* p. 16.

Publishers Weekly, January 19, 1990, p. 98; May 3, 1991, p. 62; May 10, 1991; June 1, 1992, review of *Ghostwright;* November 16, 1992; June 21, 1993; August 22, 1994, review of *Skyscape,* p. 43; July 10, 1995, review of *Taking It,* p. 59; January 8, 1996, review of *The Judas Glass,* p. 59; June 17, 1996, review of *Zero at the Bone,* p. 66; June 2, 1997, p. 72; October 13, 1997 p. 74; January 26, 1998, p. 92; July 6, 1998, p. 62; June 21, 1999, p. 69; February 21, 2000, p. 88.

School Library Journal, February, 1992, p. 121; September, 1992, Susan L. Rogers, review of *Breaking the Fall,* p. 274.

Voice of Youth Advocates, October, 1990, Mary Lee Tiernan, review of *Nightlight,* p. 225; August, 1991, Jane Chandra, review of *Calling Home,* p. 168; December, 1991, Delia A. Culberson, review of *Saint Peter's Wolf;* February, 1996, Becky Kornman, review of *Taking It,* pp. 368-369; December, 1996, Rachelle M. Blitz, review of *The Judas Glass,* p. 276; February, 1997, Carla A. Tripp, review of *Zero at the Bone,* p. 326.

Wilson Library Journal, April, 1992, Cathi Dunn MacRae, review of *Calling Home,* p. 98.

*　　*　　*

CLARE, Ellen
See SINCLAIR, Olga

*　　*　　*

CLEARY, Beverly (Atlee Bunn) 1916-

Personal

Born in 1916, in McMinnville, OR; daughter of Chester Lloyd (a fruit farmer) and Mable (a teacher; maiden name, Atlee) Bunn; married Clarence T. Cleary (an accountant), October 6, 1940; children: Marianne Elisabeth, Malcolm James (twins). *Education:* Chaffey Junior College (Ontario, CA), A.A., 1936; University of California, Berkeley, B.A., 1938; University of Washington, Seattle, B.A. (librarianship), 1939. *Religion:* Protestant. *Hobbies and other interests:* Travel, walking, needlework, reading fiction and biographies.

Addresses

Home—Carmel, CA. *Office*—c/o William Morrow & Co., 1350 Avenue of the Americas, New York, NY 10019.

Career

Public Library, Yakima, WA, children's librarian, 1939-40; U.S. Army Hospital, Oakland, CA, post librarian,

1942-45; writer for children and young people, 1950—. *Member:* Authors Guild, Authors League of America.

Awards, Honors

Young Readers' Choice Awards, Pacific Northwest Library Association, 1957, for *Henry and Ribsy,* 1960, for *Henry and the Paper Route,* 1968, for *The Mouse and the Motorcycle,* 1971, for *Ramona the Pest,* and 1980, for *Ramona and Her Father;* Dorothy Canfield Fisher Memorial Children's Book Awards, 1958, for *Fifteen,* 1961, for *Ribsy,* and 1985, for *Dear Mr. Henshaw;* Notable Book citation, American Library Association (ALA), 1961, for *Jean and Johnny,* 1966, for *The Mouse and the Motorcycle,* 1978, for *Ramona and Her Father,* and 1984, for *Dear Mr. Henshaw;* South Central Iowa Association of Classroom Teachers' Youth Award, 1968, for *The Mouse and the Motorcycle;* Nene Awards, Hawaii Association of School Librarians/ Hawaii Library Association, 1968, for *Ribsy,* 1969, for *The Mouse and the Motorcycle,* 1971, for *Ramona the Pest,* 1972, for *Runaway Ralph,* and 1980, for *Ramona and Her Father;* William Allen White Awards, Kansas Association of School Libraries/Kansas Teachers' Association, 1968, for *The Mouse and the Motorcycle,* and 1976, for *Socks.*

Georgia Children's Book Award, College of Education of University of Georgia, 1970, Sequoyah Children's Book Award, Oklahoma Library Association, 1971, and Massachusetts Children's Book Award nomination, 1977, all for *Ramona the Pest;* New England Round Table of Children's Librarians Honor Book designation, 1972, for *Henry Huggins,* and 1973, for *The Mouse and the Motorcycle;* Sue Hefley Award, Louisiana Association of School Librarians, 1972, and Surrey School Book Award, Surrey School District, 1974, both for *The Mouse and the Motorcycle;* Charlie Mae Simon Award, Arkansas Elementary School Council, 1973, for *Runaway Ralph,* and 1984, for *Ramona Quimby, Age 8;* Distinguished Alumna award, University of Washington School of Librarianship and Information Science, 1975; Golden Archer Awards, University of Wisconsin, 1977, for *Socks* and *Ramona the Brave;* Children's Choice Election Award, second place, 1978; Mark Twain Award, Missouri Library Association/Missouri Association of School Librarians, 1978, for *Ramona the Brave;* Newbery Honor Book designation, ALA, and *Boston Globe-Horn Book* Honor Book designation, both 1978, both for *Ramona and Her Father.*

Newbery Honor Book designation, International Board on Books for Young People honor list, Tennessee Children's Book Award, Tennessee Library Association, and Utah Children's Book Award, Children's Library Association of Utah, all 1980, all for *Ramona and Her Father;* Garden State Children's Choice Awards, 1980, for *Ramona and Her Father,* 1982, for *Ramona and Her Mother,* 1984, for *Ramona Quimby, Age 8,* and 1985, for *Ralph S. Mouse;* Land of Enchantment (New Mexico) Children's Award and Texas Bluebonnet Award, both 1981, both for *Ramona and Her Father;* American Book Award, 1981, for *Ramona and Her Mother;* Newbery

Honor Book designation and American Book Award nomination, both 1982, both for *Ramona Quimby, Age 8.*

California Association of Teachers of English Award and Golden Kite Award, Society of Children's Book Writers and Illustrators, both 1983, and Iowa Children's Choice Award, Iowa Educational Media Association, 1984, all for *Ralph S. Mouse;* Christopher Award, and Parent's Choice for Literature Award, both 1983, Newbery Medal, and Commonwealth Silver Medal, Commonwealth Club of California, both 1984, and Dorothy Canfield Fisher Award, 1985, all for *Dear Mr. Henshaw;* Parent's Choice for Literature Award, 1984, for *Ramona Forever;* Charles Near Simon Award, Arkansas Elementary School Council, Michigan Young Readers Award, and Buckeye Children's Book Award, all 1984, all for *Ramona Quimbly, Age 8;* Buckeye Children's Book Award, 1985, for *Ramona and Her Mother;* Reading Magic Award, 1991, for *Strider.*

Awards for body of work and for contributions to children's literature include: Laura Ingalls Wilder Award, ALA, 1975; Regina Medal, Catholic Library Association, 1980; *Everychild* honor citation, 1985; de Grummond Award, University of Mississippi, and Silver Medallion, University of Southern Mississippi, both 1982; and Jeremiah Ludington Award, Educational Paperback Association, 1988; selected as one of America's Living Legends, U.S. Library of Congress, 2000. Portland, OR, is home to the Beverly B. Cleary Children's Library and the Beverly Cleary Sculpture Garden for Children; the latter contains bronze statues of her characters Ramona Quimby, Henry Huggins, and Ribsy.

Writings

"HENRY HUGGINS" SERIES; ILLUSTRATED BY LOUIS DARLING

Henry Huggins, Morrow (New York City), 1950.
Henry and Beezus, Morrow, 1952.
Henry and Ribsy, Morrow, 1954.
Henry and the Paper Route, Morrow, 1957.
Henry and the Clubhouse, Morrow, 1962.
Ribsy, Morrow, 1964.

"BEEZUS AND RAMONA" SERIES

Beezus and Ramona, illustrated by L. Darling, Morrow, 1955.
Ramona the Pest (also see below), illustrated by L. Darling, Morrow, 1968.
Ramona the Brave, illustrated by Alan Tiegreen, Morrow, 1975.
Ramona and Her Father (also see below), illustrated by Tiegreen, Morrow, 1977.
Ramona and Her Mother (also see below), illustrated by Tiegreen, Morrow, 1979.
Ramona Quimby, Age 8 (also see below), illustrated by Tiegreen, Morrow, 1981.
Cutting up with Ramona! Paper Cutout Fun for Boys and Girls (activity book), illustrated by JoAn L. Scribner, Dell (New York City), 1983.

Beverly Cleary

Ramona Forever (also see below), illustrated by Tiegreen, Morrow, 1984.
The Ramona Quimby Diary (activity book), illustrated by Tiegreen, Morrow, 1984.
The Beezus and Ramona Diary (activity book), illustrated by Tiegreen, Morrow, 1986.
Meet Ramona Quimby (omnibus; includes *Ramona the Pest, Ramona and Her Father, Ramona and Her Mother, Ramona Quimby, Age 8,* and *Ramona Forever*), illustrated by L. Darling and A. Tiegreen, Dell, 1989.
Ramona's World, illustrated by Tiegreen, Morrow, 1999.

"RALPH S. MOUSE" SERIES

The Mouse and the Motorcycle, illustrated by L. Darling, Morrow, 1965.
Runaway Ralph, illustrated by L. Darling, Morrow, 1970.
Ralph S. Mouse, illustrated by Paul O. Zelinsky, Morrow, 1982.

"JANET AND JIMMY" SERIES

The Real Hole, illustrated by Mary Stevens, Morrow, 1960, revised edition illustrated by DyAnne DiSalvo-Ryan, Morrow, 1986.
Two Dog Biscuits, illustrated by M. Stevens, Morrow, 1961, revised edition illustrated by DiSalvo-Ryan, Morrow, 1986.
The Growing-up Feet, illustrated by DiSalvo-Ryan, Morrow, 1987.

Janet's Thingamajigs, illustrated by DiSalvo-Ryan, Morrow, 1987.

FOR CHILDREN

Ellen Tebbits, illustrated by L. Darling, Morrow, 1951.

Otis Spofford, illustrated by L. Darling, Morrow, 1953.

Leave It to Beaver (fictionalization of television series), Berkley (New York), 1960.

The Hullabaloo ABC, illustrated by Earl Hollander, Parnassus Press (Berkley, CA), 1960, illustrated by Ted Rand, Morrow, 1998.

Beaver and Wally (sequel to *Leave It to Beaver*), Berkley, 1961.

Emily's Runaway Imagination, illustrated by Beth and Joe Krush, Morrow, 1961.

Mitch and Amy, illustrated by George Porter, Morrow, 1967.

Socks, illustrated by Beatrice Darwin, Morrow, 1973.

Dear Mr. Henshaw, illustrated by Paul O. Zelinsky, Morrow, 1983.

Lucky Chuck, illustrated by J. Winslow Higginbottom, Morrow, 1984.

Muggie Maggie, illustrated by Kay Life, Morrow, 1990.

Strider (sequel to *Dear Mr. Henshaw*), illustrated by Zelinsky, Morrow, 1991.

Petey's Bedtime Story, illustrated by David Small, Morrow, 1993.

YOUNG ADULT NOVELS

Fifteen, illustrated by B. and J. Krush, Morrow, 1956.

The Luckiest Girl, Morrow, 1958.

Jean and Johnny, illustrated by B. and J. Krush, Morrow, 1959.

Sister of the Bride, illustrated by B. and J. Krush, Morrow, 1963.

OTHER

The Sausage at the End of the Nose (play), Children's Book Council (New York City), 1974.

A Girl from Yamhill: A Memoir (autobiography), Morrow, 1988.

My Own Two Feet: A Memoir (autobiography), Morrow, 1995.

Contributor of short stories to periodicals, including *Redbook, Wigwag,* and *Woman's Day,* and of articles to newspapers and periodicals, including *Horn Book Magazine, Instructor, Oklahoma Librarian,* and *New York Times.* Contributor of short stories to *A Newbery Halloween: A Dozen Scary Stories by Newbery Award-winning Authors,* edited by Martin H. Greenberg and Charles G. Waugh; *A Newbery Zoo: A Dozen Animal Stories by Newbery Award-winning Authors,* edited by Greenburg and Waugh, Delacorte, 1995; *It's Great to Be Eight!,* Scholastic, 1997; *It's Fine to Be Nine!,* Scholastic, 1998; *It's Heaven to Be Seven!,* Scholastic, 1999; and *It's Terrific to be Ten!,* Scholastic, 2000.

Cleary's works have been translated into approximately forty languages.

Adaptations

Pied Piper produced recordings and filmstrips of *Henry and the Clubhouse,* 1962, and *Ribsy,* 1964; Miller-Brody produced recordings and filmstrips of *Ramona and Her Father,* 1979, *Beezus and Ramona, Henry Huggins, Henry and Ribsy, Ramona and Her Mother,* and *Ramona the Brave,* all 1980, *Ramona Quimby, Age 8,* and *Henry and Beezus,* both 1981, *Ralph S. Mouse,* 1983, and *Dear Mr. Henshaw,* 1984. A record album of *Ramona and Her Father* was released by Newbery Award Recording, 1978. Filmic Archives released videos of several episodes from the "Ramona" series, including *Ramona's Bad Day; The Great Hair Argument; New Pajamas; Squeakerfoot; Mystery Meal; Ramona the Patient; Rainy Sunday; Goodbye, Hello; The Perfect Day;* and *Siblingitis.* Listening Library produced audio cassettes of *Henry and Beezus,* 1998 and *Ramona's World,* 1999, and has produced audio books of *Beezus and Ramona, The Mouse and the Motorcycle, Ralph S. Mouse, Ramona and Her Father, Ramona and Her Mother, Ramona the Pest, Ramona the Brave, Ramona Forever,* and *Ramona Quimby, Age 8.* McGraw-Hill Media released the video *Dear Mr. Henshaw,* 1989. Public Broadcasting System (PBS) produced the television series *Ramona,* 1988-89; actress Sarah Polley starred as Ramona. A six-episode series based on *The Mouse and the Motorcycle, Runaway Mouse,* and *Ralph S. Mouse* was produced by Churchill Films for the American Broadcasting Companies (ABC-TV); the program won a Peabody Award. Adaptations of the characters Henry Huggins and Ribsy have appeared on Japanese, Swedish, and Danish television. *Ramona Quimby,* a play by Len Jenkins, was produced by TheatreWorks U.S.A. in New York City and was published by Dramatic Publishing, 1994. The play *Henry and Ramona* was produced by the Waterloo Community Playhouse, Black Hawk Children's Theatre, Waterloo, IA. A doll based on the character of Ramona has been issued by Learning Links.

Sidelights

Acknowledged as one of the most beloved authors of children's literature, Beverly Cleary has been writing books for young people for more than fifty years, a period during which she has retained her popularity, critical acclaim, and relevance. A prolific writer with a wide range of interests who has sold over ten million books, she has written picture books, realistic fiction, historical fiction, fantasy, and nonfiction, and has written for audiences ranging from preschoolers through young adults. Cleary has received praise for her writing in all of the genres to which she has contributed; however, she is most highly regarded as the author of realistic fiction and fantasy, often humorous and in series form, that is directed to primary and middle graders.

Cleary is perhaps best known as the creator of child characters who live in and around Klickitat Street in Portland, Oregon, an area familiar to Cleary from her own childhood: Henry Huggins, a well-meaning middle grader who gets into scrapes with his dog, the lovable mutt Ribsy; and the Quimby sisters, Beatrice (nicknamed Beezus), a responsible girl who is Henry's friend, and her pesky younger sister, Ramona. Cleary's most popular creation, Ramona Quimby was first introduced as a peripheral character in the first "Henry Huggins" book, but soon took on a life—and prompted a series—of her own. Active, imaginative, independent, sometimes obnoxious, but never malicious, Ramona is generally considered a particularly well-rounded characterization.

Cleary is also well known as the creator of a fantasy series for middle graders featuring Ralph S. (for Smart) Mouse, an anthropomorphic rodent whose thirst for adventure and love for motorcycles leads him into exciting situations that take him far from home. In addition, the author has received praise for her young adult novels, pioneering works in the genre that center on young women who mature through their relationships with the opposite sex as well as their families and friends.

Characteristically, Cleary writes about the lives of ordinary middle-class children in works that are structured as collections of episodic stories and are set in Oregon and California, places in which she has lived. The problems faced by her child characters at home and school are generally those faced by most children as they face the challenges of growing up: making mistakes; feeling helpless, misunderstood, guilty, or left out; experiencing sibling rivalry; fearing a school-yard bully; mourning the death of a pet; and other tribulations. Cleary also focuses several of her works on the experiences and emotions of the only child and the children of divorced or single-parent families, and is often acknowledged as one of the first American authors to profile the latter group. Her works also feature children struggling to learn in school or to conform to society; several of her characters, including Ramona Quimby, have trouble adjusting.

Although she writes about the trials of the young, Cleary does not dwell on problems, but instead stresses the many joys of childhood in works that are filled with amusing situations and details. In addition, the author leaves her readers with hope. Her characters solve their problems through their own ingenuity or with the help of their family and friends and even their pets. Her works assure young readers that they can master their own situations and make successful transitions as they move closer to adulthood; in addition, Cleary promotes the pleasures of books and reading in her novels and stories.

Cleary is respected as an author of great perceptiveness and integrity, one who always gives her young readers something both to think about and laugh about. She is credited with turning the ordinary experiences of children into something extraordinary through her skill in translating the actions and feelings of childhood into books children can relate to easily. As a writer, she uses a flowing, conversational style often noted for its deftness, warmth, vitality, and readability as well as for its author's facility with dialogue and use of gentle satire. She is praised for the universality of her subjects,

for her understanding of children and young people, for her accuracy in depicting their world, for blending her humor with sensitivity and compassion, and for speaking to her readers honestly and without condescension. Cleary has been criticized occasionally for stereotyping and for choosing not to use a multicultural approach in her works; in addition, she has been accused of some pedestrian writing and for creating some slight plots. However, most observers consider her a national treasure, an author who has greatly influenced juvenile literature by successfully appealing to both children and adults for nearly three generations.

Reviewers have special praise for Cleary and her work. Writing in *The Beverly Cleary Handbook,* Joanne Kelly called Cleary "by many accounts, the most popular children's author in the United States today" as well as "America's favorite author for children" before concluding: "Her sharp recollections of the complex feelings of childhood and her ability to relate those feelings in a way that is both humorous and comforting to the reader make her work ever popular with children and adults." Margaret Novinger of *Southeastern Librarian* dubbed Cleary "the Boswell of the average child." Writing in *Horn Book Magazine,* Caroline Feller Bauer asked, "Who is Beverly Cleary? She is the author who has made books exciting to children—hundreds and thousands and generations of children. How can you repay Beverly Cleary for such an outstanding contribution?" Katherine Paterson, writing in *Washington Post Book World,* added that Cleary "has the rare gift of being able to reveal us to ourselves while keeping an arm around our shoulder. We laugh ... to recognize that funny, peculiar little self we were and then laugh ... with relief that we've been understood at last. Cleary is able

Ramona pesters Henry the crossing guard in Cleary's **Ramona the Pest.** *(Illustrated by Louis Darling.)*

Ramona tries to cheer up her family after her father loses his job, but only makes things worse. (Cover illustration by Alan Tiegreen.)

to sketch clearly with a few perfect strokes the inexplicable adult world as seen through a child's eyes." In *Twentieth-Century Children's Writers,* Cathryn M. Mercier concluded that Cleary's "impact as a children''s book writer cannot be overestimated.... The appeal of Cleary's work can be attributed to her extraordinary talent in creating memorable young characters whose exuberant spirit and zest for life attract young and old readers alike.... Her sensitive, penetrating awareness of individual children and their needs endures." Ilene Cooper added in *Booklist:* "When it comes to writing books kids love, nobody does it better."

Born in McMinville, Oregon, Cleary was the only child of Lloyd and Mable Atlee Bunn. Her great-grandparents on the Bunn side, Jacob and Harriet Hawn, crossed the plains in 1843 on the first covered wagon to Oregon; after they settled, Jacob Hawn built the first mill in Oregon. Their son Frederick built a home in Yamhill, Oregon, that is now a state landmark; his son John Marion Bunn then built the first fine house there. As Cleary was growing up, her mother's admonishment "Remember your pioneer ancestors" became a familiar phrase. In her autobiography *A Girl from Yamhill,* Cleary described her mother as "a classic figure of the

westward emigration movement, the little schoolmarm from the East who stepped off a train in the West to teach school." Mable Atlee Bunn was born in Michigan and came to Quincy, Washington, with two cousins in 1905. Two years later, she married Chester Lloyd Bunn, the son of a farmer. After their marriage, the couple moved to Yamhill, where Lloyd, as he preferred to be called, was working the family farm. In 1916 Cleary was born in the nearest hospital, in McMinnville. She noted in her autobiography, "McMinnville was my birthplace, but home was Yamhill."

Cleary has always been involved with paper and ink. When she was about two years old, she poured a bottle of blue ink on the tablecloth at Thanksgiving and made hand prints on it; she noted in her autobiography, "I do not recall what happened when aunts, uncles, and cousins arrived. All I recall is my satisfaction in marking with ink on that white surface." As an only child on a farm, she had plenty of freedom to explore. Her father had taught Cleary about safety, and she obeyed his rules, which seemed, in her words, "sensible and interesting." "The farm [was] my playground," she noted in *A Girl from Yamhill,* "a source of interest and delight."

From an early age, Cleary was taught by her mother, who had an interest in books and writing, that reading had power. Mable Bunn would tell Beverly, "Reading is to the mind as exercise is to the body." In an interview in *People Weekly,* Cleary once explained: "My mother had this enchanted world of reading, and I wanted in." Her mother taught Cleary scraps of literature from authors like Chaucer and Dickens and told her stories from her Michigan girlhood as well as folk and fairy tales; she also gave her daughter a list of life rules, such as to never be afraid to stand on your own two feet. Her grandmother read to Cleary from the animal stories by Thornton W. Burgess that were published in the local newspaper, and her father read her "The Katenjammer Kids" from the comics. Although she owned only two books, *Mother Goose* and *The Story of the Three Bears,* Cleary loved literature. Her mother organized a library in Yamhill that was located above a bank in a lodge hall, and soon crates of books began to arrive from the state library, including several that would become Cleary's particular favorites: Joseph Jacobs' *More English Fairy Tales* and the picture books of Beatrix Potter, most notably *The Tailor of Gloucester.*

When she was six, Cleary and her parents left the farm in Yamhill for Portland. She wrote in her autobiography, "Yamhill had taught me that the world was a safe and beautiful place, where children were treated with kindness, patience, and tolerance. Everyone loved little girls. I was sure of that." Cleary enjoyed life in the city, playing with neighborhood children and taking ballet. Then, in first grade, she got chicken pox, then smallpox. "By then," she recalled, "I was hopelessly lost in reading." Her teacher divided the class into three groups—Bluebirds, Redbirds, and Blackbirds—according to their reading ability; Cleary was placed in the lowest group, the Blackbirds. "From a country child who had never known fear, I became a city child consumed by fear." In second grade, Cleary's teacher helped her to read, but Beverly developed an aversion to reading outside of school. The family moved once again, this time to a house five blocks from Klickitat Street, a neighborhood near the city limit that Cleary would later use as the setting for many of her books. One day her mother found a case of books in the basement of the local Sunday School. One of these books was *The Dutch Twins,* a story by Lucy Fitch Perkins. Cleary recalled, "Suddenly, I was reading and enjoying what I read! It was a miracle. I was happy in a way I had not been happy since starting school." Then, Cleary received a copy of Hugh Lofting's *The Story of Doctor Dolittle,* a book she enjoyed even more than *The Dutch Twins;* she wrote a review of *Doctor Dolittle* that was published in the *Oregon Journal.* When her family moved again, this time to Hancock Street in Portland, Cleary played with the neighborhood children and went to the movies; she especially enjoyed Hal Roach's "Our Gang" comedies, noting, "To me, these comedies were about neighborhood children playing together, something I wanted to read about in books. I longed for books about the children of Hancock Street." In school, she continued to win kudos for her writing. However, tensions in the family, many of which were caused by the Depression, increased: Lloyd Bunn wanted to go back to the farm, but Mable did not; tensions also started to grow between Cleary and her mother, whom she felt was manipulating her life. Beverly escaped by going to the library. As she recalled in *More Junior Authors:* "When I had learned to read, I made regular trips to the library. As I grew up, I read almost every book in the children's collection but I could rarely find what I wanted to read most of all. That was funny stories about American boys and girls.... I wanted to read about boys and girls who lived in the same kind of neighborhood I lived in and went to a school like the one I attended."

In 1928 Lloyd Bunn sold the family farm, and the family moved to a house two blocks south of Klickitat Street. In sixth grade Cleary wrote a story for a writing assignment about a little girl who goes to Bookland and talks with some of her favorite literary characters. She remembered in her autobiography: "[A] feeling of peace came over me as I wrote far beyond the required length of the essay. I had discovered the pleasure of writing." After her teacher, Miss Smith, read the story aloud, she exclaimed, "When Beverly grows up, she should write children's books." Miss Smith's praise gave "direction to my life," Cleary maintained, adding in *More Junior Authors* that the suggestion "seemed like such a good idea that I made up my mind that someday I would write books—the kind of books I wanted to read."

In eighth grade Cleary had an experience that affected her writing more negatively. After she submitted a paragraph of description for a class assignment, her teacher returned Cleary's work covered in red corrections. "For years," Cleary recalled, "I avoided writing description, and children told me they liked my books 'because there isn't any description in them.'" However, in high school Cleary went back to receiving praise from her teachers for her writing. One of her stories, "The

Diary of a Tree-Sitter," was called very funny by a teacher, who told the budding author, "You show talent." Another story, "The Green Christmas," which describes how a boy is saved from playing the part of a Christmas angel in a school program after he falls into water containing green dye, later became a chapter in her first book, *Henry Huggins.* Cleary joined the Migwam, a school literary club, and later became its president; she also studied journalism, wrote stories for the school newspaper, and wrote a script for the Girls' League Show. At home, tensions increased between Cleary and her mother who, the author wrote in the second volume of her autobiography, *My Own Two Feet,* was struggling "to mold me into the perfect daughter." Her mother's cousin, a librarian at Chaffey Junior College in Ontario, California, offered Beverly the chance to stay with her while attending the school, which was free for California residents. Although her mother disapproved of the idea, her father stepped in, and Cleary went to California.

In her freshman English class at Chaffey, Cleary wrote an autobiography about the early years of her life in Yamhill; the teacher, who did not give out good grades easily, awarded her with what she called in her autobiography "an unadorned, unqualified A." She received another A for an assignment, written in the third person, about her difficulties in learning to read in the first grade; she noted in *My Own Two Feet,* "Without knowing it, I had begun to write the story of my life." After finishing two happy years at Chaffey, Cleary went to the University of California at Berkeley. She had worked as a substitute librarian at the Ontario, California, public library; now she wanted to become a children's librarian and write children's books. At an assembly dance at the university she met Clarence Cleary, a grad student six years her senior who was studying economics and history. Clarence was Roman Catholic, while Beverly was Protestant; consequently, Mable Bunn did not approve of her daughter's relationship. At school Beverly studied English, languages, education, and the sciences as preparation to attend the School of Librarianship at the University of Washington in Seattle. In her senior year she realized that she wanted to marry Clarence Cleary; however, she intended to keep her Protestant faith. After graduating in 1938, Cleary went to the University of Washington, where she received her bachelor of arts degree in librarianship the next year.

After graduating from the University of Washington, Cleary went to Yakima, Washington, where she became a children's librarian. Of her experience there, she wrote in *My Own Two Feet,* "Most vividly of all I remember the group of grubby little boys, nonreaders, who came once a week during school hours.... Their teacher ... said their textbooks did not interest them and perhaps library books would encourage them to read. 'Where are all the books about kids like us?,' they wanted to know. Where indeed.... As I listened to the boys talk about books, I recalled my own childhood reading, when I longed for funny stories about the sort of children who lived in my neighborhood. What was the matter with authors? I had often wondered and now wondered again."

Cleary enjoyed introducing children to books. She became a frequent storyteller, traveling to local schools and libraries and beginning a stint on her library's weekly radio broadcast. She told Shirley Fitzgibbons in *Top of the News,* "Although I told folk and fairy tales, I think I learned to write for children in those Saturday afternoon story hours. When I began *Henry Huggins,* I did not know how to write a book, so I mentally told the stories that I remembered and wrote them down as I told them. This is why my first book is a collection of stories about a group of characters rather than a novel." In 1940 Beverly married Clarence Cleary at a church in Reno, Nevada. The newlyweds moved to San Francisco, where Clarence worked for the state government and for the coast guard inspection office before being transferred to Alameda, California, to work at an office for the U.S. Navy.

Beverly began working part-time at the Sather Gate Book Shop in Berkeley, where she sold children's books. During World War II she became the librarian at Camp John T. Knight, an Army camp in Oakland, and then became post librarian at an army library in a hospital. At the end of the war, Cleary tried to write a book about "the maturing of a sensitive girl who wanted to write," but was uninspired. After having a miscarriage she returned to work at the Sather Gate Book Shop; meanwhile the Clearys moved to Berkeley and bought a house in which the previous owners had left a ream of typing paper. In the bookstore Cleary picked up a particularly lame easy reader and read, disgustedly. "Suddenly," she wrote in *My Own Two Feet,* "I knew a could write a better book and, what was more, I intended to do it as soon as the Christmas rush was over."

On the second of January, 1948, Cleary sat down to write. She thought of the boys who had come into the library in Yakima wanting books about youngsters like themselves. "Why not write an easy-reading book for kids like them?" She thought about Hancock Street in Portland, where she had lived when she was the same age as the boys who came into the Yakima library. Hancock was a street where "boys teased girls even though they played with them, where boys built scooters out of roller skates and apple boxes, wooden in those days, and where dogs, before the advent of leash laws, followed the children to school." She also recalled an incident from her days in the hospital library, where some children brought their dog into the library: "On their way home," Cleary recalled in her autobiography, "they learned that a dog was not allowed on a streetcar unless it was in a box." With all of this in mind, Cleary prepared to take the plunge. "[I]n my imagination, I stood once more before Yakima's story hour crowd as I typed the first sentence: 'Henry Huggins was in the third grade.'"

Henry Huggins was inspired by the boys on Hancock Street, who, the author recalled, "seemed eager to jump onto the page. Hancock Street became Klickitat Street because I had always liked the sound of the name when I had lived nearby." She named Henry's dog Spareribs, because she happened to have some spareribs in the refrigerator, and turned the streetcar into a bus. While writing her book, Cleary wrote to Siri Andrews, one of her former professors from library school who was now working as an editor and librarian in New Hampshire, to tell her about it. Andrews put Cleary in touch with an editor at Addison-Cokesbury publishers, who wrote back with interest. Cleary recalled in her autobiography, "I continued happily inventing stories about Henry from reality and imagination and, as I wrote, Mother's words, whenever I had to write a composition in high school, came back to me: 'Make it funny. People always like to read something funny,' and 'Keep it simple. The best writing is simple writing.'"

While continuing to write her first stories about Henry Huggins and his friends, it occurred to Cleary that all of the characters she had created thus far had no brothers or sisters. "Someone should have a sibling," she wrote in *My Own Two Feet,* "so I tossed in a little sister to explain Beezus's nickname. When it came time to name the sister, I overheard a neighbor call out to another whose name was Ramona. I wrote in 'Ramona,' made several references to her, gave her one brief scene, and thought that was the end of her. Little did I dream, to use a trite expression from books of my childhood, that she would take over books of her own, that she would grow and become a well-known and loved character."

When Cleary finished her book, she submitted it to an editor at the William Morrow publishing company, who suggested that the name of the dog be changed from Spareribs to Ribs or Ribsy because it sounded more like a name that a boy would use. *Henry Huggins* was published by Morrow in 1950. Cleary wrote in *My Own Two Feet,* "After all my years of ambition to write, of aiming both consciously and unconsciously toward writing, I had actually written. I was a real live author."

In *Henry Huggins* Henry is a third-grader who befriends a skinny stray dog he finds in a drug store. His mother, who cannot come to get him, suggests that Henry bring his new pet home on the bus. Lacking the requisite box in which to bring home the dog, which he names Ribsy, Henry uses a shopping bag to carry his new pet on the bus. Ribsy escapes from the shopping bag and wreaks havoc on the moving bus. The police arrive, looking for Henry; to his delight, they bring him and Ribsy home in a police car. *Henry Huggins* also introduces the Quimby sisters, Henry's neighbors on Klickitat Street. Henry gets along well with Beezus, whom he considers sensible, but he is irritated with Ramona, whom he considers an annoying pest.

Critics who initially reviewed *Henry Huggins* were generally appreciative of it. A *Kirkus Reviews* critic called the book "[e]nchanting small-boy adventures—a grammar-school *Odyssey* .... Cleary must have had her ear to the door many times to catch the flavor of third grade manners and mores." Mary Gould Davis of the *Saturday Review* added, "It is hard to decide which of these incidents is the funniest," while Ellen Lewis Buell, writing in the *New York Times Book Review,* concluded that *Henry Huggins* presents "everyday life as children know it. Maybe Henry is a little luckier than the average boy, but he's not really any funnier. He just seems that way, which is fine."

Cleary has written five additional volumes in her series about Henry Huggins—*Henry and Beezus, Henry and Ribsy, Henry and the Paper Route, Henry and the Clubhouse,* and *Ribsy.* In these works, the author continues the exploits of her Everyboy and his faithful mongrel. Henry tries to earn a red bicycle, tries to keep Ribsy out of trouble, takes on a paper route, builds a clubhouse, and loses—and recovers—his dog, all the while trying to outwit his nemesis, Ramona. However, in *Henry and the Clubhouse,* Ramona follows Henry into a snowstorm when he is delivering papers. He feels sorry for her, so he loads Ramona on his sled and takes her home before going back into the storm to finish his route. Henry is commended for his kindness and responsibility and, at the end of the story, is given five dollars by his dad so he can buy the new sleeping bag he wants. Reviewers favorably compared the "Henry Huggins" series to the "Little Eddie" books by Carolyn Haywood and to *Homer Price* by Robert McCloskey. They also praised the believability and unpretentiousness of the series and noted that its core is the love of a boy and his dog for each other. Writing in the *New York Times Book Review,* Ellen Lewis Buell called Henry "as typical of the present younger generation as [Booth Tarkington's] Penrod was of his.... It is part of Henry's charm that his experiences are just those that might happen to any boy you know." Writing in *Children and Books,* May Hill Abuthnot and Zena Sutherland dubbed the books about Henry and his friends "[p]ure Americana," adding, "[T]he characters are real boys and girls, convincingly alive." Margaret Novinger of *Southeastern Librarian* claimed that, with her Henry Huggins stories, Cleary "has created a world within the field of children's literature.... The world is bounded by childhood and humor and welcomes all children ... to enter and enjoy.... The characters and the setting tie [the books in the series] together. Beverly Cleary maintains their individuality as books because of her ability as a writer. To each book she brings humor and an unusual ability to understand children .... In our judgment, the 'Henry Huggins' books represent Beverly Cleary's unique contribution to the world of children's literature."

In addition to the "Henry Huggins" books, Cleary wrote two more works about children who live in or near Henry's neighborhood, *Ellen Tebbits* and *Otis Spofford.* Cleary once called *Ellen Tebbits* "probably the most autobiographical of my books." The story features Ellen, a fourth-grader who has just lost her best friend. Ellen meets Austine Allen, a new girl from California; the girls are bonded when they discover that they both have to wear horrid woolen underwear. Ellen and Austine are tormented by Otis Spofford, a schoolmate who is the son of their dancing teacher and who likes to, in his own words, "stir up a little excitement"; Otis is often considered the forerunner of Ramona Quimby. Ellen and Austine stop speaking to each other when Austine is blamed for untying the sash of Ellen's new dress, a deed actually done by Otis. Their estrangement continues for weeks until the girls' teacher asks them to clean erasers together. After Ellen rips the sash on Austine's dress, they make up and become best friends again. Writing in the *Christian Science Monitor,* Ethel C. Ince claimed, "Ellen takes her place beside Henry as an original and endearing character—a welcome addition to children's bookshelves." A *Kirkus Reviews* critic added, "It seems obvious from this entrancing successor to *Henry Huggins* that the author is well acquainted with the whisperings, weeps, and whoops of third grade distaff side as she is with the ways of young men like Henry." A reviewer in *Publishers Weekly* predicted, "The trials of an 8-year-old in school and out will be a favorite with many young readers."

Otis Spofford features the irascible title character, who lives with his mother, a single parent, in the apartment above her dance studio. A protagonist Cleary based on a sixth-grade classmate, Otis wishes for a full-time mother and a real house like the other children in his class. Otis, whose favorite person to harass is the demure Ellen Tebbits, likes to cause a scene: for example, as the front half in a bull costume in a mock bullfight staged in front of the PTA, he charges aggressively instead of falling down; he shoots spitballs; he chases Ellen; and he fills his classroom with garlic. The antihero's ultimate misdemeanor is actually an accident: playing cowboys and Indians in his classroom, Otis mistakenly cuts off a large chunk of Ellen's hair when he pretends to scalp her. Although he gets off with a reprimand from the adults, Otis is ostracized by the other children. At the ice rink, Ellen and Austine tease him and steal his shoes and boots, leaving him to come home on his skates. Otis apologizes, and they make him promise never to tease them again. However, Otis triumphs in the end: he has crossed his fingers behind his back. At the time of its publication in 1955, *Otis Spofford* was considered controversial; some critics considered Otis an amoral character, and the book was banned from some school libraries because Otis threw spitballs and did not repent. However, other reviewers were more positive: a critic in *Publishers Weekly* called *Otis Spofford* a "really hilarious story of a mischievous, impudent boy who is a classroom comedian, a show-off, and a pain, but still very lovable. Young readers will understand Otis and recognize his type." A reviewer for *Booklist* commented, "Children who find most book heroes too good to be true will be immensely taken with Otis Spofford.... As always the author's writing is marked by a freshness and naturalness stemming from an understanding of children and the brand of humor that appeals to them." Ellen Lewis Buell of the *New York Times Book Review* concluded that she "couldn't help wishing that Otis's mother had more time for him. This in itself is proof of the strength of his personality—the brasher he is, the better you like him."

In 1955 Cleary published *Beezus and Ramona,* the first of her series of books about the Quimby family. In this work, Beezus is nine years old and Ramona is four. Ramona embarrasses Beezus by scribbling all over a library book she wants to keep, by disrupting her after-school art class and a checker game she is playing with Henry Huggins, and by giving her a hard time when she is baby-sitting. When Beezus turns ten, Ramona manages to ruin two birthday cakes. Beezus decides she does not love her sister; however, when her namesake, Aunt Beatrice, arrives, she and Mrs. Quimby laugh about the trouble they caused each other while growing up. After hearing her mother and aunt, Beezus concludes that it is okay to dislike your sister every now and then. Writing in the *New York Times Book Review*, Buell called Ramona "the most exasperating little sister since Tarkington created Jane Baxter," while Heloise P. Mailloux of *Horn Book* called *Beezus and Ramona* "a very funny book; its situations are credible, and it has a perceptive handling of family relationships that is unfortunately rare in easily read books." Louise S. Bechtel noted in the *New York Herald Tribune Book Review* that *Beezus and Ramona* is "just as funny and real as [books] about Henry. It will bring wonderful comfort to nine-year-old girls who suffer from characterful, bright, naughty little sisters."

Cleary has written seven other books about the Quimbys, all of which center on Ramona: *Ramona the Pest; Ramona the Brave; Ramona and Her Father; Ramona and Her Mother; Ramona Quimby, Age 8; Ramona Forever;* and *Ramona's World.* The most recent volume was published after a fifteen-year hiatus Cleary took from writing about her most popular character. In the remainder of the series, Ramona grows from age five to nine, and matures from a kindergartner to a fourth-grader. Cleary outlines Ramona's joys and sorrows in a manner considered both poignant and hilarious: she has misunderstandings with her teachers and with other children; becomes a kindergarten drop-out; has trouble with spelling; overcomes her fear of the dark; triumphantly finds a way to make the best of being a sheep in her Sunday school Christmas pageant; tries to run away from home; deals with Willa Jean, the bratty little sister of her friend Howie; overhears a neighbor compare Willa Jean to herself at that age; throws up in class and accidentally makes a face in her class picture; is praised for her writing ability and for her creativity in making up a skit around her book report; fights and makes up with Beezus; learns about death through the passing of the family cat; finds a lost wedding ring; learns to adjust to life as a big sister to baby Roberta; gains a best friend, Daisy; and experiences the first flowering of romance with her old pal Danny, whom she calls Yard Ape. Throughout the series, Cleary depicts Ramona's emotional development as well as her adventures and misadventures. Ramona feels alone, unwanted, humiliated, angry, jealous, and betrayed. She has a hard time sticking to the rules, throws tantrums, and is often stubborn and exasperating. However, Ramona is also bright, loving, sensitive, tenacious, and forgiving. In *Ramona Forever* she assesses her progress and realizes how far she has come, while in *Ramona's World* she learns to accept being imperfect.

Parents are an integral part of the Beezus and Ramona series; in fact, the changes within the Quimby family are often thought to reflect those within U.S. society during the period covered by the books. In *Ramona the Brave,* Mrs. Quimby goes from being a full-time mother to starting a job as a part-time bookkeeper; in *Ramona and Her Father,* Mr. Quimby loses his job, and the family goes through economic difficulties as well as tensions created by his constant smoking; in *Ramona and Her Mother,* Mrs. Quimby goes to work full time so her husband can attend college; in *Ramona Quimby, Age 8,* Mr. Quimby works part-time in a supermarket warehouse while attending college; and, in *Ramona Forever,* he hopes to begin teaching art in an elementary school after receiving his teaching credentials, but accepts a position as manager in the local supermarket instead so the family can stay in Portland. In *Ramona and Her Mother* Beezus and Ramona hear their parents argue, a situation that leads the children to think that they are going to get a divorce. However, Mr. and Mrs. Quimby assure their daughters that they are just sometimes short-tempered and are far from perfect. Reviewers have noted that Mr. and Mrs. Quimby are loving and supportive parents and that they are always there for their children. As Anita Trout said in *Dictionary of Literary Biography,* "An important message which Cleary makes through Ramona is how very real are the fears which children have about their parents and family situations.... Cleary knows that children need to hear [that problems don't change the love parents have for them] often."

The character of Ramona has been appreciated by critics and readers alike. Writing in *Horn Book,* Ethel L. Heins called Ramona "[o]ne of the most endearing protagonists of children's fiction," while *Publishers Weekly* contributor Heather Vogel Frederick described her as "an indelible figure in the children's book world since she burst on the scene." Mary M. Burns claimed in *Horn Book* that, with her books about the Quimbys, Cleary developed "as memorable a cast of characters as can be found in children's literature." In his *The Marble in the Water,* David Rees stated that the Ramona books work on different levels due to "the subtle shape of the narrative, and the distinction of the author's wit." *Twentieth-Century Children's Writers* essayist Cathryn M. Mercier added: "Through Ramona, Cleary touches young readers on an emotional level which engages and challenges, but does not overwhelm. Her ability to sustain their attention over time, from book to book, remains an accomplishment beyond evaluation."

In 1955 Cleary gave birth to twins, Malcolm and Marianne. Several of her subsequent books reflected the interests and experiences of her children. For example, she wrote four picture books—*The Real Hole, Two Dog Biscuits, Janet's Thingamajigs,* and *The Growing-up Feet*—about four-year-old twins Janet and Jimmy, who are modeled on her children. In *Mitch and Amy,* a story for primary graders, Cleary again bases her protagonists on Malcolm and Marianne. The book features twins who are preparing to enter fourth grade. Mitch is good with mechanical things but has trouble with reading and spelling, while Amy is a good reader but has problems with arithmetic. Although they bicker and squabble, the twins are ultimately supportive of each other. For example, when Mitch needs to do a book report, Amy finds a title that he can enjoy. Mitch also confronts a bully, Alan, and discovers that he can stand up for himself; after the confrontation with Alan, the twins realize that he, like Mitch, has a problem with reading and spelling. Writing in *Saturday Review,* Zena Sutherland stated, "It is a rare author who can describe a sibling relationship with all the authority of a case study and have it emerge as a smoothly written and entertaining story." Ethel L. Heins added in *Horn Book,* "Probably only a parent of twins could create so convincing a pair as nine-year-old Mitch and Amy and could write about them so realistically and so unsentimentally."

Son Malcolm's fascination with motorcycles and his difficulty with learning to read led Cleary to write one of her most popular series, the realistic fantasies about Ralph S. Mouse. Cleary wrote the first volume of the series, *The Mouse and the Motorcycle,* in an attempt to capture the interest of a reluctant reader. This volume introduces Ralph, who lives with his parents and siblings in an old hotel, the Mountain View Inn, which is located in the Sierra Nevada mountains east of San Francisco. The mouse family lives in the wall of a room rented by Mr. and Mrs. Gridley and their son Keith. Ralph, who is fascinated by Keith's collection of miniature cars and a tiny toy motorcycle, becomes friends with the boy. Keith lets Ralph use the motorcycle and teaches him to make it go; this leads Ralph into a series of adventures, such as nearly being sucked up by a vacuum cleaner, being trapped in a pile of sheets headed for the laundry, being pursued by a dog, and being tossed out a window by a hotel guest. When Keith falls ill with a fever, it is Ralph who brings him the aspirin that helps him sleep. Ralph becomes a hero, and is given the motorcycle by Keith. Writing in *Young Readers Review,* Phyllis Cohen commented, "This fantasy is so realistic that it is almost plausible" before concluding, "Even boys who do not care for fantasy may find this fantasy much to their liking." Margaret Sherwood Libby added in the *New York Herald Tribune Book Week* that Cleary "has ventured into the demanding realm of fantasy. Her foray ... is a success."

In the next volume of the series, *Runaway Ralph,* the mouse takes his motorcycle to the Happy Acres summer camp, where he meets Garf, a boy who has been ostracized by the other campers. Ralph and Garf help each other, Garf by saving Ralph from a guard dog and restoring his freedom after he is caged, and Ralph by clearing Garf's name after he is accused of stealing a watch. In the third volume of the series, *Ralph S. Mouse,* Ralph leaves the Mountain View Inn after his rough-and-tumble cousins move in and disrupt his life. He turns to Ryan, the fifth-grade son of the inn's house-keeper. Ryan takes Ralph to school where his motorcycle is accidentally smashed, causing a rift between Ralph and Ryan. Wanting to leave the school, Ralph approaches Ryan's classmate, Brad; eventually, Ralph reconciles with Ryan, who works with Brad to come up with a successful plan to return Ralph to the inn. They

also present him with a sports car to replace his motorcycle. At the end of the story, Ralph organizes his cousins into a group willing to share, and Ryan and Brad become stepbrothers. Writing about the character of Ralph in *Who's Who in Children's Books,* Margery Fisher stated, "The humanizing of Ralph is carried out in a spirit of gay and practical fantasy.... In fact he remains, engagingly, both mouse and boy." In a review of *Ralph S. Mouse* in *Growing Point,* Fisher added, "In all three of Ralph's encounters with people he is a vehicle for a Gulliver-scrutiny of Brobdingnag as well as a splendidly entertaining character in his own squeakily confident right."

In 1983 Cleary produced *Dear Mr. Henshaw,* a work often praised as one of her strongest works as well as a departure in form. Directed to middle-graders and structured through letters and diary entries, the novel features Leigh Botts, a sixth-grade boy of divorced parents who is living in a new town in California. Leigh has been writing to author Boyd Henshaw since second grade. Henshaw has included a response to Leigh's last letter with a list of questions for him, so Leigh outlines his situation: he misses his father, a cross-country

BEVERLY CLEARY
RAMONA QUIMBY, AGE 8

Being a member of the Quimby family in the third grade is harder than Ramona had expected.

Now eight, Ramona has to get through third grade at a new school and put up with annoying changes at home. (Cover illustration by Alan Tiegreen.)

trucker who has his own rig but is somewhat irresponsible, and his dog Bandit, who is accompanying Mr. Botts on his runs; he is often alone while his mother studies to be a nurse and works part-time for a caterer; at school, his lunch box is being burgled; and he has made no new friends. Henshaw suggests that Leigh keep a diary, which he does. Leigh is upset when his father tells him Bandit was lost in a snowstorm; while talking to his father on the phone, Leigh hears a boy's voice telling Mr. Botts that he and his mother are ready to go out for pizza. Leigh confides his feelings to his mother, who consoles him and explains the cause of the divorce. In school, Leigh rigs a burglar alarm for his lunch box. He is praised for his work, and several of his classmates ask him to help them build alarms for their lunch boxes. He makes a new friend, Barry, wins an honorable mention in a story contest, and meets the famous author Angela Badger, who tells him he is a writer. At the conclusion of the novel, Leigh's father, who has rescued Bandit, comes to the house to leave the dog with Leigh. However, Leigh decides to let his dad keep Bandit as company on his long trucking runs.

Reviewing *Dear Mr. Henshaw* in the *Washington Post Book World,* Colby Rodowsky stated, "Epistolary novels, by their very nature, are apt to limit a writer, but Beverly Cleary ... has peopled her story with a group of fully realized characters.... The letters themselves are so real they make your teeth ache." Writing in *Dictionary of Literary Biography,* Anita Trout said, "In Leigh Botts, Cleary has brought together her years of writing experience and her ability to express the emotions, needs, and humor of a child. She has created a character that is deeper and fuller than her others because she goes further into the child's viewpoint than she has in her earlier books." Natalie Babbitt of the *New York Times Book Review* said that Cleary "has written many very good books over the years. This one is the best. It is a first-rate, poignant story in the forms of letters and a diary—a new construction for a Cleary book—and there is so much in it, all presented so simply, that it's hard to find a way to do it justice." Babbitt concluded, "What a lovely, well-crafted, three-dimensional book this is. And how reassuring to Mrs. Cleary's fellow writers to see that a 27th book can be so fresh and strong. Lots of adjectives here. She deserves them all." In 1984 Cleary received the Newbery Medal for *Dear Mr. Henshaw.*

Cleary published *Strider,* a sequel to *Dear Mr. Henshaw,* in 1991. Leigh, now an eighth-grader, begins his diary again. Leigh and Barry find an abandoned puppy on the beach that they name Strider. The boys agree to share Strider in a joint custody arrangement. However, Leigh and the dog form a special attachment to each other. Leigh's mother, who is now going to school to become a registered nurse, tells Leigh that Strider is a Queensland Heeler, an Australian herding dog. Leigh's father, still out on the road, continues to forget to call Leigh and to send child support payments, but Leigh is now better able to deal with his father's failings. When Barry goes on vacation for a month Leigh takes care of Strider, and the two grow even closer, which causes a rift with Barry

when he returns. After Leigh returns the dog to Barry, Strider escapes and returns to Leigh; finally, Barry decides to give Strider to his friend. At the conclusion of the novel, Leigh makes friends with Kevin, another boy from a divorced family, and with Geneva, a girl whom he admires. He also joins the school track team and wins the Rotary Invitational Track Meet. A reviewer in *Publishers Weekly* commented, "Although it lacks the emotional intensity that made [*Dear Mr. Henshaw*] an instant classic, this sequel offers further proof of the author's preeminence in children's fiction.... Once again Cleary demonstrates her ability to write from the heart." Mary M. Burns added in *Horn Book,* "Once again, Cleary proves that she is in complete harmony with the world view of children and adolescents."

Cleary has often included autobiographical elements in her works. *Emily's Runaway Imagination,* a book set in Oregon in the 1920s, was called "the most biographical of Cleary's work" by Joanne Kelly in *The Beverly Cleary Handbook.* Emily Bartlett lives in Pitchfork, Oregon, a thinly disguised version of Yamhill. Emily loves to read, but there are few books in Pitchfork, which does not have a library. Emily's mother requests that a library be built in the town, and the state librarians agree; consequently, Mrs. Bartlett begins preparations. Emily has a series of adventures: she feeds fallen apples to the family hogs, which then proceed to lurch around the yard, drunk on fermented juice, during her mother's elegant luncheon; she bleaches the family's plow horse to turn it into a snow-white steed; and she inadvertently wins second prize in a contest by dressing in a "costume" of an outgrown dress and her mother's high heels. At the end of the story, Emily is happy when her Chinese next-door neighbor, who is returning to China, presents his home to Mrs. Bartlett so that it can be used to house the new library. Writing in *Bulletin of the Center for Children's Books,* Zena Sutherland called *Emily's Runaway Imagination* "a truly delightful book" as well as a "pleasant story for girls, written in the artfully artless style that marks true craftsmanship." Writing in the *New York Times Book Review,* Ellen Lewis Buell added, "Friendly but shy, bumbling but sentient, [Emily] is a child other little girls will be glad to know." A reviewer in *Publishers Weekly* added, "Emily is one of Miss Cleary's most charming characters."

Cleary produced her autobiographies, *A Girl from Yamhill* and *My Own Two Feet,* in 1988 and 1995 respectively; both books are directed to middle and upper graders. The first volume describes the author's life from birth until she left for junior college in California; the second volume takes her from college to the publication of her first book. Reviewing *A Girl from Yamhill* in *Bulletin of the Center for Children's Books,* Zena Sutherland stated, "The author sees her child self with the same clarity and objectivity as she has seen her fictional characters," while Judith A. Sheriff of *Voice of Youth Advocates* added, "Cleary's memoir is every bit as delightful to read as her stories." A reviewer in *Publishers Weekly* concluded, "This is a slow, sometimes oblique story at the outset, but deeply moving by the end. A real gift to Cleary's many fans, young and old." Writing in *Horn Book* about *My Own Two Feet,* Mary M. Burns stated, "With each book, Beverly Cleary ensures her place as one of the classic writers of the twentieth century . . . . This remarkable book is written honestly without attempting to hide the difficulties that seemed to arise regularly from her parents'—particularly her mother's—attempts to control her life and the constant financial problems engendered by the Depression. Yet for all the sadness that sometimes lurks beneath the surface, it is a marvelously sensitive, often funny portrayal of a young woman's progress to adulthood and to independence. It is also the story of a writer-in-the-making." Burns concludes that, after reading Cleary's memoir, those readers "who have always admired her books will ... have an even greater admiration for the author." Ilene Cooper of *Booklist* concurred, noting, "Much of Cleary's success as a writer comes from her ability to write so honestly. She almost never makes a misstep, and that's as true here as in her fiction." Cooper concluded by suggesting that older children will find *My Own Two Feet* "a welcome change in the biography section. For one thing, it's so much better written than many titles found there; for another, the subject is much better loved."

In assessing her motivation as a author, Cleary told *Twentieth-Century Children's Writers,* "The stories I write are the stories I wanted to read as a child, and the experience I hope to share with children is the discovery that reading is one of the pleasures of life and not just something one must do in school." Cleary wrote in the *Oklahoma Librarian,* "The writer for children must fuse memory and observation and go back into childhood as he writes. He must be the child he is writing about." She noted in *Horn Book* that, as she wrote her stories, "I discovered I had a collaborator, the child within myself—a rather odd, serious little girl, prone to colds, who sat in a child's rocking chair with her feet over the hot air outlet of the furnace, reading for hours, seeking laughter in the pages of books while her mother warned her she would ruin her eyes. That little girl, who has remained with me, prevents me from writing down to children, from poking fun at my characters, and from writing an adult reminiscence about childhood instead of a book to be enjoyed by children. And yet I do not write solely for that child; I am also writing my adult self. We are collaborators who must agree." In *My Own Two Feet,* Cleary recalled her beginnings as a writer. When walking to the bank to deposit her advance royalty check for *Henry Huggins,* she found a nickel under a leaf. She wrote, "I was confident that a satisfying life of writing lay ahead, that ideas would continue to flow. As I walked, I thought about all the bits of knowledge about children, reading, and writing that had clung to me like burrs or dandelion fluff all through childhood, college, the Yakima children's room, and the bookstore. As I mulled over my past, I made two resolutions: I would ignore all trends, and I would not let money influence any decisions I would make about my books." At the bank, she deposited her check and the worn nickel, as she wrote, "for luck." She concluded, "In my years of writing, I have often thought of that nickel and now see it as a talisman of all the good fortune that has come to me: friends, readers, awards, travel, children of my own, financial security that has allowed me to return the generosity extended to me when times were hard for everyone. It was indeed a lucky nickel."

Biographical and Critical Sources

BOOKS

Arbuthnot, May Hill, and Zena Sutherland, *Children and Books,* 4th edition, Scott, Foresman, 1972, pp. 442-443.

Authors and Artists for Young Adults, Volume 6, Gale, 1991, pp. 11-23.

Berg, Julie, *Beverly Cleary: The Young at Heart,* Abdo & Daughters, 1993.

Beverly Cleary Resource Book, American School Publishers, 1988.

Children's Literature Review, Gale, Volume 2, 1976, pp. 44-51, Volume 8, 1985, pp. 34-62.

Cleary, Beverly, *A Girl from Yamhill,* Morrow, 1988.

Cleary, Beverly, *My Own Two Feet,* Morrow, 1995.

Dictionary of Literary Biography, Volume 52: *American Writers for Children since 1950,* Gale, 1986, pp. 84-91.

Fisher, Margery, *Who's Who in Children's Books: A Treasury of the Familiar Characters of Childhood,* Holt, pp. 299-300.

Kelly, Joanne, *The Beverly Cleary Handbook,* Teacher Ideas Press, 1996.

Martin, Patricia Stone, *Beverly Cleary: She Makes Reading Fun,* illustrated by Karen Park, Rourke, 1987.

More Junior Authors, edited by Muriel Fuller, Wilson, 1963, pp. 49-50.

Onion, Susan, *Beverly Cleary,* Teacher Created Materials, 1994.

Pfliger, Pat, *Beverly Cleary,* Twayne, 1991.

Rees, David, *The Marble in the Water: Essays on Contemporary Writers of Fiction for Children and Young Adults,* Horn Book, 1980, pp. 90-103.

St. James Guide to Children's Writers, St. James Press, 1999, pp. 238-240.

Scott, Elaine, *Beverly Cleary's Ramona: Behind the Scenes of a Television Show,* Dell, 1988.

The Signal Review 1: A Selective Guide to Children's Literature, 1982, edited by Nancy Chambers, Thimble Press, 1983, p. 40.

Teacher's Guide to the Novels of Beverly Cleary, Dell, 1986.

Twentieth-Century Children's Writers, edited by Laura Standley Berger, 4th edition, St. James Press, 1998, p. 216.

PERIODICALS

Booklist, September 1, 1953, review of *Otis Spofford,* p. 18; September 1, 1984, Ilene Cooper, review of *Ramona Forever,* pp. 62-63; August, 1995, Cooper, review of *My Own Two Feet,* p. 1948.

Bulletin of the Center for Children's Books, November, 1961, Zena Sutherland, review of *Emily's Runaway Imagination,* p. 40; March, 1988, Zena Sutherland, review of *A Girl from Yamhill,* p. 133.

Children's Literature in Education, March, 1999, pp. 9-29.

Christian Science Monitor, September 6, 1951, Ethel C. Ince, review of *Ellen Tebbits,* p. 13.

Creative Classroom, November/December, 1994, p. 74.

Growing Point, January, 1983, Margery Fisher, review of *Ralph S. Mouse,* pp. 4007-4008.

Horn Book, October, 1955, Heloise P. Mailloux, review of *Beezus and Ramona,* p. 364; June, 1967, Ethel L. Heins, review of *Mitch and Amy,* p. 346; June, 1975, Ethel L. Heins, review of *Ramona the Brave,* p. 266; August, 1975, Caroline Feller Bauer, in a Laura Ingalls Wilder Award presentation speech, pp. 359-360; December, 1977, Mary M. Burns, review of *Ramona and Her Father,* p. 660; October, 1982, Beverly Cleary, "The Laughter of Children"; September-October, 1991, Burns, review of *Strider,* p. 595; May-June, 1995, p. 297; November-December, 1995, Burns, review of *My Own Two Feet,* p. 75.

Kirkus Reviews, July 15, 1950, review of *Henry Huggins,* p. 386; July 1, 1951, review of *Ellen Tebbits,* p. 319.

New York Herald Tribune Book Review, November 6, 1953, Louise S. Bechtel, review of *Beezus and Ramona,* p. 8; December 5, 1965, Margaret Sherwood Libby, "Young Man's Fantasy," p. 50.

New York Times Book Review, October 22, 1950, Ellen Lewis Buell, review of *Henry Huggins,* p. 42; October 4, 1953, Buell, "The Cut-Up," p. 28; September 25, 1955, Buell, review of *Beezus and Ramona,* p. 34; September 22, 1957, Buell, review of *Henry and the Paper Route,* p. 36; November 26, 1961, Buell, review of *Emily's Runaway Imagination,* p. 50; October 23, 1983, Natalie Babbitt, review of *Dear Mr. Henshaw,* p. 34; November 12, 1995, p. 40.

Oklahoma Librarian, July, 1971, Beverly Cleary, "How Long Does It Take to Write a Book?" pp. 14-17, 28.

People Weekly, October 3, 1988, "After Forty Years, Kid-Lit Queen Beverly Cleary's Gentle Tales Are Turning up on Television," p. 59.

Publishers Weekly, August 4, 1951, review of *Ellen Tebbits,* pp. 484-485; August 15, 1953, review of *Otis Spofford,* p. 647; September 11, 1961, review of *Emily's Runaway Imagination,* p. 62; March 11, 1988, review of *A Girl from Yamhill,* p. 106; June 7, 1991, review of *Strider,* p. 66; September 16, 1996, p. 29; November 22, 1999, Heather Vogel Frederick, "Beverly Cleary," p. 21.

Saturday Review, November 11, 1950, Mary Gould Davis, review of *Henry Huggins,* p. 48; March 18, 1967, Zena Sutherland, review of *Mitch and Amy,* p. 36.

Southeastern Librarian, fall, 1968, Margaret Novinger, "Beverly Cleary: A Favorite Author of Children," pp. 194-202.

Top of the News, winter, 1977, Shirley Fitzgibbons, "A National Heroine and an International Favorite."

Voice of Youth Advocates, June, 1988, Judith A. Sheriff, review of *A Girl from Yamhill,* p. 100.

Washington Post Book World, October 9, 1977, Katherine Paterson, "Ramona Redux," p. E6; August 14, 1983, Colby Rodowsky, "Life through the Letter Box," p. 7; September 9, 1984, Michael Dirda, review of *Ramona Forever,* p. 11.

Young Readers Review, November, 1965, Phyllis Cohen, review of *The Mouse and the Motorcycle,* pp. 7-8.

ON-LINE

Beverly Cleary Home Page, http://www.upsd.wednet.educ/ (October 23, 2000).

Drennan, Miriam, "I Can See Cleary Now," *First Person Book Page,* http://www.bookpage.com/ (October 23, 2000).*

—*Sketch by Gerard J. Senick*

* * *

COLLINS, David R(aymond) 1940-

Personal

Born February 29, 1940, in Marshalltown, IA; son of Raymond A. (an educator) and Mary Elizabeth (a secretary; maiden name, Brecht) Collins. *Education:* Western Illinois University, B.S., 1962, M.S., 1966. *Politics:* Democrat. *Religion:* Roman Catholic. *Hobbies and other interests:* Lecturing, reading, tennis, bridge, people.

Addresses

Home—3403 45th St., Moline, IL 61265. *E-mail*—kimseuss@aol.com.

Career

Woodrow Wilson Junior High School, Moline, IL, English teacher, 1962-83; Moline Senior High School, Moline, English teacher, 1983-1997. Friends of the Moline Public Library, president, 1965-67; Moline

David R. Collins

Library Board, member, 1990-93; Rock Island County Historical Society Board, member, 1998—; Comm University Board, member, 1998—; Quest College Board, member, 1999—. *Member:* National Education Association (life member), Children's Reading Roundtable, Society of Children's Book Writers and Illustrators (charter member), Authors Guild, Authors League of America, Juvenile Forum (president, 1975—), Writers' Studio (president, 1968-72), Mississippi Valley Writers Conference (founder; director, 1974—), Illinois Education Association, Illinois Congress of Parents and Teachers (life member), Illinois State Historical Society (life member), Blackhawk Division of Teachers of English (president, 1967-68), Quad City Writers Club, Quad City Arts Council, Midwest Writing Center (president, 1999—), Phi Delta Kappa, Kappa Delta Pi, Delta Sigma Pi.

Awards, Honors

Outstanding Juvenile Writer Award, Indiana University, 1970; Judson College Writing Award, 1971; Writer of the Year Awards, Writers' Studio, 1971, and Quad City Writers Club, 1972; Alumni Achievement Award, Western Illinois University, 1973; Outstanding Illinois Educator Award, 1976; Junior Literary Guild Award, 1981; Midwest Writing Award, 1982; Gold Key Award, 1983; Catholic Press Writing Award, 1983; National Catholic Book Award, 1984, for *Thomas Merton: Monk with a Mission;* Veterans of Foreign Wars Teacher of the Year Award, 1987-88; Distinguished Alumni Award, Western Illinois University, 1993; Cornelia Meigs Literary Award, 1990; Louise Messer Young Authors Prize, 1994; American Legion Illinois Teacher of the Year, 1994.

Writings

FOR CHILDREN

Great American Nurses, Messner, 1971.
Walt Disney's Surprise Christmas Present, illustrated by Vance Locke, Broadman (Nashville, TN), 1971.
Football Running Backs: Three Ground Gainers, Garrard (Champaign, IL), 1976.
Illinois Women: Born to Serve, DeSaulniers, 1976.
A Spirit of Giving, illustrated by Susan Hall, Broadman (Nashville, TN), 1978.
The Wonderful Story of Jesus, illustrated by Don Kueker and Bill Hoyer, Concordia, 1980.
(With Evelyn Witter) *Notable Illinois Women,* Quest, 1982.
The Special Guest, Broadman (Nashville, TN), 1984.
Not Only Dreamers, Brethren (Elgin, IL), 1986.
The Greatest Life Ever Lived, Brethren (Elgin, IL), 1991.
Attack on Fort McHenry, Rigby Educational, 1995.
(With Rich Johnson and Bessie Pierce) *Moline: City of Mills,* Arcadia (Charleston, SC), 1998.
(With Rich Johnson, Bessie Pierce, and Bj Elsner) *Rock Island: All American City,* Arcadia (Charleston, SC), 1999.
Bettendorf: "Iowa's Most Exciting City", Arcadia (Charleston, SC), 2000.
Davenport: Jewel of the Mississippi, Arcadia (Charleston, SC), 2000.

Collins tells the story of Polish-born soldier Casimir Pulaski, who trained American soldiers on horseback and helped win the American Revolution. (Illustration from Casimir Pulaski: Soldier on Horseback, *illustrated by Larry Nolte.)*

FOR CHILDREN; FICTION

Kim Soo and His Tortoise, illustrated by Alix Cohen, Lion, 1970.
Joshua Poole Hated School, illustrated by Cliff Johnston, Broadman (Nashville, TN), 1976.
If I Could, I Would, illustrated by Kelly Oechsli, Garrard, 1979.
Joshua Poole and Sunrise, illustrated by Cliff Johnston, Broadman (Nashville, TN), 1980.
The One Bad Thing about Birthdays, illustrated by David Wiesner, Harcourt (New York City), 1981.
Joshua Poole and the Special Flowers, illustrated by Cliff Johnston, Broadman (Nashville, TN), 1981.
Ride a Red Dinosaur, illustrated by Larry Nolte, Milliken (St. Louis, MO), 1987.
Probo's Amazing Trunk, Modern Curriculum (Cleveland, OH), 1987.
Ara's Amazing Spinning Wheel, Modern Curriculum (Cleveland, OH), 1987.
Ursi's Amazing Fur Coat, illustrated by Ed Beyer, Modern Curriculum (Cleveland, OH), 1987.
Leo's Amazing Paws and Jaws, illustrated by Jim Theodore, Modern Curriculum (Cleveland, OH), 1987.
Ceb's Amazing Tail, Modern Curriculum (Cleveland, OH), 1987.
Hali's Amazing Wings, Modern Curriculum (Cleveland, OH), 1987.
The Wisest Answer, illustrated by Deborah G. Wilson, Milliken (St. Louis, MO), 1988.
Grandfather Woo Comes to School, Milliken (St. Louis, MO), 1988.

FOR CHILDREN; BIOGRAPHY

Linda Richards: First American Trained Nurse, Garrard, 1973.

Harry S. Truman: People's President, Garrard, 1975.

Abraham Lincoln, Mott Media (Milford, MI), 1976.

George Washington Carver, Mott Media (Milford, MI), 1977.

Charles Lindbergh: Hero Pilot, Garrard, 1978.

George Meany: Mr. Labor, St. Anthony Messenger, 1981.

Dorothy Day: Catholic Worker, St. Anthony Messenger, 1981.

Thomas Merton: Monk with a Mission, St. Anthony Messenger, 1982.

Francis Scott Key, Mott Media (Milford, MI), 1982.

Johnny Appleseed, illustrated by Joe Van Severen, Mott Media (Milford, MI), 1983.

Florence Nightingale, Mott Media (Milford, MI), 1983.

The Long-Legged Schoolteacher: Lyndon Baines Johnson, from the Texas Hill Country to the White House, Eakin (Austin, TX), 1985.

Collins describes the life and career of Marguerite Henry, beloved author of books about horses including Misty of Chincoteague *and* Brighty of the Canyon. *(Cover photo from Marguerite Henry Estate.)*

Country Artist: The Story of Beatrix Potter, illustrated by Karen Ritz, Carolrhoda (Minneapolis, MN), 1988.

To the Point: The Story of E. B. White, illustrated by Amy Johnson, Carolrhoda (Minneapolis, MN), 1988.

Harry S. Truman: Our 33rd President, Garrett Educational (Ada, OK), 1988.

Grover Cleveland: Our 22nd and 24th President, Garrett Educational (Ada, OK), 1988.

Woodrow Wilson: Our 28th President, Garrett Educational (Ada, OK), 1989.

Zachary Taylor: Our 12th President, Garrett Educational (Ada, OK), 1989.

Noah Webster—God's Master of Words, Mott Media (Milford, MI), 1989.

Jane Addams, Warner, 1989.

Clara Barton, Warner, 1989.

James Buchanan: Our 15th President, Garrett Educational (Ada, OK), 1990.

William McKinley: Our 25th President, Garrett Educational (Ada, OK), 1990.

Gerald Ford: Our 38th President, Garrett Educational (Ada, OK), 1990.

Pioneer Plowman: A Story about John Deere, illustrated by Steve Michaels, Carolrhoda (Minneapolis, MN), 1990.

Tales for Hard Times: A Story about Charles Dickens, illustrated by David Mataya, Carolrhoda (Minneapolis, MN), 1991.

J. R. R. Tolkien—Master of Fantasy, illustrated by William Heagy, Lerner (Minneapolis, MN), 1991.

Lee Iacocca—Chrysler's Good Fortune, Garrett Educational (Ada, OK), 1992.

Philip Knight—Running with Nike, Garrett Educational (Ada, OK), 1992.

Black Rage: The Story of Malcolm X, Dillon (New York City), 1992.

M-A-R-K T-W-A-I-N! A Story about Samuel Clemens, Carolrhoda (Minneapolis, MN), 1993.

Tad Lincoln: White House Wildcat, Discovery Enterprises, 1994.

Shattered Dreams: The Story of Mary Todd Lincoln, Morgan Reynolds (Greensboro, NC), 1994.

Arthur Ashe: Against the Wind, Dillon (New York City), 1994.

Eng and Chang: The Original Siamese Twins, Dillon (New York City), 1994.

William Jefferson Clinton: Our 42nd President, Garrett Educational (Ada, OK), 1995.

Farmworker's Friend: A Story about Caesar Chavez, Carolrhoda (Minneapolis, MN), 1995.

Casimir Pulaski: Soldier on Horseback, illustrated by Larry Nolte, Pelican (Gretna, LA), 1995.

You're Never Alone: The Thomas Merton Story, Pauline Books and Media (Boston, MA), 1996.

Got a Penny? The Dorothy Day Story, Pauline Books and Media (Boston, MA), 1997.

Beyond the Clouds: A Story about Christa Mcauliffe, Pauline Books and Media (Boston, MA), 1997.

Bix Beiderbecke: Jazz Age Genius, Morgan Reynolds, 1998.

Tiger Woods: Golf Superstar, illustrated by Larry Nolte, Pelican, 1998.

Magnificent Failure: The Story of Father Solanus Casey, Pauline Books and Media (Boston, MA), 1998.

Write a Book for Me: The Story of Marguerite Henry, Morgan Reynolds, 1999.
Tiger Woods: Golfing Champion, illustrated by Larry Nolte, Pelican, 1999.
Clara Barton: Angel of the Battlefield, Barbour, 1999.
Washington Irving: Storyteller for a New Nation, Morgan Reynolds, 2000.
(With Kris Bergren) *Ishi: The Last of His People,* illustrated by Kelly Welch, Morgan Reynolds, 2000.
Shooting Star: A Story about Michael Jordan, Eakin, 2000.
Servant to the Slaves: The Story of Henriette Delille, Pauline Books and Media (Boston, MA), 2000.
Huey P. Long: Mr. Louisiana, Pelican, 2001.

OTHER

Also contributor to periodicals, including *Catholic Boy, Catholic Miss, Child Life, Highlights for Children, Junior Discoveries, Modern Woodman, Plays,* and *Vista.*

Work in Progress

A biography of John Paul Jones; an adult novel; completion of a series of four books about the Quad Cities.

Sidelights

David R. Collins is the author of nearly one hundred titles for young readers, books that both "entertain and educate," in the words of the author. Collins has written mostly in the field of biography and has tackled subjects ranging from President Harry S. Truman to basketball superstar Michael Jordan and tennis great Arthur Ashe. His books have looked at famous social activists from Caesar Chavez to Malcolm X, and from phenomena such as the Siamese twins Chang and Eng to literary greats such as Charles Dickens and Washington Irving.

Collins, a long-time English teacher, has a healthy respect for words and for his audience. "Children are curious," Collins told *SATA.* "Their minds [are] open and flexible. A child is eager to enjoy new adventures. Anyone choosing to write for young readers faces an exciting challenge and a great responsibility. He must remember that his words and ideas may have a lasting effect on his reader's imagination, personality, even his entire character. Young readers deserve the best in reading."

Collins grew up in "a world of books and readers," as he told *SATA,* and early on "entertained thoughts about becoming an author." He also had dreams of becoming a professional football player, but by the time he reached high school he realized that his physical stature was more in tune with that of a jockey than a pulling guard. He decided to go into teaching instead, as his father and older brother had, though he continued working on the school newspaper even in college. After beginning his teaching career, he found that his time for personal writing was greatly curtailed. "I was busy working with my students on their own writing skills." It was one of Collins's students who actually got him started writing again. A seventh grader challenged him on a writing

Collins's biography of golf champion and role model Tiger Woods describes the athlete's discipline and courage in the face of adversity, and includes a glossary of golf terms. (Cover illustration by Larry Nolte.)

assignment he had given the class. The young student dared Collins to do the assignment himself, and the teacher took up the challenge. "I had motivated the group by telling them how 'fun' and 'exciting' the writing project would be," Collins said. "I discovered it was WORK and TEDIOUS, but the challenge spurred me on. Soon I was submitting manuscripts regularly, and regularly getting rejected. (Once I even received a match taped to my manuscript!) But I persisted." Persistence has paid off for Collins; eventually, one of his manuscripts was accepted and this led to a writing career that has spanned several decades and has produced nearly a hundred titles with more on the way.

Though Collins has written some fiction for young readers, as well as science books, his focus has been on biography. "People fascinate me," Collins further noted. "Always have. Therefore, my interest in biography grows even stronger. I love researching my subjects, uncovering new and interesting material. I've written about people from A to Z, from Appleseed to Zachary Taylor." One of Collins's earliest titles was *Walt Disney's Surprise Christmas Present,* which deals with a little-known moment in Disney's youth in Missouri and dramatizes the events of a Christmas when the young boy's artistic aspirations were encouraged by a loving and supportive family. A reviewer for *Library Journal* called the book "quick-moving," but also characterized it as "slight and sentimental."

This was the first of many books Collins has written on artists and writers. *To the Point,* his biography of the author of *Charlotte's Web,* E. B. White, "outlines [White's] life accurately enough," wrote a critic for *Kirkus Reviews,* but "is pedestrian in style." Beatrix Potter, the creator of the beloved "Peter Rabbit" books, has also been profiled in *Country Artist,* a book written in an "easy-to-read format," according to *School Library Journal* critic Patricia Homer. *Tales for Hard Times* follows the life and career of Charles Dickens. "The text reads smoothly and quickly," noted Eldon Younce in *School Library Journal,* "as it describes how Dickens managed to leave his poverty-stricken past behind, but not to forget it."

Nineteenth-century English author Charles Dickens never forgot his miserable childhood working in a warehouse pasting labels to pots of boot polish. (Illustration from Collins's biography Tales for Hard Times, *illustrated by David Mataya.*)

More famous writers come under the Collins lens in *M-A-R-K T-W-A-I-N!, Write a Book for Me* and *Washington Irving.* In the former title, Collins writes in an "anecdotal style" that "will appeal to readers," according to *School Library Journal* contributor Sandy Kirkpatrick, who nonetheless found the "absence of documentation" to be an "unfortunate weakness." *Booklist* critic Kay Weisman found this Mark Twain biography to be "a lively book that may well draw readers to ... Clemens' work." Newbery Award winner Marguerite Henry is profiled in *Write a Book for Me.* "Readers looking for facts about this beloved writer's life may find this account of interest," noted Kitty Flynn in *Horn Book Guide.* Reviewing the same title in *Booklist,* Carolyn Phelan felt that while the book is "not a penetrating study of the woman or writer, [it] provides intriguing insights into the inspiration and research behind" many of her works. In *Washington Irving: Storyteller for a New Nation* Collins provides a "thorough" look at Irving's life, according to Renee Steinberg in *School Library Journal.* Writing in *Booklist,* Phelan felt that "Collins' succinct biography gives a sense of Irving's personality as well as his personal history and personal accomplishments."

Collins has also profiled a wide range of political and historical personages in his brief biographies. United States Presidents Zachary Taylor, Woodrow Wilson, Harry Truman, and Bill Clinton have all been subjects, while Abe Lincoln is represented also by his mischievous son in *Tad Lincoln: White House Wildcat* and his widow in *Shattered Dreams: The Story of Mary Todd Lincoln.* "Brisk writing drives this sympathetic portrait of a vivacious woman who was probably unfairly criticized in her own day," observed a contributor for *Kirkus Reviews* of the Mary Todd Lincoln biography. "*Shattered Dreams* is highly readable and well-researched," according to Carrie Eldridge in *Voice of Youth Advocates.* "Place it into the hands of reluctant readers and put it on Hilo reading lists. But give it to your good readers too."

Social activists and thinkers also find a place in Collins's lengthy list of biographical subjects. In *Black Rage: The Story of Malcolm X* Collins attempts in the space of about a hundred pages to trace the life and career of this man who converted his anger into a political movement and was silenced by an assassin's bullet at age forty. "A book this short cannot hope to do justice to a man as complex as Malcolm X," commented *Booklist* reviewer Sheilamae O'Hara, "but Collins does a careful and evenhanded job of introducing one of the twentieth century's most influential black activists." Caesar Chavez, who dedicated his life to winning better conditions for Mexican farm workers in the United States, is portrayed in *Farmworker's Friend.* April Judge, reviewing the title in *Booklist,* found that "aspects of Chavez' personal life are smoothly blended with his continued struggles to improve the plight of his fellow man."

Additionally, names from history—recent and more distant—find their way into Collins's wide-ranging canon. Charles Lindbergh, the first man to fly solo across the Atlantic Ocean, is profiled in a biography of the same name. "The author covers the salient points in Lindbergh's life, makes very clear the role he played in aviation and science, and projects a feeling for both the man and his times," noted Ralph Adams Brown in a *School Library Journal* review of *Charles Lindbergh: Hero Pilot.* A Polish patriot who fought for the Americans in the Revolutionary War is the subject of *Casimir Pulaski: Soldier on Horseback,* a "thorough biography," according to Peter D. Sieruta in *Horn Book Guide.* "Collins' text flows smoothly and will interest history buffs," wrote Weisman in another *Booklist* review. The first famous Siamese twins are the focus of *Eng and Chang.* Born in Thailand in the early nineteenth century, the twins, who were actually ethnically Chinese, gained United States citizenship in 1839. Famous for their condition, the two refused to be separated, eventually married sisters, and had a score of children between them. "Collins presents a lively portrait of these unique brothers who traveled throughout the world," wrote Pat Katka in *School Library Journal.*

Sports figures are also a favorite subject for Collins. With his *Arthur Ashe: Against the Wind* he details the life of that famous tennis star who overcame the color barrier to become one of the best-loved players in the game. Following the course of Ashe's career from his childhood in segregated Virginia to UCLA to pro tennis and to his tragic death from AIDS in 1993, "Collins portrays this champion in a fine sports journalism style," declared Anne O'Malley in a *Booklist* review. O'Malley further dubbed the book a "sure winner in school and public libraries." Janice C. Hayes, writing in *School Library Journal,* felt that Collins's "clearly written, sensitive ... biography accurately describes" Ashe's life, and that readers "will find Collins's book interesting, informative, and readable." Collins takes on another sports star in *Tiger Woods: Golf Superstar,* a book that "vividly portrays a young man who is remarkable not just for his athletic ability and his intelligence, but for his positive attitude and demeanor," as Jackie Hechtkopf noted in *School Library Journal.* Hechtkopf further commented, "Even libraries that already have material on Tiger Woods should find space for this one." Collins returned to the same subject with another title that is for older readers, *Tiger Woods: Golfing Champion.* This second book includes a brief history of golf, employs dialogue in some parts, and is overall a "livelier" title than the first, according to Janice C. Hayes in *School Library Journal.*

After teaching full-time for thirty-five years, Collins retired in 1997 and has since devoted all his time to writing and speaking in schools. "Why did I decide to write for children?" Collins once wrote for *SATA.* "Probably because some of my best childhood adventures were discovered in books .... I owe a tremendous debt to the realm of children's literature. Perhaps if I can offer something worthwhile to young readers, part of that debt will be repaid. What advice would I give student writers? First of all, READ. Read whatever and whenever you can. In your own writing, DARE TO BE DIFFERENT .... If you are serious about writing,

THINK as a writer. The people you meet might become characters in your writing, their adventures could become plots, the places you visit could become settings. Do I like being an author? No, I don't. I LOVE being an author."

Biographical and Critical Sources

PERIODICALS

Booklist, May 1, 1989, p. 1545; October 15, 1992, Sheilamae O'Hara, review of *Black Rage,* pp. 420-421; March 1, 1994, Kay Weisman, review of *M-A-R-K T-W-A-I-N!,* p. 1256; February 1, 1995, Anne O'Malley, review of *Arthur Ashe,* p. 997; February 15, 1996, Kay Weisman, review of *Casimir Pulaski,* p. 1011; December 15, 1996, April Judge, review of *Farmworker's Friend,* p. 722; July, 1998, p. 1870; March 15, 1999, Carolyn Phelan, review of *Write a Book for Me,* p. 1325; April 1, 2000, Carolyn Phelan, review of *Washington Irving,* p. 1456.

Bulletin of the Center for Children's Books, September, 1981, p. 7; May, 1992, p. 232.

Horn Book Guide, spring, 1993, p. 137; spring, 1995, p. 149; fall, 1995, p. 381; fall, 1996, Peter D. Sieruta, review of *Casimir Pulaski,* p. 371; spring, 1997, p. 156; fall, 1998, p. 412; fall, 1999, Kitty Flynn, review of *Write a Book For Me,* p. 378.

Kirkus Reviews, April 1, 1989, review of *To the Point,* p. 544; March 15, 1992, p. 392; August 15, 1994, review of *Shattered Dreams,* p. 1124; February 15, 1999, p. 298.

Library Journal, October 15, 1971, review of *Walt Disney's Surprise Christmas Present,* p. 3484.

Publishers Weekly, April 14, 1989, p. 68; May 12, 1989, p. 293.

School Library Journal, September, 1975, pp. 74-75; May, 1976, p. 80; November, 1978, Ralph Adams Brown, review of *Charles Lindbergh,* p. 42; December, 1979, p. 94; August, 1989, Patricia Homer, review of *Country Artist,* p. 146; March, 1991, Eldon Younce, review of *Tales for Hard Times,* p. 201; March, 1994, Sandy Kirkpatrick, review of *M-A-R-K T-W-A-I-N!,* p. 227; February, 1995, Pat Katka, review of *Eng and Chang,* p. 105; March, 1995, Janice C. Hayes, review of *Arthur Ashe,* p. 209; January, 1999, p. 137; June, 1999, Jackie Hechtkopf, review of *Tiger Woods: Golf Superstar,* p. 112; September, 1999, p. 230; January, 2000, Janice C. Hayes, review of *Tiger Woods: Golfing Champion,* p. 140; May, 2000, Renee Steinberg, review of *Washington Irving,* p. 179.

Voice of Youth Advocates, May, 1992, p. 302; August, 1992, p. 183; December, 1994, Carrie Eldridge, review of *Shattered Dreams,* p. 296.

—Sketch by J. Sydney Jones

COWAN, Catherine

Personal

Female.

Addresses

Home—West Linn, OR.

Career

Freelance picture-book author.

Writings

(Reteller) Nicholai Vasilievich Gogol, *The Nose,* illustrated by Kevin Hawkes, Lothrop (New York City), 1994.

(Adaptor and translator) Octavio Paz, *My Life with the Wave,* illustrated by Mark Buehner, Lothrop (New York City), 1997.

My Friend the Piano, illustrated by Kevin Hawkes, Lothrop (New York City), 1998.

Sidelights

Through her work as a storyteller, California-based writer Catherine Cowan has allowed young people to experience the work of major world authors such as Nicholai Vasilievich Gogol and Nobel-prize winning poet Octavio Paz. Her 1994 retelling of Gogol's short story "The Nose" taps into the nineteenth-century Russian novelist's fantastic imagination without bringing to light his more obsessive edge, while in *My Life with the Wave,* the metaphysical work of Paz, a twentieth-century Mexican poet, is transformed into an imaginative story for young children through Cowan's translation. In addition to adapting the stories of Gogol and Paz for young readers, Cowan has also created a book based on an idea taken from the works of author Anibal Menterio Machado. As with *The Nose,* 1998's *My Friend the Piano* features illustrations by noted artist Kevin Hawkes.

The Nose begins with a surprising discovery by a barber named Ivan: breaking into a piece of warm bread, he discovers a nose. On the other side of the city, the Deputy Inspector of Reindeer is shocked to discover that his own proboscis has gone missing. Before the nose and its owner are reunited, a chase occurs, as the nose is none too keen to lose its new-found independence. While noting that the pointed satire of the original story was likely to be lost on young readers, *School Library Journal* contributor Donna L. Scanlon noted that Cowan's writing "captures the cadence of Russian literature." A *Kirkus Reviews* contributor praised *The Nose* as "a whimsical little number, humorous and entertaining, with all the subversive pungency gone."

Based on a story by Nobel laureate Paz, *My Life with the Wave* tells of a young boy who brings home a wave he encountered while spending his first afternoon at the beach. Translating the work from its original Spanish, Cowan makes other changes to the mature subject matter of the tale in adapting it for young readers. Many critics commended her efforts. A *New York Times Book Review* contributor dubbed the book "an earnest attempt, obviously done with deep affection"; *Horn Book* reviewer Cathryn M. Mercier praised the author's skill in "retain[ing] the metaphoric language of the Paz original." In Cowan's version, the wave is treated not as a lover as in the original tale, but as an unruly pet, and by story's end, the boy's parents help him to gently return the wave to the sea from whence she came. Taken on its own merits as a picture book, with the interjection of humor through fanciful illustrations by Mark Buehner, Wendy Lukehart noted in *School Library Journal* that *My Life with the Wave* is "a celebration of imagination from beginning to end" and will probably "delight" young listeners.

While drawing on her own skills in telling a tale, Cowan also loosely based her third book for children on a story by Machado. *My Friend the Piano* finds a young girl in league with her piano, substituting a freewheeling, creative noise for a regimented, repetitive practice routine. Criticized by her mother, who has to suffer through the exuberance of the high-spirited but atonal noise, the girl refuses to change her style of playing and, as a result, the piano is put up for sale. But the instrument refuses to behave for prospective piano-buyers, and ultimately it is sold to a woman who intends to use it as a storage trunk. Fortunately, the free-spirited piano ultimately makes its escape in a picture book that *Booklist* critic Julie Corsaro termed "funny and clever," and a perfect story for all children attempting to learn to play an instrument.

Biographical and Critical Sources

PERIODICALS

Booklist, September 1, 1998, Julie Corsaro, review of *My Friend the Piano,* p. 124.

Horn Book, September-October, 1997, Cathryn M. Mercier, review of *My Life with the Wave,* p. 555.

Kirkus Reviews, August 15, 1994, review of *The Nose,* p. 1124; August 1, 1998, review of *My Friend the Piano,* p. 1114.

New York Times Book Review, March 12, 1995, review of *The Nose,* p. 20; November 9, 1997, review of *My Life with the Wave,* p. 24.

Publishers Weekly, June 9, 1997, review of *My Life with the Wave,* p. 44; September 7, 1998, review of *My Friend the Piano,* p. 95.

School Library Journal, September, 1994, Donna L. Scanlon, review of *The Nose,* p. 208; August, 1997, Wendy Lukehart, review of *My Life with the Wave,* p. 129.

D

DANIELS, Olga
See SINCLAIR, Olga

* * *

DEFELICE, Cynthia 1951-

Personal

Born December 28, 1951, in Philadelphia, PA; daughter of William (a psychiatrist) and Ann (an English teacher and homemaker; maiden name, Baldwin) Carter; married Ralph DeFelice (a dentist), February 16, 1974; stepchildren: Michelle, Ralph. *Education:* William Smith College, B.A., 1973; Syracuse University, M.L.S., 1980. *Hobbies and other interests:* Quilt making, dulcimer playing, hiking, backpacking, bird watching, fishing, reading, watching films.

Addresses

Office—c/o Farrar, Straus and Giroux, Inc., 19 Union Square West, New York, NY 10003.

Career

Storyteller and writer. Worked variously as a barn painter, day-care provider, and advertising layout artist; Newark public schools, Newark, NY, elementary school media specialist, 1980-87. Co-founder of Wild Washerwomen Storytellers, 1980. *Member:* Authors Guild, Authors League of America, Society of Children's Book Writers and Illustrators, National Storytelling Association, Audubon Society, Nature Conservancy, Wilderness Society, Seneca Lake Pure Waters Association.

Awards, Honors

Notable Children's Trade Book for Language Arts, National Council of Teachers of English, and Teacher's Choice Award, International Reading Association, both 1989, both for *The Strange Night Writing of Jessamine*

Cynthia DeFelice

Colter; Best Children's Books of the Year, Library of Congress, Best Illustrated Children's Books of the Year, *New York Times,* and Reading Magic Award, *Parenting,* all 1989, all for *The Dancing Skeleton;* Best Books designation, School Library Journal, Notable Children's Book designation, American Library Association, Notable Children's Trade Book in the Field of Social Studies, National Council for the Social Studies-Children's Book Council, and International Reading Association and Children's Book Council Young Adult Choice Award,

A calligrapher realizes she can foretell the future through her writing and passes on the talent to her young apprentice in this picture book. (Cover illustration by Debra Lill.)

all 1990, Hodge-Podger Society Award for Fiction, 1992, and Sequoyah and South Carolina children's book awards, all for *Weasel;* Best Book of 1994, New York Public Library, for *Mule Eggs;* listed among Books for the Teen Age, New York Public Library, 1995, for *Lostman's River;* Best Book designation, New York Public Library, 1995, and Anne Izard Storytellers' Choice Award, 1996, for *Three Perfect Peaches;* South Dakota Prairie Pasque Children's Book Award and Sunshine State Young Reader's Award, both 1995, both for *Devil's Bridge;* Best Book designation, *School Library Journal,* 1996, and Notable Children's Trade Book in the Field of Social Studies designation, 1997, Notable Children's Book designation, American Library Association, Judy Lopez Memorial Award, International Honor Book, Society of School Librarians, Books for the Teen Age selection, New York Public Library, all for *The Apprenticeship of Lucas Whitaker;* Texas Bluebonnet Award, for *The Ghost of Fossil Glen;* New York State Knickerbocker Award, 1998, for body of work; Notable Children's Trade Book in the Field of Social Studies, National Council for the Social Studies-Children's Book Council, for *Nowhere to Call Home.*

Writings

JUVENILE NOVELS

Weasel, Macmillan, 1990.
Devil's Bridge, Macmillan, 1992.
The Light on Hogback Hill, Macmillan, 1993.
Lostman's River, Macmillan, 1994.
The Apprenticeship of Lucas Whitaker, Farrar, Straus and Giroux, 1996.
The Ghost of Fossil Glen, Farrar, Straus and Giroux, 1998.
Nowhere to Call Home, Farrar, Straus and Giroux, 1999.
Death at Devil's Bridge, Farrar, Straus and Giroux, 2000.

PICTURE BOOKS

The Strange Night Writing of Jessamine Colter, calligraphy by Leah Palmer Preiss, Macmillan, 1988.
The Dancing Skeleton, illustrated by Robert Andrew Parker, Macmillan, 1989.
When Grampa Kissed His Elbow, illustrated by Karl Swanson, Macmillan, 1992.
Mule Eggs, illustrated by Mike Shenon, Orchard, 1994.
(Reteller with Mary DeMarsh and others) *Three Perfect Peaches: A French Folktale,* illustrated by Irene Trivas, Orchard, 1995.
Casey in the Bath, illustrated by Chris L. Demarest, Farrar, Straus and Giroux, 1996.
Willy's Silly Grandma, illustrated by Shelley Jackson, Orchard, 1997.
Clever Crow, illustrated by S. D. Schindler, Atheneum, 1998.
Cold Feet, illustrated by Robert Andrew Parker, DK Ink, 2000.
The Real, True Dulcie Campbell, illustrated by R.W. Alley, Farrar, Straus, and Giroux, 2002.

Sidelights

Cynthia DeFelice combines the oral skills of a storyteller with the technical skills of a writer to create children's stories drawn from the folk tradition, American history, and contemporary society. Her books feature young people thrust into situations that require them to make vital decisions for themselves and to assume responsibilities far beyond their years. In her picture books and novels, DeFelice mixes the elements of suspense, drama, and humor into "crackling good storytelling," as a *Publishers Weekly* reviewer described her efforts. Whether exploring the plight of Native Americans, as in the award-winning *Weasel,* making a past way of life seem vivid and real to twenty-first century readers, or highlighting the endangered ecosystem as she does in *Lostman's River* and *Devil's Bridge,* DeFelice's primary concern is in telling a compelling story, creating the "then-what-happened?" curiosity that keeps readers turning the page. "DeFelice knows how to make history come alive by providing characters who readers will find both realistic and sympathetic," maintained *Voice of Youth Advocates* contributor Cindy Lombardo, recommending titles by DeFelice that showcase epochs from nineteenth- and early twentieth-century American history.

Born in Philadelphia, Pennsylvania, in 1951, DeFelice has credited her mother for instilling a strong storytelling tradition in her. As she once recalled, "my two brothers, my sister, and I would snuggle in Mom's lap while she read to us. She was a great storyteller and had this terrific sense of rhythm and timing. It was in that big, tan chair where we all used to curl up together that I learned to love stories and to feel their magic." Growing up in a Philadelphia suburb, DeFelice recalled her childhood as "pretty idyllic," with time spent either playing with her brothers or curled up in a chair somewhere lost in a good book. Her psychiatrist father was also supportive of his daughter's interests. "You could tell him anything. So my early years were very nourishing."

Graduating from her local high school's honors program, DeFelice enrolled at William Smith College in the town of Geneva, about forty miles southeast of Rochester, New York. She immediately fell in love with the region, and has lived there ever since. After graduating in 1973, she worked briefly as a barn painter; a year later she was married with two young stepchildren. Being a full-time mother became her priority until the children

were older; then she enrolled at Syracuse University and earned an advanced degree in library science. Graduating in 1980, DeFelice got a job as a school librarian in Newark, New York. It would be this job that sparked her interest in both storytelling and writing children's books.

DeFelice teamed up with music teacher Mary DeMarsh in a storytelling venture called the Wild Washerwomen. DeFelice and her partner began telling stories in schools throughout upstate New York, and after the sessions, intrigued members of their young audience would invariably ask her if those stories were written down somewhere so they could read them. It did not take many such requests to prompt DeFelice to put pen to paper, resulting in a series of entertaining popular picture books and, later, novels for young readers.

Her first book was *The Strange Night Writing of Jessamine Colter,* which was published in 1988. The inspiration for the story came from a nightmare DeFelice had one night. "I dreamed I saw my hand floating through space, come to rest at my desk, and then pen in

Emma has to trick crow into returning Mama's shiny keys in DeFelice's rhyming picture book **Clever Crow,** *illustrated by S. D. Schindler.*

perfect calligraphy, 'You are going to die tomorrow night at ten o'clock,'" the author recalled. Although the threatened action never materialized, a picture book did. In DeFelice's story, a calligrapher named Jessie likes to write out all the important notices for her small town. Suddenly she discovers that she has the ability to foretell the future through her writing—even her own death. Before she dies, however, she is able to pass on the art of calligraphy and the gift of her strength and love to a young girl named Callie, who has become her apprentice.

The Strange Night Writing of Jessamine Colter was a critical success. "A simple, loving story," a reviewer in *Voice of Youth Advocates* called it, and a *Publishers Weekly* contributor offered a similar opinion, stating, "DeFelice's novella has a wistful mood and a gently unwinding pace.... Thoughtful readers ... will revel in its poetic language." Roger Sutton, writing in the *Bulletin of the Center for Children's Books,* dubbed the story "sentimental in the best sense."

Encouraged by the success of her first book, DeFelice left library work and embarked on a career as a full-time writer. Her second picture book, *The Dancing Skeleton,* focuses on the difficulties a widow faces when her deceased husband refuses to stay dead; he comes back to dance about when the widow's new suitor—a fiddler—comes courting. Like several of her picture books, *The Dancing Skeleton* is a retelling of a traditional folk tale. "These stories never get old for me," DeFelice recalled. "Even if I tell them a hundred times, I find something new in them, and looking at the faces in the audience is so much fun. The kids are like my editors: I know immediately when something works or doesn't." In the case of *The Dancing Skeleton,* the tale worked. The book gained special praise for its author's technical skills. Ellen D. Warwick wrote in *School Library Journal* that DeFelice's "rhythmic prose captures the vocabulary, tone, the very cadences of the oral tradition."

With two books in as many years to her credit, DeFelice began to branch out as a writer, in part as a result of circumstances. "I was home alone one night and heard a knock at the door," the author explained in her interview. "And suddenly I wondered what a couple of kids alone might do if that happened to them. Then I asked myself who those kids in my imagination were and why they were alone. Next, I began wondering who was knocking at their door and why. Suddenly I was involved in a novel without even knowing where it was going. I had to keep writing it to see what was going to happen." Coupling her continued writing with hours of research, DeFelice set her next story in Ohio during the 1830s. Nathan, a member of a pioneering family, wakes one night to learn that a man named Weasel has wounded his father. A former Indian-hunter whose life of hunting and killing has driven him half mad, Weasel now is quick to raise a gun or knife against his own kind. Vowing to avenge his father's attack, young Nathan hunts down Weasel, but when the opportunity to strike arises, the boy realizes that such violence would make him no better than the assailant that he has been hunting.

The story of Nathan's quest for justice was published in 1990 as *Weasel,* a book that received many commendations. Calling DeFelice's rendering of her young protagonist's character "unforgettable," *School Library Journal* contributor Yvonne Frey praised the novel for addressing race relations in a new way, by "turn[ing] the results of hate back on the white race itself." *Weasel* "makes a positive contribution to a world caught up with killing and revenge," reviewer Kathryn Hackler wrote in her *Voice of Youth Advocates* review, while a contributor to Publishers Weekly pronounced the novel a "fast-paced" work that "effectively conveys the battle between good and evil."

Pleased with the critical praise for *Weasel,* DeFelice was encouraged to continue writing novels as well as picture books. Her next effort was 1992's *Devil's Bridge,* a tale that takes place off the East Coast in Martha's Vineyard. Twelve-year-old Ben Daggett hears two men scheming to cheat their way to the ten thousand dollar prize in the annual striped bass fishing derby by injecting an illegally caught fish with mercury to increase its weight. Before he perished in a hurricane the year before, Ben's fisherman father had set the record for the largest bass ever caught, and Ben doesn't want his father's accomplishments overshadowed by anyone's dishonest efforts. Since no one will listen to him when he attempts to divulge the men's scheme, Ben determines to catch the biggest fish himself. While he manages to hook the winning fish, Ben lets the creature go free at the last minute because he is unwilling to take its life.

In *Devil's Bridge,* DeFelice touches upon Ben's confusion and hurt over the death of his father, as well as several wildlife management and environmental issues, particularly as they relate to the nation's overtaxed fisheries. However, her story never becomes pedantic; as *School Library Journal* contributor Louise L. Sherman attested, *Devil's Bridge* is a "fast paced and involving" adventure yarn featuring what *Booklist* critic Janice Del Negro termed "an appealing main character" in Ben. A *Publishers Weekly* reviewer agreed, calling the novel "more than a straightforward adventure; it is a multi-layered book with feeling." *Devil's Bridge* would later find a sequel in *Death at Devil's Bridge,* which DeFelice published in 2000. In this story Ben—now thirteen—takes a job as first-mate on a fishing boat, only to find himself enmeshed in the illegal drug trade and possibly even murder.

The Light on Hogback Hill, published in 1993, started out as a typical "haunted house" mystery, taking place in the quintessential old, abandoned house on the hill, complete with boarded up windows, creaking doors, and emitting mysterious noises during the night. "But things changed with the writing," DeFelice recalled. In the published version, the author's young protagonists investigate a supposedly haunted house only to find an elderly woman whom they befriend. As DeFelice described it, *The Light on Hogback Hill* is really "a story about the shells we all build around ourselves when we get hurt, and how we can all help each other break through those shells."

The Apprenticeship of Lucas Whitaker, published in 1996, concerns a young boy who goes to work for a local physician after his entire family dies of tuberculosis. Once commonly known as "consumption," tuberculosis was one of the main causes of death prior to the turn of the twentieth century, and it was believed by some that the sickness was passed along by the dead, who acted like vampires in spreading the disease through entire households. DeFelice's historical novel takes place in Connecticut during the mid-1800s, and introduces readers to Lucas, a twelve-year-old who feels responsible for the death of his parents. Working alongside the town doctor allows Lucas to understand that the folk remedy he had failed to perform—digging up the body of the first member of the family to die of consumption, removing the heart, and burning it—could not have saved his family.

Praising DeFelice for her compelling main characters and for illustrating the harsh realities of life in New England farming communities in the nineteenth century, *School Library Journal* contributor Jane Gardner Connor noted that "Readers will experience a period when even a doctor's knowledge was very limited, and ... will come to realize how fear and desperation can make people willing to try almost anything." In her *Horn Book* review of *The Apprenticeship of Lucas Whitaker,* Elizabeth S. Watson added, "The pace of this fine piece of historical fiction is brisk in spite of a wealth of detail [about] ... health, hygiene, and witchcraft."

As it was in *The Apprenticeship of Lucas Whitaker,* the loss of both parents is a motivating factor in the life of twelve-year-old Frances Barrow in DeFelice's 1999 novel *Nowhere to Call Home.* When her father loses his Philadelphia-based business—as well as everything else—during the stock market crash of 1929, he commits suicide, leaving his daughter an orphan. Left with nothing, Frances decides to cut her hair, disguise herself as a boy, and strike out for herself by "riding the rails" westward as a train-jumping hobo, rather than going to live with an aunt she has never met. Noting that "The dialogue rings true," *Voice of Youth Advocates* critic Cindy Lombardo added that the story's "fast pace ... will keep readers turning pages until the poignant resolution." While the story takes place in the past century, Margaret A. Bush noted in *Horn Book* that DeFelice bridges the gap between her young protagonist and modern-day readers. "The story is a good adventure," Bush maintained, "presenting readers with insights into homelessness quite relevant to our own time."

DeFelice returned to the here-and-now, but with a supernatural twist, in her 1998 novel *The Ghost of Fossil Glen.* Readers are introduced to Allie Nichols, an eleven-year-old who enjoys roaming remote areas near her home in search of fossils. One day she hears a ghostly whisper, and soon becomes haunted by the voice of a girl who was murdered in that area four years earlier. Even though her friends question her sanity, Allie is determined to help the spirit, and ultimately helps bring justice to the now-departed Lucy in a story that possesses "unusual warmth" and "vivid character-

izations," according to a *Kirkus* reviewer. Praising *The Ghost of Fossil Glen* as a "beautifully crafted thriller," *Booklist* contributor Lauren Peterson added that DeFelice has skillfully crafted an "expertly paced, dynamic page-turner that never gives readers the chance to become distracted or lose interest."

While continuing to entertain young adult readers with her novels, DeFelice continues to add picture books to her bibliography, although she is quick to explain that the two genres require a different approach. "I enjoy doing both kinds of books, both novels and picture books," she once explained. "But with picture books, every word has to count. It is more like writing poetry."

Mule Eggs, DeFelice's 1994 effort, is the story of a city slicker named Patrick. Deciding to become a farmer, he buys a farm and, in addition to the challenges posed by life in the country, has to contend with a local practical joker. In her retelling of the French folktale *Three Perfect Peaches,* three brothers compete among themselves to deliver the most perfect peaches and thus win the hand of the king's daughter. In 1997's *Willy's Silly Grandma* a grandmother's folk cures prove not to be as silly as people thought. "It's grandma's turn this time," DeFelice quipped, referring to her 1992 book *When Grampa Kissed His Elbow,* an "unusual but charming inter-generational story," according to *Booklist* contributor Karen Hutt. Still another picture book, 1998's *Clever Crow,* features a battle of wits involving a young girl named Emma who becomes frustrated when a crow begins to steal small, shiny objects from around her home. When even the house keys find their way into Crow's nest, Emma hatches a plan to trick the feathered thief ... until Crow outsmarts her. Praising the story as a "sprightly takeoff on Aesop's fable 'The Fox and the Grapes,'" a *Publishers Weekly* contributor commended DeFelice for her "jaunty tone" and energetic rhymes.

Whether creating picture books or novels, DeFelice has the same basic goals. "I want to write a story to entertain, to engage the minds, hearts, and senses of young readers," she once stated. "I really think that kids are the most challenging audience to write for. They demand a satisfying story. They will not sit through something that does not please them."

DeFelice balances her time alone writing with visits to young readers. "It helps to be working with kids," she explained. "I still do storytelling at schools and it is instant feedback for me. They help me to hone my story and my language." Still, the bulk of her time is spent writing, and her focus remains straightforward: "I want my readers to come away from my books with a memory worth having, something that will enrich their lives and something that they might not otherwise have the chance to experience. But I don't like to tie up all the loose ends. I respect my readers and figure they will become part of the process if I don't answer all the questions for them. After all, life isn't like that. We can't know everything in real life. Why should we expect to in fiction?"

Biographical and Critical Sources

PERIODICALS

Booklist, March 15, 1992, Karen Hutt, review of *When Grampa Kissed His Elbow,* pp. 1386-1387; December 1, 1992, Janice Del Negro, review of *Devil's Bridge,* p. 669; March 15, 1998, Lauren Peterson, review of *The Ghost of Fossil Glen,* p. 1243.

Book Report, September-October 1999, Catherine M. Andronik, review of *Nowhere to Call Home,* p. 59.

Bulletin of the Center for Children's Books, September, 1988, Roger Sutton, review of *The Strange Night Writing of Jessamine Colter,* p. 5; November, 1992, pp. 70-71; December, 1993, p. 79; June, 1994, p. 317; October, 1996, pp. 54-55; March, 1998, p. 240.

Horn Book, January-February, 1990, Elizabeth S. Watson, review of *The Dancing Skeleton,* pp. 75-76; March-April, 1994; January-February, 1997, E. S. Watson, review of *The Apprenticeship of Lucas Whitaker,* p. 55; March-April, 1999, Margaret A. Bush, review of *Nowhere to Call Home,* p. 207.

Journal of Adolescent & Adult Literacy, May, 2000, Barbara Powell, review of *Nowhere to Call Home,* p. 778.

Kirkus Reviews, July 15, 1988, p. 1055; November 1, 1992, p. 1374.

Publishers Weekly, August 12, 1988, review of *The Strange Night Writing of Jessamine Colter,* pp. 460-61; April 27, 1990, review of *Weasel,* p. 62; September 7, 1992, review of *Devil's Bridge,* pp. 96-97; May 4, 1998, review of *Clever Crow,* p. 211; April 26, 1999, p. 84.

School Library Journal, September, 1989, Ellen D. Warwick, review of *The Dancing Skeleton,* p. 239; May, 1990, Yvonne Frey, review of *Weasel,* pp. 103-4; August, 1992, p. 134; November, 1992, Louise L. Sherman, review of *Devil's Bridge,* pp. 88-89; August, 1996, Jane Gardner Connor, review of *The Apprenticeship of Lucas Whitaker,* p. 142; July, 1998, pp. 92-93; April, 1999, p. 113.

Voice of Youth Advocates, April, 1989, review of *The Strange Night Writing of Jessamine Colter,* p. 26; June, 1990, Kathryn Hackler, review of *Weasel,* pp. 101-2; October, 1999, Cindy Lombardo, review of *Nowhere to Call Home,* p. 256.

*   *   *

DiCAMILLO, Kate 1964-

Personal

Born March 25, 1964, in Merion, PA; daughter of Adolph Louis (an orthodontist) and Betty Lee (a teacher; maiden name, Gouff) DiCamillo. *Education:* University of Florida, B.A., 1987.

Addresses

Home—2403 West 42nd St., No. 3, Minneapolis, MN 55410.

Career

Writer; St. Louis Park, MN, clerk in the children's department of a used bookstore.

Awards, Honors

McKnight artist fellowship for writers, 1998; Newbery Honor Book award, 2000, for *Because of Winn-Dixie.*

Writings

Because of Winn-Dixie (juvenile novel), Candlewick Press (Cambridge, MA), 2000.

The Tiger Rising (young adult novel), Candlewick Press (Cambridge, MA), in press.

Contributor of short fiction to periodicals, including *Jack and Jill, Alaska Quarterly Review, Greensboro Review, Nebraska Review,* and *Spider.*

Work in Progress

A collection of short stories for adults.

Sidelights

Kate DiCamillo told *SATA:* "I was a sickly child. My body happily played host to all of the usual childhood maladies (mumps and measles, chickenpox twice, and ear infections), plus a few exotic extras: inexplicable skin diseases, chronic pinkeye, and, most dreaded of all, pneumonia, recurring every winter for the first five years

Kate DiCamillo

of my life. I mention this because, at the time, it seemed like such a senseless and unfair kind of thing to me, to be sick so often, to miss so much school, to be inside scratching or sneezing or coughing when everybody else was outside playing.

"Now, looking back, I can see all that illness for what it was: a gift that shaped me and made me what I am. I was alone a lot. I learned to rely on my imagination for entertainment. Because I was always on the lookout for the next needle, the next tongue depressor, I learned to watch and listen and gauge the behavior of those around me. I became an imaginative observer.

"Also, I suffered from chronic pneumonia at a time when geographical cures were still being prescribed. I was born near Philadelphia and, after my fifth winter in an oxygen tent, the doctor gave my parents this advice: take her to a warmer climate. We moved to central Florida. There I absorbed the speech patterns and cadences and nuances of life in a small southern town. I did not know it at the time, but Florida (and pneumonia) gave me a great gift: a voice in which to tell my stories.

"When I look back on childhood, I remember one moment with great clarity. I was three years old and in the hospital with pneumonia, and my father came to visit me. He arrived in a black overcoat that smelled of the cold outdoors, and he brought me a gift. It was a little, red net bag. Inside it there was a wooden village: wooden church, house, chicken, tree, farmer. It was as if he had flung the net bag out into the bright world and captured the essential elements and shrunk them down and brought them to me.

"He opened the bag and said, 'Hold out your hands.' I held out my hands. 'No,' he said, 'like this. Like you are going to drink from them.' I did as he said, and he poured the wooden figures, piece by piece, into my waiting hands. Then he told me a story about the chicken and the farmer and the house and the church. Something opened up inside me. There was the weight of the wooden figures in my hands, the smell of my father's overcoat, the whole great world hiding, waiting in the purple dusk outside my hospital room. And there was the story—the story.

"I think of that moment often. It was another gift of my illness. When I write, I sometimes stop and cup my hands, as if I am drinking water. I try, I want desperately to capture the world, to hold it for a moment in my hands."

Biographical and Critical Sources

PERIODICALS

Booklist, May 1, 2000, Gillian Engberg, review of *Because of Winn-Dixie,* p. 1665.

Horn Book, July, 2000, review of *Because of Winn-Dixie,* p. 455.

Publishers Weekly, February 21, 2000, review of *Because of Winn-Dixie,* p. 88; June 26, 2000, Jennifer M. Brown, "Kate DiCamillo," p. 30.

School Library Journal, June, 2000, Helen Foster, review of *Because of Winn-Dixie,* p. 143.

ON-LINE

Amazon.com, www.amazon.com/ (August 26, 2000).

*   *   *

DOLSON, Hildegarde
See LOCKRIDGE, Hildegarde (Dolson)

*   *   *

DONALDSON, Stephen R. 1947-

Personal

Born May 13, 1947, in Cleveland, OH; son of James R. (an orthopedic surgeon and medical missionary) and Mary Ruth (a prosthetist and occupational therapist; maiden name, Reeder) Donaldson; first marriage ended in divorce; married Stephanie, 1980. *Education:* College of Wooster, B.A., 1968; Kent State University, M.A., 1971.

Addresses

Office—41 Broadway, New York, NY 10003.

Career

Writer. Akron City Hospital, Akron, OH, assistant dispatcher, 1968-70; Kent State University, Kent, OH, teaching fellow, 1971; Tapp-Gentz Associates, West Chester, PA, acquisitions editor, 1973-74; Ghost Ranch Writers Workshops, NM, instructor, 1973-77; University of New Mexico, teaching assistant in literature after 1982. *Member:* International Association for the Fantastic in the Arts, United States Karate Alliance, American Contract Bridge League, Duke City Bridge Club.

Awards, Honors

British Fantasy Award, 1978, for *The Chronicles of Thomas Covenant: The Unbeliever;* John W. Campbell Award, World Science Fiction Convention, 1979, for best new writer; Balrog awards for best novel, 1981, for *The Wounded Land,* and 1983, and for best collection, 1985, for *Daughter of Regals and Other Tales;* Saturn Award for best fantasy novel, 1983; Book of the Year awards, Science Fiction Book Club, 1987, for *The Mirror of Her Dreams,* and 1988, for *A Man Rides Through.*

Writings

FANTASY

The Chronicles of Thomas Covenant: The Unbeliever (*Volume I: Lord Foul's Bane, Volume II: The Illearth War, Volume III: The Power That Preserves*), Holt (New York City), 1977.

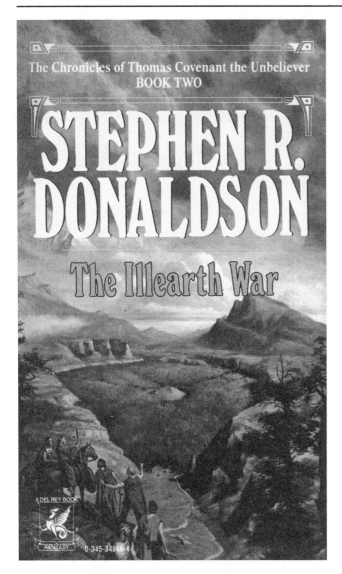

Thomas Covenant the Unbeliever is summoned back to defend the Land from Lord Foul in Stephen R. Donaldson's second book of the Covenant chronicles. (Cover illustration by Michael Herring.)

The Second Chronicles of Thomas Covenant: The Unbeliever (Volume I: The Wounded Land, 1980, *Volume II: The One Tree,* 1982, *Volume III: White Gold Wielder,* 1983), Ballantine (New York City).

Gilden-Fire, Underwood-Miller (San Francisco, CA), 1982.

Daughters of Regals and Other Tales (includes the novella *Gilden-Fire*), Del Rey, 1984.

Mordant's Need (Volume I: The Mirror of Her Dreams, 1986, *Volume II: A Man Rides Through,* 1987), Ballantine (New York City).

(Editor) *Strange Dreams: Unforgettable Fantasy Stories,* Bantam (New York City), 1993.

"THE GAP CYCLE" SERIES; SCIENCE FICTION

The Gap into Conflict: The Real Story, Bantam (New York City), 1990.

The Gap into Vision: Forbidden Knowledge, Bantam (New York City), 1991.

The Gap into Power: A Dark and Hungry God Arises, Bantam (New York City), 1992.

The Gap into Madness: Chaos and Order, Bantam (New York City), 1994.

The Gap into Ruin: This Day All Gods Die, Bantam (New York City), 1996.

UNDER PSEUDONYM REED STEPHENS

The Man Who Killed His Brother, Ballantine (New York City), 1980.

The Man Who Risked His Partner, Ballantine (New York City), 1984.

The Man Who Tried to Get Away, Ballantine (New York City), 1990.

OTHER

(Contributor) Judy-Lynn del Rey, editor, *Stellar #4,* Ballantine (New York City), 1978.

(Contributor) Terry Carr, *The Year's Best Fantasy,* Berkley Publishing (New York City), 1979.

Reave the Just and Other Tales, Bantam/Spectra (New York City), 1999.

Also contributor to science fiction magazines; both "Thomas Covenant" series have been translated for publication in other languages; author's papers are housed in the Department of Special Collections of the Kent State University Libraries.

Adaptations

White Gold Wielder is available as a recording from Camden, 1983.

Sidelights

Stephen R. Donaldson is the author of a number of lengthy, complexly plotted sagas in the science-fiction/fantasy genre that have earned him both critical praise and a devoted readership. Yet he struggled for many years as a writer, unable even to find a publisher who would work with him, before his books landed on the bestseller lists. Donaldson is perhaps best known for his *The Chronicles of Thomas Covenant: The Unbeliever,* which appeared in 1977. It sold millions, and was likened to the one of the most famous trilogies in fantasy fiction, J.R.R. Tolkien's *Lord of the Rings.*

Like all of Donaldson's subsequent novels, the "Thomas Covenant" story drew readers into a plot in which forces of good and evil battled to destroy one another; always, the author's anti-hero protagonists struggle with ethical dilemmas that echo eternal religious themes while cruelty and violence run amok. "The moral import of his fantasies is their very heart and soul," remarked fellow fantasy writer Brian Stableford in an essay about Donaldson for the *St. James Guide to Fantasy Writers.* "[F]ew other writers in the genre are capable of reaching such a terrible pitch of indignation and horror at the contemplation of the human capacity for abusing others."

Born in Cleveland, Ohio, in 1947, Donaldson was the son of Presbyterian missionaries, and at the age of three he left the Midwest with his parents to settle permanently in India. In the city of Miraj, Donaldson's orthopedic surgeon father treated victims of leprosy who had lost their extremities; his mother worked at the same hospital as a prosthetist and occupational therapist.

The exotic Asian locale, meanwhile, offered the young Donaldson the kind of adventures most children only read about in books; on one occasion, he was kept home from school because a deadly tiger was on the prowl. "India is both a mysterious and exotic place," Donaldson told Robert Dahlin in a *Publishers Weekly* interview. "And a very grim place of human misery. I grew up with wild physical beauty, strange cultural evidence of magical or spiritual events. There was a snake charmer on every corner."

A bookworm who devoured whatever English-language titles were available to him in Miraj, Donaldson became enamored with fantasy and adventure literature at an early age, reading everything from the "Hardy Boys" mystery series to the African escapade tales of Joseph Conrad; the *Chronicles of Narnia* by C.S. Lewis was also a particular favorite. Returning to Ohio at the age of sixteen, Donaldson enrolled at its College of Wooster, a small, private liberal-arts school. There, he learned that his years in India did not seem to count for much: "In my wing of the dorm, we had five National Merit scholars, five professional musicians and a guy who had already written eight novels," he told *People* writer John Neary in 1982. "I was the only person who didn't have something immense to offer the world." One Sunday, Donaldson attended church services, contemplating his future, and found a solution. "Something in my mind leapt the gap between being addicted to reading stories and wanting to write them," he explained to Neary.

After graduating in 1968, Donaldson went on to study English at Kent State University, earning his master's degree three years later. The following year, he sat in a church pew once again, listening to his father tell a congregation about the years in India and his work treating sufferers of leprosy. A chronic infectious disease that once brought on devastating physical disfigurement, leprosy was so feared in the past that its victims were often sent to die in special colonies on remote islands, to which only religious missionaries would venture as aid workers. In more modern times, the disease has proved treatable, but on that day in church, Donaldson's father was discussing the psychological trauma that leprosy sufferers still experienced. Donaldson began to think about writing a novel with a protagonist, a contemporary husband and father, who contracts the disease. From this came the Thomas Covenant character, hero of the first six of Donaldson's novels.

In the fall of 1972, Donaldson began writing the first novel in the fantasy series. Married and living in New England, he worked for a Pennsylvania publisher for a year, but spent the next four years involved in the Covenant project. His wife, a social worker, supported him both financially and emotionally, but he became dejected as his pile of rejection slips from publishers grew. The industry professionals who critiqued Donaldson's submissions voiced doubts about the potential appeal of the title character: Thomas Covenant is a successful novelist devastated by the diagnosis of leprosy; a head injury lands him in another universe where, instead of social ostracism, he is hailed as a messiah-like savior sent to keep Lord Foul from destroying The Land, as the fictional world is known.

Fully aware of the folly of his situation, Donaldson even lied to neighbors about what he did for a living. "I just immersed myself in my work," he told Dahlin in a *Publishers Weekly* interview. "It's difficult to find words to describe how bad I felt." He collected a total of 47 rejection slips from American publishers before trying, one more time, to interest Ballantine, publishers of the wildly popular fantasy novels from English medieval scholar J.R.R. Tolkien (1892-1973), *The Hobbit* and *The Lord of the Rings*. Donaldson once admitted that his perseverance was curious. As he once told Jean W. Ross, "good writers usually aren't that unlucky; bad writers usually don't try that hard."

But at Ballantine the second time around, Donaldson's manuscript luckily landed on the desk of famed editor Lester del Rey, who believed it held promise. Del Rey worked intensely with the neophyte author to edit the lengthy saga for publication. Published in 1977, the three-volume *Chronicles of Thomas Covenant: The Unbeliever,* appeared in hardcover as a Science Fiction Book Club selection, an unusual achievement in the fantasy-fiction genre for a first-time author, but one that spoke highly of del Rey's belief in Donaldson's saga.

Lord Foul's Bane, the first book in *The Chronicles of Thomas Covenant,* introduces the afflicted, unhappy writer and his sudden transcendence into another realm. Soon after Covenant regains consciousness and realizes he is in a puzzling new world called The Land, he is mistaken for one of its mythical heroes, Berke Halfhand. He also encounters Lord Foul, a powerful, destructive figure who is determined to ruin The Land and kill off its populace by unleashing environmental toxins. Though he was an outcast in his previous life, Covenant is hailed by denizens of The Land as their long-awaited savior, the hero with the power to foil Lord Foul.

In the first volume, Donaldson creates a complex, intricate realm with a long history, highly stratified social organization, and series of alliances and enmities among its many life forms. The narrative and cast are expanded across the other two volumes, *The Illearth War* and *The Power That Preserves.* Covenant discovers early on that he possesses magical powers, but the realization does not heighten his sense of self-esteem to any degree. He emerges as an anti-hero, an unlikely messiah uncomfortable with his role, an embittered man still plagued by the cynicism and pessimism that marked his earthly existence. He begins to call himself "the Unbeliever," and at times even doubts that the fantastical adventures are occurring outside of his own imagination.

In the end, he is offered a choice between the two worlds.

"The real surprise of the tale," wrote John Calvin Batchelor in a review of the trilogy for the *Village Voice,* "comes not when Foul is unexpectedly undone, but rather when Covenant is returned by the Creator to Earth to die of an allergic reaction." Other assessments were positive, though some faulted the first-time author's ornate prose style—a criticism that would follow Donaldson throughout his career. A *Publishers Weekly* review declared that the work possesses "riches and excitements a plenty for the fantasy minded," while Judith Yamomoto declared that the trilogy "shows promise and makes absorbing reading" in her *Library Journal* review.

The "Covenant" series quickly reached the two-million sales mark in paperback, was translated into several other languages, and earned Donaldson comparisons to Tolkien. In the United Kingdom, the three-part series won the British Science Fiction Society's top award for 1978. A surge in popularity in the works of Tolkien—related to the posthumous publication in 1977 of his *Silmarillion* manuscript—coincided with Donaldson's debut as an author, and the two authors seemed to share a readership. When asked about the influence of Tolkien upon his work, Donaldson told Ross that "there are obviously many details in Covenant which purportedly show the influence of Tolkien. But almost without exception those details were consciously chosen because what I could gain by them was worth the risk that my readers might think I was imitating Tolkien."

Despite the professional and financial rewards that Donaldson had finally achieved, success also brought unexpected changes to his life. As he explained to Dahlin in the *Publishers Weekly* interview, his wife had become "so used to taking care of me that when she didn't have to anymore, she saw me going away from her"; their marriage ended in divorce. Eager to immerse himself in writing another series—he had spent the years between 1972 and 1976 creating the Covenant trilogy—Donaldson was instead cajoled by Lester del Rey to write a second trilogy. The author was initially reluctant to do so, but then began to think that perhaps there were more complex moral issues left unexplored in the first series, whose battles between good and evil were conducted in a physical arena with a great deal of violent, bloody action.

The Second Chronicles of Thomas Covenant: The Unbeliever, which began with the publication of *The Wounded Land* in 1980, returns Covenant to The Land a few millennia later; Lord Foul has been resurrected and again threatens it. Accompanying Covenant this time is Dr. Linden Avery, a female physician plagued by a guilty conscience related to the untimely death of her parents. In the second volume, 1982's *The One Tree,* the pair set out on a granite ship to an island called the One Tree Land; a delegation of giants and Elohim, considered holders of "Earth Power," come along. Here Covenant and Linden fall in love, adding a romantic twist to the series and centering some of the plot development around issues of love and trust, as Donaldson wanted to do for this second series. Throughout this novel and Volume III, *White Gold Wielder,* which appeared in 1983, Covenant suffers from a poison venom that Lord Foul used against him. Once again, the reluctant hero utilizes his powers to save The Land, which has been afflicted with a Foul-induced plague.

Reviews for this second Covenant trilogy were mixed. "As one burrows deeper into the inflated text it soon becomes apparent that the rules, not to mention the standards, of good fiction are violated repeatedly on every page," decreed Timothy Robert Sullivan in a *Washington Post Book World* review of *White Gold Wielder.* Still, the second trilogy was equally popular among Donaldson's fans. As Stableford noted in the *St. James Guide to Fantasy Writers* essay, both series "demonstrated that vast numbers of readers were not only prepared to immerse themselves in the plight of a man with a particularly horrible disease, but were avid to do so.... They were enthusiastic to participate in his quest, which was explicitly stated to be a hard battle against his own unbelief, primarily directed against an enemy which personified the determination of others to despise him."

By now Donaldson had spent over a decade writing draft upon draft of his fantastical, allegorical tales, which drew heavily upon religious themes in their explorations of timeless moral quandaries. As he told Ross, "Science fiction and fantasy try to answer the question 'What does it mean to be human?' by altering the context (the world) in order to test real conceptions of humanness against alien definitions of reality or alien conceptions of humanness against normal or familiar ones. Science fiction, in fact, takes an explicitly speculative approach to the great theme of literature. Fantasy, on the other hand, does the same thing by delving explicitly into the human imagination. (I don't mean to be confusing about this. Imagination is, of course, the tool of all creative vision. In fantasy, imagination is the subject as well as the tool.) It follows—naturally—that I consider science fiction and fantasy (but especially fantasy) to be the fundamental form of literature. Lacking the imaginative immediacy of fantasy (or the rational rigor of science fiction), 'mainstream fiction' is a bastardized art form, 'a genre apart.'"

During the early 1980s, Donaldson concentrated on two other series of fantasy novels. The first volume of *Mordant's Need,* titled *The Mirror of Her Dreams,* was published by Ballantine in 1986. His unlikely hero this time is a heroine, Terisa Morgan. A wealthy New Yorker with a conflicted relationship with her parents, Terisa possesses a great deal of material wealth but little self-esteem. She is so insecure that inside her home is a room completely walled in mirrors, to prove to herself her very existence. An *Alice in Wonderland*-type encounter with an unusual mirror transports her to the land of Mordant. Her emissary is Geraden, an inept sorcerer who was attempting to follow an edict to bring a strong male warrior to help Mordant through a particularly trying time of political instability.

The denizens of Mordant exhibit disbelief when the bumbling Geraden presents Terisa, a meek and anxious young woman, as their savior. King Joyse, ruler of the tenuously united kingdom, seems dismissive of her as well, though many in Mordant think that the monarch might be suffering from dementia. In the second and concluding volume of the saga, *A Man Rides Through,* the king continues to be obsessed with playing a game called hopboard, similar to chess, while his empire disintegrates. Terisa, finding herself in the middle of political battle, realizes that in Mordant she possesses special powers that can indeed help its people. A romance develops between she and Geraden, King Joyse is not at all deranged, and the army of High King Festten is defeated; Mordant rejoices.

Susan Shwartz, reviewing the first volume of the Mordant series for the *New York Times,* wrote favorably of Donaldson's maturation as a writer. The 1986 tome, Shwartz noted, "demonstrates steady growth. Though he has replaced the tortuous, almost impenetrable, language that proved such heavy going in the Chronicles with the leaner, suppler prose of his novellas, Mr. Donaldson still focuses on outcasts."

Donaldson, who retreated to New Mexico to write after his flush with success, spent the latter half of the 1980s working on a third saga, *The Gap Cycle.* The first volume of this space opera, *The Real Story,* was published by Bantam in 1990. A trio of characters—a villain, a victim, and a rescuer—are introduced, but over the course of the series they often exchange roles as plot and character developments warrant. Nick Succorso and Angus Thermopyle are space pirates who despise one another; Morn Hyland is a female law-enforcement official for the United Mining Companies. Thermopyle kidnaps Hyland, setting in motion a series of space chases, unlikely alliances, and fantastical inventions. An evil force called Amnion hopes to achieve complete control over the galaxy. A review of this first volume by Faren C. Miller in *Locus* compared Donaldson's effort to the seventeenth-century dramas of the English stage. "Like those early masters, he esteems nothing better than villainy writ so large, and so charged with anguish, it calls for pity as well as horror," Miller observed.

In the second volume in the series, *The Gap into Vision: Forbidden Knowledge,* Morn and Nick must flee to one of the galaxy's forbidden zones. Amnion and its agents remain determined to take over the realm. The plot reveals that Morn is haunted by a terrible secret—she once suffered from something called "Gap Sickness," which caused her to wreck a vessel that belonged to her family. A more ominous secret is also disclosed: Morn is expecting a child, the result of a liaison with Angus.

In the 1992 entrant to the series, *The Gap into Power: A Dark and Hungry God Arises,* Nick—less of a hero than before—considers trading Morn to Amnion; meanwhile, Angus has been brainwashed and is now a far more

honorable person. Both men arrive at a trading post, Billingate, with plans to sabotage it. A *Publishers Weekly* review of this volume found Donaldson's plot beyond intricate, and conceded that "through it all runs Donaldson's trademark sadism, betrayal, amorality and purposeless cruelty."

The plot of the Donaldson's fourth volume, 1994's *The Gap into Madness: Chaos and Order,* takes the reader further into Amnion's devious plan to mutate Earth's inhabitants into a race of aliens. Both the United Mining Police and agents of Amnion are desperately trying to locate people whose blood contains antibodies that will become the basis for a drug to prevent the alienization. Morn's son, Davies, begins to take on a more integral role in the action, while Nick and a scientist develop the immunity drug. Aliens from Amnion pursue a space ship with Davies aboard, but UMC personnel are also on the trail in an attempt to rescue Morn.

In the concluding volume, *The Gap into Ruin: This Day All Gods Die,* Donaldson ties up the complex story and its related subplots. A showdown in Earth's orbit takes place between Morn's forces and an Amnion faction. A review of the final novel in the series from *Publishers Weekly* termed it "a crowd-pleasing story told on a grand scale, SF adventure with a genuinely galactic feel."

Donaldson has also written several other shorter works, as well as a few detective novels. In 1984, a volume of stories titled *Daughters of Regals and Other Tales* was issued by the Del Rey imprint. Included in it was *Gilden-Fire,* an outtake from the second volume of the first "Thomas Covenant" series, *The Illearth War,* that had to be excised because of length and plot considerations. *Daughters of Regals* also contained several unusual shorter works from the writer, such as "Animal Lover," the tale of a scientist with plans to create an army of genetically modified, weapons-proficient creatures.

Another story in the collection, "The Conqueror Worm," tracks the speedy disintegration of an already-faltering marriage when an enormous centipede appears in the home; Donaldson has said that this story was perhaps the most difficult writing experience of his career. A *Publishers Weekly* assessment of the volume compared *Daughters of Regals* to the work of Donaldson's "Thomas Covenant" series, and concluded that overall, the pieces "demonstrate that his intense style and offbeat approach can be quite effective in other realms."

Under the pseudonym "Reed Stephens," Donaldson has also written a series of detective novels. The first, *The Man Who Killed His Brother,* was issued by Ballantine in 1980, and introduces another unlikely hero, Mick Axbrewder. A heavy drinker nicknamed "Brew," Mick is approached by his ex-wife, Ginny, a private investigator. Brew's 13-year-old niece has vanished, and Ginny and others fear that a serial killer is at work. A *Publishers Weekly* review observed that while the plot of this amateur detective story offers no surprises, the author "fits the pieces together neatly."

Eight mythical short stories and novellas including "The Woman Who Loved Pigs" and "The Djinn Who Watches Over the Accursed" make up Donaldson's insightful collection. (Cover illustration by Gerald DiMaccio.)

In the second Reed Stephens book, 1984's *The Man Who Risked His Partner,* a sobered Brew and a devastated Ginny—who has lost her hand in an accident—again join forces when a banker hires them, fearing he is the target of a local organized crime ring. *The Man Who Tried to Get Away,* a third in the series, appeared in 1990.

Donaldson is also the author of the 1998 collection, *Reave the Just and Other Tales,* his first since 1984's *Daughters of Regals.* The work contains a number of short stories and novellas, many of them previously published in anthologies or magazines, and garnered its creator the customary critical plaudits. Writing for *Booklist,* Roberta Johnson noted that though a few of the stories were characteristically bleak, like Donaldson's longer works, the tales in *Reave the Just* were "more often exciting, moving and even comic."

The writer may return to his Thomas Covenant hero for one final trilogy. As he once told Ross, "I do have some ideas I like for a new large fantasy. But I have trouble dealing with all the expectation surrounding such a project—other people's as well as my own. My publishers (and maybe my readers) expect me to change the clothes and the names and a few other details and serve up Covenant again," Donaldson said. "I, on the other hand, expect myself to do both 'totally different' and 'better' than Covenant. This exerts a lot of pressure (it's one of the problems that comes with success) and I still have to learn to deal with it."

Biographical and Critical Sources

BOOKS

Contemporary Literary Criticism, Volume 46, Gale, 1988.
Stableford, Brian, "Stephen R. Donaldson" *St. James Guide to Fantasy Writers,* first edition, edited by David Pringle, St. James Press, 1996.

PERIODICALS

Booklist, April 15, 1994, p. 1484; December 1, 1998, Roberta Johnson, review of *Reave the Just and Other Tales,* p. 655.
Fantasy Review, November, 1986, p. 28.
Galileo, January, 1978.
Kirkus Reviews, February 15, 1996, p. 265; November 15, 1998, review of *Reave the Just and Other Tales,* p. 1637.
Library Journal, October 15, 1977, Judith Yamomoto, review of *The Chronicles of Thomas Covenant,* pp. 2184-2185.
Locus, December, 1990, Faren C. Miller, review of *The Gap into Conflict: The Real Story,* p. 17; June, 1994, p. 27.
Los Angeles Times, January 29, 1978.
Los Angeles Times Book Review, May 1, 1983.
Magazine of Fantasy and Science Fiction, February, 1979.
Montreal Star, December 13, 1977.
New York Times, November 30, 1986, Susan Shwartz, review of *Mirror of Her Dreams,* section 7, p. 16.
New York Times Book Review, February 18, 1979; August 14, 1983.
People, July 26, 1982, John Neary, "Both Sales and Sagas Are Fantastic for Stephen Donaldson and His Leper Hero," p. 58.
Publishers Weekly, August 15, 1977, review of *The Chronicles of Thomas Covenant,* p. 56; June 27, 1980, Robert Dahlin, interview with Stephen R. Donaldson, p. 12; October 31, 1980, review of *The Man Who Killed His Brother,* p. 83; February 19, 1982, p. 62; March 2, 1984, review of *Daughters of Regals,* p. 86; November 16, 1990, p. 48; May 3, 1991, p. 66; September 28, 1992, review of *The Gap into Power: A Dark and Hungry God Arises,* p. 69; March 4, 1996, review of *The Gap into Ruin: This Day All Gods Die,* p. 58; December 14, 1998, review of *Reave the Just and Other Tales,* p. 61.
San Francisco Examiner, October 5, 1977.
Science Fiction and Fantasy Book Review, May, 1982; November, 1983, p. 24-25.

Science Fiction Review, September-October, 1978; November, 1982; May 1983.

Village Voice, October 10, 1977, John Calvin Batchelor, "Tolkien Again: Lord Foul and Friends Infest a Morbid but Moneyed Land," pp. 79-80.

Voice of Youth Advocates, June, 1988, p. 95; June, 1993, p. 100-101; October, 1996, Diane G. Yates, review of *The Gap into Ruin: This Day All Gods Die,* p. 216; August, 1999, D. Yates, review of *Reave the Just and Other Tales,* p. 190.

Washington Post, August 12, 1980; August 21, 1980.

Washington Post Book World, December 11, 1977; June 26, 1983, Timothy Robert Sullivan, review of *White Gold Wielder,* p. 10; November 23, 1986, p. 9.*

* * *

DURANT, Alan 1958-

Personal

Born September 6, 1958, in Sutton, Surrey, England; son of Christopher (a sales manager) and Joy (Simpson) Durant; married Jinny Johnson (a primary school teacher), May 25, 1985; children: Amy, Kit, Josie. *Education:* Attended Trinity School, Croydon; Keble College, Oxford, B.A. (English language and literature). *Politics:* "Leftish." *Religion:* Christian.

Addresses

Home—46 Poplar Grove, New Malden, Surrey, KT3 3DE, England. *Office*—Walker Books, 87 Vauxhall Walk, London, SE11 5HJ, England. *E-mail*—aland@ walker.co.uk.

Career

Writer. Publicist for the Spastics Society; senior copywriter for Walker Books, 1986—.

Awards, Honors

Twice winner of the Kingston Borough/Waterstone's Poetry Competition.

Writings

Hamlet, Bananas and All That Jazz (young adult), Red Fox, 1991.

Jake's Magic (easy reader), Walker, 1991.

Little Dracula's Fiendishly Funny Joke Book, Walker, 1992, published as *Little Dracula's Joke Book,* 2000.

Blood (young adult), Red Fox, 1992.

Nightmare Rave (young adult), Fantail, 1994.

The Fantastic Football Fun Book, illustrated by Cathy Gale, Walker, 1994, published as *Football Fun,* 1999.

Snake Supper (picture book), illustrated by A. Parker, Walker, 1994, Western (New York City), 1995.

Mouse Party (picture book), illustrated by Sue Heap, Walker, 1995, Candlewick Press (Cambridge, MA), 1995.

The Good Book (young adult), Red Fox, 1995.

Creepe Hall (easy reader), illustrated by Hunt Emerson, Walker, 1995.

Prince Shufflebottom (picture book), illustrated by Nick Schon, Dutton (New York City), 1995.

Angus Rides the Goods Train (picture book), illustrated by Chris Riddell, Viking, 1996.

Spider McDrew (easy reader), illustrated by Martin Chatterton, HarperCollins, 1996.

Big Fish, Little Fish (picture book), illustrated by A. Parker, Macmillan, 1996, Golden Books, 1996.

Hector Sylvester (picture book), illustrated by A. Parker, HarperCollins, 1996.

A Short Stay in Purgatory (young adult), Red Fox, 1997.

Happy Birthday, Spider McDrew (easy reader), illustrated by Martin Chatterton, HarperCollins, 1997.

The Return to Creepe Hall (easy reader), illustrated by Hunt Emerson, Walker, 1997.

Publish or Die (young adult mystery), Scholastic, 1998.

(Compiler) *The Kingfisher Book of Vampire and Werewolf Stories,* Kingfisher (New York City), 1998.

Little Troll (picture book), illustrated by Julek Heller, HarperCollins, 1998.

Little Troll and the Big Present (picture book), illustrated by Julek Heller, HarperCollins, 1999.

A Good Night's Sleep (picture book), Walker, 1999.

Star Quest: Voyage of the Greylon Galaxy (easy reader), illustrated by Mick Brownfield, Walker, 1999.

Creepe Hall For Ever! (easy reader), illustrations by Hunt Emerson, Walker, 1999.

(Compiler) *The Kingfisher Book of Sports Stories,* Kingfisher, 2000.

Big Bad Bunny (picture book), Dutton (New York City), 2000.

(Contributor) *Ways of Reading: Advanced Reading Skills for Students of English Literature,* 2nd edition, Routledge (New York City), 2000.

"LEGGS UNITED" SERIES; ILLUSTRATED BY CHRIS SMEDLEY

The Phantom Footballer, Macmillan, 1998.

Fair Play or Foul, Macmillan, 1998.

Up for the Cup, Macmillan, 1998.

Spot the Ball, Macmillan, 1998.

Red Card for the Ref, Macmillan, 1998.

Team on Tour, Macmillan, 1998.

Sick as a Parrot, Macmillan, 1999.

Super Sub, Macmillan, 1999.

OTHER

Also contributor of stories to *Toddler Time, Centuries of Stories,* HarperCollins; *Same Difference,* Egmont; *Gary Lineker's Favourite Football Stories* and *More of Gary Lineker's Favourite Football Stories,* Macmillan; *Football Shorts,* Orion; *Nice One, Santa, On Me 'Ead, Santa,* and *Thirteen Murder Mysteries,* Scholastic; *The Walker Treasury of First Stories;* and *Stories for Me!,* Candlewick. Also author of poetry. Durant's work has been translated into Danish, Norwegian, Finnish, French, Greek, Italian, Spanish, Dutch, Welsh, Korean, Chinese, and Japanese.

VAMPIRE
AND
WEREWOLF
STORIES

CHOSEN BY
ALAN DURANT

Alan Durant chose folktale, gothic, and contemporary stories for this introductory horror collection. (Cover illustration by Nick Hardcastle.)

Work in Progress

Tiger Wood and *Leila's Shel,* (picture books); *Bad Boyz* (easy reader series); *That's Not Right!* (easy reader); *The Ring of Truth* (young adult thriller for reluctant readers); *Clownfish,* a novel.

Sidelights

Alan Durant is an English writer of picture books, chapter books for young readers, young adult novels, and short stories for children and young adults. His earliest efforts were teen novels such as *Hamlet, Bananas and All That Jazz* and *Blood,* but since the birth of his three children he has concentrated more on picture books and short stories. "I'm a versatile writer," Durant told *SATA:* "As a professional publishing copywriter I have to be; and I like turning my hands to different forms of book[s]. Also, when I first started writing books, they were very much for me, but since I've had children their preoccupations have come to the fore. They are my inspiration." This inspiration has produced such popular picture books as *Mouse Party, Snake*

Supper, and *Angus Rides the Goods Train,* and easy readers and juvenile novels such as *Jake's Magic, Little Troll,* the "Creepe Hall" books, and the "Leggs United" sports series.

Born in Surrey in southern England, Durant attended Trinity School in Croydon, which later became the model for the school in his first novel, *Hamlet, Bananas and All That Jazz.* "I started writing seriously at the age of fourteen," Durant noted, "because that was the only way I could express myself. The book that had the most influence on me was J. D. Salinger's *The Catcher in the Rye.* Reading that book was so inspiring. My first books were novels about the trauma of adolescence and were, I guess, a kind of catharsis. I really didn't enjoy being a teenager at all."

Durant graduated from Keble College, Oxford, with a degree in English. He then lived in Paris for a couple of years, working at a school for spontaneous expression "run by one of the shortest, fattest, most volatile couples the world has seen," as he told *SATA.* Returning to England, Durant took work as a writer and publicist for the Spastics Society, married, and then in 1986 became a copywriter for Walker Books, a position he still holds. Working in publishing, it was logical that Durant's own passion for writing would come to the fore.

Durant's first novel was published in 1991, and that same year his first book for young readers, *Jake's Magic,* also appeared. Ann G. Hay, writing in *School Librarian,* found the book to be a "short but delightful tale ... about a boy unable to have a pet because his family has no settled home." Jake desperately wants to keep the stray cat he has found, despite all the logical arguments against the idea. His family moves often and might even be emigrating soon to Canada. But Jake knows he must keep the cat at all costs and finds a way to do so. Pam Harwood, reviewing the title in *Books for Keeps,* called it a "delightfully gentle story" and "sensitively written." Harwood concluded that "we share Jake's dilemma right up to the unexpected ending." Hay also noted that the "language is simple enough for the newly independent reader" and that the book would find a "welcome place" on the school or home library shelf.

Further books for young readers include the popular "Creepe Hall" series, which begins with 1995's *Creepe Hall.* When young Oliver is sent to stay with distant relatives, they turn out to be a host of ghosts and mummies straight out of a horror film. "These are the chilling monsters of the cinema screen," observed Julia Marriage in a *School Librarian* review, "but also friendly characters who can scare the villains of the story when necessary." Oliver soon finds himself allied with the servant, "Mummy," an ancient Egyptian mummy, to save Creepe Hall from poachers. As his new family weans Oliver off television, he in turn gently nudges them into late twentieth century technology. Marriage commented that the story "moves rapidly" and that the characters "are larger than life but never improbable or unbelievable," and further noted that this "fun" and "decidedly lively" read will appeal to those children who "do not find reading an enjoyable process." *Magpies* reviewer Russ Merrin wrote, "While this isn't exactly the 'Addams Family Revisited,' we really are in the same territory." Merrin concluded, "Middle primary school aged children will enjoy *Creepe Hall* enormously. It is lightweight, but it is also lots of fun!" Durant has reprised the cast and setting of Creepe Hall in two further installments: *Return to Creepe Hall* and *Creepe Hall For Ever!.*

Little Troll is another story book for young readers, this time featuring the protagonist named in the title. In the first story of the book, Little Troll wakes up grumpy and he stays so throughout the day. A monster—invisible of course—pushes our troll to excesses of naughtiness that get him sent to the headmistress of the school. Contrition results and Little Troll agrees to take part in the class activities. In the second tale, Little Troll sets off to see the world and have adventures. But on his way and with loneliness setting in, he discovers that home is quite the most fun place to be. "These small vignettes of childhood told with tongue-in-the-cheek humour are just right for the intended audience," commented Margaret Phillips in a *Magpies* review. "Short simple sentences will encourage new readers," Phillips added. Durant has continued the adventures of Little Troll in *Little Troll and the Big Present.*

Additionally, Durant has often written about sports for middle grade readers. "I believe in writing about things you know about," Durant said "and, even more, things that you are passionate about. I'm passionate about sport—and soccer in particular. Like it or loathe it, sport plays a massive role in many children's lives. It's a great subject for fiction, too, because you can address many different issues through it—bullying, self-confidence, friendship, justice." Durant's sports books for young readers include *The Fantastic Football Fun Book, The Kingfisher Book of Sports Stories,* and the eight-book series, "Leggs United," which is about a soccer team.

Picture books from Durant include *Snake Supper, Mouse Party,* and *Angus Rides the Goods Train.* In *Snake Supper* a hungry snake slithers through the forest, swallowing up all the animals in its path until finally it is stymied by an ingenious elephant. Writing in *Books for Keeps,* Liz Waterland called *Snake Supper* an "entertaining tale" and a "simple and enjoyable book with amusing illustrations." After the snake's undoing, all the animals he has swallowed survive unharmed, and the snake himself is happily unrepentant, ready to slither off to find new prey. *School Library Journal* reviewer Alexandra Marris was not so convinced of the story's merits, however. She wrote that the "text is minimal and predictable" and that this "offering can easily be skipped." A contributor for *Publishers Weekly,* on the other hand, felt that kids "will likely applaud the solution achieved by an ingenious elephant."

Reviews of Durant's *Mouse Party* were more favorable on both sides of the Atlantic. The book tells the story of a mouse who moves into a deserted house and invites all his friends to a party: there is the Owl with a towel and

the Hare with a chair, among others. Yet an unexpected arrival—the elephant who lives in the house and is returning from vacation—surprises Mouse. "The text will delight those who are doing their first reading," commented a contributor for *Kirkus Reviews,* who felt that the book is "[l]aced with humor and incident," and gives "new meaning to the phrase 'party animal.'" *Booklist*'s Ilene Cooper found the text "clever" and the illustrations full of "visual excitement." Cooper called the book an "energetic offering that has Party! written all over it."

Angus Rides the Goods Train is a picture book that tells of a train chugging across the bedclothes after little Angus falls asleep. Entering this dream, Angus is angered at the adult driver, who refuses to stop for hungry people along the train route. He tells Angus that their goods are for the king, but soon Angus takes over the train and delivers food to the hungry people. Waking the next morning and seeing hungry people on the television as he eats breakfast, Angus feels he has done the right thing in his dream. "This is an unusual picture

Athletes from a variety of sports triumph over hardship in Durant's **The Kingfisher Book of Sports Stories.** *(Illustrated by David Kearney.)*

book with a text suitable for older infants and juniors," wrote a reviewer for *Junior Bookshelf.* George Hunt, writing in *Books for Keeps,* noted how "refreshing it is to find an imaginatively undidactic picture book ... which vigorously and unashamedly celebrates that antiquated notion, the redistribution of wealth." Hunt further commented that Durant's book, with its "highly idealistic message," should be given out free "by the World Health Organization."

Among Durant's novels and story collections for young adult readers are *The Good Book, A Short Stay in Purgatory,* and *Publish or Die.* In *The Good Book* Durant portrays a fifteen-year-old gang leader, Ross, who follows his local football team and with his gang members participates in all manner of hooliganism. Ironically, he takes inspiration from the Old Testament and also has his own ideas about subjects from the Gulf War to redemption. Enter a Youth Peace Mission and one of its members, Morgan, to whom Ross is romantically drawn. Ross begins to leave his violent life behind, until his drunken and cruel father returns and ratchets up the violence one more. Steve Rosson, reviewing the novel in *Books for Keeps,* called it an "unrelentingly grim read." The dozen stories collected in *A Short Stay in Purgatory* "focus on the special hell which only teenage years can bring," according to Val Randall in *Books for Keeps.* In these tales, Durant focuses on themes from first love to crime, and from homosexuality to an unwanted pregnancy. Randall went on to mention that the "writing is clear and well-focused." *Publish or Die* is a mystery dealing with a new publisher's assistant, young Calico Dance, who is fresh out of school and who encounters the worst sort of writer: a threatening one. An anonymous writer sends chapters of a book with a note that warns, "publish or die." When the publisher refuses such blackmail conditions, it becomes clear that the writer is very serious. Then it is up to Calico to try to stop matters before they turn deadly. "The plot moves at a good pace with plenty of red herrings along the way," noted Felicity Wilkins in *School Librarian.* Wilkins concluded that *Publish or Die* "is bound to be enjoyed by ... fans in the secondary school."

Durant is a frequent speaker in schools and also gives writing workshops. Much of his personal motivation comes, as he has noted, from his faith and beliefs. "Religion has been a preoccupation throughout my writing life," Durant told *SATA,* "I don't come from a religious background, but I started singing in a church choir at the age of nine or ten and most of my closest friends as a teenager were connected with the youth group attached to a number of churches in the area where I grew up. I've always believed in God, but my faith has fluctuated in intensity over the years. Whether or not there's an after life and what form it might take is the most persistent thorn in my flesh. There's barely a day goes by without me worrying about it. Given this, it's maybe surprising that I don't write about religion more; death, though, pops up quite regularly."

Biographical and Critical Sources

PERIODICALS

Booklist, September 1, 1995, Ilene Cooper, review of *Mouse Party,* p. 84; January 1, 1999, p. 857.
Books for Keeps, March, 1993, Pam Harwood, review of *Jake's Magic,* p. 9; March, 1995, Liz Waterland, review of *Snake Supper,* p. 9; March, 1996, Steve Rosson, review of *The Good Book,* p. 13; July, 1996, p. 6; January, 1997, George Hunt, review of *Angus Rides the Goods Train,* p. 20; September, 1997, Val Randall, review of *A Short Stay in Purgatory,* p. 29.
Junior Bookshelf, August, 1995, p. 134; December, 1996, review of *Angus Rides the Goods Train,* p. 230.
Kirkus Reviews, August 1, 1995, review of *Mouse Party,* p. 1108.
Magpies, September, 1995, Russ Merrin, review of *Creepe Hall,* p. 29; March, 1996, p. 27; July, 1996, p. 45; March, 1999, Margaret Phillips, review of *Little Troll,* pp. 28-29.
Observer, July 23, 1995, p. 12.
Publishers Weekly, April 24, 1995, review of *Snake Supper,* p. 70; July 10, 1995, review of *Mouse Party,* p. 57; February 5, 1996, p. 90.
School Librarian, February, 1992, Ann G. Hay, review of *Jake's Magic,* p. 19; August, 1995, Julia Marriage, review of *Creepe Hall,* p. 108; March, 1998, Felicity Wilkins, review of *Publish or Die,* p. 156.
School Library Journal, September, 1995, Alexandra Marris, review of *Snake Supper,* p. 169; August, 1998, p. 146; November, 1999, p. 67.
Times Educational Supplement, January 29, 1993, p. 10; May 27, 1994, p. 12; March 8, 1996, p. 4158; May 29, 1998, p. 857.

—Sketch by J. Sydney Jones

F–G

FITZGIBBON, Terry 1948-

Personal

Born Terence David Fitzgibbon, January 3, 1948, in Christchurch, New Zealand; son of David Ronald (a bus driver) and Rita Gwendolene (Sullivan) Fitzgibbon; married Carol Ann Wilson (a physiotherapist and school teacher); children: Zoe Mae, Anna Bella, Mollie Grace, Tessa Shannon. *Education:* Otago University, Dip.L.S., 1972; Auckland University, M.T.P, 1976; St. Kevin's College, Oamaru, certificate. *Politics:* Green. *Hobbies and other interests:* Nature, tramping, fishing, surfing, art, and reading.

Addresses

Office—Making Waves Design Co. Ltd., Box 7115, Whangarei, New Zealand. *Agent*—Penguin Books, Private Bag 102902, NSMC, Auckland, New Zealand. *E-mail*—fitz@makingwaves.co.nz.

Career

Graphic artist, director, designer, illustrator, cartoonist, and writer, 1986—. Royal Forest and Bird Protection Society, Wellington, NZ, conservation advocate and officer, 1984-86; also works as a conservation planning consultant to community trusts, the New Zealand Department of Conservation, and private individuals. *Member:* Royal Forest and Bird Protection Society, Native Forest Action Council, Youth Hostel Association (life member).

Awards, Honors

Planning Institutes Award, 1976, for university thesis, "Native Forest Protection"; finalist, Aim Children's Book of the Year Award, for *Estralita.*

Writings

SELF-ILLUSTRATED

Count and Colour Our Wildlife, GraFitz, 1991.
Who's Wild and Free?, Puffin, 1999.
Who's Wild and Wacky?, Puffin, 2000.

ILLUSTRATOR

Grant Hindin Miller, *Estralita,* Hodder & Stoughton New Zealand, 1984.
Exploring Time: A History of New Zealand for Children, Jackie Arbury, 1993.
Jacque Piggot and Robyn Williams, *Creative Time,* Creative Mums, 1997.

Terry Fitzgibbon

Work in Progress

Educational posters for Penguin Books New Zealand in association with Whitcoulls New Zealand; "developing writing skills, exploring illustrative styles and communication mediums (e.g., the Internet, etc.)".

Sidelights

Author and illustrator Terry Fitzgibbon told *SATA:* "I am an enthusiastic, highly motivated person. Living in the country and interacting with my family provides me with the inspiration to develop concepts and bring them into fruition in both words and illustration. I admire the works of New Zealanders—authors such as Margaret Mahy and illustrators such as Russell Clark. Overseas writers such as Paul Jennings and Ron Brooks, also inspire.

"I aim to make my works accessible to as many children as possible from infants (I am now doing a 'cotbook' series called *Baby's World* for Penguin Books), reluctant readers through to accomplished readers. I believe in the strength of originality and that as artistic communicators, we have to sow the seeds of a love of books to inspire everyone who comes in contact with our works."

*   *   *

GALLOWAY, Owateka (S.) 1981-

Personal

Born June 24, 1981, in Ashton, ID; daughter of Marc Fretty and Sandra Ward. *Hobbies and other interests:* Song writing, environmentalism, gardening.

Addresses

E-mail—owateka@hotmail.com.

Career

Author.

Awards, Honors

Editor's Choice Award, National Library of Poetry, 1998, for poetic excellence.

Writings

Revelations: The Power of Youth in Blue Jeans Poetry, Coda Publications (San Diego, CA), 1999.

Sidelights

Owateka Galloway told *SATA:* "I was inspired to become a writer when I was four years old. I have held steadfast to that dream ever since. In school I would always finish my lessons early so I was motivated to write short stories while I was waiting for the other students. In exploring different writing styles, I took

Teenager Owateka Galloway writes from the perspective of youth in her first poetry collection.

notice of my older sister's intense self-expression through poetry. At twelve years old I became impatient with long-hand writing and started exploring the world of poetry. I liked what I discovered there.

"Inspiration is a process of its own. I sometimes feel like I am not writing but inspiration is forming itself into a stunning expression through me and my feelings. It is also very fleeting, so if I don't have silence and a pen on time, it will slip away as suddenly as it came. To me inspiration cannot really be found. It comes and it goes. I like to write about things that I care and have strong feelings about. I feel that everyone has the right to be listened to and to be heard. In a way I believe that most destructive behavior comes from people's attempts to be noticed and approved of by other people. This idea can expand to include every situation that arises in the universe from our inherent disrespect for our environment to self-destructive behavior. My writing has changed because as I have grown my feelings have grown. As an adolescent I sometimes felt more angry and depressed about my environment. I felt that people were harming me with their behavior. Through realizing that I will be the only person that will be with me throughout my life, I am learning that not everything needs to be painful. When I decide to I can give myself everything that I need. Thus I am learning to notice and appreciate the circumstances that are beautiful to me.

"The way that I appreciate things is writing about them. Maybe this way I will go back and experience them again. I also think writing is important because I can express feelings that everyone has. This is a link between myself and the reader. I like to think that we are never alone in our experiences."

* * *

GEDALOF, Robin
See McGRATH, Robin

* * *

GIFF, Patricia Reilly 1935-

Personal

Born April 26, 1935, in Brooklyn, NY; daughter of William J. and Alice Tiernan (Moeller) Reilly; married James A. Giff, January 31, 1959; children: James, William, Alice. *Education:* Marymount College, B.A., 1956; St. John's University, M.A., 1958; Hofstra Uni-

Patricia Reilly Giff

versity, professional diploma in reading, 1975. *Religion:* Roman Catholic.

Addresses

Home—15 Fresh Meadow Rd., Weston, CT 06883. *Agent*—George Nicholson, Sterling Lord Literistic, 65 Bleecker St., New York, NY.

Career

Public school teacher in New York City, 1956-60; Elmont Public Schools, Elmont, NY, teacher, 1964-84. Freelance writer, 1979—. The Dinosaur's Paw (children's book store), Fairfield, CT, cofounder and partner, 1994—. *Member:* Society of Children's Book Writers and Illustrators, Authors Guild.

Awards, Honors

Honorary D.H.L., Hofstra University, 1990; Newbery Honor award, American Library Association, 1997, for *Lily's Crossing.*

Writings

FOR CHILDREN

Fourth-Grade Celebrity (also see below), illustrated by Leslie Morrill, Delacorte (New York City), 1979.
The Girl Who Knew It All (also see below), illustrated by Morrill, Delacorte (New York City), 1979.
Today Was a Terrible Day, illustrated by Susanna Natti, Viking (New York City), 1980.
Next Year I'll Be Special, illustrated by Marylin Hafner, Dutton (New York City), 1980.
Left-handed Shortstop: A Novel, illustrated by Morrill, Delacorte (New York City), 1980.
Have You Seen Hyacinth Macaw?: A Mystery, illustrated by Anthony Kramer, Delacorte (New York City), 1981.
The Winter Worm Business: A Novel, illustrated by Morrill, Delacorte (New York City), 1981.
The Gift of the Pirate Queen, illustrated by Jenny Rutherford, Delacorte (New York City), 1982.
Suspect, illustrated by Stephen Marchesi, Dutton (New York City), 1982.
Loretta P. Sweeny, Where Are You?: A Mystery, illustrated by Kramer, Delacorte (New York City), 1983.
Kidnap in San Juan, Dell (New York City), 1983.
The Almost Awful Play, illustrated by Natti, Viking (New York City), 1984.
Rat Teeth, illustrated by Morrill, Delacorte (New York City), 1984.
Watch Out, Ronald Morgan, illustrated by Natti, Viking (New York City), 1985.
Love, from the Fifth Grade Celebrity, Delacorte (New York City), 1986.
Mother Teresa: A Sister to the Poor (nonfiction), illustrated by Ted Lewin, Viking (New York City), 1986.
Happy Birthday, Ronald Morgan, illustrated by Natti, Viking (New York City), 1986.

Laura Ingalls Wilder: Growing Up in the Little House (nonfiction), illustrated by Eileen McKeating, Viking (New York City), 1987.

Tootsie Tanner Why Don't You Talk? An Abby Jones Junior Detective Mystery, illustrated by Kramer, Delacorte (New York City), 1987.

Columbus Circle, Dell, 1988.

Ronald Morgan Goes to Bat, illustrated by Natti, Viking (New York City), 1988.

I Love Saturday, illustrated by Frank Remkiewicz, Viking (New York City), 1989.

Poopsie Pomerantz, Pick Up Your Feet, Delacorte (New York City), 1989.

Matthew Jackson Meets the Wall, Delacorte (New York City), 1990.

The War Began at Supper: Letters to Miss Loria, Delacorte (New York City), 1991.

Diana: Twentieth-Century Princess (nonfiction), illustrated by Michele Laporte, Viking (New York City), 1991.

Show Time at the Polk Street School: Plays You Can Do Yourself or in the Classroom, illustrated by Blanche Sims, Delacorte (New York City), 1992.

Shark in School, illustrated by Sims, Delacorte (New York City), 1994.

Ronald Morgan Goes to Camp, illustrated by Natti, Viking (New York City), 1995.

Good Luck, Ronald Morgan, illustrated by Natti, Viking (New York City), 1996.

Lily's Crossing, Delacorte (New York City), 1997.

Katie Cobb Two, Viking (New York City), 1999.

Louisa May Alcott (nonfiction), Viking (New York City), 1999.

Nory Ryan's Song, Delacorte (New York City), 2000.

Fourth-Grade Celebrity and The Girl Who Knew It All, Dell, 2000.

Edith Stein: Sister Teresa Benedicta of the Cross, Holiday House (New York City), 2001.

"KIDS OF THE POLK STREET SCHOOL" SERIES

The Beast in Ms. Rooney's Room, illustrated by Blanche Sims, Delacorte (New York City), 1984.

The Candy Corn Contest, illustrated by Sims, Delacorte (New York City), 1984.

December Secrets, illustrated by Sims, Delacorte (New York City), 1984.

Lazy Lions, Lucky Lambs, illustrated by Sims, Delacorte (New York City), 1985.

Say "Cheese", illustrated by Sims, Delacorte (New York City), 1985.

Purple Climbing Days, illustrated by Sims, Delacorte (New York City), 1985.

In the Dinosaur's Paw, illustrated by Sims, Delacorte (New York City), 1985.

Snaggle Doodles, illustrated by Sims, Delacorte (New York City), 1985.

The Valentine Star, illustrated by Sims, Delacorte (New York City), 1985.

Sunny-Side Up, illustrated by Sims, Delacorte (New York City), 1986.

Fish Face, illustrated by Sims, Delacorte (New York City), 1986.

Pickle Puss, illustrated by Sims, Delacorte (New York City), 1986.

Casey determines to change her image, starting with being elected class president. *(Cover illustration by Leslie Morrill.)*

"NEW KIDS AT THE POLK STREET SCHOOL" SERIES

The Kids of the Polk Street School, Dell, 1988.

B-E-S-T Friends, Dell, 1988.

If the Shoe Fits, Dell, 1988.

Watch Out! Man-eating Snake, Dell, 1988.

All about Stacy, Dell, 1988.

Fancy Feet, Dell, 1988.

Stacy Says Good-Bye, Dell, 1989.

Spectacular Stone Soup, Dell, 1989.

Beast and the Halloween Horror, Dell, 1990.

Emily Arrow Promises to Do Better This Year, Dell, 1990.

Monster Rabbit Runs Amuk!, Dell, 1990.

Wake Up Emily, It's Mother Day, Dell, 1991.

"POLKA DOT, PRIVATE EYE" SERIES

The Mystery of the Blue Ring, Dell, 1987.

The Powder Puff Puzzle, Dell, 1987.

The Riddle of the Red Purse, Dell, 1987.

The Secret at the Polk Street School, Dell, 1987.

The Case of the Cool-Itch Kid, Dell, 1989.

Garbage Juice for Breakfast, Dell, 1989.

The Clue at the Zoo, Dell, 1990.

The Trail of the Screaming Teenager, Dell, 1990.

"LINCOLN LIONS BAND" SERIES

Meet the Lincoln Lions Band, illustrated by Emily Arnold McCully, Dell, 1992.

Yankee Doodle Drumsticks, illustrated by McCully, Dell, 1992.

The Jingle Bells Jam, illustrated by McCully, Dell, 1992.

The Rootin' Tootin' Bugle Boy, illustrated by McCully, Dell, 1992.

The Great Shamrock Disaster, illustrated by McCully, Dell, 1993.

"POLK STREET SPECIAL" SERIES

Write Up a Storm with the Polk Street School, Dell, 1993.

Turkey Trouble, Dell, 1994.

Count Your Money with the Polk Street School, illustrated by Blanche Sims, Dell, 1994.

Postcard Pest, illustrated by Sims, Dell, 1994.

Look Out, Washington, D.C.!, illustrated by Sims, Dell, 1995.

Pet Parade, illustrated by Sims, Dell, 1996.

Green Thumbs, Everyone, illustrated by Sims, Dell, 1996.

Oh Boy, Boston!, illustrated by Sims, Dell, 1997.

Next Stop, New York City! The Polk Street Kids on Tour, illustrated by Sims, Dell, 1997.

Let's Go, Philadelphia!, illustrated by Sims, Dell, 1998.

"BALLET SLIPPERS" SERIES

Dance with Rosie, illustrated by Julie Durrell, Viking (New York City), 1996.

Rosie's Nutcracker Dreams, illustrated by Durrell, Viking (New York City), 1996.

Starring Rosie, illustrated by Durrell, Viking (New York City), 1997.

A Glass Slipper for Rosie, illustrated by Durrell, Viking (New York City), 1997.

Not-So-Perfect Rosie, illustrated by Durrell, Viking (New York City), 1997.

Rosie's Big City Ballet, illustrated by Durrell, Viking (New York City), 1998.

"FRIENDS AND AMIGOS" SERIES

Good Dog, Bonita, illustrated by DyAnne DiSalvo-Ryan, Gareth Stevens (Milwaukee, WI), 1998.

Adios, Anna, illustrated by DiSalvo-Ryan, Gareth Stevens (Milwaukee, WI), 1998.

Happy Birthday, Anna, Sorpresa!, illustrated by DiSalvo-Ryan, Gareth Stevens (Milwaukee, WI), 1998.

Ho, Ho, Benjamin, Feliz Navidad, illustrated by DiSalvo-Ryan, Gareth Stevens (Milwaukee, WI), 1998.

It's a Fiesta, Benjamin, illustrated by DiSalvo-Ryan, Gareth Stevens (Milwaukee, WI), 1998.

Say Hola, Sarah, illustrated by DiSalvo-Ryan, Gareth Stevens (Milwaukee, WI), 1998.

"THE ADVENTURES OF MINNIE AND MAX" SERIES

Kidnap at the Catfish Cafe, illustrated by Lynne Cravath, Viking (New York City), 1998.

Mary Moon Is Missing, illustrated by Lynne Cravath, Viking (New York City), 1998.

OTHER

Advent: Molly Maguire, Viking (New York City), 1991.

Adaptations

Several of Giff's books, including *Happy Birthday, Ronald Morgan, Today Was a Terrible Day,* and *The Almost Awful Play,* have been recorded on audio cassette and released by Live Oak Media. Many of Giff's books have been translated into Spanish.

Sidelights

A prolific author, Patricia Reilly Giff specializes in writing humorous books for middle-grader readers. In both her novels and her multi-book series, Giff explores situations that are readily familiar to young people: putting on a class play, having a pet, and getting along with family and friends. Giff's background as a teacher and reading consultant has given her a unique perspective on her readers. Although she did not begin writing until her early forties, Giff always had a clear idea of her objectives. She once commented, "I had worked with so many children who had terrible problems that I wanted to say things that would make them laugh. I wanted to tell them they were special.... I wish I had started sooner."

Born in Brooklyn, New York, in 1935, Giff recalled her childhood as an adventure in reading. As she once told *SATA,* "While the rest of the kids were playing hide and seek, I sat under the cherry tree reading. On winter evenings I shared an armchair with my father while he read *Hiawatha* and *Evangeline* to me. I read the stories of my mother's childhood and every book in our little library in St. Albans. I wanted to write. Always."

After graduating from high school, Giff enrolled at Marymount College, where she studied the classic authors of English literature, such as Keats, Poe, Pope, and Dryden. Intimidated by such masterworks, she changed her major from English to business, "and then to history, where I listened to a marvelous man named Mullee spin tales about the past. I fell into teaching because my beloved dean, who had no idea I wanted to write, saw that it was a good place for me." Teaching would be her main focus for close to two decades, her time too full of work and family to grant a place to writing. Married with three children, a master's degree in history, and a professional diploma in reading, Giff rounded the corner to age forty when it hit her: "I hadn't written a story; I hadn't even tried."

Determined to pursue her childhood dream, she said, "I dragged myself out of bed in the early morning darkness to spend an hour or two at my typewriter before I had to leave for school. Slowly and painfully, I began to write." Her first published book, *Fourth Grade Celebrity,* appeared in 1979, and its success convinced Giff to dedicate herself to her craft. Along with a number of Giff's books for school-age readers, *Fourth Grade Celebrity* has been through a number of printings, a reflection of its author's ability to connect with the interests of young people. In many of her series, Giff teams with an accomplished illustrator who uses a light, humorous touch to bring to life each of the author's likeable, realistic characters.

Several of Giff's series books have featured the popular students of her fictional Polk Street School. In 1992's *Show Time at the Polk Street School* pivotal teacher Ms. Rooney decides to have her students stage plays. Three play scripts, along with the student's efforts to make them come to life, are included in the volume, which serves as "a solid introduction for aspiring thespians," according to a *Kirkus Reviews* contributor. Bring-your-pet-to-school week becomes the focus of *Pet Parade,* as student Beast looks for another pet to take to Ms. Rooney's class because his own dog, Kissie Poo, does nothing well except sleep. In *Next Stop, New York City!* and *Look Out, Washington, D.C.!* the Polk Street School gang descends on some of the nation's largest cities, with humorous chaos the expected result. Serving as both a story and a tour guide of sorts, the books feature maps of their subject cities, as well as phone numbers of the most favorite tourist attractions for kids.

In the "Ballet Slippers" series, Giff introduces young readers to Rosie O'Meara, an aspiring dancer whose enthusiasm for ballet sometimes gets her into trouble. In *Starring Rosie,* although unhappy about finding herself cast as the evil witch rather than the star in *Sleeping Beauty,* Rosie rebounds, offers to find a boy to play the handsome prince, and then must make good on her promise. But finding a boy willing to wear tights on stage in front of all his friends proves to be no easy task in what *School Library Journal* contributor Eva Mitnick characterized as a "breezy and fun" read. *A Glass Slipper for Rosie* finds the young dancer involved in another class production, although disappointment follows when she realizes her grandfather may not be in town to see the show. Calling the book a "delightful addition to the series," *School Library Journal* critic Janet M. Bair praised *A Glass Slipper for Rosie* as "a well-rounded story about family and friends."

In addition to seeing many of her popular stories translated into Spanish for Hispanic students, Giff has also written a series that incorporates children from Spanish-speaking cultures. In *Ho, Ho, Benjamin, Feliz Navidad* a young boy shares the holiday season with his homesick Ecuadorian neighbor and learns about Christmas celebrations in other countries. *Adios, Anna,* another installment in Giff's "Friends and Amigos" series, finds Sarah Cole dejected after her best friend, Anna Ortiz, goes away for summer vacation. Deciding to occupy her time by trying to learn to speak Spanish, Sarah borrows Anna's house key to use one of her books and then mislays the key. "Children are sure to enjoy Sarah's funny adventures as they also learn some Spanish," commented *School Library Journal* reviewer Maria Redburn, who also praised Giff's inclusion of basic Spanish vocabulary words. Sarah appears again in *Say Hola, Sarah.* Here her progress in learning Spanish is being aided by Anna, although she is frustrated at how slowly she is advancing in another book that includes short lessons in the language.

Fifteen-year-old Lily tells a lie that may cost the life of a young Hungarian refugee during World War II in Giff's award-winning historical fiction. (Cover illustration by Kamil Vojnar.)

In the late 1990s, with over sixty books for young readers to her credit, Giff changed gears somewhat by penning *Lily's Crossing,* a coming-of-age story for older readers. In the poignant story, which takes place during the summer of 1944 as World War II rages across Europe, fifteen-year-old Lily is left behind with her grandmother as her widowed father joins the army to fight the Nazi threat overseas. The novel draws on Giff's own memories of the war years and took four year to complete. "When I sat down to write the book," Giff told a *Publishers Weekly* interviewer, "I wanted to see what I remembered. I made a list of everything I could think of—posters I had seen, the banner in our church with names of who was missing and who was dead. I was surprised by how much I remember." While grounded in her own life, the story's protagonist, Lily, is not modeled after Giff, as many readers might think. The character just "took over" at one point, the author explained in her interview. Praising the work as "a fine piece of historical fiction that evokes a time and place without taking advantage of its characters' emotional lives," *Bulletin of the Center for Children's Books* contributor Janice M. Del Negro noted that *Lily's Crossing* "coalesces [plot and characters] into an emotional whole that is fully satisfying."

Since she began her career as a children's author in the late 1970s, Giff has enjoyed the writing process more and more, particularly when it involves a young audience. "Writing became one of the most important parts of my life, a part that now I couldn't do without," she once recalled. "I hope to say to all the children I've loved that they are special ... that all of us are special ... important just because we are ourselves." In 1994 she and several members of her family started a hometown bookstore entirely devoted to children's books. Giff views her new enterprise, named The Dinosaur's Paw, as "a community that brings children and books together."

Biographical and Critical Sources

BOOKS

Holtze, Sally Holmes, editor, *Fifth Book of Junior Authors,* H. W. Wilson, 1983, pp. 132-133.

PERIODICALS

Booklist, January 15, 1993, Kay Weisman, review of *Meet the Lincoln Lions Band,* p. 907; July, 1994, Stephanie Zvirin, review of *Shark in School,* p. 1947; December 1, 1994, Carolyn Phelan, review of *Turkey Trouble,* pp. 680-681; June 1, 1995, Kay Weisman, review of *Look Out, Washington, D.C.!,* p. 1770; July, 1995, Julie Yates Walton, review of *Ronald Morgan Goes to Camp,* p. 1878; September 1, 1996, Carolyn Phelan, review of *Dance with Rosie* and *Rosie's Nutcracker Dreams,* p. 125; September 15, 1996, Susan Dove Lempke, review of *Pet Parade,* p. 238; December 15, 1996, Carolyn Phelan, review of *Starring Rosie,* p. 726; May 1, 1997, Carolyn Phelan, review of *Not-So-Perfect Rosie,* p. 1493; October 1, 1997, Carolyn Phelan, review of *A Glass Slipper for Rosie,* p. 329; October 15, 1999, Barbara Baskin, review of *Lily's Crossing,* p. 467.

Bulletin of the Center for Children's Books, May, 1984; September, 1984; March, 1985; April, 1986; January, 1992, review of *Diana: Twentieth-Century Princess,* p. 125; July-August, 1995, review of *Look Out,*

Washington, D.C.!, pp. 383-384; October, 1996, review of *Good Luck, Ronald Morgan,* p. 59; April, 1997, Janice M. Del Negro, review of *Lily's Crossing,* pp. 282-283.

Horn Book, July-August, 1993, Maeve Visser Knoth, review of *Next Year I'll Be Special,* p. 442; September-October, 1994, Maeve Visser Knoth, review of *Shark in School,* p. 611; March-April, 1997, Mary M. Burns, review of *Lily's Crossing,* p. 198.

Kirkus Reviews, November 15, 1992, review of *Show Time at Polk Street,* p. 1442; September 1, 1993, review of *Next Year I'll Be Special,* p. 1143; September 15, 1994, p. 1271; October 15, 1998, review of *Kidnap at the Catfish Cafe,* p. 1531.

New York Times Book Review, September 2, 1984; May 18, 1997, Jane Langton, review of *Lily's Crossing,* p. 24.

Publishers Weekly, November 2, 1992, review of *Meet the Lincoln Lions Band* and *Yankee Doodle Drumsticks,* p. 71; July 5, 1993, review of *Next Year I'll Be Special,* p. 72; April 18, 1994, Sally Lodge, "The Author as Bookseller: Patricia Reilly Giff's Career Comes Full Circle," p. 26; October 7, 1996, review of *Dance with Rosie,* p. 76; January 20, 1997, review of *Lily's Crossing,* p. 403; April 27, 1998, "On the Road with Patricia Reilly Giff," p. 29; May 4, 1998, review of *Love, from the Fifth Grade,* p. 216; November 9, 1998, review of *Kidnap at the Catfish Cafe,* p. 77; December 13, 1999, review of *Kidnap at the Catfish Cafe,* p. 32; July 24, 2000, review of *Nory Ryan's Song,* p. 94.

School Library Journal, January, 1992, April L. Judge, review of *Diana: Twentieth-Century Princess,* p. 102; September, 1994, Mary Ann Bursk, review of *Shark in School,* p. 184; June, 1995, Pamela K. Bomboy, review of *Ronald Morgan Goes to Camp,* p. 80; October, 1995, Maria Redburn, review of *Ho, Ho, Benjamin, Feliz Navidad,* p. 37, and *Adios Anna,* p. 38; March, 1996, Eunice Weech, review of *Say Hola, Sarah,* p. 174; August, 1996, Anne Parker, review of *Pet Parade,* p. 122; September 1, 1996, pp. 125, 130; March, 1997, Eva Mitnick, review of *Starring Rosie,* p. 152; October, 1997, Suzanne Hawley, review of *Next Stop, New York City!,* pp. 95-96; December, 1997, Janet M. Bair, review of *A Glass Slipper for Rosie,* p. 90; January, 1999, Janie Schomberg, review of *Mary Moon,* p. 88.*

H

HAFNER, Marylin 1925-

Personal

Born December 14, 1925, in Brooklyn, NY; daughter of Mark (an artist) and Francis (Cisin) Hafner; married Harvey B. Cushman, June 9, 1950 (marriage ended); married Rudolf G. de Reyna (a painter and writer), August 17, 1970; children: (first marriage) Abigail, Jennifer, Amanda. *Education:* Pratt Institute, B.Sc., 1947; attended New School for Social Research, 1948-50, School of Visual Arts, Silvermine School of Art, and Slade School, London, England. *Politics:* Democrat. *Religion:* Unitarian Universalist. *Hobbies and other interests:* Cooking, antiques, travel, gardening, music.

Addresses

Home—98 Woodland Rd., New Canaan, CT 06840.

Career

Artist, illustrator, and designer. *McCall's* magazine, New York City, art director, 1950-54; Famous Schools, Inc., Westport, CT, art instructor, 1968-70. Has taught art to children, designed advertising materials and textiles, and worked in graphic design. *Member:* Society of Illustrators, Westport Artists Guild, Silvermine Guild of Artists.

Awards, Honors

New York Herald Tribune Children's Spring Book Festival award (with Alvin Tresselt), 1949, for *Bonnie Bess: The Weathervane Horse.*

Writings

FOR CHILDREN; SELF-ILLUSTRATED FICTION

Mommies Don't Get Sick, Candlewick (Boston, MA), 1995.
A Year with Molly and Emmett, Candlewick (Boston, MA), 1997.

Molly and Emmett's Camping Adventure, McGraw-Hill, 2000.

ILLUSTRATOR

Alvin Tresselt, *Bonnie Bess: The Weathervane Horse,* Lothrop (Boston, MA), 1949.
Hal Dareff, *Fun with ABC and 1-2-3,* Parents' Magazine Press, 1965.
Mabel Watts, *The Story of Zachary Zween,* Parents' Magazine Press, 1967.
Marguerite Staunton, *That's What* (poetry), Random House (New York City), 1968.
Charlotte Reynolds and Barbara Parker, *Poetry Please,* Random House (New York City), 1968.
Eleanor Felder, *X Marks the Spot,* Coward, 1971.
Lou A. Gaeddert, *Too Many Girls,* Coward, 1972.
Sally Cartwright, *Water Is Wet,* Coward, 1973.
Cartwright, *Sunlight,* Coward, 1974.
Anne Edwards, *P. T. Barnum,* Putnam, 1977.
Charlotte Pomerantz, *The Mango Tooth,* Greenwillow, 1977.
Jack Prelutsky, *It's Halloween,* Greenwillow, 1977.
Pauline Watson, *Cricket's Cookery,* Random House, 1977.
Peggy Parish, *Mind Your Manners!,* Greenwillow, 1978.
Velma and Barry Berkey, *Robbers, Bones, and Mean Dogs,* Addison Wesley, 1978.
Janet Schulman, *Jenny and the Tennis Nut,* Greenwillow, 1978.
Wilson Gage, *Mrs. Gaddy and the Ghost* (also see below), Greenwillow, 1979.
Barbara Power, *I Wish Laura's Mommy Was My Mommy,* Lippincott, 1979.
Steven Kroll, *The Candy Witch,* Holiday House, 1979.
Schulman, *Camp KeeWee's Secret Weapon,* Greenwillow, 1979.
Patricia Reilly Giff, *Next Year I'll Be Special,* Dutton, 1980.
Parish, *I Can—Can You?,* Greenwillow, 1980.
Prelutsky, *Rainy Rainy Saturday,* Greenwillow, 1980.
Pat Ross, *M & M and the Haunted House Game,* Pantheon, 1980.
Marjorie Weinman Sharmat, *Little Devil Gets Sick,* Doubleday, 1980.

Abby tries to take care of things while her mother is sick in bed in Hafner's self-illustrated **Mommies Don't Get Sick!**

Sharmat, *Rollo and Juliet Forever!,* Doubleday, 1981.

Meredith Tax, *Families,* Little, Brown, 1981.

Prelutsky, *It's Christmas,* Greenwillow, 1981.

Ross, *M & M and the Big Bag,* Pantheon, 1981.

Morse Hamilton, *Big Sisters Are Bad Witches,* Greenwillow, 1981.

Florence Parry Heide, *Time's Up!,* Holiday House, 1982.

Prelutsky, *It's Thanksgiving,* Greeenwillow, 1982.

Kroll, *Are You Pirates?,* Pantheon, 1982.

Joan M. Lexau, *The Poison Ivy Case,* Dial, 1983.

Elizabeth Winthrop, *Katharine's Doll,* Dutton, 1983.

Nanette Newman, *That Dog!,* Crowell, 1983.

Ross, *M & M and the Bad News Babies,* Pantheon, 1983.

Gage, *The Crow and Mrs. Gaddy* (also see below), Greenwillow, 1984.

Heide, *Time Flies!,* Holiday House, 1984.

Gage, *Mrs. Gaddy and the Fast-growing Vine* (also see below), Greenwillow, 1985.

Melvin Berger, *Germs Make Me Sick!,* Crowell, 1985.

Kroll, *Happy Mother's Day,* Holiday House, 1985.

Lexau, *The Dog Food Caper,* Dial, 1985.

Ross, *M & M and the Mummy Mess,* Viking, 1985.

Ross, *M & M and the Santa Secrets,* Viking, 1985.

Joanna Cole and Stephanie Calmenson, compilers, *The Laugh Book: A New Treasury of Humor for Children,* Doubleday, 1986.

Joan Robins, *My Brother, Will,* Greenwillow, 1986.

Terry Wolfe Phelan, *Best Friends, Hands Down,* Shoe Tree (Belvidere, NJ), 1986.

David A. Adler, *The Purple Turkey and Other Thanksgiving Riddles,* Holiday House, 1986.

Peggy Charren and Carol Hulsizer, *The TV-smart Book for Kids,* Putnam, 1986.

Ross, *M & M and the Super Child Afternoon,* Viking, 1987.

Kroll, *Happy Father's Day,* Holiday House, 1988.

Ross, *Meet M & M,* Putnam, 1988.

Jean Rogers, *Dinosaurs Are 568,* Greenwillow, 1988.

Vicki Cobb, *Feeding Yourself,* Lippincott, 1989.

Everett Hafner, *Sports Riddles,* Viking, 1989.

Cobb, *Getting Dressed,* Lippincott, 1989, revised as *Snap, Button Zip: Inventions to Keep Your Clothes On,* HarperCollins, 1993.

Cobb, *Keeping Clean,* Lippincott, 1989, revised as *Brush, Comb, Scrub: Inventions to Keep You Clean,* Harper-Collins, 1993.

Cobb, *Writing It Down,* Lippincott, 1989.

Cole, *Bully Trouble,* Random House (New York City), 1989.

Rogers, *Raymond's Best Summer,* Greenwillow, 1990.

Sharmat, *I'm Santa Claus and I'm Famous,* Holiday House, 1990.

Roni Schotter, *Hanukkah!,* Joy Street, 1990.

Gage, *My Stars, It's Mrs. Gaddy!: The Three Mrs. Gaddy Stories* (contains *Mrs. Gaddy and the Ghost, Mrs. Gaddy and the Fast-growing Vine,* and *The Crow and Mrs. Gaddy*), Greenwillow, 1991.

Ross, *M & M and the Halloween Monster,* Viking, 1991.

Mary Ann Hoberman, *Fathers, Mothers, Sisters, Brothers: A Collection of Family Poems,* Joy Street, 1991.

Riki Levinson, *Me Baby!,* Dutton, 1991.

Edith Kunhardt, *Red Day, Green Day,* Greenwillow, 1992.

Martine Davison, *Kevin and the School Nurse,* Random House (New York City), 1992.

Davison, *Maggie and the Emergency Room,* Random House (New York City), 1992.

Nancy Evans Cooney, *Chatter-Box Jamie,* Putnam, 1993.

Jake Wolf, *And Then What?,* Greenwillow, 1993.

Judith Mathews, *An Egg and Seven Socks,* HarperCollins, 1993.

Pat Lowery Collins, *Don't Tease the Guppies,* Putnam, 1994.

Cole and Calmenson, compilers, *A Pocketful of Laughs: Stories, Poems, Jokes, and Riddles,* Doubleday, 1995.

Schotter, *Passover Magic,* Little, Brown, 1995.

Kathryn Laski, *Lunch Bunnies,* Little, Brown, 1996.

Wolf, *Daddy, Could I Have an Elephant?,* Greenwillow, 1996.

Schotter, *Purim Play,* Little, Brown, 1997.

Laski, *Show and Tell Bunnies,* Candlewick (Boston, MA), 1998.

Laski, *Science Fair Bunnies,* Candlewick (Boston, MA), 2000.

Laski, *Lucille's Snowsuit,* Crown, 2000.

Sid Fleischman, *A Carnival of Animals,* Greenwillow, 2000.

Johanna Hurwitz, *Ethan at Home,* Candlewick (Boston, MA), 2001.

Laski, *Starring Lucille,* Crown, 2001.

Hurwitz, *Ethan Out and About,* Candlewick (Boston, MA), 2001.

Hafner's illustrations have appeared in periodicals, including *Good Housekeeping* and *Humpty Dumpty's Magazine.*

Sidelights

Illustrator Marylin Hafner has brought to life the works of such noted children's book authors as Florence Parry Heide, Steven Kroll, and Marjorie Weinman Sharmat through her drawings and paintings. In addition to her work as an artist, Hafner has also created original stories that carry the same light, humorous touch as her drawings. With the original picture book *Mommies Don't Get Sick,* as well as the books *A Year with Molly and Emmett* and *Molly and Emmett's Camping Adventure,* Hafner has added a whole new dimension to her work for the ready-to-read set. Originally published serially in a children's magazine, Hafner's comic strip-style tales about Molly and the cat that magically came to life through one of Molly's drawings have proved popular with readers, prompting their release in book form both in the United States and England.

Born in Brooklyn, New York, in 1925, Hafner attended the Pratt Institute and the New School for Social Research before getting a job at *McCall's* magazine as an art director in 1950. Four years later she left to raise her three children; by 1968 she was back at work teaching at a correspondence school and doing freelance design work. Her first picture book effort, Alvin Tresselt's *Bonnie Bess: The Weathervane Horse,* was published in 1949. Awarded the *New York Herald Tribune*'s Children's Spring Book Festival award, Hafner knew that she had found her niche; in the five decades since, she has contributed to over eighty-five books.

Popular characters, Molly and Emmett, share seasonal events and celebrate the holidays in their first picture book, **A Year with Molly and Emmett,** *written and illustrated by Hafner.*

In her characteristic softly shaded style and using a variety of mediums—from pen and ink to watercolor to pencil—Hafner has contributed drawings to three books by author Wilson Gage, among them *The Crow and Mrs.*

Gaddy. "Hafner makes the happenings visible," commented a *Publishers Weekly* critic, who enjoyed the artist's "softly shaded drawings of the dumpling-round ... farmer." The ability to adapt her rounded style to suit each of her illustration projects has been one of Hafner's skills: in Patricia Reilly Giff's *Next Year I'll Be Special,* the "rosy tones in Hafner's buoyant pictures match the dreams of glory" harbored by Giff's young protagonist, observed a *Publishers Weekly* reviewer. *School Library Journal* contributor Carolyn Noah praised the artist's treatment of Steven Kroll's *Are You Pirates?* by noting that her "black-and-sepia pen-and-ink illustrations are full of wily detail and bring the pirate antics to life." In Vicki Cobb's *Feeding Yourself,* the author's discussion about the use of eating utensils around the world is enhanced by Hafner's interpretation of "their origins and uses in many cultures" through humorous and "lively watercolor illustrations," according to *School Library Journal* contributor Janie Schomberg.

Hafner's pen and ink illustrations for Joanna Cole and Stephanie Calmenson's *The Laugh Book* portray "comic characters running pell-mell over the pages; ... just the kind of silly stuff kids love," remarked a *Publishers Weekly* contributor. *School Library Journal* critic Jane Saliers praised the artist's use of a quite different medium in *Happy Father's Day* by Steven Kroll, noting that the book featured "colorful line and wash illustrations ... filled with active people, pets, and homey details." And *Horn Book* reviewer Mary M. Burns also found appropriate Hafner's use of a full-color palette in illustrating Morse Hamilton's *Big Sisters Are Bad Witches,* remarking that the artist's "slightly caricatured figures and vivid use of color complement [the protagonist's] personality without losing the sense of warmth appropriate to a family story."

Hafner once told *SATA,* "My most important influences in my work are Saul Steinberg, Ronald Searle, Andre Francois, John Birmingham. I do not apply a 'formula' to illustration (using the same style or technique for every book)—but instead let the author's concept and general attitude decide what 'look' the book should have. I try to use the limitations of budget and color, etc., as a challenge to create a unity between words and pictures. My feeling about picture books is that the pictures can add another dimension without overpowering the author's intention."

Biographical and Critical Sources

PERIODICALS

Booklist, June 15, 1992, Deborah Abbott, review of *Red Day, Green Day,* p. 1847; May 1, 1993, Kay Weisman, review of *Chatterbox Jamie,* pp. 1601-1602; December 1, 1993, Elizabeth Bush, review of *And Then What?,* Greenwillow, p. 1993.

Bulletin of the Center for Children's Books, November, 1995, Susan Dove Lempke, review of *Mommies Don't Get Sick,* p. 91.

Horn Book, August, 1980, review of *Meet M & M,* p. 402, and *Next Year I'll Be Special,* p. 397; October, 1980, Paul Heins, review of *Rainy, Rainy Saturday,* p. 533;

August, 1981, Mary M. Burns, review of *Big Sisters Are Bad Witches,* p. 414; December, 1981, Karen M. Klockner, review of *It's Christmas,* p. 654; December, 1983, Karen Jameson, review of *Katharine's Doll,* p. 706; July-August, 1986, review of *Germs Make Me Sick,* p. 474; January-February, 1992, Hanna B. Zeiger, review of *Hanukkah!,* p. 95.

Publishers Weekly, February 15, 1980, review of *Little Devil Gets Sick,* p. 110; May 16, 1980, review of *Next Year, I'll Be Special,* p. 211; June 6, 1980, review of *Meet M & M,* p. 82; May 1, 1981, review of *Families,* p. 67; December 22, 1982, review of *Rollo and Juliet Forever,* p. 63; February 3, 1984, review of *The Crow and Mrs. Gaddy,* p. 403; August 22, 1986, review of *The TV-smart Book for Kids,* p. 102; October 31, 1986, review of *The Laugh Book,* pp. 68-69.

School Librarian, November, 1997, Catriona Nicholson, review of *A Year with Molly and Emmett,* p. 186.

School Library Journal, January, 1980, Reva Pitch, review of *The Candy Witch,* p. 57; May, 1980, Kathy Coffey, review of *Little Devil Gets Sick* and *Meet M & M,* pp. 83-84; July, 1980, Nancy Palmer, review of *I Wish Laura's Mommy Was My Mommy,* p. 124; February, 1983, Carolyn Noah, review of *Are You Pirates?,* p. 68; May, 1984, Nancy Palmer, review of *The Poison Ivy Case,* p. 98; May, 1986, Carolyn Noah, review of *My Brother, Will,* p. 84; November, 1986, Annette Curtis Klause, review of *The Purple Turkey and Other Thanksgiving Riddles,* p. 71; January, 1987, Craighton Hippenhammer, review of *The Laugh Book,* p. 72; May, 1988, Jane Saliers, review of *Happy Father's Day!,* p. 85; December, 1988, Lisa Smith, review of *Dinosaurs Are 568,* p. 92; October, 1989, Janie Schomberg, review of *Feeding Yourself* and *Writing It Down,* pp. 102-103; October, 1990, Susan Hepler, review of *Hanukkah!,* p. 39; December, 1991, Alexandra Marris, review of *M & M and the Halloween Monster,* p. 100; April, 1998, Libby K. White, review of *Purim Play,* p. 110.*

*   *   *

HALE, Kathleen 1898-2000

OBITUARY NOTICE—See index for *SATA* sketch: Born May 24, 1898, in Scotland; died January 26, 2000, in Bristol, England. Illustrator, author. Kathleen Hale was the creator, writer, and illustrator of numerous children's books, including the "Orlando the Marmalade Cat" series. Her first book, *Orlando the Marmalade Cat: A Camping Holiday,* was published in 1938. That book was followed by nearly twenty others, including the stories *Orlando's Magic Carpet, Orlando's Invisible Pyjamas,* and *Henrietta's Magic Egg.* Hale's writing was often based on events in her own life; whether she traveled, bought a farm, or watched man set foot on the moon, these experiences were conveyed on paper as her characters' lives, families, and adventures. Early in life she set out to be an artist, and her first experiences as an illustrator came in the early 1920s when she began designing book jackets and wrote and illustrated stories for *Child Education.* Hale's artwork has been exhibited at various locales, including the Vermont and Leicester Galleries. In 1994 she published the autobiography *A Slender Reputation.*

OBITUARIES AND OTHER SOURCES:

BOOKS

Who's Who, 1998, St. Martin's (New York City), 1998, p. 830.

PERIODICALS

Chicago Tribune, January 28, 2000, section 2, p. 10.
Los Angeles Times, January 31, 2000, p. A14.
Times (London), January 28, 2000.
Washington Post, January 29, 2000, p. B7.

*   *   *

HEFFERNAN, John 1949-

Personal

Born June 15, 1949, in Sydney, Australia; married, 1975; wife's name, Victoria (a grazier); children: Hermione Callista, Ophelia Agnes. *Education:* University of New England, B.A., Dip. Education, Bachelor of Education, and M.A. (honors; in education).

Addresses

Home and office—"Roamville," Walcha, New South Wales 2354, Australia.

Career

Author and grazier.

Awards, Honors

Notable Book Award, Children's Book Council of Australia, for *Spud;* shortlist, Environmental Award for Children's Literature, Wilderness Society, for *Rachael's Forest.*

Writings

Spud, Margaret Hamilton (Sydney, Australia), 1997.
Rachael's Forest, Margaret Hamilton (Sydney, Australia), 1998.
Pete Paddock-Basher, illustrated by Stephen Axelsen, Margaret Hamilton (Sydney, Australia), 1999.
CBD (science fiction; volume 1 of "Mythos" trilogy), Margaret Hamilton/Scholastic Australia (Sydney, Australia), 2000.
More than Gold, Margaret Hamilton/Scholastic Australia (Sydney, Australia), 2000.
My Dog, illustrated by Andrew McLean, Margaret Hamilton/Scholastic Australia (Sydney, Australia), 2000.
CHIPS (science fiction; volume 2 of "Mythos" trilogy) Margaret Hamilton/Scholastic Australia (Sydney, Australia), 2001.

Contributor of full-length story version of *My Dog* to *Cricket* magazine, November, 2000.

John Heffernan

Sidelights

John Heffernan told *SATA:* "I live on a sheep and cattle property in northern New South Wales (Australia) with my wife, Victoria, my two daughters, Hermione and Ophelia, three cats, a house dog and seven working ones, a swag of horses, hundreds of cattle, and thousands of sheep. Perhaps understandably therefore, my first three books have a solid rural setting.

"My first book, *Spud,* is about a blue heeler, and gives a picture of life on the land through the dog's eyes. It was chosen as a Notable Book by the Children's Book Council of Australia. My second book, *Rachael's Forest,* takes up the theme of rural recession, and a family's fight to save their farm. This book was shortlisted by the Wilderness Society for the Environment Award for Children's Literature. My third book, *Pete Paddock-Basher,* is for younger readers, and tells three fast-moving stories about an old farm car who dreams of kicking his heels up and going to town.

"My fourth book, *CBD,* is a conscious change in emphasis. It still has a rural component, but is largely set in the city. A futuristic book for young adult readers, *CBD* tells the tale of a powerful tribe that has built its tiny walled city in the ruins of what had been Sydney's central business district. It is the first book in the 'Mythos' trilogy.

"I have two more books coming out in 2000. The first, titled *More than Gold,* is the start of an Olympic journey—not just for one boy, but for a whole town. The other book, *My Dog,* is an illustrated story set in Bosnia Herzegovina, around a young boy, his dog, and their search for the boy's family. The illustrator is Andrew McLean.

"I am at present working on two books. One is a sequel to *Spud,* and the other is the second book in the Mythos trilogy. And after that? Well, there is such a vast fountain of stories to be told that material is not a worry. Telling the stories well is the difficult part."

Biographical and Critical Sources

PERIODICALS

Magpies, November, 1997, review of *Spud,* p. 35; November, 1998, review of *Rachael's Forest,* pp. 34-35; November, 1999, review of *Pete Paddock-Basher,* p. 34.

*   *   *

HOLUBITSKY, Katherine 1955-

Personal

Surname is pronounced Hall-oo-*bit*-skee; born June 25, 1955, in Toronto, Ontario, Canada; daughter of F. Donald (an aeronautical drafter) and Marion B. (a teacher; maiden name, Buchanan) James; married Jeffrey M. Holubitsky (a newspaper writer and editor), March 20, 1976; children: Maxwell James, Paul Jeffrey. *Education:* Attended Simon Fraser University, 1973-75; Grant MacEwan College, graduated, 1992.

Addresses

Office—Centre High School, Edmonton, Alberta, Canada.

Career

Edmonton Public School Board, Edmonton, Alberta, library technician, 1992—. *Member:* Young Alberta Book Society.

Awards, Honors

Cited among "pick of the lists," American Booksellers Association, 1999, "best books for young adults," American Library Association, "books for the teen age," New York Public Library, Young Adult Book of the Year, Canadian Library Association, and I.O.D.E. Violet Downey Award, all 2000, all for *Alone at Ninety Foot.*

Writings

Alone at Ninety Foot (novel), Orca (Custer, WA), 1999.

Work in Progress

Last Summer in Agatha, publication expected in 2001.

Sidelights

Katherine Holubitsky told *SATA:* "I'm not sure what prompted me to begin writing, except that books and reading have always been a part of my life. I guess it was a natural progression. It wasn't until I turned thirty, however, that I began to write in earnest.

"I write about adolescent life because I really *like* young adults, and I have a lot of empathy for that age. I remember the extremes of emotion so well. Developing teens need to be reassured that what they are feeling is

Katherine Holubitsky

normal. As well as entertaining them, this is what I hope to accomplish in writing for teens. It was certainly the driving motive behind *Alone at Ninety Foot.*

"I can never complain of being lonely when I write and, in fact, the room is often quite crowded. My Clumber spaniel discovered long ago that it's the perfect opportunity to get his head scratched, one of my Siamese cats loves the warmth of the monitor, and the other one makes himself comfortable in my lap. I know I become very single-minded when I am writing. I think of the story and the characters constantly. Luckily, my family has learned to ignore me when I become that intense!

"There are so many writers of fiction who have influenced me, and they are a very diverse group. Common elements in the work of authors I return to, however, are strong characterization, terrific imagery, and wit. I think humor is a great equalizer, something every age understands.

"The one piece of advice I would give to aspiring writers is to read good literature, not just in the genre in which you are writing, but everything you can. You will soon learn to recognize bad writing when you pick it up and, hopefully, when you've typed it out. Then—persevere!"

Biographical and Critical Sources

PERIODICALS

Booklist, March 15, 2000, review of *Alone at Ninety Foot,* p. 1340.

Prairie Books Now, Summer, 2000, Irene D'Souza, "Alone at any Age."

Publishers Weekly, September 13, 1999, review of *Alone at Ninety Foot,* p. 85.

Quill and Quire, August, 1999, Maureen Garvie, review of *Alone at Ninety Foot.*

ON-LINE

Amazon.com, www.amazon.com/ (August 26, 2000).

CM Magazine, www.umanitoba.ca/cm/ (March 3, 2000).

I–J

ISADORA, Rachel 1953(?)-

Personal

Born c. 1953 in New York, NY; married Robert Maiorano (a ballet dancer and writer), September 7, 1977 (divorced, May, 1982); married James Turner; children: (second marriage) Gillian Heather. *Education:* Attended American School of Ballet.

Addresses

Home—c/o William Morrow and Co., 1350 Avenue of the Americas, New York, NY 10019.

Career

Dancer with Boston Ballet Company, Boston, MA; free-lance author and illustrator of children's books.

Awards, Honors

Children's Book of the Year awards, Child Study Association, 1976, for *Max*, 1985, for *I Hear* and *I See*, and 1986, for *Flossie and the Fox* and *Cutlass in the Snow;* Children's Choice award, International Reading Association and Children's Book Council, 1976, Children's Book Showcase award, Children's Book Council, 1977, American Library Association (ALA) notable book citation, and Reading Rainbow selection, all for *Max;* ALA notable book citation, 1979, for *Seeing Is Believing; Boston Globe-Horn Book* honor book for illustration citation, 1979, Best Book for Spring award, *School Library Journal,* 1979, and Caldecott Honor Book award, ALA, 1980, all for *Ben's Trumpet; A Little Interlude* was included in American Institute of Graphic Arts Book Show, 1981; Best Book award, School Library Journal, and ALA notable book citation, both 1982, both for *The White Stallion;* Children's Book award, New York Public Library, 1983, for *City Seen from A to Z;* Outstanding Science Trade Book citation, National Science Teachers Association and Children's Book Council, 1985, for *I Touch; Horn Book* honor list citation, 1987, for *Flossie and the Fox;* ALA notable book, 1991, for *At the Crossroads;* Junior Literary Guild citation, for *Willaby.*

Writings

FOR CHILDREN; SELF-ILLUSTRATED

Max, Macmillan, 1976.
The Potters' Kitchen, Greenwillow, 1977.
Willaby, Macmillan, 1977.
(With Robert Maiorano) *Backstage,* Greenwillow, 1978.
Ben's Trumpet, Greenwillow, 1979.
My Ballet Class, Greenwillow, 1980.
No, Agatha!, Greenwillow, 1980.
Jesse and Abe, Greenwillow, 1981.
(Reteller) *The Nutcracker,* Macmillan, 1981.
City Seen from A to Z, Greenwillow, 1983.
Opening Night, Greenwillow, 1984.
I Hear, Greenwillow, 1985.
I See, Greenwillow, 1985.
I Touch, Greenwillow, 1985.
The Pirates of Bedford Street, Greenwillow, 1988.
(Adaptor) *The Princess and the Frog* (based on *The Frog King* and *Iron Heinrich* by Wilhelm and Jacob Grimm), Greenwillow, 1989.
(Adaptor) *Swan Lake: A Ballet Story* (based on the ballet *Swan Lake* by Pyotr Ilich Tchaikovsky), Putnam, 1989.
Friends, Greenwillow, 1990.
Babies, Greenwillow, 1990.
At the Crossroads, Greenwillow, 1991.
Over the Green Hills, Greenwillow, 1992.
Lili at Ballet, Greenwillow, 1993.
(Adaptor) *Firebird,* Putnam, 1994.
My Ballet Diary, Penguin Putnam, 1995.
Lili on Stage, Penguin Putnam, 1995.
(Adaptor) *The Steadfast Tin Soldier* (based on the story by Hans Christian Andersen), Penguin Putnam, 1996.
(Adaptor) *The Little Match Girl* (based on the story by Hans Christian Andersen), Penguin Putnam, 1996.
Lili Backstage, Penguin Putnam, 1997.
Young Mozart, Penguin, 1997.
(Adaptor) *The Little Mermaid* (based on the story by Hans Christian Andersen), Penguin Putnam, 1998.

Isadora Dances, Viking Penguin, 1998.
A South African Night, HarperCollins, 1998.
Caribbean Dreams, Putnam, 1998.
Listen to the City, Putnam, 1999.
ABC Pop!, Viking Penguin, 1999.
Sophie Skates, Penguin Putnam, 1999.
123 Pop!, Penguin Putnam, 2000.
Bring on the Beat, Putnam, 2001.

FOR CHILDREN; ILLUSTRATOR

Robert Maiorano, *Francisco,* Macmillan, 1978.
Elizabeth Shub, *Seeing Is Believing,* Greenwillow, 1979.
Maiorano, *A Little Interlude, Coward,* McCann & Geoghegan, 1980.
Shub, *The White Stallion,* Greenwillow, 1982.
Shub, *Cutlass in the Snow,* Greenwillow, 1986.
Patricia C. McKissack, *Flossie and the Fox,* Dial, 1986.
Ruth Young, *Golden Bear,* Viking, 1990.
Sandol Stoddard, editor, *Prayers, Praises, and Thanksgivings,* Dial, 1992.
Reeve Lindbergh, *Grandfather's Lovesong,* Viking, 1993.

OTHER

Also author of *Fulton Fish Market,* Putnam.

Adaptations

Ben's Trumpet has been adapted into both a videocassette and a filmstrip with audiocassette.

Sidelights

After a short-lived career as a professional dancer, Rachel Isadora turned to children's book illustration and writing, fashioning a career notable both for its achievements and variety. From such award-winning titles as *Max* and *Ben's Trumpet,* to biographies, to retellings of fairy tales and ballet stories, to the "Lili" series of tales of a little girl's association with the world of ballet, and to distant corners of the world such as South Africa and the Caribbean, Isadora has turned a painterly eye and an artist's perception to retrieve lasting images and playful voices. Recipient of a Caldecott Honor award as well as numerous "notable book" and "honor book" citations, Isadora features people of various races, nationalities, and ages in her works and draws and paints in many styles, from black and white to soft pastel washes to bright icons of pop art. Often her illustrations complement simple texts about such characters as novice ballerinas, hopeful musicians, and promising artists. "Work like this is a dancer's fantasy," she once noted in *SATA.* "Because ballet is so demanding, dancers' stage careers are short. They can only dream of going on and on forever. With art, I can go on and on, and for me it's the only work that compares in intensity and joy."

Isadora began dancing as a toddler, after wandering into her older sister's dance class. By age eleven she was performing professionally and also studying at the American School of Ballet on a scholarship. Throughout the years, though, she was troubled by extreme shyness. While in class, for instance, she wouldn't practice new movements until she could rehearse in an empty studio. She struggled, too, with the great pressures that came from training professionally. To release tension, she began drawing. "Ballet was very real to me: my world," she revealed to Elaine Edelman in a *Publishers Weekly* interview. "To escape it, I drew—so that became my fantasy world. I could express my thoughts in it, I could even express my anger. I couldn't do that as a dancer."

Max joins his sister's dance class one morning and warms up for his baseball game. (Illustration from Max, *written and illustrated by Rachel Isadora.)*

Seven years of study finally culminated in an offer to dance with the New York City Ballet; however, instead of accepting, Isadora broke down. "I went into my room," she told Edelman, "and didn't come out for three months." A few years later she joined the Boston Ballet Company, but a foot injury ended her brief career, and she was forced to establish herself in another vocation. So she loaded a paper bag with her sketches—all "odds and ends on bits of paper," she told *SATA*—and took them to New York, hoping to obtain work as an illustrator. Her venture proved successful, for almost immediately she was assigned to work on her first book.

Both written and illustrated by Isadora, *Max* received considerable attention. Winner of the 1976 Child Study Association Children's Book of the Year award, the story revolves around the title character, a young baseball player who one day joins his sister at her ballet class. Clad in his uniform, the boy exercises along with the young ballerinas and soon realizes that ballet training could improve his athletic skills. He then becomes a regular pupil. Many reviewers praised Isadora for the nonsexist message they found in *Max* that ballet can be enjoyed by all. They also commended the author for her black-and-white illustrations, finding them graceful, lively, and lifelike. The dancers are "poised but fetchingly unpolished," decided a reviewer for *Publishers Weekly.*

In 1979 Isadora incorporated music and dance in what is one of her best-known works, *Ben's Trumpet.* Winner of the 1980 Caldecott Honor award, the book is set during the 1920s Jazz Age and centers on Ben, a young boy who lives in the ghetto. Ben longs to play the lively music that emanates from a neighborhood club, but he cannot afford to buy a trumpet. His dream comes true, though, when a seasoned jazz musician not only gives the youngster an instrument, but also teaches him to play. *Ben's Trumpet* is a "poignant, spare story," observed Marjorie Lewis in *School Library Journal.* Reviewers also lauded Isadora for the story's inventive artwork, which is reminiscent of the art deco style popular during the 1920s and 1930s. Bold outlines, dancing silhouettes, keyboards, and zigzag lines cover the pages of the book, forming a pictorial image of the music. "Jazz rhythms visually interpreted in black and white fairly explode," proclaimed Mary M. Burns in *Horn Book,* while Linda Kauffman Peterson, writing in *Newbery and Caldecott Medal and Honor Books,* declared that the drawings possess a "swinging, throbbing beat."

Isadora returned to the world of ballet in subsequent books, many of which have been praised for their realistic portrayals of dancers' movements. Among these are 1978's *Backstage,* which Isadora wrote with her first husband, ballet dancer Robert Maiorano. The story describes a young girl's trek through the theater to meet her mother, who is rehearsing for the famous ballet *The Nutcracker. Opening Night* features a nervous and excited young dancer who is braving her first performance. The book traces her steps from the time she walks backstage, to her first leap in front of the

audience, to the moment she finds roses in her dressing room after the production. Yet another book, *My Ballet Class,* portrays young ballerinas of all nationalities, who are depicted laughing, cluttering the dressing room floor, putting on their tights and ballet slippers, and stretching out and practicing. The dancers are sketched "with fluid agility," judged *Booklist* reviewer Barbara Elleman. "Facial expressions and body movements are surely and thoughtfully captured."

Lili at Ballet is also about dance class, but centers on one young girl who dreams of becoming a serious ballerina. It outlines the practical aspects of learning ballet, such as clothing, exercises, and some of the classic steps. A *Kirkus Reviews* contributor praised Isadora's illustrations for "nicely capturing [the dancers'] poise and grace." Deborah Stevenson, writing in *Bulletin of the Center for Children's Books,* noted that "[a]ctual young dancers may want more sweat and less gossamer," but she also felt that *Lili at Ballet* "is a nice Nutcrackery treat for armchair Giselles." "Isadora's own background in ballet is evident in the abundance and precision of her illustrations and in her understanding of the enthusiasm of the young dancer," concluded *Horn Book* reviewer Hanna B. Zeiger. Isadora has followed the adventures of her young ballerina through several more picture books. In *Lili on Stage,* Lili performs in *The Nutcracker* ballet as a party guest in act one. Once home, she dreams of her next performance. "The book's charm lies partly in the subject, but mainly in the simplicity and realism of both text and illustrations," wrote Carolyn Phelan in a *Booklist* review. Zeiger noted in *Horn Book* that the "watercolor illustrations are like confections and will be a delightful reminder for children who have seen the ballet performed." Lili next leads the reader to the excitement that goes on behind the curtains in *Lili Backstage,* a book that captures the "excitement of putting on a show," according to *Booklist*'s Hazel Rochman. "For the stagestruck," Rochman further commented, "even the technical names will be magical, and they will pore over the graphic details of professionals at work."

Isadora did for professional skating with *Sophie Skates* what she has done for ballet with her "Lili" books. Eight-year-old Sophie desperately wants to become a professional skater and religiously practices five mornings a week and three afternoons after school. Now she is preparing for a competition and is back at the rink for a further lesson. "The story line gracefully shares space with watercolor sidebars that give behind-the-scenes background," noted a reviewer for *Publishers Weekly.* "A winning score for Isadora once again," the same reviewer concluded. *Booklist* contributor Susan Dove Lempke felt that *Sophie Skates* "provides an excellent balance between information ... and a profile of a believable little Asian American girl living the exhausting, exhilarating life many little girls dream of." "Young skaters—armchair or otherwise—will glide through this one," commented a contributor to *Horn Book.*

The real lives of artists are explored in two biographies for young readers, *Young Mozart* and *Isadora Dances.*

Flossie outwits a vain fox in Patricia C. McKissack's **Flossie and the Fox,** *illustrated by Isadora.*

Reviewing the former title, a writer for *Publishers Weekly* commented, "Biographies for the very young can be a tricky business. In this absorbing account of the great composer's life, Isadora adroitly navigates the potential hazards." The same reviewer also commented on Isadora's "[s]erene watercolors," which "provide an almost impressionistic backdrop to the unfolding events." Writing in *Booklist*, Rochman called *Young Mozart* an "upbeat picture-book biography," as well as a "handsome introduction" to the subject. Isadora presents the same sort of introduction for the American dancer Isadora Duncan in *Isadora Dances,* "another highly accessible biography," according to a contributor to *Publishers Weekly.* In a *Booklist* review, Rochman suggested that "dance lovers ... will feel the excitement and joyful freedom of Duncan's expressive style."

Isadora explores themes unrelated to music or the ballet in other books, such as *Willaby* and *The Pirates of Bedford Street,* two narratives about young artists. Among her more distinctive "non-music" works, though, is 1983's *City Seen from A to Z.* An urban alphabet book, *City* is a collection of street scenes—all drawn in gray, black, and white—depicting the moods, settings, and ethnic diversity of New York. Black, Asian, and Jewish people populate the pages, caught in such activities as window shopping, relaxing in the sun, and strolling through city streets. Isadora also incorporates an element of surprise into many of her scenes: "L," for example, points to the picture of a ferocious lion ironed onto the back of a young boy's t-shirt, while "Z" stands for the chalk-drawn zoo that two children have sketched on the sidewalk. She also portrays elderly people sharing ice cream with their grandchildren or minding them at the beach. "Young and old people of different cultures and individual tastes all seem snugly at home," wrote Leonard S. Marcus in the *New York Times Book Review.* And Beryl Lieff Benderly concluded in the *Washington Post Book World* that "Isadora's elegant, perceptive pictures capture small realities of city life."

The sounds of the city are evoked in the 1999 title, *Listen to the City,* rendered in pop art that captures "the sights and sounds of the city," according to a *Horn Book* reviewer. "In keeping with the Lichtenstein look, the text is limited to painted onomatopoeic words and brief utterances enclosed in dialogue bubbles," noted the same writer. Grace Oliff called *Listen to the City* an "exuberant picture book" in *School Library Journal.* "The use of rich primary colors, coupled with the unique design of the pages, sometimes juxtaposing images in oddly angled segments, captures the energy of urban life," Oliff further observed. With *ABC Pop!* and *123 Pop!,* Isadora also utilized pop art imagery in a novel manner to produce an alphabet and a counting book respectively. Reviewing the former title, *Horn Book* contributor Lolly Robinson noted, "Isadora has created a striking alphabet book in homage to the pop art she admired as a child .... But the pacing is pure Isadora, revealing a vitality that harks back to *Ben's Trumpet* and *City Seen from A to Z.*" Also reviewing *ABC Pop!,* *Booklist* critic Michael Cart felt that "Isadora's artfully energetic book will appeal to eyes of all ages." Writing about Isadora's *123 Pop!,* *Booklist* reviewer Gillian Engberg found it to be a "sophisticated, playful introduction to numbers," while Robinson noted in another *Horn Book* review that the artist "manages to maintain her spontaneous style with vibrant gestural lines, surprising color choices, and unexpected whimsical touches."

Isadora has also gone farther afield with three picture books about South Africa: *At the Crossroads, Over the Green Hills,* and *A South African Night.* In the first title, an ALA notable book, South African children gather to welcome home their fathers, who have been away for several months working in the mines. The second, *Over the Green Hills,* "is a loving portrait of the Transkei and its people," according to a critic for *Junior Bookshelf. A South African Night* is a "simply written picture book [that] focuses on the transition from day to night" in Kruger National Park, according to Gebregeorgis Yohannes in *School Library Journal.* Yohannes further observed that "Isadora's vibrant watercolor illustrations are evocative of both the human bustle and the wild untamed life force of the animals." More exotic locations are served up in *Caribbean Dreams,* an "evocative" book, according to *Booklist*'s Ilene Cooper, and one that "captures the mood of an island and the spirit of children." A writer for *Publishers Weekly* called this same book a "simple, rhythmic paean to the Caribbean."

Whether depicting young children in love with the stage or the arts, or creating picture books that both inform and entertain, or telling tales of faraway lands, or dealing in fairy tales retold, Isadora has created a body of work that critics have praised, award committees have honored, and, most importantly, that children have taken to their hearts.

Biographical and Critical Sources

BOOKS

Children's Literature Review, Volume 7, Gale (Detroit, MI), 1984, pp. 102-109.

Holtze, Sally Holmes, editor, *Fifth Book of Junior Authors and Illustrators,* H. W. Wilson, 1983, pp. 159-160.

Peterson, Linda Kauffman, and Marilyn Leathers Solt, *Newbery and Caldecott Medal and Honor Books: An Annotated Bibliography,* G. K. Hall, 1982, p. 372.

St. James Guide to Children's Writers, fifth edition, St. James (Detroit, MI), 1999.

PERIODICALS

Booklist, January 15, 1980, Barbara Elleman, review of *My Ballet Class,* p. 720; November 15, 1995, Carolyn Phelan, review of *Lili on Stage,* March 15, 1997, Hazel Rochman, review of *Lili Backstage,* p. 1247; May 1, 1997, Hazel Rochman, review of *Young Mozart,* p. 1500; February 15, 1998, p. 1019; March 15, 1998, Hazel Rochman, review of *Isadora Dances,* p. 1246; November 1, 1998, Ilene Cooper, review of *Caribbean Dreams,* p. 503; July, 1999, Michael Cart, review of *ABC Pop!,* p. 1949; December 1, 1999, Susan Dove Lempke, review of *Sophie Skates,* p. 711; May 1, 2000, Gillian Engberg, review of *123 Pop!,* p. 1672; June 1, 2000, p. 1909.

Bulletin of the Center for Children's Books, April, 1993, Deborah Stevenson, review of *Lili at Ballet,* p. 253; September, 1997, p. 14; April, 1998, p. 82; July, 1998, p. 386; June, 1999, p. 354.

Horn Book, June, 1979, Mary M. Burns, review of *Ben's Trumpet,* pp. 293-294; May-June, 1993, Hanna B. Zeiger, review of *Lili at Ballet,* p. 318; January-February, 1996, Hanna B. Zeiger, review of *Lili on Stage,* p. 98; July-August, 1997, p. 443; May-June, 1999, Lolly Robinson, review of *ABC Pop!,* p. 315; January-February, 2000, review of *Sophie Skates,* p. 66; March-April, 2000, review of *Listen to the City,* p. 186; May-June, 2000, Lolly Robinson, review of *123 Pop!,* p. 294.

Junior Bookshelf, August, 1993, review of *Over the Green Hills,* pp. 127-128.

Kirkus Reviews, May 15, 1991, p. 672; January 1, 1993, review of *Lili at Ballet,* p. 61; April 1, 1997, p. 558; January 15, 1998, p. 113; April 1, 1998, p. 496; October 1, 1998, p. 1460; May 1, 1999, p. 722.

New York Times Book Review, May 22, 1983, Leonard S. Marcus, review of *City Seen from A to Z,* p. 39; November 11, 1984, p. 55; January 15, 1995, p. 25; July 20, 1997, p. 22.

Publishers Weekly, August 2, 1976, review of *Max,* p. 114; February 27, 1981, Elaine Edelman, "Rachel Isadora and Robert Maiorano," pp. 66-67; October 10, 1994, p. 70; February 13, 1995, p. 79; March 31, 1997, review of *Young Mozart,* p. 73; March 2, 1998, review of *Isadora Dances,* p. 67; October 26, 1998, review of *Caribbean Dreams,* p. 65; October 11, 1999, review of *Sophie Skates,* p. 74.

School Library Journal, February, 1979, Marjorie Lewis, review of *Ben's Trumpet,* p. 43; June, 1991, p. 80; March, 1998, p. 196; August, 1998, Gebregeorgis Yohannes, review of *A South African Night,* p. 140; April, 1999, p. 99; June, 1999, p. 116; August, 1999, p. 39; November, 1999, p. 143; May, 2000, Grace Oliff, review of *Listen to the City,* p. 144; June, 2000, p. 133.

Teacher Librarian, May, 1999, p. 47.

Washington Post Book World, May 8, 1983, Beryl Lieff Benderly, "This Is the Way the World Works," pp. 16-17.*

—Sketch by J. Sydney Jones

*   *   *

JEAN-BART, Leslie 1954-

Personal

Born January 28, 1954, in Haiti; son of Humel (a customs official) and Andrea (Dambreville) Jean-Bart. *Education:* Columbia University, B.A., 1976, M.S.J., 1977.

Addresses

Home—310 West 107th St., No. 4-C, New York, NY 10025.

Career

Freelance corporate and industrial photographer, c. 1980—. Sotheby's, New York City, staff photographer, 1995—. Work represented in group shows, including

Leslie Jean-Bart

exhibits at Smithsonian Institution, 1998, Society of Illustrators, 1999, Brooklyn Museum of Art, 2001, and Peterson Automotive Museum, Los Angeles, CA, 2001.

Writings

ILLUSTRATOR

Washington, Abrams (New York City), 1982.

The Nanny Book, Prentice-Hall (Englewood Cliffs, NJ), 1988.

Drive to Survive, Prentice-Hall (Englewood Cliffs, NJ), 1988.

Ken Wose, *Blue Guitar,* Chronicle Books (San Francisco, CA), 1998.

John Coy, *Strong to the Hoop* (juvenile fiction), Lee & Low (New York City), 1999.

Contributor of illustrations to periodicals, including *Newsweek, New York Times, Smithsonian,* and *Business Review Weekly.*

Biographical and Critical Sources

ON-LINE

Leslie Jean-Bart—Photographer, http://www.lesliejean-bart.com/ (February 1, 2001).

K

KAY, Guy Gavriel 1954-

Personal

Born November 7, 1954, in Weyburn, Saskatchewan, Canada; son of Samuel Kopple (a surgeon) and Sybil (an artist; maiden name, Birstein) Kay; married Laura Beth Cohen (a marketing consultant), July 15, 1984; children: two sons. *Education:* University of Manitoba, B.A., 1975; University of Toronto, LL.B., 1978.

Addresses

Home—Toronto, Ontario, Canada.

Career

Worked as editorial consultant on posthumous book by J. R. R. Tolkien, *The Silmarillion,* 1974-75; practiced law, 1981-82; Canadian Broadcasting Corporation (CBC-Radio), Toronto, Ontario, writer and producer in drama department, 1982-89; writer. *Member:* Association of Canadian Television and Radio Artists, Law Society of Upper Canada.

Awards, Honors

Scales of Justice Award for best media treatment of a legal issue, Canadian Law Reform Commission, 1985, for *Second Time Around;* Casper Award for best speculative fiction novel in Canada, 1986, for *The Wandering Fire;* Casper Award, 1987; World Fantasy Award nominee and Aurora Award, 1991, both for *Tigana.*

Writings

(Editor with Christopher Tolkien) J. R. R. Tolkien, *The Silmarillion,* Houghton, 1977.
The Summer Tree, (first volume of "The Fionavar Tapestry"), McClelland & Stewart, 1984, Arbor House, 1985.

The Wandering Fire, (second volume of "The Fionavar Tapestry"), Arbor House, 1986.
The Darkest Road, (third volume of "The Fionavar Tapestry"), Arbor House, 1986.
Tigana, Viking, 1990.
A Song for Arbonne, Crown, 1992.
The Lions of Al-Rassan, Viking, 1995.
Sailing to Sarantium: Book One of The Sarantine Mosaic, HarperPrism, 1999.
Lord of Emperors: Book Two of The Sarantine Mosaic, HarperPrism, 2000.

Also author of radio drama *Second Time Around.*

Guy Gavriel Kay

Five university students are transported to Fionavar, the first of all worlds, to join forces with magical beings against the wrath of the Unraveller.

Sidelights

The fantasy novels of Canadian writer Guy Gavriel Kay have become bestsellers and have won critical acclaim for their appealing protagonists, lively pacing, and deft interweaving of complex plot lines. Best known for "The Fionavar Tapestry" trilogy from the mid-1980s, Kay has progressed from the pure fantasy genre into works of fiction that mine the treasures of medieval European history for inspiration. "Guy Kay creates complex psychological characters and a rich sense of ambience, place and time," declared *Washington Post Book World* writer John H. Riskind, who has also hailed Kay's novels as being "resonant and powerful, almost impossible to put down, satisfying the reader on multiple levels."

Kay was born in a small town in the prairie province of Saskatchewan in 1954, and he grew up in nearby Winnipeg, Manitoba. His father was a surgeon, and his

mother an artist. Kay went on to pursue a degree in philosophy from the University of Manitoba, but his education was interrupted by a fortuitous opportunity. Through a connection to the family of the woman who had become the second wife of famed British novelist J. R. R. Tolkien, Kay was introduced to Tolkien's son, Christopher. A medievalist by profession, Tolkien had gained a cult following with his 1937 fantasy novel *The Hobbit,* and continued the story about the mythological Middle Earth kingdom with a trilogy of books in the 1960s known as *The Lord of the Rings.* Tolkien left behind a cache of other fantasy writings when he died in 1973, and Kay, a devoted enthusiast of the Tolkien books, was invited by the son to England to help assemble the materials for publication. The result was *The Silmarillion,* published in 1977 to great success; Kay and Christopher Tolkien were listed as joint editors. "The public didn't have any idea who I was, except for the dyed-in-the-wool Tolkien junkies," Kay told *Maclean's* writer Ann Jansen in 1992. "But the industry did, because *The Silmarillion* was a monstrous success."

Kay went on to earn a law degree from the University of Toronto in 1978, but practiced only briefly. Instead, he found an opportune way to merge his literary ambitions with his training, taking a job with the Canadian Broadcasting Corporation in 1982 as a writer and producer of radio and television dramas. Kay was particularly associated with the television series "The Scales of Justice," which dramatized landmark cases in Canadian history, for seven years.

However, the publication of *The Silmarillion* incited a spate of fantasy novels, and Kay was dismayed by the second-rate imitators of Tolkien and the other masters of the genre that he found on bookstore and library shelves. Thus he went to work on writing his own series, "The Fionavar Tapestry." Its first installment, *The Summer Tree,* was published in 1984, and like all of Kay's books it became a tremendous commercial success. The novel introduced five University of Toronto students who find themselves suddenly immersed in an entirely different realm—that of Fionavar—and must fight to save both it and themselves.

As *The Summer Tree* opens, the students have been invited to a Celtic studies conference by a reclusive academic named Lorenzo Marcus, but Marcus is actually an ambassador from Fionavar who has been charged with the task of bringing representatives from other universes back to Fionavar for a royal jubilee. Thus the students find themselves in a meta-world that possesses characteristics of many other worlds and mythologies; Fionavar is the "Weaver's World" where all of these other belief systems—Celtic tenets, Norse legends, matriarchal practices—find common ground. A magical Tapestry of Life is the repository for the answers as to how and why all these philosophies are interrelated.

Each of the five Toronto characters has distinctive strengths and weaknesses, which find a way to interweave on Fionavar as well: Dave's self-esteem has been damaged by a father who favors his brother over him;

Paul's girlfriend died in an accident; Kevin is handsome and well-liked, but realizes his world is shallow; Jennifer's heart has been saddened by the end of a relationship; and Kim is a loner. As *The Summer Tree* gets underway, the students learn that Fionavar is in grave danger: the malevolent Rakoth Maugrim, imprisoned for a thousand years, has escaped, and plans to abscond with the Tapestry of Life. The group of five ally with an exiled prince to save Fionavar, and find that they each possess a special power. In the end, one has sacrificed his life, and Jennifer has been sexually assaulted by Rakoth.

Booklist reviewer Sally Estes found *The Summer Tree* "an ambitious undertaking that succeeds in itself and as a precursor of what is to come." Though the work did invoke some comparisons to Tolkien's books, in her essay for the *St. James Guide to Fantasy Writers* Maureen Speller called Kay "among the foremost modern fantasy writers on the strength of the Fionavar Tapestry." Speller noted that while Kay's books and Tolkien's classic cycle shared some similarities, the former "nevertheless set a new standard in what could be achieved in original fantasy writing."

The second installment of the Fionavar trilogy, *The Wandering Fire,* was published in 1986. Here the students return to Fionavar a year later, and Jennifer is carrying Rakoth's child, which is not expected to survive. A perpetual winter has descended upon Fionovar, the curse of a wicked magician who has allied with Rakoth. However, the students have brought with them representatives from the Arthurian legends to assist them in saving the Tapestry of Life. Jennifer emerges as the Arthurian female Guinevere, and a cabal of virtuous deities help the students shatter the magic cauldron and end the winter on Fionavar. Another student, Kevin, loses his life—sacrificed to the Mother Goddess on Midsummer's Eve—but like Paul, he remains a guiding spirit in the plot. *Booklist* reviewer Estes termed *The Wandering Fire* "a most satisfying sequel" and a book "rich in mythological lore."

Critics also commended Kay for creating a believable cast of innocents who, like readers, were utterly new to the strange universe of Fionavar. Kay's deft and full delineation of each character is considered one of the trilogy's primary strengths, and his convincing description of a complex world won additional praise. Kay concluded the trilogy with another book published in 1986, *The Darkest Road.* As it opens, spring has finally arrived, but the rains bring disease. Kim persuades a nation of giants known as the Paraiko to take their side, and the armies of good arrive at Rakoth's fortress to do battle.

"Even the prose weighs a ton," noted a *Kirkus Reviews* assessment of The Darkest Road, commenting upon the very intricate layer of plot, action, and cast created by Kay, "a density that's often impenetrable." Jennifer's son Darien, feeling that the pro-Fionavar forces have rejected him because of his mixed heritage, steals a dagger with magical properties and heads off, ostensibly,

to fight for Rakoth's side. Darien becomes "the random thread in the Weaver's story, the one who can control many destinies by his choice," explained Penny Blubaugh in *Voice of Youth Advocates.* "Like Tolkien, Kay recognizes that there must be sacrifice as well as a happy ending and the Fionavar trilogy is more successful than most modern fantasies for acknowledging this," observed Speller in *St. James Guide to Fantasy Writers.*

The Fionavar books were a success for Kay both in English and in foreign-language editions. By 1989 he had quit his job with the CBC, but later said that his years writing radio and television drama, especially for "The Scales of Justice," helped give his works their gripping pace so often cited by critics. "I proudly acknowledge my sense of the operatic and theatrical," he told Ann Jansen of *Maclean's.* "I want to give the readers that page-turning energy." As a writer, Kay has been fortunate enough to be able to ensconce himself in a psychically rich part of the world to inspire his prose. He traveled to Crete and New Zealand to write two of

Fionavar faces its final days in this concluding book of the series.

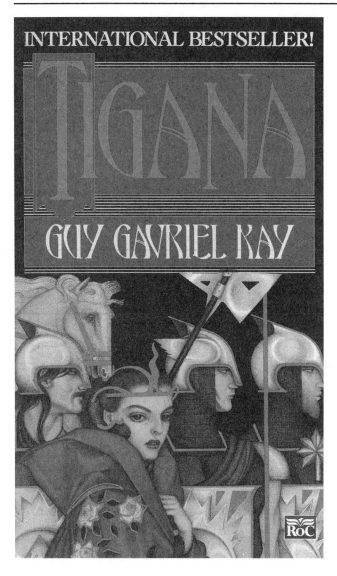

INTERNATIONAL BESTSELLER!

TIGANA

GUY GAVRIEL KAY

RoC

The last prince of Tigana, a land removed from human memory, battles to release the curse.

the Fionavar books, and then arrived in Tuscany to research and write his next project, *Tigana,* which was published in 1990. Here he created another fantasy world, but one which bears some resemblance to Renaissance Italy.

Tigana is threatened by sorcerer-king Brandin, who battles to erase from history the very word "Tigana." The Mediterranean realm was once a powerful and noble kingdom, but Brandin's beloved son died in a battle against it, and he has made its destruction his revenge. After erasing its borders, he has been able to cast a spell that renders the very word Tigana unhearable. A few surviving Tiganans band together to fight him, and their lost prince, Alessan, and a troubadour named Devin also join the cause. The courtesan Dianora becomes a spy in Brandin's camp, and achieves in the end what bloodshed could not. Reviewing the novel for *Voice of Youth Advocates,* Edith S. Tyson termed *Tigana* an even more intricate creation than the Fionavar trilogy. "This well crafted, fully realized mega-fantasy is designed to appeal

to the fans of Tolkien and Donaldson," Tyson wrote. "It is not for casual readers or for the faint of heart."

Other reviewers found problems with Kay's post-Fionavar effort, and commented that the characters did not emerge as the well-rounded personalities who saved Fionavar. The troubadours, outlaws, exiles, and magicians who made up the large cast of *Tigana* were faulted for being too attractive and heroic. Some critics also found that the intersection of an array of mythologies and worlds was confusing. "There is a sense that this novel was intended to be much more closely related to the Fionavar trilogy than it is now," assessed Speller in the *St. James Guide to Fantasy Writers.*

Kay set his next book in the Mediterranean world as well. The 1992 fantasy, *A Song for Arbonne,* takes place in a medieval Europe where Christianity never took hold. Arbonne is in Provence, a place in modern times that is part of the south of France; here, a more progressive outlook on gender issues fostered the rise of the troubadour in the twelfth century. These wandering poets/musicians sang verse, in a dialect called langue d'oc, about romantic love, nature, and war. In Kay's novel, the most famous among them is Bertran of Arbonne. In contrast, the disintegrating patriarchal kingdom of Gorhaut to the north is ruled by the brutal, corrupt King Ademar. Blaise, an honorable young man from Ademar's court, flees this world to Arbonne, where he becomes a mercenary soldier in the war ignited by his own father against Arbonne and its heretical system that worships a female deity. Blaise eventually challenges Ademar for the throne.

The liberal climate and revolutionary rethinking of masculine and feminine behaviors in Provence and the Languedoc region—before they became an actual part of France—came to a repressive close with the events surrounding the Albigensian Crusade. Kay's novel, however, has a more positive ending. As the author explained to Ann Jansen of *Maclean's,* "I'm basing my works on a period, but I'm not writing about that period. I reinterpret it in order to allow for some reflection on how we didn't have to end up where we are today," Kay stressed.

A Song for Arbonne was published to positive reviews. "This panoramic, absorbing novel beautifully creates an alternate version of the medieval world," a *Publishers Weekly* reviewer wrote. Candace Smith of *Booklist* described it as a "lush, lengthy medieval saga" with a "compelling narrative." However, a later assessment in the *St. James Guide to Fantasy Writers* faulted *A Song for Arbonne* for its scope. "The novel is strong on background flavor, and many of its characters are as attractive as those in *Tigana,* but the plot might easily have been accomplished in half the pages," Speller remarked.

Kay's next novel also tackled a historically significant epoch, though here he created a complex series of nations and alliances under entirely fictitious names. However, many critics remarked that *The Lions of Al-*

Rassan (1995) was entirely reminiscent of a period of Spanish medieval history, when Christians, Moors, and Jews enjoyed a tenuous but culturally rich coexistence. The novel is set on a peninsular land called Esperana, ruled by Asharites who had come from desert lands. As the story opens, this once powerful group's hold on the conquered land is waning. Esperana has disintegrated into rival city-kingdoms, and a holy war against the imperialist Jaddites seems imminent. The Jaddites are led by Rodrigo Belmonte, and two other characters who play crucial roles: a female physician and a poet-courtier. The novel comes to an emotionally wrenching conclusion. Margaret Miles, writing in *Voice of Youth Advocates,* called Kay's sixth book "yet another monumentally impressive historical novel." His heroes and the wide cast of other figures, Miles noted, "come vividly to life, set in the matrix of an equally vivid and complex society and involved in a plot as intricate and subtle as the characters themselves."

Kay began another trilogy with his 1999 novel, *Sailing to Sarantium: Book One of The Sarantine Mosaic.* Again, the Mediterranean landscape provides the backdrop. The book's protagonist is a mosaic artisan living in Rome at the time of the Visigoths in the sixth century. The Roman Empire has fallen, but the center of power has shifted eastward to Sarantium—an ersatz Byzantine empire. The artist, Caius Crispin, has been invited to Sarantium's capital to work on a massive mosaic project for its famous church. Since Crispin has recently lost his entire family in a plague, he accepts the mission. Before he departs the queen learns of his plans, however, and she sends with him a secret message to deliver to Sarantium's brutal emperor. Along the way, Crispin rescues a prostitute, and once in Sarantium, becomes embroiled in political and religious discord. "*Sarantium* also harbors intriguing elements of magic, adding the chiaroscuro of pagan blood-worship and alchemic transmutation to this tale about a people terrified of darkness and night," observed John Burns, writing in *Quill & Quire.* A *Publishers Weekly* review remarked that "Kay is at his best when describing the intertwining of art and religion or explicating the ancient craft of mosaic work." In 2000 Kay published the second book in the trilogy, *Lord of Emperors.*

Kay told *Locus,* "The aspect of fantasy I'm most interested in now is the most difficult to explain. I'm beginning to see fantasy as a way of looking at history, as an antidote to what they call 'faction'—fiction using real people, real lives, and embedding them in narrative." He added, "In *Sailing to Sarantium* and *Lord of Emperors,* the reign of Justinian and Theodora, with Count Belisarius and the eunuch Narses, is clearly my source, but I'm saying right from the beginning that this is not even pretending to know what the real people were like. It's a fantasy on themes."

Kay has said that his novels usually take him nearly a year to research, and another to write. Creating entirely fictional characters, who participate in actual historic events and sometimes even alter their outcome, has allowed his creativity to flourish. "I lack the utter autonomy some writers have," Kay told *Maclean's.* "I don't want to write on the back of a real person. THAT SMACKS OF HUBRIS."

Biographical and Critical Sources

BOOKS

Speller, Maureen, "Guy Gavriel Kay," *St. James Guide to Fantasy Writers,* St. James Press, 1996, pp. 318-319.

PERIODICALS

Booklist, September 1, 1985, Sally Estes, review of *The Summer Tree,* p. 4; May 15, 1986, S. Estes, review of *The Wandering Fire,* p. 1361; January 15, 1993, Candace Smith, review of *A Song for Arbonne,* p. 878; January 1, 1999, p. 842; March 15, 2000, review of *Lord of Emperors,* p. 1335.
Fantasy Review, January, 1985; December, 1986.
Financial Post, July 8, 1995, Shlomo Schwartzberg, review of *The Lions of Al-Rassan,* p. 23.
Globe and Mail (Toronto), February 9, 1985; June 28, 1986; September 8, 1990.
Kirkus Reviews, May 15, 1986, p. 752; October 1, 1986, review of *The Darkest Road,* p. 1475.
Library Journal, October 15, 1985, p. 104; November 15, 1986, p. 112; August, 1990, p. 147; December, 1998, p. 161.
Locus, June, 1990; September, 1992; November, 1992; May, 2000, "Guy Gavriel Kay: Lord of Fantasy," pp. 6-7, 63-64.
Maclean's, March 23, 1987; December 14, 1992, Ann Jansen, "Castles in the Air: Guy Gavriel Kay Mixes History and Fantasy;" July 1, 1995; October 26, 1998, "Playing Fast and Fun with Past Events," p. 82; April 3, 2000, Brian Bethune, "The Man Who Sailed to an Alternate Byzantium," p. 58.
Magazine of Fantasy and Science Fiction, December, 1995; October, 2000, Charles DeLint, review of *The Lord of Emperors,* p. 39.
New Statesman, November 28, 1986.
Publishers Weekly, May 16, 1986, pp. 72-73; October 10, 1986, p. 81; November 23, 1992, review of *A Song for Arbonne,* pp. 56-57; February 8, 1999, review of *Sailing to Sarantium,* p. 199.
Quill & Quire, May, 1995, p. 33; October, 1998, John Burns, review of *Sailing to Sarantium,* p. 35.
Time International, March 13, 2000, Katherine Govier, "Fantastic Voyager," p. 54.
Voice of Youth Advocates, December, 1986, p. 237; April, 1987, Penny Blubaugh, review of *The Darkest Road,* p. 38; April, 1991, Edith S. Tyson, review of *Tigana,* p. 44; October, 1995, Margaret Miles, review of *The Lions of Al-Rassan,* p. 234.
Washington Post Book World, July 28, 1996, John H. Riskind, review of *The Lions of Al-Rassan,* p. 8.

ON-LINE

Guy Gavriel Kay's Web site, http://www.brightweavings.com.*

KENNETT, David 1959-

Personal

Born October 5, 1959, in Adelaide, Australia; son of Dean Daniel (a building contractor) and Peggy Lenore (a nurse; maiden name, Hoile) Kennett. *Education:* Underdale College of Advanced Education, B.A. (design and illustration), 1985.

Addresses

Home—6/354 Greenhill Rd., Glenside, South Australia 5065, Australia. *E-mail*—davidckennett@hotmail.com.

Career

Author and illustrator.

Writings

SELF-ILLUSTRATED

Polar Bear, Omnibus (Norwood, South Australia), 2000.
Wolf, Omnibus (Norwood, South Australia), 2000.

ILLUSTRATOR

Gwen Pascoe, *Two Feet,* Era, 1986.
Pascoe, *Huggly, Snuggly Pets,* Era, 1987.
Harry Breidahl, *Ecology: The Story of Life, the Earth, and Everything,* Macmillan Australia (South Melbourne), 1987.
Kath Lock, *Jennifer and Nicholas,* Keystone (Flinders Park, South Australia), 1989.
Yvonne Winer, *Herbertia the Vile,* Era, 1990.
Edel Wignell, *Voices,* Era, 1990.
Jane O'Loughlin, reteller, *Folk Tales: A Short Anthology,* Era, 1991.
Beryl Ayers, *Lucky I Have My Umbrella,* Martin International, 1992.
Josephine Croser, *Baleen,* Era, 1992.
J. Croser, *Patrick,* Era, 1992.
Lock, reteller, *Little Burnt-Face,* Keystone (Flinders Park, South Australia), 1994.
Lock, reteller, *The Tiger, the Brahmin, and the Jackal,* Keystone (Flinders Park, South Australia), 1994.
Lock, reteller, *The Sea of Gold,* Keystone (Flinders Park, South Australia), 1994.
Nigel Croser, *Changing Shape,* Era, 1994.
June Loves, *One Week with My Grandmother,* Era, 1995.
Lock, reteller, *Anansi and the Rubber Man,* Era, 1995.
Lock, reteller, *The King's Gift,* Era, 1995.
N. Croser, *Cats,* Era, 1996.
Telene Clarke-Giles, *Molly McClog,* Era, 1996.
Dave Luckett, *The Best Batsman in the World,* Omnibus (Norwood, South Australia), 1996.
J. Croser, *Grandpa's Breakfast,* Era, 1997.
Loves, *One Wild Weekend with My Grandmother,* Era, 1997.
Luckett, *The Last Eleven,* Omnibus (Norwood, South Australia), 1997.
Loves, *One Slow Saturday with My Grandmother,* Era, 1998.

Jonathan Harlen, *The Crescent Moon,* Lothian (Port Melbourne, Australia), 1998.
Dyan Blacklock, *Olympia: Warrior Athletes of Ancient Greece,* Omnibus (Norwood, South Australia), 2000.

Work in Progress

Two self-illustrated fact books for young children, *Lion* and *Elephant;* research on the Roman Empire, 54 B.C. to 9 A.D.

Sidelights

David Kennett told *SATA:* "My maternal grandfather had a wonderful library—many books on mythology, ancient history, and natural history. I particularly remember some illustrations that I now suppose were Dore's Bible illustrations.

"My childhood and a lot of my adolescence were spent in a perpetual daydream of Vikings, Native Americans, and Greek myths. In the later '60s and '70s the work of Frank Frazetta overwhelmed me and I tried unsuccessfully to draw and paint just like him. I still regard him as my most important and lasting influence.

"Rosemary Sutcliffe and Henry Treece are the two authors whose books have meant most to me. Rosemary Sutcliffe was particularly helpful to me as I was a very shy boy and she wrote very well of outsiders and I felt that at least one person understood how I felt. She also wrote me two very nice letters telling me about her latest projects and research. I did feel like her special friend. As an adult I realise it was also a very kind and generous amount of time to spend on a complete stranger on the other side of the world. The work of Victor Ambrus, Charles Keeping, N. C. Wyeth, and Howard Pyle have also had a lasting and continuing influence on my work.

"I hope that some of the pictures I draw will leave some kind of lasting impression on some child in much the same way that pictures of my childhood have stayed with me."

*   *   *

KER WILSON, Barbara 1929-

Personal

Born September 24, 1929, in Sunderland, County Durham, England; daughter of William and Margaret Ker Wilson; married Peter Richard Tahourdin (a composer), December 15, 1956; children: Julia, Sarah. *Education:* Attended North London Collegiate School, 1938-48. *Religion:* Christian.

Addresses

Home—Moreton Bay, Australia.

Career

Oxford University Press, London, England, junior children's editor, 1949-54; Bodley Head, London, managing editor in children's books section, 1954-57; William Collins, London, managing editor, 1958-61; Angus & Robertson, Sydney, Australia, children's books editor, 1965-73; Hodder & Stoughton, Sydney, children's books editor, 1973-76; *Readers Digest* Condensed Books, Sydney, editor, 1978-84; editor for University of Queensland Press. *Member:* Australian Society of Authors.

Writings

FICTION; FOR CHILDREN

Path-through-the-Woods, illustrated by Charles Stewart, Constable, 1957, Criterion, 1958.

The Wonderful Cornet, illustrated by Raymond Briggs, Hamish Hamilton, 1958.

The Lovely Summer, illustrated by Marina Hoffer, Dodd, 1960.

Last Year's Broken Toys, Constable, 1962, published as *In Love and War,* World, 1963.

Ann and Peter in Paris (and in London), two volumes, illustrated by Harry and Ilse Toothill, Muller, 1963-65.

A Story to Tell: Thirty Tales for Little Children, illustrated by Sheila Sancha, J. Garnet Miller, 1964.

Beloved of the Gods, Constable, 1965, published as *In the Shadow of Vesuvius,* World, 1965.

A Family Likeness, illustrated by Astra Lacis Dick, Constable, 1967, published as *The Biscuit-Tin Family,* World, 1968.

Hiccups and Other Stories: Thirty Tales for Little Children, illustrated by Richard Kennedy, J. Garnet Miller, 1971.

The Willow Pattern Story, illustrated by Lucienne Fontannaz, Angus & Robertson, 1978.

(With Jacques Cadry) *The Persian Carpet Story,* illustrated by Nyorie Bungey, Methuen, 1981.

Kelly the Sleepy Koala, illustrated by Lorraine Itannay, Golden, 1983.

Molly, Golden, 1983.

Kevin the Kookaburra, illustrated by Sue Price, Golden, 1983.

Acacia Terrace, illustrated by David Fielding, Ashton Scholastic, 1988.

RETELLER; FOR CHILDREN

Scottish Folk Tales and Legends, illustrated by Joan Kiddell-Monroe, Oxford University Press, Walck, 1954, published as *Fairy Tales from Scotland,* Oxford University Press, 1999.

Fairy Tales of Germany, illustrated by Gertrude Mittelmann, Dutton, 1959.

Fairy Tales of Ireland, illustrated by G. W. Miller, Dutton, 1959.

Fairy Tales of Russia, illustrated by Jacqueline Athram, Dutton, 1959.

Fairy Tales of England, illustrated by J. S. Goodall, Dutton, 1960.

Fairy Tales of France, illustrated by William McLaren, Dutton, 1960.

Fairy Tales of India, illustrated by Rene Mackensie, Dutton, 1960.

Fairy Tales of Mexico, illustrated by G. W. Miller, Dutton, 1960.

Fairy Tales of Persia, illustrated by G. W. Miller, Dutton, 1961.

Legends of the Round Table, illustrated by Marra Calati, Hamlyn, 1966.

Greek Fairy Tales, illustrated by Harry Toothill, Muller, 1966, Follett, 1968.

Animal Folk Tales, illustrated by Mirko Hanak, Hamlyn, 1968, Grosset & Dunlap, 1971.

Tales Told to Kabbarli: Aboriginal Legends Collected by Daisy Bates, illustrated by Harold Thomas, Angus & Robertson, Crown, 1972.

The Magic Fishbones and Other Fabulous Tales of Asia, illustrated by Susanne Dolesch, Angus & Robertson, 1974.

The Magic Bird and Other Fabulous Tales from Europe, illustrated by S. Dolesch, Angus & Robertson, 1976.

The Turtle and the Island: Folk Tales from Papua New Guinea, edited by Donald S. Stokes, illustrated by Tony Oliver, Hodder & Stoughton, 1978.

Wishbones: A Folk Tale from China, illustrated by Meilo So, Macmillan, 1993.

OTHER; FOR CHILDREN

Look at Books (nonfiction), illustrated by John Woodcock, Hamish Hamilton, 1960.

(Compiler) *The Second Young Eve,* Blackie, 1962.

(Editor) Bernhardt Gottlieb, *What a Girl (and Boy) Should Know about Sex,* two volumes, Constable, 1962.

(Editor) *Australian Kaleidoscope,* illustrated by Margery Gill, Collins, 1968, Meredith Press, 1969.

Australia, Wonderland Down Under (nonfiction), Dodd Mead, 1969.

(Compiler) *A Handful of Ghosts: Thirteen Eerie Tales by Australian Authors,* Hodder & Stoughton, 1976.

(Editor and author of notes) *Alitji: In the Dreamtime* (Aboriginal Pitjantjatjara version of Lewis Carroll's *Alice's Adventures in Wonderland*), adapted and translated by Nancy Sheppard, illustrated by Byron Sewell, Adelaide University Press, 1976.

Just for a Joyride (reader), Holt Rinehart, 1977.

(Editor) *Illustrated Treasury of Australian Stories and Verses for Children,* Nelson, 1987.

(Compiler) *Brief Encounters: Short Stories,* University of Queensland Press, 1992.

(Compiler) *Hands Up!: Who Enjoyed Their Schooldays,* University of Queensland Press, 1994.

NOVELS; FOR ADULTS

Jane Austen in Australia, Secker & Warburg, 1984, published in the United States as *Antipodes Jane,* Viking, 1985.

The Quade Inheritance, Secker & Warburg, 1988, St. Martin's Press, 1989.

NONFICTION; FOR ADULTS

Writing for Children, Boardman, 1960, Watts, 1961.

Noel Streatfeild: A Monograph, Bodley Head, 1961, Walck, 1964.

Adaptations

A Story to Tell: Thirty Tales for Little Children has been adapted for radio and television.

Sidelights

Barbara Ker Wilson has blended a career as an editor and a writer both in her native England and in her adopted country of Australia. Writing mainly for a juvenile audience, she has produced picture books, young adult novels, retellings of myths and folk tales from around the world, and a miscellany of story collections. Writing for adults, she has produced two popular novels, also read by teens: the speculative history *Jane Austen in Australia,* published in the United States as *Antipodes Jane,* and the historical romance *The Quade Inheritance.* As an editor, she has worked for the publishers Bodley Head and William Collins in England, as well as for Angus & Robertson, Hodder & Stoughton, *Reader's Digest,* and the University of Queensland Press in Australia; she has served as children's editor at most of these houses. From both sides of the editorial desk, Ker Wilson has produced a long list of publications.

Knights, witches, wizards, and Gaelic magic abound in these Scottish tales. (Cover illustration by Joan Kiddell-Monroe.)

"Like a number of publisher's editors who are also authors, I am never sure which facet of this double career should come first," she once told *SATA.* "As a writer, my primary interest is to tell a story, and time and again I find myself returning to the refreshing vigor of the world's oldest stories, folk tales—the springboard for all fiction, including the most sophisticated modern novel. As a publisher's editor, it is often very satisfactory to be able to suggest ideas which are not right for my own style of authorship to other writers, and see them used successfully."

Born in Sunderland, County Durham, England, in 1929, Ker Wilson grew up during the depression in a family that was in the shipbuilding industry. Luckier than other families, the Ker Wilson's maintained employment during those difficult years, though her father worked at a reduced salary. Growing up near the sea a few hours from Norway, Ker Wilson formed an early love for distant horizons and the charm and fantasy of imagined worlds. "From an early age I was always within hearing of stories and poetry," the author wrote in the *Something about the Author Autobiography Series* (SAAS). "My mother and my aunts read me bedtimes stories, and my father, who had spent his boyhood in India, loved to recite Rudyard Kipling's *Just So Stories.*" Another favorite childhood activity was visiting the toy shop managed by an uncle on Wednesday, which was early closing day. Then she would have the doll houses, the entire play land, to herself. "I was free to explore this magic territory, alone," she noted.

All this changed in 1939. The family moved to a London suburb when Ker Wilson's father became a chief research assistant for an aircraft company. "It seemed almost as though we had moved to a foreign country," Ker Wilson commented in *SAAS.* But there were benefits to this relocation: London, with all its museums and galleries, was only a subway trip away. Ker Wilson and her older half-sister attended the North London Collegiate School for Girls, where scholarship was emphasized and expectations were high. Graduates assumed careers in law, medicine, science, and the arts. Ker Wilson soon became editor of the school magazine. Working on the magazine suited her literary bent. "I knew that I wanted to write from an early age," the author reported to *SATA.* She had begun writing as early as primary school, when she composed plays and had them performed at the school. "My father wrote erudite scholarly works on engineering science, and I used to accompany him on visits to his publishers, from time to time. This is how I became interested in publishing, as well, from an early age."

Soon events from the larger world intruded; England went to war in 1939 and the Blitz began the following year. The Ker Wilsons slept in an air raid shelter in their garden and spent much of their school time below ground as well. "The worst years of the war in England were 1940-43," Ker Wilson wrote. "The air-raid siren sounded by day as well as by night, and at school we spent quite a lot of our time in the huge air-raid shelter below the new building." At home, after a night spent in the air-raid shelter, the family would emerge to find the lawn "littered with pieces of shrapnel from the thunderous gunfire." The war had a profound influence on Ker Wilson, as she noted in *SAAS:* "To spend one's childhood in a time of war, amid bombing raids and with the very real threat of invasion from across the English Channel, gave those growing years an extra dimension which contained an undeniable element of excitement, but, more importantly, somehow emphasized one's significance as a human being." As a result, she felt "an uplifting awareness of people united in a common cause, with the absolute conviction that we were striving against the power of evil." She would draw upon this inspiration later in her novel *Last Year's Broken Toys.*

After the war, and failing to gain a scholarship to study English or history, Ker Wilson went to a secretarial college. "But now I was determined to carve out a career in book publishing—as well as to become a published writer myself," she wrote. She first took a position at Oxford University Press, ultimately becoming a junior editor in the children's book section. During these years she also became familiar with all aspects of the publishing business, from editing to typography and book design. She also joined the ranks of published writers, contributing *Scottish Folk Tales and Legends* to the Oxford University Press "Myths and Legends" series. Next, she moved on as managing editor of the children's book list at Bodley Head. From Bodley Head, Ker Wilson went to William Collins, where she was the managing editor of the children's division. But by 1961, with two daughters and a distinguished publishing career, Ker Wilson decided to leave Collins and get on with her own writing.

Her first novel for teenagers, *Path-through-the-Woods,* was published in 1958 and gave her the confidence to strike out on her own as a writer. The novel deals, on one level, with the position of women in society. The story behind a patchwork quilt, the novel is a series of vignettes from Victorian life with a young girl breaking tradition to become a pioneering female doctor. A contributor to the *St. James Guide to Children's Writers* noted that the "middle-class atmosphere is well conveyed" in this novel. Ker Wilson also wrote many titles on fairy tales from around the world before turning her hand to a second novel. Also dealing with the social issue of women's rights, *The Lovely Summer* appeared in 1960. Here Ker Wilson focuses on suffragettes and the enfranchisement of women. The "lovely summer" of the title was the summer of 1914, when World War I began. "This is a convincing and readable book," noted the *St. James Guide to Children's Writers* writer.

Moving to a house in Surrey, Ker Wilson published several more volumes in the next few years: *Beloved of the Gods, Last Year's Broken Toys,* and *A Story to Tell: Thirty Tales for Little Children.* Ancient Rome and the destruction of Pompeii is at the center of *Beloved of the Gods,* while Ker Wilson's own experiences in World War II inform *Last Year's Broken Toys,* an episodic novel with dozens of characters but with the war itself taking center stage. *A Story to Tell* was written for her

children and has become a popular standard for radio broadcasts and television adaptations.

Moving to Australia in 1965, Ker Wilson found new inspiration in her adopted country. She quickly saw that there were few books available on the shelves for children with stories told from an Australian or Aboriginal point of view. She began writing such books herself. *A Family Likeness* is a dual tale, looking at the lives of a contemporary Australian girl, Debbie, and her nineteenth-century ancestors during the Australian gold rush. "The starting off point for this story occurred," Ker Wilson recalled, "when I visited a friend who told me that the small looking-glass in my bedroom had been used by her great-great-grandmother in a tent on the goldfields." Another popular story collection also followed, *Hiccups and Other Stories: Thirty Tales for Little Children.*

Soon, however, Ker Wilson found herself back in publishing, as an editor for Angus & Robertson, to produce a children's list of international quality that also focused on Australian and Asian themes. Further work in publishing took Ker Wilson from Adelaide to Sydney to work with Hodder & Stoughton and then *Reader's Digest* in the Condensed Books division. After what she thought would be a final retirement from editing in 1984, she took up writing again full time, but returned to publishing for one last stint. This time she worked for the University of Queensland Press in the young adult and newly formed children's sections.

Throughout these years, Ker Wilson was pursuing the dual career of writer and editor, retelling folk tales from around the world and compiling story collections. One of her most popular children's titles has been *Acacia Terrace,* a history of one corner of Sydney. Built in 1860, this neighborhood has undergone many changes over the years. Ker Wilson tells the story of this neighborhood through its buildings and the people who lived there. "Will the saga close with its demolition, or is there a chance for it to be restored?" asked Susan Wolfe in a *Wilson Library Bulletin* review of the book. "Listen to an old house's memories—a story waiting to be heard." Shirley Wilton, writing in *School Library Journal,* felt that it "is refreshing to have this glimpse of Australia and its history."

Working as compiler and editor, Ker Wilson assembled a potpourri of Australian tales and poetry for *Illustrated Treasury of Australian Stories and Verses for Children,* an "excellent anthology" that offers "a valuable perspective on Australian culture," according to Belle Alderman in *Booklist.* Jeanette Larson commented in *School Library Journal* that "overall the collection offers a good balance of material not readily available in other sources." Two of her popular retellings in picture book format are *The Turtle and the Island* and *Wishbones.* The first is the story of how Papua New Guinea was brought up from the bottom of the ocean by an ambitious turtle and also how the native people of the island came to live there. Adapted from a Papuan myth, the story is "a classic type of creation myth," according to Sonja Bolle, writing in the *Los Angeles Times Book Review*. With *Wishbones* Ker Wilson retells a folk tale from China that is something of a Cinderella motif. Betsy Hearne, reviewing the book in *Bulletin of the Center for Children's Books,* noted Ker Wilson's "ironic twist at the end," while *School Library Journal* critic John Philbrook felt the book was a "clever retelling."

Ker Wilson has also written two novels for adults that have proven popular with adult audiences. Her *Antipodes Jane* tells the what-if story of Jane Austen down under when she accompanies her uncle and aunt (accused of shoplifting); it is also the tale of a lost love in Australia. Mixing some fact with a great deal of historical fiction (Austen was never in Australia), Ker Wilson came up with a "vastly entertaining" story, according to John Espey in the *Los Angeles Times Book Review*. A writer for *Kirkus Reviews* felt that though this "fictional fling" might be "irritating to Janites," Ker Wilson nonetheless "has produced an amusing and even illuminating view of Australia's colonial beginnings." *Times Literary Supplement* contributor Lindsay Duguid, reviewing the English publication of the same book, titled *Jane Austen in Australia,* concluded that the novel "offers some rewarding contrasts; incongruity is part of its appeal."

Ker Wilson's *The Quade Inheritance* began life as an attempt at a spoof gothic, but it emerged as a straight historical story set in 1860s England, with reverberations both in Australia and America. The story of the acquisition and continued possession of a perfect country house over several centuries, "this captivating gothic ... throbs with the singleminded malevolence of a possessive gentlewoman," character Imogen Quade, according to a reviewer for *Publishers Weekly*. Reviewing the same novel in *School Library Journal,* Keddy Outlaw noted that the book was written in a "crisp literary style, with certain gothic overtones and vivid detail," and it "moves through the lives of its characters with compelling sureness."

Whether retelling folk tales and myths from around the world, writing children's novels and short stories, dealing with more adult themes in novels and nonfiction, or compiling the work of others, Ker Wilson has always maintained an editor's eye for detail and audience. She has combined the skills of able editor and creative writer in her fifty books for both children and adults, but children's books remain closest to her heart. "Both as a children's writer and as an editor, I see children's literature as a great force for international understanding," she told *SATA*. "My work with children's writing has taken me all over the world, and I have seen this branch of literature grow and develop significantly in extent and depth."

Biographical and Critical Sources

BOOKS

Something about the Author Autobiography Series, Volume 18, Gale (Detroit, MI), 1994, pp. 165-184.

St. James Guide to Children's Books, fifth edition, St. James (Detroit, MI), 1999.

PERIODICALS

Booklist, October 19, 1988, Belle Alderman, review of *The Illustrated Treasury of Australian Stories and Verses for Children,* p. 423; April 15, 1989, p. 1435; February 15, 1990, p. 90; January 15, 1991, p. 1033.

Bulletin of the Center for Children's Books, February, 1994, Betsy Hearne, review of *Wishbones,* p. 204.

Kirkus Reviews, April 15, 1985, review of *Antipodes Jane,* p. 350; September 15, 1990, p. 1334.

Los Angeles Times Book Review, July 21, 1985, John Espey, review of *Antipodes Jane,* pp. 1, 6; January 27, 1991, Sonja Bolle, review of *The Turtle and the Island,* p. 8.

Magpies, May, 1994, p. 27; July, 1994, p. 24; September, 1999, p. 20; November, 1999, p. 29.

New York Times Book Review, July 21, 1985, p. 12.

Observer, November 25, 1990, p. 6.

Publishers Weekly, April 5, 1985, p. 65; March 3, 1989, review of *The Quade Inheritance,* p. 87; September 13, 1993, p. 128.

School Library Journal, April, 1988, Jeanette Larson, review of *The Illustrated Treasury of Australian Stories and Verses for Children,* p. 111; September, 1989, Keddy Outlaw, review of *The Quade Inheritance,* p. 286; March, 1990, Shirley Wilton, review of *Acacia Terrace,* p. 233; January, 1991, p. 87; March, 1994, John Philbrook, review of *Wishbones,* p. 219.

Spectator, January 19, 1985, p. 23.

Times Educational Supplement, November 2, 1990, p. R4; September 10, 1993, p. 11.

Times Literary Supplement, October 26, 1984, Lindsay Duguid, review of *Jane Austen in Australia,* p. 1224.

Wilson Library Bulletin, September, 1990, Susan Wolfe, review of *Acacia Terrace,* p. 4.

—*Sketch by J. Sydney Jones*

*   *   *

KIERSTEAD, Vera M. 1913-

Personal

Born March 14, 1913, in Bainbridge, IN; daughter of George E. (an agriculturalist) and Nelly Bernice (a homemaker; maiden name, Hillis) Knauer; married Roger H. Kierstead (died May 26, 1983); married Robert H. Farber (an educator and university administrator), June 26, 1998. *Education:* DePauw University, B.S.Mus.; Villanova University, M.S.Mus; certified by the Famous Artists School and the Institute of Children's Literature. *Politics:* Democrat. *Religion:* Methodist. *Hobbies and other interests:* Choral music, piano, oil painting, gardening.

Addresses

Home and office—210 West Poplar St., Greencastle, IN 46135. *E-mail*—rfarber@CCRTC.com.

Vera M. Kierstead

Career

Worked as a music teacher at a school in Radnor, PA for many years. DePauw Festival Chorus, member; also served as pianist at a retirement village and as art director at a senior citizens' center; active with local council for the aging. *Member:* American Guild of Organists, American Association of Retired Persons, P.E.O. Sisterhood, Mu Phi Epsilon.

Awards, Honors

Freedoms Foundation Award for *Jamie's Journey.*

Writings

Jamie's Journey: An Early American Adventure, Dorrance (Pittsburgh, PA), 2000.

Author of musical plays.

Work in Progress

Research for a sequel to *Jamie's Journey;* adapting four historical plays (previously produced) into books.

Sidelights

Vera M. Kierstead told *SATA:* "The eagerness of my students and the interest of present readers has encouraged me to keep writing early American stories."

Biographical and Critical Sources

ON-LINE

Amazon.com, www.amazon.com/ (August 26, 2000).

*   *   *

KIMELDORF, Martin (R.) 1948-

Personal

Born April 3, 1948, in Eugene, OR; son of Donald (a scientist) and Fay (a homemaker) Kimeldorf; married August 5, 1976; wife's name, Judith (a teacher). *Education:* Portland State University, B.A., 1970, M.S. (education), 1979. *Politics:* "Left Center and Independent." *Religion:* "Personal." *Hobbies and other interests:* Carving, magic, cooking.

Addresses

Home—6705 Gold Creek Dr. S.W., Tumwater, WA 98512. *E-mail*—martinkim@aol.com.

Career

Author.

Awards, Honors

Literary award from *Career Management Journal;* educator award from Washington Special Needs Group; various playwriting awards.

Writings

FOR YOUNG ADULTS

Pathways to Leisure (nonfiction), Meridian Education, 1989.
Pathways to Work (nonfiction), Meridian Education, 1989.
Creating Portfolios for Success in School, Work, and Life (nonfiction), Free Spirit Publishing (Minneapolis, MN), 1994.
Exciting Writing, Successful Speaking: Activities to Make Language Come Alive (nonfiction), Free Spirit Publishing, 1994, Kids In Between (Ballwin, MO), 1999.
A Teacher's Guide to Exciting Writing, Successful Speaking: Activities to Make Language Come Alive (nonfiction), Free Spirit Publishing (Minneapolis, MN), 1994.

FOR ADULTS

(With Rod Lathim) *Open Auditions: Scripts and Methods for Theatre by, with, and for Handicapped Individuals,* Ednicks Communications (Portland, OR), 1982.

Special Needs in Technology Education: A Resource Guide for Teachers, Davis Publications (Worcester, MA), 1984.

Job Search Education, Educational Design, 1988.

Write into a Job, Meridian, 1990, PublishingOnline.com, c. 2000.

Educator's Job Search, National Education Association, 1993.

Serious Play: A Leisure Wellness Guidebook, foreword by Richard Nelson Bolles, Ten Speed Press (Berkeley, CA), 1994, PublishingOnline.com, 2000.

Portfolio Power: The New Way to Showcase All Your Job Skills and Experiences, foreword by Joyce Lain Kennedy, Peterson's (Princeton, NJ), 1997, PublishingOnline.com, 2000.

Grandfriends Project, Fairview Press, 1999.

FOR ADULTS; ONLINE

Authoring Your Days, PublishingOnline.com, 1999.

A Bad Boy's Cookbook, PublishingOnline.com, 1999.

Bike Notebook, PublishingOnline.com, 1999.

Bike-a-Demics, PublishingOnline.com, 1999.

Camping on the Edge, PublishingOnline.com, 1999.

Cycle Journal, PublishingOnline.com, 1999.

The Last Thing I Build, PublishingOnline.com, 1999.

Write Off the Page, PublishingOnline.com, 1999.

Friends across the Divide: Creating Community and Learning Experiences One E-mail at a Time, PublishingOnline.com, 2000.

Also author of essays, plays, and nonfiction published by PublishingOnline.com.

Work in Progress

Gourmet Aging, Flourishing in Your Second Career.

Sidelights

Martin Kimeldorf told *SATA:* "I write about things that interest me, then I go find a publisher. It's a backwards approach, but it suits me just fine. I am now interested in how we provide lifelong learning to people after they retire."

* * *

KIMENYE, Barbara 1940(?)-

Personal

Born c. 1940 in Uganda. *Education:* Educated in Uganda.

Addresses

Home—38 Florence St., London N1, England.

Career

Writer. Worked as private secretary for government of the Kabaka of Buganda; journalist and columnist with

Uganda Nation (Kampala); social worker in London, 1974—.

Writings

FOR CHILDREN

The Smugglers, illustrated by Roger Payne, Thomas Nelson, 1966.

Moses, illustrated by Rena Fennessy, Oxford University Press, 1967.

Moses and Mildred, illustrated by Fennessy, Oxford University Press, 1967.

Moses and the Kidnappers, illustrated by Fennessy, Oxford University Press, 1968.

Moses in Trouble, illustrated by Fennessy, Oxford University Press, 1968.

The Winged Adventure, illustrated by Terry Hirst, Oxford University Press, 1969.

Moses in a Muddle, illustrated by Fennessy, Oxford University Press, 1970.

Moses and the Ghost, illustrated by Fennessy, Oxford University Press, 1971.

Paulo's Strange Adventure, illustrated by Olga J. Heuser, Oxford University Press, 1971.

Set in Africa, Paulo's Strange Adventure *begins when he falls off a ladder onto a lorry. (Written by Barbara Kimenye and illustrated by Olga J. Heuser.)*

Moses on the Move, illustrated by Mara Onditi, Oxford University Press, 1973.

Martha the Millipede, Oxford University Press, 1973.

Moses and the Penpal, illustrated by Onditi, Oxford University Press, 1973.

Moses, the Camper, illustrated by Onditi, Oxford University Press, 1973.

The Runaways, illustrated by Onditi, Oxford University Press, 1973.

Sarah and the Boy, Oxford University Press, 1973.

Moses in a Mess, illustrated by George Mogaka, Heinemann Kenya, 1991.

The Mating Game, Macmillan, 1992.

The Money Game, Heinemann, 1992.

Kayo's House, Macmillan, 1995.

Moses and the Movie, Macmillan, 1996.

Beauty Queen, East African Educational (Nairobi, Kenya), 1997.

Prettyboy; Beware, East African Educational, 1997.

SHORT STORIES

Kalasanda, illustrated by N. Kagwa, Oxford University Press, 1965.

Kalasanda Revisited, Oxford University Press, 1966.

FICTION; FOR ADULTS

The Gemstone Affair, Thomas Nelson, 1978.

The Scoop, Thomas Nelson, 1978.

OTHER

The Modern African Vegetable Cookbook, Kenway (Nairobi, Kenya), 1997.

Sidelights

Barbara Kimenye is well known in Africa for her column in *Uganda Nation,* a newspaper based in the Nairobi area. In addition to her journalistic endeavors, Kimenye has published a number of books for children, featuring subjects ranging from schoolboys to a confused millipede who learns that millipedes do not wear shoes. As an author of children's stories, however, Kimenye is best known for her "Moses" series of boys' adventure tales. Beginning with *Moses* and *Moses and Mildred* in 1967 and including a host of other books spanning more than two decades, the collection centers on a young boy full of spunk and energy who attends a school designed to care for those who are unable to attend more reputable institutions.

Moses and his friends encounter all sorts of trying situations, usually resulting in clashes with authority. Kimenye offers a sympathetic portrayal of boys in a negative environment, attempting to illustrate that some boys are not necessarily bad, but merely mischievous or the victims of circumstance. *Twentieth-Century Children's Writers* contributor Mabel D. Segun observed, "With her humorous style Kimenye manages to keep everything in proportion. The boys' escapades are narrated with indulged amusement, most of them being simply unfortunate, not wicked." At the same time, Kimenye demonstrates the difference between well-meaning boys such as Moses and his friends, and truly bad boys such as the bully Magara. "The adventures of Moses and his friends are most exciting," continued Segun, "and sound so probable that the reader is drawn into the stories. This is why the books have been so successful.... Kimenye is at her best when she writes stories with an authentic African background about real people whose trials and tribulations she portrays with human understanding."

Biographical and Critical Sources

BOOKS

Twentieth-Century Children's Writers, 4th edition, St. James Press, 1995; 5th edition, 1999.

PERIODICALS

African Studies Review, September, 1976.*

*   *   *

KURCZOK, Belinda 1978-

Personal

Surname is pronounced Kur-zok; born February 11, 1978, in Armidale, New South Wales, Australia; daughter of Anton (an electronics technician) and Lynette Ann (a dressmaker; maiden name, Melbourne) Kurczok. *Education:* TAFE, Hobart Institute, associate diploma, 1996. *Religion:* Jehovah's Witness. *Hobbies and other interests:* Bush walking, reading, taxidermy, music, bookbinding, sewing.

Addresses

Home—83 Kingstons Rd., Koonya, Tasmania 7187, Australia. *E-mail*—kurczok_belinda@hotmail.com.

Career

Artist, 1996—. Tasmanian Devil Park and Wildlife Rescue Centre, Taranna, Australia, shop assistant and animal rescue worker, 1995—.

Awards, Honors

Prize for paintings and drawings, Tasman Peninsula Art Society, 1994; Tomasetti Paper House Award, 1997, for achievement in printmaking; runner-up, Royal Hobart Show Art Award, 2000; shortlist, Australian Environment Children's Book of the Year, 2000, for *The Glow Worm Cave.*

Writings

ILLUSTRATOR

Anne Morgan, *The Glow Worm Cave,* Aboriginal Studies Press (Canberra, Australia), 1999.

Carey Denholm, *How Albert Saved Kathleen the Cat,* Kazzabooks, 1999.

Artwork of artist and illustrator Belinda Kurczok.

Work in Progress

Illustrations for a children's book, tentatively titled *Tiger Trail: A Tasmanian Epic,* by Patrick and Harriot Gambles, for Regal Press.

Sidelights

Belinda Kurczok told *SATA:* "I guess my interest in illustrating began with sketching horses and faces in primary school. Over the past ten years my sisters and orphaned marsupials that we've raised have also 'posed' to be painted. Prior to *The Glow Worm Cave,* I illustrated two unpublished books for fun.

"I love working alone, therefore generally at night, in country surroundings, and listening to music. I find inspiration in nature, sketching and observing the techniques and composition that other artists have used. I admire detailed and accurate paintings, but creation even more so, because along with looking beautiful, it works!

"There are many brilliant artists. Among my favorite are Jane Tanner and Raymond Ching.

"My advice to aspiring illustrators is to allow your work to be seen. Send examples to publishing companies and related associations. Enter open exhibitions, and keep learning and practicing."

L

LANNIN, Joanne (A.) 1951-

Personal

Born January 19, 1951, in Rockland, MA; daughter of William A. (an auto dealer) and Alice (a homemaker; maiden name, Swiriduk) Lannin; married Rikki Devin O'Neal (a writer), August 5, 1984; children: Michael Lannin O'Neal. *Education:* University of New Hampshire, B.A. (English education), 1973; Boston University, M.S. (journalism), 1985.

Addresses

Home—48 Fessenden Street, Portland, ME 04103. *E-mail*—jlannin@worldnet.att.net.

Career

Portland Press Herald, Portland, ME, sportswriter, reporter, 1980—; English teacher, 1973-78; journalism instructor, 1980, 1992-96; middle school girls' basketball coach, 1992—. *Member:* Portland Newspaper Guild, president, 1990—.

Awards, Honors

Maine Press Association, first place, 1984, for newspaper feature writing, 1986, for feature writing; New England Women's Press Association, best sportswriting, 1985.

Writings

Billie Jean King: Tennis Trailblazer (juvenile nonfiction), Lerner Publications (Minneapolis, MN), 1999.
The History of Basketball for Girls and Women: From Bloomers to Big Leagues (young adult nonfiction), Lerner Publications (Minneapolis, MN), 2000.

Magazine articles published in *Yankee Magazine, Boston Magazine,* and *Women's Sports and Fitness.*

Sidelights

Joanne Lannin told *SATA:* "I've been on a mission since I left teaching and began writing full-time 20 years ago to make people, kids especially, aware of the wonderful world and rich history of women's sports. I've always been an athlete and a lover of sports but as a kid growing up in the '50s and '60s, I didn't know about all the women who'd come before me, often playing in the shadows of sports, without publicity, fanfare, or remuneration—simply playing for the love of sports. Now there are many female athletes and careers in sports to aspire to, but I still want to let people know about the pioneers, the women who came before and in many ways made today's boom in women's sports possible."

* * *

LARSON, Jean Russell 1930-

Personal

Born July 25, 1930, in Marshalltown, IA; daughter of Charles Reed and Myrtle (Koester) Russell; married Richard Larson (deceased); married Harold Parks (deceased); children: (first marriage) M. Kathleen McCord, Richard Jr., David Larson, Rosemarie, William, Michael; (second marriage) Patrick, Daniel. *Education:* Attended Winthrop College (Rock Hill, SC), 1948-49; Buena Vista University, B.A. (English); Iowa State University, M.A. (English). *Politics:* Democrat. *Religion:* Roman Catholic. *Hobbies and other interests:* Genealogy, environment, animal welfare, protection of wildlife, classical music.

Addresses

E-mail—Reed@marshallnet.com.

Career

Educator and author. Former college instructor. County Red Cross, secretary. Former member of County Central

Democrat Committee, Democrat State Platform Committee, County Coalition for Social Justice (chair), Health and Nutrition Board, United Nations Year of the Child committee (county chair), Catholic Peace Movement, and St. Henry Library (chair).

Awards, Honors

Notable Book designation, American Library Association; Lewis Carroll Shelf Award; William Allen White award nominee.

Writings

Palace in Bagdad: Seven Tales from Arabia, illustrated by Marianne Yamaguchi, Scribner's (New York City), 1966.
The Silkspinners, illustrated by Uri Shulevitz, Scribner's (New York City), 1967.
Jack Tar, illustrated by Mercer Mayer, Macrae Smith (Philadelphia, PA), 1970.
The Glass Mountain and Other Arabian Tales, illustrated by Donald E. Cooke, Macrae Smith (Philadelphia, PA), 1971.
(Reteller) *The Fish Bride and Other Gypsy Tales,* illustrated by Michael Larson, Shoe String Press, 1999.

Contributor to *Scholastic News* and *Junior Great Books.* Poetry published in *Massachusetts Review, Michigan Quarterly,* and *Literary Review.*

Work in Progress

A collection of folk tales.

Sidelights

Former college professor Jean Russell Larson explained to *SATA:* "When I stopped teaching, I decided to write all the folk tales I grew up with. *The Fish Bride and Other Gypsy Tales* is the first of these collections.

"People from many parts of the world passed through Iowa and many settled here. My own storytelling family included Norwegians, Irish, Dutch, and some of the first settlers of Connecticut. I believe the preservation of folk tales is important, because those stories are culture-bearing and values-laden."

Biographical and Critical Sources

PERIODICALS

Booklist, November 1, 1972, review of *The Glass Mountain,* p. 245; November 1, 2000, John Peters, review of *The Fish Bride and Other Gypsy Tales,* p. 533.
Horn Book Magazine, November, 2000, Mary M. Burns, review of *The Fish Bride and Other Gypsy Tales,* p. 765.
Kirkus Review, May 1, 1972, p. 540; August 15, 2000, review of *The Fish Bride and Other Gypsy Tales,* p. 1199.
Library Journal, May 15, 1972, p. 1914.
School Library Journal, September, 2000, Ginny Gustin, review of *The Fish Bride and Other Gypsy Tales,* p. 251.

Autobiography Feature

Dom Lee

1959-

I grew up in Seoul, Korea. I was the youngest of three children. My family constantly moved from one home to another as did most others who lived in Korea at that time. We were poor then—my father was an artist and there were not many job opportunities for him—and the small rental costs rose higher and higher. Since we were moving very often over long distances, it was impossible for me to make friends. Drawing was my only form of entertainment. I drew upon the brightly colored walls of our landlords' properties. I was glad that my parents, instead of restraining me, painted their hosts' walls every time we departed. It

was there that I first stumbled upon art.

When I was three years of age, my father founded an art institute where he taught drawing and painting to his students. His business took an unexpected rise, and, two years later, our travelling came to an end. We settled into a house of our own. It was a one-storied, suburban dwelling with a backyard. It was so much larger than our previous ones, and that pleased me.

There, at our new home, I began to practice on actual paper. During the days of my first year there, I stayed indoors drawing and, unknowingly, developing into a shy,

Dom Lee, self-portrait, 1993.

lonesome character. My brother, Youl, who was three years older than me, stayed indoors as I did, but he was focused mainly on reading. However, my sister, Hae-kyung (now known as Helen), was five years older than me and was very playful and energetic. My father was a kind and gentle man. He was always polite to everyone. I thought it odd for my father to respect even the homeless when I was young. I later realized the equality between all people and understood his behavior. He never fought with my mother, who was also very nice and quiet. (She was also an artist at the time. Although she was merely an amateur back then, she has come much closer to being a professional now. She has, in fact, had an exhibition of her own.) She was never too busy for me and never got angry with me. That's what I liked about my parents. They weren't rich or famous, but they were great parents and were always there when I needed them.

I spent my days drawing. I got my inspiration from my surroundings. Whenever I saw something that I liked, I observed it carefully, returned home, and drew it. I rarely left out any detail of any subject. So when someone came around and saw my drawings, they didn't think it had been drawn by a youngster such as myself.

Another childhood hobby of mine was making my own little toys. I enjoyed drawing what I observed outside, then, if I chose, I might make a small paper figurine (later, I used wood to construct other things). I made small cars, ships, animals, and people, painting over them to make them look realistic, some things even to the point where they could drive one to the false belief that they were made by an excellent manufacturer. I preferred constructing my own childhood playthings since I could shape them into the forms of my choice.

I enjoyed touring my father's art room, but I didn't do so while he was working, for I didn't want to disturb him. I admired the realism of his sketches, but I couldn't understand his abstract paintings. There was also the clay that I enjoyed working with. I modeled ships, tanks, cars, planes, animals, and other things. As the days went on, I gradually began to explore the outside world. For the first time in my life, I started to make friends. I smelled flowers, rolled in the dirt, chased butterflies, and watched the oxen plowing the fields. I watched the sun set over the horizon, an orange and purple ring of fields and clouds all around it, and the sparkling stars in the void of the deep night sky. Such experiences were all so new to me, and that pleased me as well.

I met my very first friend at a local playground. She was about two years older than I. I cannot recall her real name but her nickname was "Jaap Jaap." She was very thin and had very large eyes and dark skin. We met while digging holes, linking tunnels in the sand, and chanting a children's rhyme. In this way we came to be friends. We remained close friends for two years; we met each other's families and visited each other's homes. But, when the time for my first admittance to elementary school drew near, she moved away. The night before she left, she visited my house. We played and had fun, but when her parents came to pick her up, the two of us parted in tears. At that point, I wondered if we would ever be reunited in the future. To this day, unfortunately, I have never met my old friend again.

It was here that I started to attend first grade. I had never received any previous school education, so it was my first time. My teachers fixed their eyes on me as I fixed my eyes on my mother, fearful of being left alone. It was hard for me to adjust to this new life. Everything was so confusing: announcements, assignments, tests, and quizzes. The teachers became stricter by the grade, the stress was

"*My mother, Young Sook Lee, my brother, Youl Lee, and me.*"

worse by the day. The one thing about school that I felt comfortable about was the art class. There lay my field of expertise, where I had confidence and where I won many contests. (Such contests were held during the spring and fall months when we were to prepare artwork at a specific location such as a famous park, palace, or other such landmark.) I attended extracurricular art classes to improve upon my skills and in order to challenge myself. I was encouraged by my teachers in such classes to take up a career as an artist. But I didn't receive my compliments for the pictures of an ordinary child, with big suns or stick figures. I drew lifelike people and realistic landscapes. At times, I was told that my pictures looked too professional to have been drawn by me. Perhaps by a mentor or a professional artist, people said, but as time went on, they finally believed that these were my works.

I made another very close friend here. His name was Nahm-soo Oh. He was as good a friend as my very first friend had been to me. And, just as before, he moved away. At this stage in my life, I could catch a bus ride to wherever my friend might have moved, as long as it wasn't too far away.

Unfortunately, instead of moving to another town or province, Nahm-soo and his family emigrated to Toronto, Canada. This time, however, he became my pen pal and I retained contact with him by mail for the next three years. But, as time went by, Nahm-soo became more and more accustomed to life in a North American country, so as his English became better and his native tongue grew worse, it became more difficult to write to one another. As the two of us moved to different homes, I attempted to keep in touch with him. It became harder and harder to do so each time one of us moved. Eventually, I lost contact with him entirely. And to this day, I have not seen him again, just as with my other very good friend. Today, I could have caught a plane to Canada or I might have been able to make a car ride there. I regret, now, having let another close friend slip out of my reach.

A few years later, I began to take up certain hobbies. I played sports such as baseball and soccer with my friends whenever I was out of school. We formed teams and scheduled days for practice like the teams that were supported by the local school systems did, against whom we often competed. I also enjoyed games of table tennis. I frequently spent several months on one sport (when I really got interested in a sport, I concentrated on it for a very long time and didn't do much else other than that sport) before realizing that I could not depend on a hobby for the rest of my life.

Even with all of my other interests, I was mainly attracted to stamp collecting. While my friends spent their money on snacks and comic books, I spent most of my money and my time on my stamp collection. At such times I was glad that my parents didn't mind that I spent more time on my hobbies than my school work. Stamp collecting stayed as one of my greatest joys until I reached high school.

Another important hobby of mine was, of course, art. I enjoyed drawing the faces of my friends. Whenever I made a new friend, I drew his or her face (quite accurately), signed it, and gave it to the person (some of my old classmates from those days might yet have my old artwork). Some portraits took a very short time—say, ten to

"My father, Myung Eui Lee," about 1962.

twenty minutes—and came out splendidly; others took much longer—maybe about an hour or so—and they hardly looked like my subjects at all.

By the time I reached high school, my sister was already attending a college and my brother, being only three years older than I, had just recently entered one to start off his future career as a doctor. I started to look for something to major in, something that I would enjoy. I knew art to be the right choice for me. However, my father was worried about me becoming an artist. He knew from his own experience that it wouldn't be easy for an artist to gain a steady income. I, myself, was curious as to whether or not I had other talents that I had not yet realized. So, I looked into other fields in a search for something better. I thought about sports and music and spent two years on them. They turned out to be a waste. In my last year of high school, I knew that I would have to find something. There was nothing left for me but art. So, with the time I had before I graduated, I had my father aid me in preparing for the university of my choice at his art institute. I wanted to attend the College of Fine Arts. It was at my father's institute where I became friends with a former classmate, Keunhee Kim, who also had her eyes on the College of Fine Arts. I remembered her from elementary and high school, though we weren't very close back then. All we knew about each other were our names and our faces, but meeting someone familiar, one that had the same major and university in mind, started a friendship.

During that last year of high school, I realized that I had not efficiently spent my years in school on education. With twelve months before graduation, I studied harder than I had ever done before. In order to improve my skills, I

concentrated on everything that I wanted to capture in my artwork. I studied the shape of the objects in my environment, drawing the lines of the faces of my family members and my classmates in my mind, even looking at the bites that I took out of the food that I ate. I used every minute of every day, save when I slept, to work on my technique. All in all, every moment that I spent practicing then helped me become what I am today.

One of my main reasons for choosing the College of Fine Arts of Seoul National University was because it was the best art college in the country. Aside from that fact, I also wanted to be with Keunhee, with whom I had made a strong friendship by then. I didn't want for us to be separated as I had been from my other childhood companions.

Competition for admittance into the university was very stiff. The college was very selective and sent new students through several examinations that included all of the various subjects taught in school: Korean language and literature, English, world history, geometry, mathematics, biology, algebra, and even physical education. But, most importantly, they examined your technique (at the College of Fine Arts of Seoul National University, as with any other art college in Korea, one's technique or individual style was as important as one's portfolio here in the United States). They tested our technique in representational art and compositional design for two days, and we were given three hours to complete each test on a drawing pad with sheets of paper that were twenty by thirty inches (for drawing) or fifteen by twenty inches (for painting). Every year, they changed the subjects between human models and Greek or Roman statues when drawing. The materials required also varied by the year, perhaps from pencils to charcoal and oil paints to watercolor. This test was valued the highest among all the tests that one took in order to enter the school. These tests felt as though they were of no use at the time, as if all they were doing was ruining my

The family at the new house, 1967: (clockwise) Dom working on a clay ship at the table; his sister, Helen; father, Myung Eui; mother, Young Sook, holding brother Youl; and Aunt Sook Young Park.

technique by concentrating too hard on one subject and not giving enough attention to another. These tests differed so much from the tests taken here in the United States. Here, tests are taken throughout the course of one's life as a student to determine his or her future. But where I was at the time in Korea, two days' worth of tests decided my future. Imagine the fear and frustration that one would experience if the conditions weren't right or if they didn't have enough time. That was how I felt then. There were students who had completed their high school years and failed at attending an art college more than half a dozen times before deciding to attend my father's art institute to improve their skills before trying again. (Many students usually gave up after a second and third failed attempt, though there were others stubborn and determined enough to keep trying, even after seven and eight tries.)

When it came time, I entered the College of Fine Arts of Seoul National University. What made it an even more joyous victory was that I entered with Keunhee. But my entrance lost its glory when I had to adapt myself to another life. As before it wasn't easy. Before I entered the College of Fine Arts, I thought it to be an exciting and triumphant experience, but I took a long time experimenting with different techniques. I tried sculpting, drawing, painting, print making, and even oriental brush painting. None of them fit me. None of them fit my needs or my desires. None of them felt right. Another problem was that I was paying more attention to Keunhee than my responsibilities at the college. So, after two years of confusion, I finally left to serve my time in the army. Although I still had another two years left at the college, I felt that if I continued the way I was performing at the time, my entire college experience would be ruined. I had to serve my time in the army at some point in my life, anyhow. This, I decided, was the best time to go.

I wondered what I would achieve in the army and whether or not I would come out as a new man. In a way, I welcomed the experience of being in the army. Still, it was an odd situation for me. As before, I had trouble adjusting to a strange environment. I met many different people and it was all new. Most of those three years felt like three years as a prisoner, and the only things that I looked forward to were the visits from Keunhee and the day when I would finally leave the service. When my three years in the army ended, I wasn't quite sure whether to think of the whole period as insane or exciting—perhaps both.

During the years of servitude in the army, I was engaged to marry Keunhee, who had become more than just a friend to me. After my three years there, in the few months that I had left before I had to return to complete my two years in college, I married her. She was a friend in my work and a friend in my life. We taught and helped each other in our times of need. She was there for me as much as art was there for me from my childhood, and both are equally important.

During my remaining years in college, I focused on narrative and realistic form. Most of my paintings included cityscapes and the people of Seoul. And though oil paints and acrylic paints did not feel right for me, I continued on with those methods.

"A picture of me, enjoying the scent and sight of a flower," about 1969.

At that time, I was also involved in my father's work. When I graduated, I knew that I would have to run his art institute. My sister moved to the United States through marriage, and my brother became a doctor. I knew that my father would have to pass his work down to me if he wanted to keep the business in the family. And I accepted that, but I wondered whether it was the right line of work for me. I thought to myself, What if there is someone better than I am, and what if I can't handle it? I had a family that I had to take care of as well. The institute would give me financial support, but I didn't want to live out the rest of my life managing a business. I wanted to become an artist. Yet, I knew how important it was to my father who had owned the business for thirty years.

At first I thought that I could do both, but after the first five years there, I realized that I would have to sacrifice one of them—I chose to give up art. However, as time went on, I felt that I shouldn't have given up my dream of becoming an artist. And with the encouragement from Keunhee, I gathered enough confidence to become an artist. I told my father of my proposal, and though at first he was reluctant, he soon agreed to close the institute. Its succession was later given to one of its early graduates. At first, we both regretted the decision. However, after much time, thinking, and more risks, giving up the institute seemed like a good choice. It was because of this that both my father and I were able to become artists.

I wished to paint narrative artwork and to visualize stories about people, especially those who live in the city. Their surroundings constantly change as the city grows and expands, but they don't. They are usually the subject of my artwork. I wanted to share my artwork and spread them around, but such works were inaccessible to many people. Illustration, on the other hand, provided the consumers with a much easier and cheaper way of seeing my work, but I wanted to do fine art as well as illustrations. I became very fond of books dealing with American illustration. I heard that there were many American artists who did both fine art and illustrations. I wished to learn more about the styles of such American artists. I needed more information on colleges where I could graduate from a master's course in illustration and fine arts. I learned that the best place to go was to the School of Visual Arts M.F.A. Program

"Illustration as Visual Essay." Its location, New York City, was the center of illustration. Besides, my sister, Helen, lived there and encouraged me to come. Now, I asked myself this question: Can I leave for New York City? I had a family—my wife, my six-year-old son, and my three-year-old daughter—to take care of. I worried about whether or not they would survive. Another problem was the fact that my English was very poor. However, Keunhee encouraged me to go to New York City. It was a high risk and anything could go wrong at any time, but I thought to myself, Life is a gamble sometimes, and this is one of those times.

On the flight to New York City, I looked back on my life. Here I am, I thought. Here I am, thirty years old, with my family in a plane in the year 1990. So much of my life has gone by so quickly, and so much of it has been a waste. With almost every decision that I had made, there followed a negative result. I'm leaving that life behind. I have a new life to live, a family to take care of, and a country to be explored. Soon I'll land on a nation exotic to me, one that I've never actually seen, but only heard and read about.

During the summer of 1990, we rented a small room in an apartment. We all had trouble adjusting to our new life here. The single window parallel to the entrance gave me a negative feeling, as though I was trapped inside. It made me uncomfortable. I felt this way because in Korea, in my native land, I was able to afford a nice home for my family. But here I was, in a new land. I was just a student, so was worried that I would not be able to provide for my family. The window was supposed to give a feeling of enlightenment, but it didn't. Nevertheless, Keunhee and I stuck to our plans to remain here for a few years to study and then return to Korea.

Our first year in New York City was a hard one. My son had trouble adjusting to a new school system and having to make new friends, I was usually at the School of Visual Arts, and we had problems when we had to speak English. The whole family had to learn the language of this new land, and I had to adjust the subjects of my art to match my environment. But eventually, as time went on, we got used to our new home. I was lucky enough to be

The author's wife, Keunhee Lee, as a college student, 1977.

taught by someone like Marshall Arisman, the chairman of the M.F.A. Programs. He was a great painter and an illustrator and he inspired me a good deal. I wanted to be as good an artist as he was. And being able to see great masterpieces in person and to walk into museums like the Metropolitan Museum of Art, the Museum of Modern Arts, and the Whitney Museum of American Art furthered my inspiration, as did the fact that I lived in New York City, the center of the world's art community at the time. I enjoyed the works of artists like Vermeer, Rembrandt, George Bellows, and Andrew Wyeth and the museums' retrospective exhibitions dedicated to such artists as Rucian Freud and Edward Hopper. It was all so much better than mere books and pictures.

In my earlier days as an artist, I painted on canvas with oil and acrylic paint, but such two-dimensional artwork did not satisfy me. So I sought a new form of art. I thought back to my childhood, to the times when I would model realistic objects out of clay. While going to the College of Fine Arts of Seoul National University, I enjoyed printmaking, especially etching. In New York City, I sought a technique that would be right for me, but I wasn't sure what that technique was. I went to Pearl Paint for the supplies I might need. I was overwhelmed at the immensity of size and the variety of material provided by the five-storied building. I was sure that I would find just what I needed.

With my new supplies, I began to experiment with different techniques and materials. In this way, I developed my encaustic wax technique by the second semester of the M.F.A. Program, in which I start by covering paper with a thick coating of melted beeswax. After it cools down, I take a tool and scratch out images into the dark box. Afterwards, I paint over it with colored pencils or oil paint or even paint the paper before I cover it with the wax. When it is finished, the artwork has a slight three-dimensional feel to it, though it remains on a two-dimensional surface. I knew that this was the technique that I was looking for. It was comfortable and gave me the feel of both painting and sculpturing.

Around the end of the second semester, I held a solo exhibition called "Generations" at the school's gallery. It was based on a story that I had heard of an old Chinese man who lived through many hardships and died a lonesome death in a dark corner of Chinatown. This was my first official opportunity to prepare artwork using my ever developing technique. (I originally thought of etching for the project, but I found that my wax technique was better and more suitable than etching.)

In order to research my subject, I went sightseeing in Chinatown. While there, my surroundings gave me a familiar feeling. The people's faces reminded me of those in Korea, and the signs made me think of the Chinese calligraphy that I had seen on the signs in Seoul. After living for about a year apart from a community with people from my country, it felt a little bit like home. It wasn't the best of the feelings that I had gotten from the time I arrived here up to this point—like I was starving but had only gotten a taste of food. After all, they weren't of my people. Another factor that gave me mixed feelings was the irony of the fact that I couldn't communicate with the people. Here, I saw familiar faces, but I couldn't get through to the people since I didn't know their language.

"Urban Landscapes, 1996."

Before the show, I was nervous, because it was the first solo exhibition I had ever had in my life. I was worried that my guests wouldn't understand what I was trying to express through my artwork. I was worried that someone along the way might notice a flaw in my works. But I tried my best to keep myself from altering my pieces out of fear. The exhibition was a success and as I saw the admiration in the sightseers' faces, I gained more confidence in myself.

It was after my solo exhibition that I met Moe Foner, the executive director of 1199's Bread and Roses Cultural Project, a nonprofit organization. From him, I received an editorial illustration project for a cover story of *1199 News Magazine,* which was my first real commissioned job using my wax technique.

In the spring of 1991, my family and I moved out of Manhattan to the adjacent state of New Jersey. Our new home was in the small town of Demarest. One of the several reasons for our departure was because we needed more space. Compared to our previous one-bedroom-sized apartment space, our new home had several times more space for me, my wife, and my two children who grew ever taller. I also moved for my children's sake, for they had no place to play. My son's school may have been conveniently nearby, but there was no playground in which to run around and be active. My children had nowhere else nearby where they could be energetic; everywhere you turned, a car flashed by and there was no grass. Everything was just too

urban. But we knew that moving to a rural environment would solve these problems; the schools had playgrounds, there were trees and grass and a lovely pond of ducks. And my children would make many friends. Besides, the rent wasn't much different from what we had originally been paying in Manhattan. At the outset, I needed some time to adjust to life in the country, while I needed to be near the school that I attended. But as I became more and more accustomed to my new life, I found the routine much easier. I felt that sacrificing a small portion of myself for the rest of my family was simply the right thing to do. Even though I found my new home far better than my old one, when I look back to my life in Manhattan, I know that it was all worth it. I came out of there with more experience, more knowledge, and more skill. There, for the first time, while working and studying alongside complete strangers, isolated from family and friends, Keunhee and I found that we tended to look more into our true selves.

The program later held a group exhibition at the Art Directors' Club of New York City. Among the viewers of this exhibition was Arthur Levine, an editor for G. P. Putnam's Sons. He complimented me on my artwork and asked me if I would like to illustrate a children's book. Arthur introduced me to Philip Lee, publisher for Lee and Low Books. The company was just starting and was in search of new, talented illustrators. I was chosen to illustrate *Baseball Saved Us.* It was a story about a Japanese American boy who played baseball while confined to an internment camp with his family during World War II. I hadn't expected to become a children's book illustrator, but because of this project, I was carried over to my new line of work.

I was very impressed with Ken Mochizuki's manuscript *Baseball Saved Us.* When I first read of the main character's hardships, his obstacles reminded me of my own hard times and, more importantly, the troubles that my family experienced adjusting to their new life during their first year in America. Aside from these reasons, I've always liked the sport of baseball. I enjoyed playing the sport and watching the professional players playing baseball at the stadium. So I agreed to illustrate the book. I was busy preparing my workroom to set the mood of the setting of the story and in finding photographs from the time. I searched through bookstores and libraries, especially the

Dom Lee (left) with Moe Foner, Marshall Arisman, and Keunhee at Gallery 1199 in 1993.

New York Central Library. I looked through the photographs of internment camps that had been taken by Ansel Adams. Now that an appropriate environment had been laid out in my own home and most of the necessary resources were gathered, a new problem arose: a model. I needed someone to model for the part of the main character. At first, I attempted to use my son as a model, but he simply refused to take the job. For one thing, he had never liked baseball and, to this day, he still dislikes the sport. Luckily, I recalled that our next-door neighbor, Takeshi Kashima, routinely practiced baseball. He was of the right age, and he enjoyed the sport, not to mention the fact that he and the main character of *Baseball Saved Us* were both Japanese. He gladly agreed to model for the book.

I had my hands full as I prepared my artwork for the school's final graduation exhibition and my illustrations for *Baseball Saved Us*. The show was called "Contests" and included scenes based on fighting such as boxing, bullfighting, and cockfighting. I did my best to concentrate on both duties equally. The results of my divided attention were not what I had pictured: *Baseball Saved Us* was a big success, but my work at the graduation exhibition was not as good as it should have been.

After graduating, I sent the Contests series, which I used during my final exhibition at the School of Visual Arts, as a portfolio to many different magazine offices. I didn't have any luck there, but my job working for Lee and Low Books made up for that. *Baseball Saved Us* received the 1993 Parents' Choice Award, 1993 Choices Award from Cooperative Children's Book Center, Pick of the List award from the American Bookseller, and Best Multicultural Title, 1993 Cuffies Award from *Publishers Weekly,* and was translated into Japanese and Spanish. Through it, I gained an agent, a career, a green card, and exhibitions at the San Francisco International Airport Museum, the Society of Illustrators Museum of American Illustration, and others.

A few months after my graduation from the School of Visual Arts, my wife became a student of the M.F.A. Programs "Illustration as Visual Essay." And because of this, I had to switch duties with Keunhee. While she went to the School of Visual Arts, I worked on my illustrations and took care of the children. In this way, we took another gamble by staying here. We hadn't financially prepared for this. If we had returned home, we could have been with our family and we would have had better chances of getting steady jobs. And if we didn't return in time, it would be too late. Our children were getting more and more accustomed to their new lives. Even so, we knew of the hope that lay here for us. We thought of the benefits that would come in the future of staying in this country. In the end, we remained in Demarest.

With his son, Brian, and daughter, Eun, while traveling through the Korean countryside, 1994.

Keunhee's experience was better than mine. She had watched me perform my two years there, so she had a better idea of what she might go through than I did when I was a student. As I spent the next two years here with my wife, I learned new things from watching her performance as a student of the School of Visual Arts and old things that I had missed. It was as though we had both spent four years in study.

Around her first semester, Keunhee met Moe Foner. She met with him in hopes of gaining an editorial illustration project for *1199 News Magazine* as I had. To her surprise, Foner suggested that she hold an exhibition with me. It came as a shock to the both of us. It was an even greater opportunity than an editorial. The exhibition was supported in part by the New York City Department of Cultural Affairs, the Aaron Diamond Foundation, and the Joyce Mertz Gilmore Foundation.

The coming exhibition was titled "Urban-scapes: Images of New York City." It was the first major exhibition that either my wife or I had ever held and the perfect opportunity to develop my wax technique. I was determined to perfect my technique at that point and I did. I felt that New York City, the subject of much of my artwork, was like a quilt pieced together from thousands of different fabrics. Much like such a quilt, New York City harbored thousands of different people from different lands, people whose thoughts and purposes varied. Joy and sadness, excitement and nervousness, all of this I felt while walking down the streets of the huge metropolis. As I walked down the lonely paths, I asked myself several questions. "Why am I here?" I thought. "Why are these people here? And what are their goals in life within this city?" Life back in Seoul had prepared me for life in a large city. But somehow, this place felt as though it was even more urban than my old home. As I melt the hot wax for my artwork, I get the feeling that parts of my life somehow get mixed with the dark brown liquid when I pour it on the surface on which I would scratch out my thoughts and form them into descriptive images. The exhibition was a success. Our audience understood our art, and it helped to know that many of them, being immigrants like ourselves, might have known how we felt. When the show was over, I realized I had truly found my own form of art.

The Lafayette (Indiana) School Corporation and Purdue University's School of Education were sponsoring a nonprofit organization based on promoting the desire to read and learn in young children called TELL (Teachers Encouraging a Love of Literature). Every year, TELL selected three books and invited the authors and illustrators of those books to a workshop, and *Baseball Saved Us* was one of the books chosen. So, I made a trip to Lafayette. It was at the workshop that I met Ken Mochizuki for the very first time. I had spoken with him in the past, over the phone due to the long distance that separated the two of us, but this was the first time that I came face to face with the author of *Baseball Saved Us*. He looked to be of my age and we became friends quickly. Although we had just met (not including speaking over the phone), I felt as though he was an old friend whom I had not seen for a long time. We discussed the progress of our second upcoming book, *Heroes,* during the period of three days and four nights of the workshop.

By 1994, Keunhee graduated from the School of Visual Arts, and I had finished my second picture book for Lee and Low Books called *Heroes,* which tells of a Japanese American boy in the 1960s who learns of heroism from his father and his uncle. It was here that I used my son, Brian, as a model for the very first time. Even though he was just as reluctant as before (football wasn't one of his favorite sports either), he agreed to model for the new book. *Heroes* wasn't quite the success that *Baseball Saved Us* was, but it did receive several awards: the 1996 Teacher's Choice Award, the Notable Children's Book, Smithsonian, "Editor's Choice," San Francisco, and the Notable Children's Trade Book in the Field of Social Studies.

I also made an illustration for a book called *On the Wings of Peace,* a book that was published in the memory of the people who had perished during the Second World War in the bombings of the two Japanese cities of Hiroshima and Nagasaki and dedicated to reminding us just how important it is to keep peace, to which a group of sixty writers and illustrators contributed. My illustration was based on a story written by Ken Mochizuki about a survivor of the bombing of Hiroshima.

In 1995, I held an exhibition in Seoul. I separated my work into two groups, my children's book illustrations and artwork from my previous exhibition "Urban-scapes." The show was successful and my audience's responses pleased me. I was interviewed by many different newspapers and magazines. It felt good to be back in my native land after having lived five long years abroad.

During my stay in Seoul, I was contacted by a publisher, Gilbut Children's Publishing Company, who offered my wife and me a new project. So, after the exhibition, Keunhee and I traveled to China to meet with the author and do some research on the setting of the story, which happened to be in China. The story of the new book, *Fireworks,* took place in the late eighteenth century. When a young Korean girl was abandoned by her parents, she was raised by a Chinese family. At the time, many Korean people were victims of famine and the foreign invasions that plagued their native country and were forced to travel to other lands in order to survive. When *Fireworks* was printed, it was chosen to be one of the eighty selected books at the 1996 Bologna International Children's Book Fair. *Fireworks* was the first project where I worked with Keunhee on the illustrations.

After the completion of *Fireworks,* my agent suggested that my wife and I cooperate more often. Our teamwork resulted in four elementary school reading books for Macmillan/McGraw-Hill: *A Railroad on Gold Mountain* by Fay Chiang, *Flat as a Pancake* by Sheila Black, *Grandmother and I* by Anne Miranda, and *Quinto's Volcano* by Aileen Friedman. I also received another project, this time for book jackets for the book *After the War,* the story of Ruth Mendenberg, the sole survivor of her entire family, who attempts to smuggle a group of children from her village in Poland to Palestine, and its sequel, *The Garden,* from Simon and Schuster. After that, I did illustrations for *Cricket* magazine, as well as the cover illustration for the August 1997 issue. My most recent work was for *Passage to Freedom: The Sugihara Story.* It tells the true tale of a Japanese diplomat by the name of Chiune Sugihara, who saved the lives of thousands of Jews in Lithuania during

Dom Lee (far right) with wife Keunhee and Ho-Baek Lee, publisher of Gilbut Children, at Tiananmen Gate in Beijing, China, 1995.

World War II. I worked for the third time alongside my old colleague, Ken Mochizuki, with whom I worked on *Baseball Saved Us* and *Heroes.*

Two of my recent fine art exhibitions were "Purest Forms" and "Works on Paper." "Purest Forms" took place at the Park Avenue Armory in March 1997. I used paintings from my Urban-scapes series in both of them. I now found myself able to earn money through my illustrations and fine art exhibitions. I had a good response from my audience and I sold some paintings during both events. Up until that point, I had made a living mostly through illustrating children's books. But with these two exhibitions, I gained confidence that I could make money through both activities.

After "Purest Forms" and "Works on Paper," my most recent exhibition took place at the Elizabeth Stone Gallery in Birmingham, Michigan, a gallery based on the illustrations of children's books. I got the job after my father paid us a visit from Korea. He wished to see an old student who now works in Birmingham as a psychologist, whom he hadn't met in thirty years. My father met him on a rainy day. Doctor Kim suggested that, since there were few other places to go in the rain, they tour the Elizabeth Stone Gallery. They looked around and saw that it was full of children's books. There they met the owner of the gallery, Elizabeth Stone. The trio discussed my line of work and Elizabeth Stone became interested. She contacted me and asked me to hold an exhibition at her gallery. After the

workshop based on *Heroes,* I caught a flight from Detroit to return home. Before I left, I met Elizabeth Stone at the airport. I showed her my works as well as those done by Keunhee and I suggested that we hold a two-person exhibition at the Elizabeth Stone Gallery. She agreed with me and the show was set for the month of May of 1997. During the exhibition, the audience seemed mostly impressed with our preparation of the slide presentations. I came out with Keunhee to meet our guests at the exhibition. We met many different people and made many new friends.

I wanted to become a painter and an illustrator. I found that I could do both. As my life went on, I continued on my path surely and with confidence. While I was on my flight from Korea to the United States, I thought of my past life as a waste, but the more I think about it, the more I realize that I needed that part of my life as something to look back on. The choices that I made and the risks that I took were all a part of my experience. I'm glad that I had a family to support me and share my experience with. And I am very grateful for my children, Brian and Eun. They're both growing up to be good artists and have helped Keunhee and me in our work. They help me remember what it was like to be a child and serve as models for the illustrations. That is a part of my past that I enjoy remembering.

In my old life, I recall that almost everything that I sincerely prepared for didn't go the way that I had wanted it to, but instead, many of my successes in life came to me by chance or fate. In America, I was always given the chance to prepare for what needed to be done, and much of my success here came through good preparation. During the two years at the School of Visual Arts, I felt that I knew what I would be going through and was fully prepared for the tasks ahead. My time spent there turned out, from my point of view, much better than my time spent in Seoul. It was by chance that I found my own technique through experimentation. I had to sacrifice my old life in Korea, or I may never have discovered my art. It was also through the sacrifice of my father's art institute that I was able to become the artist that I am today. I never expected to illustrate children's books. I didn't think about becoming a resident of the United States when I first flew here. And yet, all of my fortune is somehow connected to my past. I first discovered art by drawing on walls as a child. If that hadn't happened to me, I may never have become an artist in the first place. I was never very good at talking to people, especially people that I didn't know, but through my art, I was able to speak as I wanted to. And it was my art that led me through my life to where I am now.

Writings

FOR CHILDREN; ILLUSTRATOR

Ken Mochizuki, *Baseball Saved Us,* Lee & Low, 1993.
Ken Mochizuki, *Heroes,* Lee & Low, 1995.

Works on Wax, Zamimazu, 1995.
Ken Mochizuki, *Passage to Freedom: The Sugihara Story,* Lee & Low, 1997.
Carol Matas, *The Garden,* Simon & Schuster, 1997.
Kirk Douglas, *Young Heroes of the Bible: A Book for Family Sharing,* Simon & Schuster, 1999.

FOR CHILDREN; ILLUSTRATOR WITH WIFE KEUNHEE LEE

Hae-sun Lee, *Fireworks,* Gilbut, 1996.
Sheila Black, *Flat as a Pancake,* Macmillan/McGraw-Hill, 1996.
Fay Chiang, *A Railroad on Gold Mountain,* Macmillan/McGraw-Hill, 1996.
Aileen Friedman, *Quinto's Volcano,* Macmillan/McGraw-Hill, 1996.
Anne Miranda, *Grandmother and I,* Macmillan/McGraw-Hill, 1996.
Lawrence McKay, et al., *Journey Home,* Lee & Low, 2000.

OTHER

Lee has held a number of exhibitions of his work and joint work with his wife, including: "Urban-scapes: Images of New York City," at 1199 Gallery, New York City, 1994, and in Seoul, Korea, 1995; "The Art of Dom and Keunhee Lee," at Elizabeth Stone Gallery, Birmingham, Michigan, 1997; and has participated in two exhibitions of Old Master to Contemporary, Park Avenue Armory, New York City, the Ninth Annual Works on Paper, 1997, and Tenth Annual Works, on Paper, 1998.

One of many contributing artists to *On the Wings of Peace,* Clarion, 1995. Also creator of book jackets, including *After the War* and *The Garden,* and editorial illustrations for *Cricket* magazine.

LETTS, Billie 1938-

Personal

Born May 30, 1938, in Tulsa, OK; daughter of Bill and Virginia (a secretary; maiden name, Barnes) Gipson; married Dennis Letts (a professor of English); children: Shawn, Tracy (son). *Education:* Attended Northeastern State College (now Northeastern Oklahoma State University), 1956-58; Southeast Missouri State College (now University), B.A., 1969; Southeastern Oklahoma State University, M.A., 1974.

Addresses

Home—Durant, OK. *Agent*—Elaine Markson, Elaine Markson Literary Agency, Inc., 44 Greenwich Ave., New York, NY 10011.

Career

Teacher and novelist. *Member:* Writers Guild of America, Authors Guild, Oklahoma Federation of Writers.

Awards, Honors

Walker Percy Award, 1993; Oklahoma Book Awards, 1995, for *Where the Heart Is,* and 1998, for *The Honk and Holler Opening Soon.*

Writings

Where the Heart Is (novel), Warner Books (New York City), 1995.
The Honk and Holler Opening Soon (novel), Warner Books (New York City), 1998.

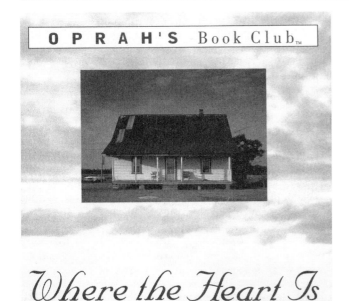

Stranded at an Oklahoma Wal-Mart, seventeen years old and pregnant, Novalee is taken to heart by caring town folk in Billie Letts' Where the Heart Is.

Contributor of stories to magazines, including *Good Housekeeping* and *North American Review.*

Adaptations

Where the Heart Is was adapted as a feature film.

Work in Progress

A novel, completion expected in 2001.

Biographical and Critical Sources

BOOKS

Griffis, Molly Levite, *You've Got Mail, Billie Letts,* Eakin Publications (Austin, TX), 1999.

PERIODICALS

Booklist, September 1, 1995, Kathleen Hughes, review of *Where the Heart Is,* p. 41. May 1, 1998, Donna Seaman, review of *The Honk and Holler Opening Soon,* p. 1487; August, 1999, review of *Where the Heart Is,* p. 2025.

Chicago Tribune, August 12, 1998, review of *The Honk and Holler Opening Soon.*

Kirkus Reviews, May 15, 1998, review of *The Honk and Holler Opening Soon.*

Library Journal, July, 1995, Barbara E. Kemp, review of *Where the Heart Is,* p. 121; June 1, 1998, Kimberly G. Allen, review of *The Honk and Holler Opening Soon,* p. 154; November 15, 1998, review of *The Honk and Holler Opening Soon,* p. 124.

New York Times Book Review, August 6, 1995, Dwight Garner, review of *Where the Heart Is,* p. 20.

People Weekly, February 22, 1999, Peter Ames Carlin and Carlton Stowers, "Never Too Late: At 60, Small-Town Novelist Billie Letts Knows Success Was Worth Waiting For," p. 101.

Publishers Weekly, May 15, 1995, review of *Where the Heart Is,* p. 55; May 11, 1998, review of *The Honk and Holler Opening Soon,* p. 50.

School Library Journal, April, 1996, Pamela B. Rearden, review of *Where the Heart Is,* p. 168; January, 1999, Carol Clark, review of *The Honk and Holler Opening Soon,* p. 160.

Southern Living, August, 1998, Carly L. Price, review of *The Honk and Holler Opening Soon,* p. 48.

*   *   *

LEWIS, Elizabeth Foreman 1892-1958

Personal

Born May 24, 1892, in Baltimore, MD; died August 7, 1958, at Briar Cliff-on-Severn, Arnold, MD; daughter of Joseph Francis and Virginia D. (Bayly) Foreman; married John Abraham Lewis, January 28, 1921 (died, 1934); children: John Fulton. *Education:* Attended Maryland Institute of Fine Arts, 1909-10, secretarial school in Baltimore, MD, 1916-17, and Bible Seminary of New York, 1917; also studied in China. *Religion:* Methodist.

Career

Woman's Foreign Missionary Society, Shanghai, China, associate mission treasurer, 1917-18; district supervisor of schools in Chunking, China, and teacher for schools in Nanking, China, 1918-21; writer.

Awards, Honors

John Newbery Medal, American Library Association, 1933, for *Young Fu of the Upper Yangtze.*

Writings

FICTION FOR CHILDREN

Young Fu of the Upper Yangtze, illustrations by Kurt Wiese, Winston (Philadelphia, PA), 1932, revised edition with introduction by Pearl Buck, illustrations by Ed Young, Holt, 1973.

Ho-Ming, Girl of New China, illustrations by Kurt Wiese, Winston (Philadelphia, PA), 1934.

China Quest, illustrations by Kurt Wiese, Winston (Philadelphia, PA), 1937.

When the Typhoon Blows, illustrations by Kurt Wiese, Winston (Philadelphia, PA), 1942.

To Beat a Tiger, One Needs a Brother's Help, illustrations by John Huehnergarth, Winston (Philadelphia, PA), 1956.

OTHER

Portraits from a Chinese Scroll, illustrations by Virginia Hollinger Stout, Winston (Philadelphia, PA), 1938.

(With George C. Basil) *Test Tubes and Dragon Scales,* Winston (Philadelphia, PA), 1940.

Work represented in anthologies. Contributor to periodicals.

Adaptations

A recording and filmstrip have been made of *Young Fu of the Upper Yangtze.*

Sidelights

Elizabeth Foreman Lewis was recognized for her various writings, notably children's books, regarding China. She was probably best known for her first literary effort, *Young Fu of the Upper Yangtze,* which concerns a young Chinese boy apprenticed to a coppersmith in the busy city of Chunking. For this story, Lewis received the prestigious Newbery Medal in 1933. She was also known for such titles as *Ho-Ming, Girl of New China* and *To Beat a Tiger, One Needs a Brother's Help.* In addition, Lewis penned a few works about China for adults, including a collaboration with George C. Basil entitled *Test Tubes and Dragon Scales.*

Lewis was born on May 24, 1892, in Baltimore, Maryland. She had a happy childhood as the daughter of devout Methodist parents who valued knowledge. In Bertha Mahony Miller and Elinor Whitney Field's *Newbery Medal Books: 1922-1955,* Lewis recalled, "My sister and I grew up in a world of books, country life, horses, dogs and a variety of other pets, a background threaded by colorful strands of wit, hearty laughter, singing, hospitality, and, naturally in Maryland, good food."

Although Lewis read considerably as a child, she did not always aspire to become a writer. One of her earliest ambitions was to become a doctor, but by late adolescence she had opted for art school instead. She attended the Maryland Institute of Fine Arts for a few years, then occupied herself drawing architectural plans for doll houses. In 1916, Lewis attended a secretarial school in Baltimore. The following year she enrolled at the Bible Seminary in New York. After a period of training, she traveled to China to serve as a missionary.

During her time in China, Lewis worked as an educator in the cities of Shanghai, Chunking, and Nanking. She became greatly enamored of the ways of the Chinese people, noting for Miller and Field that the Chinese "far

outstripped us in reverence for learning and beauty" and that in China "the written word was a sacred thing." She added: "Printed matter does not litter the streets of China, each scrap is salvaged from mire and trampling, and placed in boxes on the walls to be preserved, or if in hopeless condition to be burned. And a refuse-coolie, bent under the load, or a satin-clothed merchant is just as likely to rescue these bits as is a teacher or a schoolboy." Lewis further recalled that "when the high school girls in Nanking happened to enter the room in which I kept my personal effects, trinkets and clothing interested them but a brief moment. Soon someone would glance at the meager collection of books I had shipped from home, and exclaim, 'How rich you are, Teacher!'"

In 1921 Lewis became the wife of John Abraham Lewis. That was also the year that, due to illness, she had to depart from her beloved China and head home to the United States. "By the time illness forced me home," Lewis related to Miller and Field, "China and her people had become almost an obsession. In time, having worn out the ears of most of my listeners, I was literally driven to writing about them."

Friends eventually suggested to Lewis that she write a book about China for young people, and so she began *Young Fu of the Upper Yangtze* with the intention of both highlighting the interesting cultural differences between China and the United States and displaying the underlying similarities between young people in the two countries. As Lewis explained for Miller and Field, "My own opinion is that youth is much the same the world over, regardless of race or color. Differences there are in ways of thinking and habits of living, but for the most part these seem artificial. The determination to succeed motivates Small Chang of Nanking just as strongly as it does Johnny Brown of Philadelphia; thwarted impulses, ridicule, a sense of injustice stir him as hotly to anger and rebellion." She concluded, "If I had any one desire or purpose in writing *Young Fu* it was that this same Johnny Brown and his contemporaries in America might recognize in the youth of China this kinship to themselves."

In *Young Fu of the Upper Yangtze* the thirteen-year-old protagonist, training as an apprentice coppersmith, probes portions of lively Chungking while delivering his mentor's works. Young Fu learns that a great deal of superstition and prejudice flourishes among the citizens of Chungking, and he finds that social conflicts exist everywhere. Mary Lystad, writing in *Twentieth-Century Young Adult Writers,* observed that Young Fu "is not an idealized hero: he is brave and honest, but he also wastes his master's time and his own." Lystad described *Young Fu of the Upper Yangtze* as Lewis's "most important novel for children."

After winning the Newbery Medal for *Young Fu,* Lewis published her second book, *Ho-Ming, Girl of New China,* which relates the experiences of a girl who must overcome the superstitious upbringing of her village to become a modern nurse. As a consequence of her endeavors, Ho-Ming runs afoul of her conservative relations. Lystad, in her *Twentieth-Century Young Adult*

Writers entry on Lewis, affirmed that *Ho-Ming, Girl of New China,* like Lewis's other children's books, is concerned with "individual response to social change."

In between the publishing of *Young Fu of the Upper Yangtze* and *Ho-Ming, Girl of New China,* Lewis sustained the loss of her husband in 1934. Left alone to raise their only son, she continued writing books about China. She published *China Quest* for young readers in 1937, then she worked on two adult nonfiction volumes, *Portraits from a Chinese Scroll* and *Test Tubes and Dragon Scales.* Her last book, *To Beat a Tiger, One Needs a Brother's Help,* is a young adult novel about two boys of different social classes who become friends during the Japanese invasion of China. In their efforts to survive the invasion, the two boys observe the ravages of disease and starvation, and also witness scenes of violence and death.

With the seven books that she produced during her literary career, Lewis proved effective in fostering interest in China. Lystad concluded in *Twentieth-Century Young Adult Writers* that "through her sympathetic character portrayal, her swift plots, and her compelling prose, [Lewis] has affected many young readers for several decades."

Biographical and Critical Sources

BOOKS

Chevalier, Tracy, editor, *Twentieth-Century Children's Writers,* 3rd edition, St. James Press, 1989.
Kunitz, Stanley J., and Howard Haycraft, editors, *Junior Book of Authors,* 2nd edition, H. W. Wilson, 1951.
Miller, Bertha Mahony, and Elinor Whitney Field, *Newbery Medal Books: 1922-1955,* Horn Book, 1955.
Twentieth-Century Young Adult Writers, St. James Press, 1994, pp. 398.
Yesterday's Authors of Books for Children, Volume 2, Gale, 1978, pp. 243-244.

*　　　*　　　*

LOCKRIDGE, Hildegarde (Dolson) 1908-1981
(Hildegarde Dolson)

Personal

Born August 31, 1908, in Franklin, PA; died January 15, 1981, in Columbus, NC; daughter of Clifford and Katharine (Brown) Dolson; married Richard Lockridge (a writer), May, 1965. *Education:* Attended Allegheny College, 1926-29.

Career

Advertising copywriter in New York City at Gimbel's, Macy's, Franklin-Simon, and Bamberger stores, 1933-38; freelance writer, 1938-81. *Member:* Authors League, American Civil Liberties Union.

Writings

UNDER NAME HILDEGARDE DOLSON

How about a Man, Lippincott (Philadelphia), 1938.
(Self-illustrated) *We Shook the Family Tree* (collection of sketches for children), Random House, 1946.
The Husband Who Ran Away, Random House, 1948.
The Form Divine, Random House, 1950.
Sorry to Be So Cheerful (humorous essays), illustrated by Paul Galdone, Random House, 1955.
(With Elizabeth Stevenson Ives) *My Brother Adlai,* Morrow (New York City), 1956.
A Growing Wonder, Random House, 1957.
The Great Oildorado: The Gaudy and Turbulent Years of the First Oil Rush: Pennsylvania 1859-1880, Random House, 1959.
William Penn: Quaker Hero (for children), Random House, 1962.
Guess Whose Hair I'm Wearing, Random House, 1963.
Disaster at Johnstown: The Great Flood (for children), Random House, 1965.
Open the Door, Lippincott (Philadelphia), 1966.
Heat Lightning, Lippincott (Philadelphia), 1968.
To Spite Her Face (mystery), Lippincott (Philadelphia), 1971.
A Dying Fall (mystery), Lippincott (Philadelphia), 1973.
Please Omit Funeral, Lippincott (Philadelphia), 1975.
Beauty Sleep, Lippincott (Philadelphia), 1977.

Contributor of articles to *New Yorker, Harper's, Ladies Home Journal, McCall's, Reader's Digest, Good Housekeeping,* and other popular magazines.

Sidelights

Writing primarily under her maiden name Dolson, Hildegarde Lockridge is credited with humorous contributions to magazines such as the *New Yorker,* historical and other nonfiction books, writings for children, and mysteries. Before her death in 1981, Lockridge published nearly twenty books, including her popular story collection *We Shook the Family Tree,* an anecdotal offering of memories of the author's youth in a small Pennsylvania town, and her experiences as a young adult with her first jobs in New York. A *Kirkus Reviews* critic described *We Shook the Family Tree* as "zippy, humorous, [and] light-hearted," and a *New York Times* commentator asserted: "Unmitigated cheerfulness is the hallmark of this tidy little accumulation of Dear-Family items."

Lockridge followed the success of *We Shook the Family Tree* with her 1948 novel *The Husband Who Ran Away,* which tells of a man who, unliked by his in-laws, moves to New York City and, through some luck, becomes a successful designer. Eventually the man's mother-in-law recognizes that he is making her daughter happy. "Readers who enjoyed Hildegarde Dolson's humorous sketches in *We Shook the Family Tree* will find [*The Husband Who Ran Away*] diverting and amusing," declared a *Kirkus Reviews* contributor. The story "follows the pattern of a shriveled life expanding under special conditions, and the crispness of the writing, the pleasantness of the situation make it amusing," judged a *Christian Science Monitor* critic.

The humorous essays collected in *Sorry to Be So Cheerful* address a wide range of topics. "The majority of [the pleasant satires] have appeared in *The New Yorker* or *Good Housekeeping*, but they re-read amusingly," maintained a *New York Herald Tribune Book Review*. "All the stories are written with skill and wit and altogether no one is sorry to have Miss Dolson so cheerful," praised *New York Times* reviewer Jane Cobb. "To be enjoyed to the fullest," asserted Richard Blakesley in the *Chicago Sunday Tribune*, the stories comprising *Sorry to Be So Cheerful* "should be read over a space of several days—they're too stimulating to be taken at one gulp." "She can pick up a subject," explained *San Francisco Chronicle* critic J. H. Jackson, "take a brief, highly personal look at it, and when she puts it down again it will never be quite the same . . . . Dolson is right at the top when it comes to doing this sort of thing deftly, wittily and with just the right dash of residual common sense which makes a funny piece stick in the reader's mind."

Lockridge turned to the writing of history with *The Great Oildorado: The Gaudy and Turbulent Years of the First Oil Rush: Pennsylvania 1859-1880*. "Marking oil's centennial, being celebrated in 1959, *The Great Oildorado* deals with the inventors, creators, speculators, and oil kings of western Pennsylvania," summarized Gerald Carson in his *Chicago Sunday Tribune* review. *Christian Science Monitor* contributor Nate White maintained that "[w]henever Hildegarde Dolson punches a typewriter key it is never dull," noting that her "objective, while historically inclined, is always to amuse and entertain." At the same time, S. T. Williamson noted in the *New York Times* that "the many anecdotes which make Miss Dolson's story as free-flowing as a Titusville gusher are the result of research as prodigious as for a more solemn 'definitive' history." Concluding his favorable assessment of *The Great Oildorado*, Carson asserted: "The author skillfully ties the oil rush to the general social setting—to popular music, the theater, the merchandise in the stores, politics, and the Civil war . . . . *The Great Oildorado* is crowded with stories, all authentic Americana, and not a hackneyed anecdote in the bookful."

Lockridge also wrote well-regarded studies of Pennsylvania subjects for middle-graders, including her biography *William Penn: Quaker Hero* and her nonfiction *Disaster at Johnstown: The Great Flood*. The latter examines the 1889 Johnstown flood, which took the lives of more than 2,000 people. "Hildegarde Dolson has written a fresh, swiftly paced account of a well-documented disaster," declared *New York Times Book Review* contributor Robert Berkvist, who added: "Dozens of moving vignettes animate her pages—poignant glimpses of how the people of Johnstown met the terrible trial-by-water."

Biographical and Critical Sources

PERIODICALS

Best Sellers, September 1, 1966; May 15, 1973; August, 1975.
Booklist, October 1, 1948; September 1, 1955; March 1, 1959; September 15, 1966; September 15, 1975; July 15, 1977.
Chicago Sunday Tribune, July 10, 1955, Richard Blakesley, review of *Sorry to Be So Cheerful,* p. 3; March 1, 1959, Gerald Carson, review of *The Great Oildorado,* p. 4.
Christian Science Monitor, September 23, 1948, review of *The Husband Who Ran Away,* p. 15; June 18, 1959, Nate White, review of *The Great Oilderado,* p. 11.
Horn Book, December, 1955.
Kirkus Reviews, February 1, 1946, review of *We Shook the Family Tree,* p. 62; July 15, 1948, review of *The Husband Who Ran Away;* May 15, 1955; December 1, 1958; July 1, 1966; November 15, 1969; February 15, 1973; May 1, 1975; March 15, 1977.
Kliatt, March, 1997.
Library Journal, August, 1948; September 15, 1955; May 15, 1965; July, 1966; November 1, 1969; May 1, 1973; August, 1975; June 1, 1977.
New York Herald Tribune Book Review, September 19, 1948; July 10, 1955, review of *Sorry to Be So Cheerful,* p. 6; March 1, 1959.
New York Times, July 14, 1946, review of *We Shook the Family Tree,* p. 19; August 21, 1955, Jane Cobb, review of *Sorry to Be So Cheerful,* p. 20; February 22, 1959, S. T. Williamson, review of *The Great Oilderado,* p. 6.
New York Times Book Review, May 9, 1965, Robert Berkvist, review of *Disaster at Johnstown: The Great Flood,* p. 22; August 21, 1966; February 8, 1970; April 22, 1973; July 3, 1977.
Publishers Weekly, November 10, 1969; February 26, 1973; March 21, 1977.
San Francisco Chronicle, October 3, 1948; July 12, 1955, J. H. Jackson, review of *Sorry to Be So Cheerful,* p. 15.
Saturday Review, July 30, 1955; March 7, 1959.
Saturday Review of Literature, November 27, 1948.
Times Literary Supplement, November 19, 1938, review of *How about a Man,* p. 746.
Washington Post Book World, April 15, 1973; July 20, 1975.

Obituaries

PERIODICALS

New York Times, January 17, 1981.

*   *   *

LORBIECKI, Marybeth 1959-

Personal

Born August 3, 1959, in Nueremberg, Germany; daughter of Rudolph John (a dentist) and Marilyn (a medical technician; maiden name, Schneider) Lorbiecki; married David Peter Mataya (a creative director and illustrator), November 24, 1990; children: Nadja Marie, Mirjiana, Dmitri Peter. *Education:* College of St. Catherine, St. Paul, MN, B.A. (English), 1981; Mankato State University, Mankato, MN, M.A. (English literature), 1985; University of Essex, Colchester, England, postgraduate study, 1985-86.

Addresses

Home—Hudson, WI. *Office*—c/o Publicity Director, Dial Books for Young Readers, 375 Hudson St., New York, NY 10014.

Career

Freelance writer, editor, teacher, and speaker. Marycrest High School, Denver, CO, theology teacher, 1982-83; Mankato State University, Mankato, MN, composition instructor, 1983-85; Carbil Communications, Inc., Roseville, MN, marketing copy director, 1986-88; Carolrhoda Books, Inc., Minneapolis, MN, children's book editor and author, 1988-93; College of St. Catherine, GRE/GMAT verbal and logic prep instructor, 1994-2000. Volunteer in youth ministry in Hispanic community in Colorado, 1981-82; past president of Western Wisconsin

Marybeth Lorbiecki

Prairie Project, 1998-99; board of trustees for Carpenter St. Croix Valley Nature Center.

Awards, Honors

International Rotarian Scholarship, 1985-86; *Boston Globe* Best Environmental Picks, and *Science Books and Films* Best Picks, both 1993, both for the three titles in the "Earthwise" series; Distinguished Service to History award, State Historical Society of Wisconsin, and John Burroughs Nature Book, both 1993, both for *Of Things Natural, Wild, and Free: The Story of Aldo Leopold;* *Chicago Tribune,* New York Public Library, and American Library Association Pick of the Lists citations, all 1996, and Children's Choice award, 1997, all for *Just One Flick of a Finger;* Distinguished Service to History Award, State Historical Society of Wisconsin, and Minnesota Book Award in Biography and History, both 1996, both for *Aldo Leopold: A Fierce Green Fire;* *Children's Literature* Choice List, 1998, for *My Palace of Leaves in Sarajevo;* Notable Trade Book for Young People in Social Studies, 1998, for *The Children of Vietnam;* Notable Trade Book for Young People in Social Studies and in Literary Arts, 1999, Best Books of the Year, Bank Street College, 1999, Storyteller World's Award, International Reading Association, 1999, and Living the Dream Award, Manhattan Country School, 2000, all for *Sister Anne's Hands.*

Writings

FOR CHILDREN

(With Linda Lowery) *Earthwise at School: A Guide to the Care and Feeding of Your Planet,* illustrated by husband, David Mataya, Carolrhoda (Minneapolis, MN), 1993.

(With Lowery) *Earthwise at Play: A Guide to the Care and Feeding of Your Planet,* illustrated by David Mataya, Carolrhoda (Minneapolis, MN), 1993.

(With Lowery) *Earthwise at Home: A Guide to the Care and Feeding of Your Planet,* illustrated by David Mataya, Carolrhoda (Minneapolis, MN), 1993.

Of Things Natural, Wild, and Free: The Story of Aldo Leopold, illustrated by Kerry Maguire, Carolrhoda (Minneapolis, MN), 1993.

Just One Flick of a Finger, illustrated by David Diaz, Dial, 1996.

My Palace of Leaves in Sarajevo, illustrated by Herbert Tauss, Dial, 1996.

The Children of Vietnam, photographs by Paul P. Rome, Carolrhoda (Minneapolis, MN), 1997.

Sister Anne's Hands, illustrated by Wendy Popp, Dial, 1998.

Painting the Dakota: Seth Eastman at Fort Snelling, illustrated by Seth Eastman, Afton Historical Society Press, 2000.

FOR ADULTS

(With Sarah Boehme and Christian Feest) *Seth Eastman: A Portfolio of North American Indians,* Afton Historical Society Press, 1995.

Aldo Leopold: A Fierce Green Fire, Falcon Press, 1996, Oxford University Press, 1999.

Lorbiecki's writing of her award-winning historical biography for older readers coincides with the fiftieth anniversary of the publication of Leopold's classic **A Sand County Almanac.** *(Cover photo courtesy of the University of Wisconsin Archives.)*

Contributor of essay "Prairie Spirits on the Wing" in *Stories from WHERE WE LIVE: The Great North American Prairie,* Milkweed Editions, 2001; Lorbiecki also co-authored, with Kathe Crowley Conn, the script for the video documentary *Aldo Leopold: Learning from the Land.* Contributor to periodicals, including *New Mexico Magazine, Eau Claire Leader-Telegram, Pioneer Press, New Mexico Historical Society Review,* and *Wisconsin Academy Review.*

Work in Progress

Several books for children, including *Jackie's Bat,* for Simon & Schuster; (with Julie Dunlap) *Louisa May and Mr. Thoreau's Flute,* illustrated by Mary Azarian, for Dial; (with Dunlap) *Stickeen and the Ice Chief,* for Orchard Books; and *The Ant in My Bellybutton,* for Golden Books. Also a middle grade novel and a book of adult essays on Christianity and the Land Ethic.

Sidelights

Marybeth Lorbiecki is the author of children's picture books, easy readers, young adult novels, and nonfiction books that often explore themes of nature conservancy and social problems. Tackling subjects ranging from the life of the naturalist and conservationist Aldo Leopold to guns at school, and from young children in Vietnam to one young child's life in war-torn Sarajevo, Lorbiecki attempts to provide a broad range of subject matter for young readers. As the author told *SATA,* "Children deserve the full range of literature just as adults do: comedy, tragedy, poetry, information, drama, and adventure (plus more!). If their choices are narrowed solely to quick-to-read fiberless stories of flash and glitter, they will be cheated. We need to trust them to give them more. Sometimes it takes more than 300 or 500 or 800 words to spin magic or spark curiosity or answer questions or touch the heart."

Born at a U.S. Army hospital in Germany, Lorbiecki went to college in Minnesota and worked in Colorado and Minnesota before taking up residence in Wisconsin. A varied career in writing, teaching, editing, and marketing led to her first published books in 1993, the three titles of the "Earthwise" series that were illustrated by her husband and published by Carolrhoda Books, her employer at the time. In these books, *Earthwise at Play, Earthwise at School,* and *Earthwise at Home,* Lorbiecki, along with her co-writer, Linda Lowery, suggested ideas that can help save our planet, from smart shopping to recycling, and provided information about various animals and plants. Reviewing the series in *School Library Journal,* Eva Elisabeth Von Ancken thought the books would be a "most welcome and valuable set and ... an excellent addition to library collections." Von Ancken further commented, "Emphasizing positive attitudes and actions, these books encourage readers to become environmentally aware in all aspects of their lives."

Sticking with an environmental theme, Lorbiecki next penned an "appealing biography" on the naturalist Aldo Leopold, according to Carolyn Angus in *School Library Journal. Of Things Natural, Wild, and Free* tells the story of that pioneering wildlife conservationist and author of the well known *A Sand County Almanac.* "The author effectively communicates a sense of Leopold's vision and chronicles his achievements and setbacks in an accessible style," Angus noted. Reviewing the same title in *Booklist,* Sheilamae O'Hara felt that the book might be "of use in a unit on careers or the environment." Lorbiecki also wrote an adult title about Leopold called *Aldo Leopold: A Fierce Green Fire,* and she co-authored the script for a video about the conservationist. Reviewing the adult book, Nancy J. Moeckel, writing in *Library Journal,* declared, "Those unfamiliar with Leopold will relish this book; those who already know him will enjoy the retelling." Moeckel concluded, "This highly readable, lavishly illustrated biography is recommended for all environmental collections, public and academic." Writing in *Choice,* S. A. Carlson called the same title "well-researched," and concluded that "Lorbiecki successfully examines the more private Leopold and his family as well as his life as a scholar, teacher, hunter, and policy ethicist."

With her 1996 picture book *Just One Flick of a Finger,* Lorbiecki touched on another hot topic, school violence. In this story, a young boy, Jack, takes his father's gun to school to scare away a bully, Reebo, who has been bothering him. During an ensuing confrontation and scuffle, the gun is accidentally discharged, wounding Jack's friend who is trying to intervene. Though no one is seriously hurt, all the boys learn a lesson from this near tragedy and become closer because of it. "The issue of adolescents taking guns to school is intensely played out in narrative and depiction," observed Julie Cummins in a *School Library Journal* review of the book. Cummins paid special attention to the "verse-like text" in the characters' "hip street talk." While noting "the book ends on a positive note," another reviewer for *School Library Journal* did warn that "the bold, provocative illustrations and disturbing subject matter make this a book to share with an adult." A reviewer for *Publishers Weekly* called *Just One Flick of a Finger* a "stark picture book for middle graders" and further noted that as a result of the shooting all the boys "obviously learn a lesson, which Lorbiecki unequivocally passes on to readers." *Booklist*'s

Hazel Rochman claimed that the "writing is terse, the standoffs dramatic."

Several reviewers, including Rochman, however, considered the action to be too pat and the ending too unrealistically happy. Rochman noted the "contrived" feeling of the story, and the "heavy-handed" message, while Janice M. Del Negro complained of the "naively unrealistic ... happily-ever-after conclusion" in *Bulletin of the Center for Children's Books.* A critic for *Kirkus Reviews,* on the other hand, found that "[b]oth text and images capture the tension and fear of an urban schoolyard menaced by guns; the implied acceptance of the ease of obtaining a firearm is utterly chilling," and Bette Ammon, writing in *Voice of Youth Advocates* noted that though the message is "somewhat simplistic and moralist, the point is well taken and immediate."

Contrasting views of children around the world are presented in the middle-grade books *My Palace of Leaves in Sarajevo* and *The Children of Vietnam.* In the former novel, pen pals in the United States and Sarajevo exchange their hopes, dreams, and fears. Ten-year-old Nadja begins to write to her American cousin, Alex, in 1991, about her life, particularly the camping and skiing

Lorbiecki introduces readers to the often violent history and daily life of growing up in Vietnam in her 1997 Children of Vietnam. *(Photographs by Paul P. Rome.)*

she enjoys. Then in April, 1992, when her native Sarajevo is bombed by the Yugoslav Army, the tone of the letters changes considerably, describing food shortages, deprivation, and death. Alex, safe in Minnesota, soon begins to become emotionally involved with his cousin's fate. Finally, Alex's family hires a lawyer to try and obtain visas for Nadja and her family. In the introduction and afterword, Lorbiecki summarizes the historical and political setting of the book and brings readers into the contemporary context. "Lorbiecki personalizes the experiences of war in this epistolary novel," wrote a contributor for *Publishers Weekly*. Reviewing the same novel in *School Library Journal*, Karen MacDonald concluded, "Young readers will be moved by the plight of Bosnians and Alex's determination to help his cousin." Betsy Hearne, reviewing the novel in *Bulletin of the Center for Children's Books*, thought that the "suspense of constant danger" would "draw younger readers," and that overall the book "is informative by virtue of the dramatic situation."

The Children of Vietnam introduces the history, geography, and culture of that country through the daily lives of children who live there. Lorbiecki takes readers on a north-south journey through Vietnam, from the mountain-dwelling Lac Viet people to the Black Thai, Hmong, and Cham cultures, in a kaleidoscope of customs, beliefs, and lifestyles. Shirley N. Quan, writing in *School Library Journal*, observed that "this photo-essay describes the diversity of the country's population and focuses on the lives of its children" and that the "numerous full-color photographs enhance a text that is rich with historical and cultural details." Quan concluded that for libraries seeking a "broad overview," Lorbiecki's title "will make a welcome addition."

With *Sister Anne's Hands* Lorbiecki treats the subject of racism from a unique perspective. Seven-year-old Ann gets her first taste of racism in the 1960s when an African-American nun comes to teach at her Catholic school. Sister Anne challenges the preconceptions of children in her second-grade classroom, especially when a note about the nun's skin color written on the wings of a paper airplane literally lands on her desk. Though some of the parents pull their children from the school because of the nun's race, those that remain are introduced by Sister Anne to African-American culture and what it means to grow up black in America. Lorbiecki based the story on an actual incident that happened to her as a youth. A writer for *Publishers Weekly* called the picture book "thought-provoking" and one with "considerable emotional appeal." *Booklist*'s Rochman commented, "There is an idyllic quality to the story and the period pictures of the nun and her classroom, but the hurt is there, too, and the message of tolerance grows out of the personal experience, which confronts the racism and gets beyond it." "The story has honesty and integrity," noted Jody McCoy in *School*

Library Journal. Lorbiecki has also written the text for the middle-grade nonfiction book *Painting the Dakota: Seth Eastman at Fort Snelling*, an introduction to the work of that soldier-artist, who married a Dakota woman and chronicled much of the history of the Dakota people in the territory that became known as Minnesota.

Lorbiecki continues to be busy at work on a number of projects, from picture books to middle-grade novels and nonfiction. She also has thoughtful advice for aspiring writers. As she told *SATA:* "It helps to work on assignments for others. You are always handed projects that seem impossible to do well. Yet, if you push on, you'll find a way through them because you have to. If you take this attitude toward your book or story ideas, you can push through the points of frustration and despair."

Biographical and Critical Sources

PERIODICALS

Booklist, November 1, 1993, Sheilamae O'Hara, review of *Of Things Natural, Wild, and Free*, p. 520; June 1, 1996, Hazel Rochman, review of *Just One Flick of a Finger*, p. 1718; April 1, 1997, p. 1308; June 1, 1997, p. 1675; March 13, 1998, p. 1238; October 1, 1998, Hazel Rochman, review of *Sister Anne's Hands*, p. 345.

Bulletin of the Center for Children's Books, September, 1996, Janice M. Del Negro, review of *Just One Flick of a Finger*, pp. 20-21; March, 1997, Betsy Hearne, review of *My Palace of Leaves in Sarajevo*, p. 252; November, 1998, p. 105.

Choice, May, 1997, S. A. Carlson, review of *Aldo Leopold*, p. 1520.

Kirkus Reviews, June 1, 1996, review of *Just One Flick of a Finger*, p. 826.

Library Journal, November 1, 1996, Nancy J. Moeckel, review of *Aldo Leopold*, p. 105.

Publishers Weekly, August 19, 1996, review of *Just One Flick of a Finger*, p. 67; April 14, 1997, review of *My Palace of Leaves in Sarajevo*, p. 76; September 21, 1998, review of *Sister Anne's Hands*, p. 84.

School Library Journal, July, 1993, Eva Elisabeth Von Ancken, review of "Earthwise" series, p. 93; November, 1993, Carolyn Angus, review of *Of Things Natural, Wild, and Free*, p. 117; September, 1996, Julie Cummins, review of *Just One Flick of a Finger*, p. 204; June, 1997, Karen MacDonald, review of *My Palace of Leaves in Sarajevo*, p. 122; February, 1998, Shirley N. Quan, review of *The Children of Vietnam*, p. 120; January, 1999, Jody McCoy, review of *Sister Anne's Hands*, p. 98; January, 2000, review of *Just One Flick of a Finger*, p. 43.

Voice of Youth Advocates, June, 1997, Bette Ammon, review of *Just One Flick of a Finger*, p. 110.

—Sketch by J. Sydney Jones

M

McDANIELS, Pellom III 1968-

Personal

Born February 21, 1968, in San Jose, CA; son of Pellom, Jr. and Mary McDaniels; married, wife's name, Navvab. *Education:* Oregon State University, B.S., 1990.

Addresses

Home—875 Louisville Suwanee Rd., Suite 310-353, Lawrenceville, GA 30043. *E-mail*—Pellom@Pellom.com.

Career

Professional football player, 1991—, including affiliations with Kansas City Chiefs and Atlanta Falcons. Pellom McDaniels III Enterprises, Inc., president. Painter. Arts for Smarts Foundation, founder. *Member:* Kappa Alpha Psi.

Awards, Honors

Selected among "thirty leaders thirty and under" by *Ebony.*

Writings

My Own Harlem, Fish out of Water Publications (Kansas City, MO), 1997, 2nd edition, foreword by Marcus Allen, photographs by Gary Carson, Addax Publishing (Lenexa, KS), 1998.

So, You Want to Be a Pro?, Addax Publishing (Lenexa, KS), 1999.

Work in Progress

In That Place Called Heaven.

Sidelights

Pellom McDaniels III told *SATA:* "As a professional athlete, I have had the opportunity to observe, document,

Pellom McDaniels III

and change the perception that America has of the African-American male. My work as a researcher, writer, and educator has culminated in several articles and two books, *So, You Want to Be a Pro?* being the most recent. My desire to pursue an advanced degree has been nurtured by my interest in the evolution of the African-American male athlete into a social icon. Looking for concrete answers to the why, what, and how, sports have become so important to a particular group of people. These questions and a critical inventory of my life experiences, life goals, and academic aspirations has led me to pursue the apex of educational progress, the Ph.D.

"Although I didn't play baseball, I am a product of the expectations my grandfather's generation had of its heroes. Through their collective efforts, they taught me that community matters, and all it takes is one individual to make a difference. Today the circumstances that led his generation to follow those athletes has changed. Those morals and values, once held in high esteem, have seemingly all but disappeared. Society is still trying to integrate, and the African American is trying to figure out where he/she fits in.

"The circumstances, traditions, and situations that I have been a part of have, without a doubt, shaped my future. This is why I write."

Biographical and Critical Sources

PERIODICALS

Booklist, November 15, 1999, Chris Sherman, review of *So, You Want to Be a Pro?,* p. 612.

Knight-Ridder/Tribune News Service, April 26, 1999, Joe Posnanski, "Pellom McDaniels Leaving Chiefs Because Falcons Made Him Feel Wanted," p. K4001.

School Library Journal, March, 2000, Diane P. Tuccillo, review of *So, You Want to Be a Pro?,* p. 257.

*   *   *

McGRATH, Robin 1949-
(Robin Gedalof)

Personal

Born March 29, 1949, in Newfoundland, Canada; daughter of James M. F. (a doctor) and Anita (Kearney) McGrath; married Allan J. Gedalof (divorced October 28, 1987); married John L. Joy (a lawyer), July 12, 1995; children: (first marriage) Michelle Gedalof Labrecque, Ze'ev, Eli. *Education:* Attended Memorial University of Newfoundland, 1966-68, and University of Alberta, 1968-69; University of Western Ontario, B.A., M.A., Ph.D., 1983. *Religion:* Jewish.

Addresses

Home—131 Beachy Cove Rd., Site E, Box 39, Portugal Cove, Newfoundland, Canada A0A 3K0. *Agent*—John L. Joy, P.O. Box 5457, St. John's, Newfoundland, Canada A1C 5W4.

Career

Writer. University of Western Ontario, London, lecturer, 1981; Fanshawe College, instructor, 1982-84; University of Western Ontario, assistant professor of English, 1984-85; McGill/Arctic College, Iqaluit, assistant professor, 1985; University of Western Ontario, assistant professor of English, 1987-89; University of Alberta, Edmonton, assistant professor, 1989-92, associate professor of English, 1992-93; Memorial University of Newfound-

land, St. John's, instructor, 1992 and 1994, research associate at Centre for Cold Ocean Resources Engineering, 1993-99. Hebrew University of Jerusalem, visiting professor at Halbert Center for Canadian Studies, 1996-97; University of Alberta, adjunct associate professor, 2000. Geological Survey of Canada, camp manager in the western Arctic, 1986 and 1988. Hebrew Congregation of Newfoundland and Labrador, executive. Guest on Canadian radio programs; gives readings from her works; appears in television documentaries. *Member:* Writers Alliance of Newfoundland and Labrador, Writers Union of Canada, Portugal Cove-St. Philip's Heritage Society (president).

Awards, Honors

Explorations grant, Canada Council, 1984; fellow, Social Sciences and Humanities Research Council of Canada, 1985-86; grant from Royal Canadian Geographical Society, 1988; first place in Great Fire Story Contest, Canadian Broadcasting Corp., 1992; Newfoundland and Labrador Arts and Letters Awards, first place awards for nonfiction, 1995, 1998, and 1999, first place award for poetry, 1998; Henry Fuerstenberg Poetry Prize, Canadian Jewish Book Awards, 1999; Canadian National Magazine Award nomination, 2000.

Writings

An Annotated Bibliography of Canadian Inuit Literature, Department of Indian and Northern Affairs (Ottawa, Ontario), 1979.

(Editor, under name Robin Gedalof) *Paper Stays Put: A Collection of Inuit Writing,* illustrated by Alootook Ipellie, Hurtig (Edmonton, Alberta), 1980.

Canadian Inuit Literature: The Development of a Tradition, National Museums of Canada (Ottawa), 1984.

(Author of foreword) Agnes Nanogak, *More Tales from the Igloo,* Hurtig, 1986.

Robin McGrath

(Contributor) T. King, C. Calvert, and H. Hoy, editors, *The Native in Literature: Canadian and Contemporary Perspectives,* ECW Press (Toronto, Ontario), 1987.

(Contributor) John Carlsen and Bengt Streijffert, editors, *The Canadian North: Essays in Culture and Literature,* Nordic Association for Canadian Studies (Lund, Sweden), 1989.

(Contributor) Arnold E. Davidson, editor, *Studies on Canadian Literature: Introductory and Critical Essays,* Modern Language Association of America (New York City), 1990.

Trouble and Desire (stories), Killick Press (St. John's, Newfoundland), 1995.

A Heritage Guide to Portugal Cove-St. Philip's, Oceanside Press (Pouch Cove, Newfoundland), 1996.

(Contributor) Streijffert, editor, *Essays on Arctic Canada,* Nordic Association for Canadian Studies, 1996.

A Heritage Guide to Torbay, Oceanside Press (Pouch Cove, Newfoundland), 1997.

Escaped Domestics (poems), Killick Press (St. John's, Newfoundland), 1998.

Hoist Your Sails and Run (young adult novel), Tuckamore Books (St. John's, Newfoundland), 1999.

Author of teaching aids, pamphlets, and indexes. Contributor of more than 100 articles, poems, stories, and reviews to periodicals, including *Inuit Art Quarterly, Canadian Journal of Native Education, Newfoundland Quarterly, Canadian Woman Studies, Blue Buffalo, Room of One's Own,* and *Prairie Journal of Canadian Literature.*

Work in Progress

A poetry collection, *On the Long Finger.*

Sidelights

Robin McGrath told *SATA:* "As a reader and as a writer, I do not limit myself to any one genre of literature. I write fiction, nonfiction, poetry, drama, and I even compose poetry and prose for recitation rather than publication. I am always puzzled by novelists who have never attempted to write a poem, or by poets who shun prose. I choose the genre according to the material, and sometimes I will use the same material in several different ways before finding the right format for it. Similarly, I do not consider myself a children's author or an adult's author. My target audience varies according to the piece I am working on. I read and enjoy children's books with the same enthusiasm now as I did forty years ago, and I am sure that many young readers can appreciate material that I have aimed at older readers.

"As a child, I had great difficulty with writing. I was ten years old before I could spell my own name, and I repeated two grades at school. I believe that I suffered from a mild dyslexia, and while I still have difficulty with both letters and numbers, I no longer feel that I am at a disadvantage because of it. Over time, I have developed coping mechanisms that are usually adequate to the job at hand. I am very aware, however, that not all readers are comfortable with complex sentence structures and jargon. As an academic I tried to make my work accessible to general readers as well as to my colleagues. I now try to do the same thing in my creative writing. I read and write with a dictionary at hand, but I aim for plain language. It is sometimes necessary to use obscure words to make a specific point, but usually such obfuscation is merely self-indulgent.

"The first book I published was a collection of Inuit writing. I was drawn to the material because Inuit had a strong oral tradition that was struggling to shift into a written form, rather as I was myself. My work in the Arctic and with Aboriginal people has strongly influenced my writing, but they rarely feature in my fiction as I believe there are Inuit and Indian writers who are far better able to express the Aboriginal cultural perspective. After many years of working with Aboriginal people, I was drawn back into my own culture and a need to find my own voice. That voice is centered in Newfoundland, and has—even on paper—a clearly Newfoundland accent. I love Newfoundland English. I love the unique words, the cadence of the sentence structures, and the humor. I don't try to write in dialect, but I try to convey the language through the rhythms and speech patterns. When I am in doubt about a sentence or a phrase, I try to imagine one of my parents saying the words, and if it rings true to my inner ear, I let it stand.

"I do not consider myself to be primarily a poet, but I think my most successful work is my poetry. I love giving readings, and my work is often broadcast on radio, so I suppose there is a strength in the 'orality' that comes from my Anglo-Irish tradition, and perhaps from my dyslexia. My father was a gifted storyteller, and my ten sisters and brothers are all great talkers, so it is natural for me to give my poems a narrative shape. Each one is a little snapshot or drama, and often I simply record what I have heard in the post office or at the grocery store. Of course, the narrative is shaped, trimmed, and condensed down, but the inner core is the same. In my first collection, *Escaped Domestics,* there are a number of these 'found' poems. My next book of poems, *On the Long Finger,* will contain even more."

Biographical and Critical Sources

PERIODICALS

Canadian Forum, June, 1996, Julie Mason, review of *Trouble and Desire,* p. 850.

Newfoundland Studies, volume 12, number 2, 1996, Joan Strong, review of *Trouble and Desire,* pp. 149-152.

Pottersfield Portfolio, volume 19, number 5, 1999, Susan Tileson, review of *Escaped Domestics,* p. 4.

Quill & Quire, January, 1999, Ruth Panofsky, review of *Escaped Domestics,* p. 38.

Resource Links, volume 5, number 5, Margaret Mackey, review of *Hoist Torn Sails and Run,* p. 37.

TickleAce, number 36, 1999, Susan Drodge, review of *Escaped Domestics,* pp. 105-108.

ON-LINE

Amazon.com, www.amazon.com/ (August 26, 2000).

MONAGLE, Bernie 1957-

Personal

Born March 10, 1957, in Melbourne, Australia; son of Frank (an accountant) and Mary (Dornom) Monagle; married Marisa Hook (a nurse), 1983; children: Phoebe, Hannah. *Education:* Earned teaching diploma. *Hobbies and other interests:* Bush walking, rock climbing, music.

Addresses

E-mail—monagle@gcom.net.au.

Career

High school teacher in Kyneton, Australia, 1988—. Also works as drama consultant.

Writings

Blue Girl, Yella Fella, Lothian Books (Port Melbourne, Australia), 2000.
Monstered, Lothian Books (Port Melbourne, Australia), 2001.

Work in Progress

A young adult novel dealing with teenage pregnancy, completion expected in 2001; research on native birds and drop-tail lizards.

*   *   *

MORGAN, Anne 1954-

Personal

Born November 16, 1954; daughter of Eamonn Joseph and Claire Therese (Travers) Morgan; married David N. Harries; children: Nicholas, Miranda. *Education:* Earned teaching certificate, 1977; University of Tasmania, M.Ed., 1987. *Politics:* Green. *Hobbies and other interests:* Table tennis, bush walking.

Addresses

Home—32 D'Arcy St., South Hobart, Tasmania 7004, Australia. *E-mail*—amorgan@netspace.net.au.

Career

Drama tutor for Apprentice Theatre and Tasmanian Youth Theatre, Hobart, Australia, 1972-75; schoolteacher in Burnie, Australia, 1976, and Ramangining, Australia, 1977-78; Hobart Technical College, teacher and coordinator of education program for unemployed youth, 1979 and 1982; Service Civil International, community development worker in France, Belgium, and England, 1980; Sacred Heart College, teacher, 1983; Australian Department of Employment, Education, and Training, Aboriginal education officer, 1984-88; Community Aid Abroad, Hobart, development education officer, 1989-

Anne Morgan

90; Australian Department of Employment, Education, and Training, executive officer for Aboriginal employment, 1990-91, state equal employment opportunity coordinator, 1991-92, training officer for youth affairs, 1994-98; University of Tasmania, Hobart, tutor in Aboriginal studies, 1999, research assistant at Centre for Research and Learning in Regional Australia, 1999—. TAFE, Hobart Institute, writer for Tikiri Adult Learning Project, 1996-97. Television and radio actress, 1979 and 1980. *Member:* Australian Society of Authors, Fellowship of Australian Writers (executive member), Tasmanian Writers Centre.

Awards, Honors

Banjo Paterson Literature Award, open poetry section, Orange Arts Council, 1999, for the poem "An Unknown Wreck, Macquarie Island"; Colin Knight Memorial Poetry Award, Fellowship of Australian Writers, 1999, for "The Moss-Bearded Apple Tree"; shortlist, Australian Environment Children's Book of the Year, 2000, for *The Glow Worm Cave.*

Writings

The Glow Worm Cave, illustrated by Belinda Kurczok, Aboriginal Studies Press (Canberra, Australia), 1999.

Contributor of poems to periodicals, including *Australian, Countdown,* and *Blast Off.* Short fiction has been broadcast on Australian media programs.

Work in Progress

The Rats of Rumbarrel Island, based on her story of the same title; *The Lights Went Out in Blackberry Lane;* a multimedia piece, *Shipwrecks, Sealers, and Scientists on Macquarie Island,* for Tasmanian Parks and Wildlife Service.

Sidelights

Anne Morgan told *SATA:* "As a 'bookworm' big sister to a family of eight children, I used to read bedtime stories to my young brothers in the early 1970s. Our favorites were the Finn Family Moomintroll series by Tove Jansson, Frank L. Baum's *The Wizard of Oz,* A. A. Milne's *Winnie the Pooh,* and later C. S. Lewis's Narnia books. From big sister to teacher seemed a natural progression for me. Since leaving teaching I have worked in children's theater, staff training, corporate journalism, research and freelance writing—all of which require skills in storytelling in one form or another.

"As a young teacher I was lucky enough to be able to work on a remote settlement in Arnhem Land, Australia, where indigenous people spoke their own languages and practiced traditional lifestyles. This experience, and my subsequent involvement with environmental protests in Tasmania, provided the inspiration for my first published children's book, *The Glow Worm Cave.*

"By the time I had my own children, there was a vast smorgasbord of children's literature for us to sample. My children loved the 'musical' picture books of Mem Fox, Pamela Allen, and Lynley Dodd, and enjoyed the bizarre humor of Roald Dahl and Paul Jennings. Despite the proliferation of modern children's literature, however, my son remained a devoted fan of Rudyard Kipling's classic, *The Jungle Book.*

"I started writing in the 1990s after becoming a 'Ph.D. widow.' My husband was working long hours completing his doctoral thesis while I stayed home at nights looking after the children. I've never been fond of television, so I wrote children's stories. My children were trenchant critics of my work, but they also gave me the confidence to continue the daunting process of submission to publishers. If my son Nick hadn't read *The Glow Worm Cave* and declared, 'You will get this one published, Mum,' the manuscript would still be in my bottom drawer. I am also grateful to publishers who, when rejecting my manuscripts, also wrote brief notes of encouragement to me.

"My prime motivation in writing is to entertain the shy child within myself. A secondary motivation is to open up new worlds for children that are the same as their own, only different. I also like to challenge children to think about some of the moral dilemmas that are part of everyday life.

"These days I spend more time writing poetry and short stories than children's books. I have also developed an interest in multimedia and have recently worked on an Internet education project on the shipwrecks, sealers, and scientists of Macquarie Island.

"My advice to aspiring writers is to avoid the approach I took when I first started writing. I wrote covertly, too embarrassed to admit that I was a secret scribbler—or keyboard tapper, until I had my first book published. I wish now that I had sought out a community of writers much earlier and gained some sound advice about the craft of writing and the expectations of publishers before sending off submissions."

N

NOBISSO, Josephine 1953-
(Nuria Wood, Nadja Bride)

Personal

Born February 9, 1953, in Bronx, NY; daughter of Ralph (a mason contractor) and Maria (a homemaker; maiden name, Zamboli) Nobisso; married Victor Jude (an antiques restorer), July 26, 1981; children: one daughter. *Education:* Attended Universita di Urbino, Italy, 1971-74; State University of New York, New Paltz, B.S. (foreign languages; cum laude), teaching certification, 1974. *Religion:* Roman Catholic. *Hobbies and other interests:* Hiking, reading, collecting children's books, family days, contemplative walks.

Addresses

Home and office—P.O. Box 1396, Quogue, NY 11959. *E-mail*—ghbooks@optonline.net.

Career

Freelance writer, publisher, and educational consultant, 1971—. Winslow Press, New York City, senior editor, 1995-99; Gingerbread House (publishing house), Westhampton Beach, NY, founder and publisher, 1999—; writing instructor and creator of copyrighted writing program "The Nobisso Recommendations: Guiding Students to Write in Their Authentic Voices"; lecturer and workshop presenter at numerous schools. *Member:* Society of Children's Book Writers and Illustrators (former group co-chair), Authors Guild, Authors League of America.

Awards, Honors

"Best Kid's Book of the Year" citation, *Parents* magazine, 1989, for *Grandpa Loved;* Verna Mulholland Friend of Education award, Delta Kappa Gamma Beta Pi, 1991; Distinguished Graduate award, National Catholic Education Association, 2000.

Josephine Nobisso

Writings

FOR YOUNG READERS

Grandpa Loved, illustrated by Maureen Hyde, Green Tiger Press (San Diego, CA), 1989, second edition, Gingerbread House (Westhampton Beach, NY), 2000.

Grandma's Scrapbook, illustrated by Maureen Hyde, Simon & Schuster (New York City), 1991, second edition, Gingerbread House (Westhampton Beach, NY), 2000.

Shh! The Whale Is Smiling, illustrated by Maureen Hyde, Simon & Schuster (New York City), 1992.

For the Sake of a Cake, illustrated by Anton Krajnc, Rizzoli (New York City), 1993.

Hot-cha-cha!, illustrated by Joan Holub, Winslow Press, 1998.

John Blair and the Great Hinkley Fire, illustrated by Ted Rose, Hougton (Boston), 2000.

Forest Fires: Run for Your Life!, Mondo Publishing (Greenvale, NY), 2000.

The Yawn, illustrated by Glo Coalson, Orchard (New York City), 2001.

FOR ADULTS

(Under name Nuria Wood) *With No Regrets,* Berkley (New York City), 1983.

(Under name Nuria Wood) *The Family Plan,* Berkley (New York City), 1984.

(Under name Nadja Bride) *Hide and Seek,* Quest (New York City), 1985.

OTHER

Contributor of articles, short stories, and reviews to periodicals, including *Instructor, Fiction Writer's Monthly,* and *SCBWI Bulletin.*

Work in Progress

Time Travels Well, a novel for young adults; a screenplay and novelization for adults titled *The Psychic Life of Esther Cane;* numerous picture books; *Miracle of the Americas: Our Lady of Guadalupe.*

Sidelights

With a teaching certification in early childhood education, author and lecturer Josephine Nobisso has authored a number of picture books that capture the joys of childhood. Beginning with her first published book for children, 1989's *Grandpa Loved,* Nobisso has imbued her stories with both deep emotions and an uplifting sense of wonderment. In addition to her picture books for children, she has also authored several adult novels and has created a writing curriculum used in many schools in her native New York State.

Born in the Bronx, New York, in 1953, Nobisso once explained to *SATA* that she was "raised on both sides of the Atlantic (and sometimes *on* the Atlantic as my fortuitous adventures included many things from luxury ocean liners to twelve-passenger freighter crossings)." The reason? Her parents, both Italian immigrants, returned to Italy for long visits every year to touch base with the family and friends they had left behind. Attending Catholic schools until her junior year of high school, Nobisso excelled at her English studies, even though Italian, not English, was spoken in her home. After high school graduation, she enrolled at the State University of New York at New Paltz, earning a bachelor's degree, with honors, in foreign languages in only three years. In 1981 she married her childhood

An older boy remembers the times he and his grandpa shared in **Grandpa Loved.** *(Written by Nobisso and illustrated by Maureen Hyde.)*

***An older girl shares a scrapbook of her summers with her grandmother in* Grandma's Scrapbook.** *(Written by Nobisso and illustrated by Maureen Hyde.)*

sweetheart, Victor Jude, and together the couple has raised one daughter. Nobisso is also a certified teacher with a specialization in early childhood education.

"The incidents in my family are the stuff of legend," Nobisso once told *SATA.* "There was the grandfather who appeared to his ten children even though he was hundreds of miles away, the grandmother who unearthed an ancient urn that toppled every dish in the farmhouse in its fury to be re-buried, and the perfectly healthy grandfather whose prediction to die upon seeing the birth of a certain grandchild (me, I'm afraid to say), came true." From this rich family life, it is easy to see where stories like *Grandpa Loved* and *Grandma's Scrapbook* have their roots. In *Grandpa Loved* Nobisso follows a boy and his grandfather as they explore the seaside and the forest, walk along busy city streets, and enjoy the bustle of a family gathering. Throughout the story, the relationship between the two grows stronger, and it is only at the end of the book that readers learn the old man has died and the boy is actually recalling happy

memories. *Grandma's Scrapbook* follows much the same pattern, as a girl shares with readers the pages of a scrapbook kept by her elderly—and now deceased—grandmother to hold memories of summers spent together.

Family interaction is also central to *For the Sake of a Cake,* as a koala and an alligator, all dressed in pajamas and tucked into bed, quibble over whose turn it is to toss off the covers, get up, and check the cake baking in the oven. As each tries to top the other's list of arduous tasks already done that day, the cake shows signs of transforming into a cinder-block in Nobisso's humorous tale, comically illustrated by artist Anton Krajnc. As a special bonus, the author ends her story with a recipe for a Viennese cake. In another story for bedtime reading, *Shh! The Whale Is Smiling* finds a girl soothing her afraid-of-the-dark little brother with a story about a singing whale. Calling the book "a gentle, nocturnal fantasy" in her *School Library Journal* review, Kate McClelland praised Nobisso's text for its "lilting cadence."

In a more upbeat vein, Nobisso's 1998 picture book *Hot-cha-cha!* is pure fun as Maria and her friends discover a lost playground key in a cookie jar, then rush the gates, ready to swing, jump, roller-skate, toss the ball, and laugh. A *Kirkus Reviews* critic praised the "infectious rhythm of Nobisso's rhymes," while *School Library Journal* contributor Carolyn Jenks enjoyed the author's use of "rap" rhythms and the portrayal of both children and adults engaged in energetic activity. As with her other books, *Hot-cha-cha!* draws on what Nobisso once explained to *SATA* as "the densely atmospheric and passionately happy world that was my childhood. If an author's voice is a function of her personality, then I can hope that mine is 'sharply original' for that's what my work is often called."

"It has taken some of my stories up to twenty years to see the light of day as published books," Nobisso once admitted. "But I persevere, believing, as a playwright once said, that 'hope is an orientation of the heart. It is not the conviction that something will turn out well, but the certainty that something makes sense, regardless of how it turns out.'" In 1999 the author decided to take matters into her own hands by founding her own publishing house, called Gingerbread House, which has issued revised editions of several of Nobisso's most popular picture books.

Nobisso's success is due, in part, to the fact that she made a "full-time commitment" to her writing; "I'm writing all the time (even in my dreams!), planning workshops, running my office and home, and waking up very early to accomplish it all!" In addition to writing, she also finds time to present an average of forty creative writing workshops each year at elementary schools near her home in Long Island, New York.

Biographical and Critical Sources

PERIODICALS

Children's Book Review Service, February, 1999, Pamela L. Simon, review of *Hot-cha-cha!,* p. 70.
Kirkus Reviews, October 15, 1998, review of *Hot-cha-cha!,* p. 1535.
School Library Journal, August, 1992, Kate McClelland, review of *Shh! The Whale Is Smiling,* p. 145; December, 1998, Carolyn Jenks, review of *Hot-cha-cha!,* p. 88.

ON-LINE

Gingerbread House, http://www.gingerbreadbooks.com/ (February 2, 2001).

P–R

PERROW, Angeli 1954-

Personal

Born February 7, 1954, in Rockland, ME; daughter of Joseph and Elsie (maiden name, Rogers; present surname, Savage) Seavey; married Mark Perrow (a carpenter), July 27, 1974; children: Gabriel, Ariel. *Education:* Westfield State College, B.S.E., 1976. *Hobbies and other interests:* Drawing, photography, gardening, hiking.

Addresses

Home—24 Western Ave., Hampden, ME 04444.

Career

Katahdin Times, Millinocket, ME, reporter and photographer, 1977-78; schoolteacher in Hermon, ME, 1989-98; Mainely Buoys, Holden, ME, artist, 1998-2000; art teacher in Hampden, ME, 2000—. *Member:* Maine Writers and Publishers Alliance.

Writings

Maine Lighthouses Coloring Book, privately printed, 1994.
Captain's Castaway, illustrated by Emily Harris, Down East Books (Camden, ME), 1998.
Lighthouse Dog to the Rescue, illustrated by Harris, Down East Books (Camden, ME), 2000.

Work in Progress

Great Adventures of New England Lighthouses, an illustrated collection of true stories about storms, rescues, and other adventures at lighthouses in New England.

Sidelights

Angeli Perrow told *SATA:* "I have a passion for lighthouses. The flame was lit during my years as an elementary schoolteacher in Hermon, Maine, as I attempted to develop a Maine studies unit that would pull in our science topic of lights and lenses. Material about lighthouses for children was sparse. I researched our state's lighthouses and created a coloring book as an educational tool for my students. Out of the research sprang fascinating people of the past (light-keepers and their families) and tantalizing tidbits of history. One of these, a paragraph about a shipwrecked dog rescued by a lighthouse keeper's daughter, sparked the idea for my first picture book, *Captain's Castaway.* Another account inspired my second picture book, *Lighthouse Dog to the Rescue.* It is my hope that by my writing about real people and events, not only will children be entertained,

Angeli Perrow

but they will come to appreciate our lighthouses and desire to preserve them for future generations."

Biographical and Critical Sources

PERIODICALS

Publishers Weekly, December 7, 1998, review of *Captain's Castaway,* p. 59.

School Library Journal, March, 1999, Sally R. Dow, review of *Captain's Castaway,* p. 183.

ON-LINE

Amazon.com, www.amazon.com/ (August 26, 2000).

* * *

REYNOLDS, Marilyn (M.) 1935-

Personal

Born September 13, 1935, in California; daughter of Fay (a meat market owner) and Esther (a homemaker) Dodson; married, c. 1956 (divorced); married Michael Reynolds (a musician), 1967; children: (first marriage) Cindi, Sharon; (second marriage) Matthew. *Education:* California State University, Los Angeles, B.A. (English), 1965, teaching credential, 1967; Pepperdine University, M.S. (reading education), 1981; attended Pacific Oaks College, 1980, and California State University, 1997-98.

Addresses

Home—2135 Promontory Point Ln., Gold River, CA 95670. *E-mail*—mmreynolds@earthlink.net.

Career

Teacher and writer. Glen A. Wilson High School, Hacienda Heights, CA, English teacher, 1967-69; Alhambra and Monrovia, CA, public schools, English-as-a-second-language teacher, 1969-72, teacher at Century High School, Alhambra, 1972-93, writer-in-residence, consultant and tutor, 1993-98; Pacific Oaks College, Pasadena, CA, undergraduate writing instructor, 1982-83; lecturer, workshop presenter, and freelance writer, 1998—; Calvine High School, Elk Grove, CA, teacher, 1999—. *Member:* PEN, National Education Association, National Council of Teachers of English, Assembly of Literature for Adolescents, California Teachers Association, California Reading Association, Screen Writers' Association of Santa Barbara, Altadena Writers Association; Sacramento Area Library Association.

Awards, Honors

Best Books for Young Adults citation, American Library Association (ALA), 1994, for *Detour for Emmy;* South Carolina Young Adult Book Award, 1995-96, for *Detour for Emmy;* Best Books for the Teen Age designation, New York Public Library, for *Detour for Emmy;* Best Books for Young Adults citation, American Library Association (ALA), for *Too Soon for Jeff;* Quick Picks for Young Adults, American Library Association (ALA), 1995, for *Too Soon for Jeff;* Best Books for the Teen Age designation, New York Public Library, 1996, for *But What about Me?* and *Beyond Dreams;* Quick Picks for Young Adults, American Library Association (ALA), 1997, for *Telling;* Daytime Emmy Award nomination for Writing in a Children's Special, 1997, for teleplay *Too Soon for Jeff;* Best Books for the Teen Age designation, New York Public Library, 1998, for *Beyond Dreams;* Best Books for the Teen Age designation, New York Public Library, 1999, for *Baby Help;* 2000 Popular Paperbacks for Young Adults, Short Takes, American Library Association (ALA), 2000, for *Beyond Dreams;* Best Books for the Teen Age designation, New York Public Library, 2000, for *If You Loved Me.*

Writings

"TRUE-TO-LIFE" FICTION SERIES; FOR YOUNG ADULTS; BOOKS INCLUDE TEACHING GUIDES

Telling, Peace Ventures Press, 1989, revised edition part of "True-to-Life" series, Morning Glory Press, 1996.

Twelve-year-old Cassie learns to deal with being molested by the father of the children she baby-sits in Marilyn Reynolds's realistic and informative story.

Detour for Emmy, Morning Glory Press, 1993.
Too Soon for Jeff, Morning Glory Press, 1994.
Beyond Dreams, illustrated by Laura Manriquez, Morning Glory Press, 1995.
But What about Me?, Morning Glory Press, 1996.
(With David Doty) *True-to-Life Series from Hamilton High Teaching Guide*, Morning Glory Press, 1996.
Baby Help, Morning Glory Press, 1998.
If You Loved Me, Morning Glory Press, 1999.
Love Rules, Morning Glory Press, 2001.

OTHER

Contributor to *Among Us*, Peace Ventures Press, 1989. Contributor of essays and short fiction to periodicals, including *Sonoma Mandala*, *Event*, *English Journal*, *Chicago Tribune*, *Los Angeles Times*, and *Pasadena Magazine*. Contributor of essays to anthologies, including *Filtered Images*, *Fathers and Daughters*, and *Mothers and Sons*.

Adaptations

Too Soon for Jeff (teleplay; "ABC Afterschool Special"), first broadcast on ABC-TV, 1997.

Sidelights

Marilyn Reynolds worked as a teacher for many years before putting pen to paper to begin what has become a fulfilling second career as a writer. In 1989 her first novel, *Telling*, was published; it would be the first of several books Reynolds would author that focus on the troubled lives of modern teens. Among her most popular works are the "True-to-Life" series from Hamilton High books, novels that focus on specific problems common to teens and which are accompanied by a teacher's guide to make them convenient for classroom use.

Born in 1935, Reynolds was raised in Temple City, California, where her father owned a meat market. While not exactly a motivated student during high school, she returned to college in her late twenties, graduated, and earned her teaching certificate, as well as an advanced degree. In 1978, after the second of her three children left home, she finally indulged in a long-held desire to write, and three years later witnessed the publication of her first work, an essay in the *Los Angeles Times*. With her name now in print in such a lofty publication, Reynolds was energized; her byline has appeared on numerous short stories, essays, and articles since.

Reynolds published her first teen novel, *Telling*, in 1989; it would eventually become the first of her "True-to-Life" novels. In this story, when the Sloane family move to a new town, twelve-year-old neighbor Cassie Jenkins believes she has found cool new babysitting clients. However, Mr. Sloane makes a sexual advance toward her while bringing her home from babysitting his children. Cassie is embarrassed and confused about her feelings; after she tells a confidant, it seems like everyone suddenly knows what happened. Frances Bradburn dubbed this novel, "sad, frightening, ultimate-

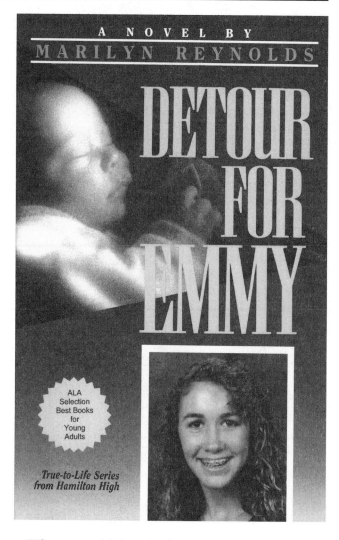

Fifteen-year-old Emmy's plans for the future change after she becomes an unmarried mother.

ly hopeful, and definitely worthwhile" in a *Booklist* assessment. Critic Marilyn Makowski also praised Reynolds' debut novel, commenting in *School Library Journal* that the author does "a superb job of weaving the complexities of difficult issues into the life of an innocent child." In *Voice of Youth Advocates* contributor Joyce A. Litton believed *Telling* could be "very helpful to girls who have been sexually abused."

In another installment in Reynolds' series, a young woman must struggle between remaining true to her core beliefs or retaining the love of her boyfriend. *But What about Me?* introduces Erica Arrendondo, a high school senior, who, with a spot on the school volleyball team, a part-time volunteer job at the local animal shelter, and a dream of becoming a veterinarian, seems to have it together. But her boyfriend is headed straight downhill and wants to drag her along with him. "The characters are compelling and the novel itself [is] almost impossible to put down," said *School Library Journal* reviewer Robyn Ryan Vandenbroek, who called Reynolds' writing "superb."

Baby Help finds a young teen mother living with her baby's teen father at his mother's house. In this 1998 novel, Melissa suddenly confronts the fact that her boyfriend is becoming as abusive to their child as he once was to her. "Reynolds carefully explores the problem of partner abuse," noted Bradburn in another *Booklist* review. In *School Library Journal*, Melissa Gross praised the dialogue as "authentic" and "likely to hold the interest of reluctant readers." Reynolds explores the problem of a drug-addicted parent as seen through seventeen-year-old Laura's eyes as she tries to hold the line against a boyfriend enticing her to break her long held promise to remain a virgin until marriage in *If You Loved Me.*

In an essay for the *Something about the Author Autobiography Series,* Reynolds offered the following advice to young people: "First, pay attention to your innermost hopes and dreams. If someone tells you you're not good enough to be an artist, a dancer, or whatever, know that the important thing is the strength within you, not another person's judgment. Find people with whom you can feel safe exchanging thoughts and feelings on the deepest level available to you, and cherish such people above all else." And, most importantly, "Love yourself, even when you are tormented by stupid mistakes and the consequences they bring."

Biographical and Critical Sources

BOOKS

Something about the Author Autobiography Series, Volume 23, Gale (Detroit), 1996, pp. 247-265.

PERIODICALS

Arizona Republic, March 6, 2000, David Madrid, "Teen Sex Enough for Dysart to Ban Book from Schools," p. B1.
Booklist, September 15, 1994, Jeanne Triner, review of *Too Soon for Jeff,* p. 126; November 15, 1995, Jeanne Triner, review of *Beyond Dreams,* p. 548; April 2, 1996, Frances Bradburn, review of *Telling,* p. 1356; February 1, 1998, Frances Bradburn, review of *Baby Help,* p. 911; September 1, 1999, Shelle Rosenfeld, review of *If You Loved Me,* p. 124.
Publishers Weekly, June 28, 1993, review of *Detour for Emmy,* p. 79.
School Library Journal, July, 1993, Alice Casey Smith, review of *Detour for Emmy,* p. 102; September, 1994, Judy R. Johnston, review of *Too Soon for Jeff,* p. 241; September, 1995, Susan R. Farber, review of *Beyond Dreams,* p. 220; May, 1996, Marilyn Makowski, review of *Telling,* p. 116; October, 1996, Robyn Ryan Vandenbroek, review of *But What about Me?,* p. 148; May, 1998, Melissa Gross, review of *Baby Help,* p. 216; December, 1999, Susan R. Farber, review of *If You Loved Me,* p. 140.
Voice of Youth Advocates, December, 1993, Anne Liebst, review of *Detour for Emmy,* p. 298; February, 1996, Carrie Eldridge, review of *Beyond Dreams,* p. 376; June, 1996, Joyce A. Litton, review of *Telling,* p. 99; February, 1997, Jacqueline Rose, review of *But What about Me?,* p. 332; June, 1998, Carrie Eldridge, review of *Baby Help,* p. 124.
Wilson Library Bulletin, May, 1995, review of *Too Soon for Jeff,* p. 110.

S

Anne Shelby

1948-

If you leave Kentucky before daylight and drive straight through, you can make Myrtle Beach by late afternoon, check into a motel, and run for the water. Surrounded by mountains the rest of the year, on summer vacations we headed straight for the sea. That first sight of the water, wider and deeper and more luminescent than dreams, thrilled beyond measure. After days of screaming in the surf and baking our skins in the sun, we headed back, red as tomatoes, with sand in our shoes and underwear, with suitcases full of seashells, wet bathing suits, and souvenirs. We had been to a different place and we were changed, so changed we shed our skins and grew new ones. I never meant to become a writer. I have shed several skins on the way to becoming one and hope to shed more before it's over.

As a kid my ambitions ran along the lines of preacher, cowgirl, and movie star. Most of the grown-ups I knew were tobacco farmers, schoolteachers, or preachers. Of the three, preaching held by far the most appeal. The preachers seemed to be having more fun than the farmers and teachers, and they got to talk about interesting topics like sin, hell, miracles, and idol worship, which sounded a lot more interesting to me than leaf mold and mixed fractions. We went to the Gray Hawk Baptist Church, a white wooden structure with a steeple and old-fashioned benches. Sunday mornings the church house would be full, men on one side, women on the other, children roving freely and noisily between. Mrs. Humes played an introduction on the piano, and we all stood up and set the walls to ringing with "Higher Ground," "Standing on the Promises," or "Leaning on the Everlasting Arms." I learned to read, moving my finger along the lines in the hymnbook. The words were poems, with meter, rhyme, repetition, metaphor, image, and symbol. They spoke of joy and sorrow, love, forgiveness, and life beyond the grave. Long before I started school, I learned these songs by heart and sang them as I played.

After Mrs. Humes left the piano bench and went back to sit in the pew with Mr. Humes, after the whispers and the coughs and the rustle of dresses and the slap and zip of hymnals being shut and slid into their racks, the congregation settled and the preacher rose in the pulpit. "Reading from the *King James* ... " he began. Whether the *King James* was the definitive version of the Bible, dictated and therefore preferred by God Himself, was a subject of some debate, since if you actually *believe* the Bible exact wording becomes important. My mother, who had studied religion in college, was considered something of a radical, as she could be seen entering Sunday school carrying, along with her best pocket book, a suspiciously modern-looking *Revised Standard Version.*

Whether from her influence or my own common sense, I never thought that our religion was the only one. And while I did hear from the pulpit occasional warnings of the dangers of hell, short shorts, and rock 'n' roll, more often the sermons earnestly examined the teachings of Jesus and exhorted us to try to be more like Him. And then there were the stories, grand tales of beasts and floods and miracles, Daniel in the lions' den, manna falling from heaven, Jesus walking on the water. I listened, wide-eyed. I heard other stories, but nothing could touch this stuff. I decided to become a preacher.

I gave up the idea later, when I kept picking up hints from grown-ups that what I should be was not a preacher but a preacher's wife, and I failed to see much attraction in that. The number of possible adult occupations to observe and emulate was somewhat limited, particularly for girls, in that time and place. The world I knew was small and far removed from the world of concerts, opera, ballet, art museums, and poetry readings. Yet in some ways it was a world rich in art and culture.

More clearly than yesterday, I remember a summer afternoon more than forty years ago. I was, perhaps, seven.

Anne Shelby

We lived in Jackson County, Kentucky, in McKee, the county seat (population 100), a town which had, it seemed to me then, exactly what it needed with nothing extra left over. There was one bank, one grocery store, one five-and-dime, a restaurant, filling station, two funeral homes, and half a dozen churches. Throw a rock from the courthouse steps and you could hit about anything in McKee.

The town lay in a flat narrow valley between two ridges. On one ridge sat the high school, a majestic WPA structure where my father taught agriculture; my mother, English. They had gone to school together and had met again after the war at a Berea College reunion. They married in 1947 and came to McKee, my father's hometown, to teach. I was born a year later at Berea College Hospital.

The hillside opposite the school in McKee was dotted with small frame houses, and we lived in one, near the top of the hill. In our yard my father put up a swing set for my sister and me, and this particular summer afternoon I spent swinging, as high and as long as I wanted to—for some reason no one came out that day to warn me of the dangers of swinging too high—and looking out on the treetops and the rooftops of the town, on women and children and men and dogs on the courthouse lawn, on a world that seemed to make perfect sense. I sang, as long and as loudly as I wanted.

I love my rooster, my rooster loves me.

I'll cherish my rooster in a greenberry tree . . . .

Songs and music seemed to me then as natural and certain a thing as rocks in the creek. At that time most of my relatives did not have indoor plumbing. They did have stacks of 78 rpm records—the Carter Family, Mainer's Mountaineers, Fiddlin' John and Moonshine Kate—and wind-up Victrolas which filled the house with music so loud you had to go out in the yard to listen to it.

Uncles Arnold and James picked guitar. Aaron played harmonica. Don sang in a gospel quartet. Myrna and Glenna harmonized, washing the supper dishes. Mother sang in the kitchen, too, while she cooked, "I'll Fly Away" and "Somewhere Listening" accompanied by the sizzle of grease and the clatter of pot lids. Dad sang Hank Williams and Ernest Tubb. Uncle Millard preferred cowboy songs— "Streets of Laredo" and anything by the Sons of the Pioneers. At one grandmother's house there was an old organ, where great-aunts sang sentimental songs, weeping while pumping vigorously on the foot pedals. My grandfather, usually stern-faced and dignified, sometimes erupted unexpectedly:

Get out of the way, Old Dan Tucker
You're too late to get your supper
Supper's over, breakfast cookin'
Old Dan Tucker, stand there lookin'

Decades after his death, neighbors still talk about how that man could whistle. You could hear him, they say, on "Little Birdie," all the way from the lower field clear up to the Road Run Gap. He'd once played for Saturday night dances, but traded his banjo to a mantel clock when he joined the church. I imagine the time went by a little slower after that.

We sang on the porch, in the car, and at family reunions, songs from church, records, and the radio. And when we sang all the songs we knew, we made up our own, sad songs, mostly, but we had fun singing them, about dying cowboys, lost love, and the hope of heaven.

I do not think my family was unusual in this way. I remember talent shows in the high school gym and at the county fair. Music flowed out the windows, summer evenings, of the Pentecostal Church down the road, and pulled me from the playhouse and the TV "Hit Parade" to stand on the rock steps and listen. And one of the highest forms of praise, right up there with "He'd do anything in the world to help you out" and "She's not one bit stuck up" was "She has got the prettiest voice" or "He can hear a tune one time and play it. Never had a lesson in his life."

Music still seems to me as present and as necessary as air. I've never understood, in fact, some people's objections to musicals, to the notion that, standing in line or on a street corner in the rain, people might suddenly burst into song. I'm surprised, in fact, that this doesn't happen rather more often in real life. As someone who learned to read out of a hymnbook, music and writing are to me, not distant relatives in the family of the arts, but close kin, like double first cousins. Unlike some of my own cousins, I don't have perfect pitch. I can't play guitar or piano by ear. I try to write that way.

There were, in addition to music, other art forms in that little country place. I remember plays at church and at school, and while they might not have been well reviewed had they been reviewed at all, they were lively productions which attracted large and enthusiastic audiences. Dance was perhaps the most neglected of the arts, being associated as it was with elitism on one hand and sin on the other. I can report, however, that my aunt Mildred delighted nieces, puzzled hounds, and scattered chickens, dancing the Charleston on the porch.

Many people I knew worked in the visual arts, though they did not call it that. They called it "piddlin'." As a boy my father's brother James wanted only crayons for Christmas. Later, if he couldn't afford canvas, he painted on the window shades. Pull down the ring with the crocheted cover, and there was a mountain lake, a snow-covered cabin, a tree full of birds. Aaron went to the hills and brought back pieces of wood he "just liked the looks of." Under his hands they turned into vases, tables, twisted abstract sculptures. Jack set up a woodworking shop in an old storehouse in McKee and made doll furniture from scraps of walnut he salvaged from the lumber yard. "I just can't stand to see good walnut go to waste," he said.

The aunts piddled, too, drying wildflowers to arrange under glass, creating room-size displays of antique furniture, dolls, and dishes they collected. My grandmother and great-grandmother pieced so many quilt tops they died before they got them all quilted. My mother finished them and made her own quilts from patterns she drew herself. She painted, too, barns and cardinals in acrylics, and made bolder patterns of line and color in the yard in the medium of marigolds, petunias, and scarlet sage.

Nobody I knew claimed to be an artist—or a philosopher—but as much a part of the air we breathed as Saturday soup beans or the bubby bush in the yard were abstract questions, posed earnestly and often, which entered our experience through the church or arose from a heightened awareness of death, which was always as close and as real as the family graveyard. *How can we know God's will in our lives? Are we free or are our lives predetermined in some way? How can we tell the right from the wrong action? What is our duty to others? Will all sins be forgiven, come the end of time? Will we know one another, on the other side?* I've never found convincing answers, but the questions have stayed with me, and any occupation which does not include them has seemed frivolous somehow.

There were books, too, which were regarded with great respect, if not actual attention. Our greatest reader was perhaps my grandmother Pearlie, who, after raising nine children and burying her husband, lived by herself in a little house across the creek, which War on Poverty photographers would have taken pictures of if they had found out about it, and which we unself-consciously called "the shack." There she proceeded to catch up on some thirty years of reading. For me, while kick-the-can and hoopey-hide with the cousins had their pleasures, so too did slipping off to Mamaw's shack, to sit for a while in her gentle presence and leaf through old copies of *The Saturday Evening Post.*

There were books, but the language that seeped into my bones did not come from them. My father's family, his eight brothers and sisters and their children, gathered most evenings at the homeplace at Gray Hawk. In warm weather while the children played in the yard, the men pitched horseshoes or drew a ring for marbles. The women, supper over, sat on the porch with glasses of iced tea. Winter nights were for playing Rook, making fudge, tending fire, and telling tales.

Well, you know what Granddad Cornett said before he died. He was bad off, very low, not expected to make it through the night. Talking out of his head, craziest stuff you ever heard in your life. They was all gathered around the deathbed there, and Kermit bent over him real quiet and whispered, said, "Dad, can you hear me? Do you know who I am?" Grandad never moved nor opened his eyes, just answered, said, "What's the matter, Kermit? Don't you know who you are?"

My mother, a great talker and storyteller, had grown up in a time and place in which talking constituted the main source of entertainment. Women talked while they quilted, broke beans or churned butter, men as they hoed corn or mended fences. Evenings when the work was done they talked on the porch or in front of the fire. In those days before radio, TV, and personal stereos, they talked to pass the time, to liven up monotonous chores, to fill the silence.

Anne with her father, Luther Gabbard, 1948.

Anne with her mother, Jessie Bishop Gabbard, 1951.

The skills of a good talker, who remembered stories and knew how to tell them, were highly valued.

Weekends we crossed the county line from Jackson into Clay, clouds of white gravel dust billowing behind the car, to visit her side of the family. There were no cousins at that end of the road, but there was a store, a tiny country store my grandparents kept, full of pop, candy, plug tobacco, nails, flies, and talk, mostly talk, which included spirited debates over politics, hunting dogs, and who was the laziest man in the county.

> I heard of a feller one time, boys, too lazy to breathe. Set down under a shade tree, leaned up against it there, said, "Breath, you can come and go as you please. I've pushed and I've pulled all I'm a-goin' to."

Sunday afternoons in summer, the store spilled over into the yard—there being no real distinction between customers and company—and we sat on benches under the apple tree or lay on pallets in its shade. Men whittled, women fanned, and talk flowed like Teges Creek, a little slower here, a little faster there, pooling quiet for a spell, then cascading into laughter like water over a falls.

Shade and Dewey Fox, Virgil Webb, Morris and Tildy Allen, my parents and grandparents, uncles and aunts— these were my first and most important literary influences. I spent my childhood among people who laughed and cried easily, who wrote songs, laboriously drawing the notes on homemade staff paper, who worried about predestination and could not stand to see good walnut go to waste. They showed me, humbly and without ever speaking of it, the necessity of such activities. I can't do much with walnut. I piddle with words.

These memories are early ones, from the time before I was eight. Something was about to happen that would change our lives in ways we are still trying to figure out. Some parts of the world were about to open up, while others would close down forever.

My grandmother had been cooking all morning, throwing sticks of wood into the blazing stove, raising clouds of flour dust as she poured from the sack into the sifter. When the biscuits were brown, the chicken fried, and all of us gathered round, she dried her hands on her apron and addressed us as a group, something she had not done before and would not do again. "Well, I won a television," she announced abruptly. My grandmother had picked up the lucky flour sack, and things would never be quite the same.

My father and uncle planted an antenna on top of the hill and ran wire from the antenna to the house and in the front window to the back of the set. I held the hall mirror in front of the TV so Uncle could see it while he fiddled with the knobs in the back, trying to get a picture. We claimed to get two stations, 6 and 10 out of Knoxville, but you could never really see Channel 10, you could only hear it, and occasionally make out a blurry figure, bantering brightly despite being caught in a blinding snowstorm.

At this time my grandparents had electricity but no telephone or plumbing, and they still heated with coal and cooked on a wood stove. They took pride in the television as evidence of their modernity, but were largely disinterested in the proceedings surrounding its installation and clearly disappointed with the results. After watching for a few minutes, my grandmother yawned, mumbled something with the word "foolish" in it, and went to bed. My grandfather retired to the front porch to sit in the dark, rolling cigarettes and listening to the crickets. Mother, Dad and Uncle, while enamored of science and its promise of a bright tomorrow, predicted that the television would make people so lazy, after a while they wouldn't even want to get up to change the channel, and something would have to be invented to do it for them, an idea we found so ridiculous it struck us as highly amusing at the time.

But I was hooked. Suddenly new career possibilities seemed to present themselves, such as riding horses, carrying guns, singing in a saloon, or having my own weekly variety show. The unglamorous growing of potatoes and teaching of grade school arithmetic were definitely out. Even the dream of becoming Jackson County's first woman preacher dissolved in that flickering light, where beautiful men and ladies in tuxedoes and sparkly dresses danced with champagne glasses in their hands and sang of romantic love. My sister and I still played but our play changed. Now we pretended we lived in apartments in the city, where we entertained splendidly-dressed gentlemen who mixed martinis and never tracked in garden dirt.

I learned new songs from TV, songs that were not in the Broadman Hymnal, and sang them under the apple trees and down by the creek. I learned something else, too. According to TV, the place where we lived was small and insignificant, comical somehow, and my neighbors and family, who had seemed so lovely and interesting to me, so different one from the next, were just so many hillbillies and hicks.

School was a disappointment, failing to measure up in interest level to staying home playing all day. Since I could already read the only book the Board of Education offered first graders at the time, I was doomed to spend the rest of the school year listening in misery as classmates whose talents lay in areas other than reading struggled with the tedious monosyllabic adventures of Alice and Jerry and Jip. Though literally bored to tears, I loved my teacher Mrs. Boggs and my friends Carolyn and Loretta and Brenda Sue, and I loved the alphabet. Warm days during long recess, while the others ran and yelled and fought on the hot noisy playground, I slipped back into the cool dark classroom to visit the letters, which danced on grass-green rectangles above the blackboard. They were my friends, all twenty-six, from friendly A, reliable B and sassy C to dangerous X, quiet Y and crazy old Z.

When I was eight my father left teaching to take a job with the Department of Agriculture Soil Conservation Service, and we packed up and moved to Burkesville in Cumberland County, on the Tennessee line. The change was hard but people in the new town were friendly and made us feel at home. My dad settled into his new job, and Mother was teaching eighth grade. It was here, about 1957, that my parents bought the new house. Having lived in old dark houses with leaky roofs and uneven floors, they fell in love with the new brick ranch, with its smooth white walls, polished hardwood floors, and big picture window.

I don't remember writing during this time, or even reading much for that matter. I am sure there was no bookstore, and if there was a library in town I do not remember it. The only children's books I remember having at home were *The Three Billy Goats Gruff* and *Little Black Sambo*. I cannot say with any degree of certainty how these particular works influenced me, though come to think of it, I am extremely fond of pancakes, and I tend to tromp loudly over bridges, in case of trolls underneath.

Most of the books in our house were my parents' college textbooks and, though the words were big and the print small, there was something in Mother's art and poetry books which kept me coming back for more, and Dad's agriculture texts included some very interesting photographs of various veterinary procedures being performed on bulls. My parents never said anything to me about sex, hoping, perhaps, that I wouldn't find out about it, so I went to my only other source of information, my uncle's college science texts, where I found the whole thing laid out in dispassionate scientific language, giving me a rather clinical view of the topic for a small child. The term *zygote*, for example, turned out later to assume a far lesser role in the proceedings than I had initially surmised.

I do not remember ever writing a poem or a story at home or being asked to write one for school. I do remember one wonderful teacher, Mrs. Fudge in sixth grade, who in that period of rampant modernization seemed to have walked into the low brick rectangle that was Cumberland County Elementary directly from a one-room schoolhouse of a century before. Mrs. Fudge paddled fiercely when she thought it necessary, every day she wore a dark dress with an old-fashioned brooch, and every Friday she required each member of the class to recite an assigned poem from memory. Other teachers had given up poetry recitations

"Swinging at McKee," Kentucky, 1954.

along with paddles and brooches, but Mrs. Fudge continued in her time-proven ways.

I loved Fridays, not just because they meant the end of the school week, but because they meant getting to hear poems all afternoon, forty-two stumbling recitations of "Paul Revere's Ride," and I relished every one. While the boys in the back of the room rolled their heads on their desks in agony, I kept alert so as not to miss anything. I can still recite more Longfellow at parties than anyone wants to hear, and I am grateful to Mrs. Fudge, though I never told her, for having those verses in my head.

In high school my primary interests, like those of everyone else I knew, lay less in literature than in trying to get (1) a date and (2) out of the house with the keys to the family car without arousing too much suspicion. The writing I did was for English class at London High School, where we were required to write one verbose theme per day on an abstract topic. I made good grades and was sometimes referred to by my classmates as "a brain," which I knew was not a compliment, intelligence not being regarded as attractive in a teenage girl at the time. To compensate I acted as silly as possible, a habit that after all these long years I am still trying to break.

I started college in 1966 at Kentucky Southern, a small liberal arts school in Louisville, which unfortunately folded for financial reasons the next year. My freshman English teacher was Wade Hall, who has written and published many books since then. At the time I believe he had one, *The Smiling Phoenix,* which I bought and carried around with me. He was a southerner studying and writing about the South, and the first person I knew who had written a book. In his class we wrote poems, stories, essays, experiments in the theater of the absurd. On one of my papers Dr. Hall wrote, "You have a flair."

I transferred to another small liberal arts school, St. Andrews Presbyterian College in Laurinburg, North Carolina, arriving there in the fall of 1968, when the times were a-changing and so was I. Two weeks later, on my twentieth birthday, I had a date with a guy from Fort Bragg, a big army base about forty miles away. There was quite a lot of traffic in those days between the base and the girls' dorms at the college. His name was Jim Godwin, and he was handsome and fun and more than a little dangerous and represented the opposite of everything my parents had tried to teach me so I fell in love with him right away. We married three months later, on the day after Christmas, and in January he went to Vietnam.

I stayed in school, majoring in English because it was the subject I did best in, and finished my degree the year Jimmy was gone. I had no particular ambitions nor even a vague plan. It seems dumb now, I know, but many of us did not plan for the future in those days. We thought that the future, when it came, would be so unlike the past that there was no use doing anything to get ready for it. My friends' plans involved hitchhiking to California or around Europe for a while. I thought I would just hang out around my life and see what happened. I won't trouble you with details, but as you might guess I have had more than one occasion over the years to question the wisdom of this approach.

Jimmy and I wrote letters which I wish now I had kept. Mine were about rock lyrics and protest marches, his about

"My grandmother, Carrie Bishop, making biscuits," 1955.

firefights and ambushes, about having to be sick and scared all the time, about having to kill people and seeing your friends killed around you. Though others were protesting, Jim had felt that if his country was fighting a war, then that must be the right thing to do. It was the reality that changed his mind.

We lived together for a year after he came back, in Charleston, South Carolina, where he was from, and Graham was born there in January 1971. Five weeks later I took the baby and went back to Kentucky. The nightmares which had followed Jimmy home from Vietnam were more than I could handle. We divorced, had little contact for a long time, and are now good friends. He was featured on the CBS Evening News one Memorial Day, an example of a Vietnam vet in the lifelong process of healing.

Back in London, Kentucky, with Graham and living with my parents, I got a job teaching ninth grade English. Since I had no teaching certificate, I was taking education classes at a nearby college, where I met Edmund Shelby. We have been married since 1972, and he has become Graham's father, my best buddy, and the most ardent supporter of my writing.

At Morehead State University where Edmund was finishing a degree in journalism, I worked at the Appalachian Adult Education Center. My job was typing proposals, letters, and reports that had to do with various experimental education projects in the region. I was not very good at this, since I refused to type anything I considered awkward, ungrammatical, or smacking of stereotype. I rewrote everything I typed, and either in recognition of my contributions or in self-defense, my bosses gave me a raise and changed my title from secretary to writer.

University employees could take one free class a semester. I worked my way through the writing classes, but it was an Appalachian History course taught by Stuart Sprague that set me thinking in ways which have influenced my life and work ever since. Until then the political and social movements of the time, which had to do with the war and the economy, with civil rights and women's rights, seemed to have little to do with the people I knew, mostly white and mostly poor, in Eastern Kentucky. With the class and the works of Harry Caudill, I began studying Appalachian history and culture, and found that other people from the mountains—journalists, scholars, writers, activists, artists, and musicians—were also looking at the region in new ways and, like me, were electing to live and work here. Since then, Appalachian studies programs have grown up around the region, and new artists continue to emerge. Their work has not yet permeated the national consciousness, however, and the persistence in the popular mind and media of ill-informed generalizations and negative stereotypes about our region continues to be a source of frustration.

When Edmund got a job as a reporter with the *Hazard Herald*, we were glad to be moving to that part of Kentucky. Perry County was the scene of dramatic confrontations between environmentalists, citizens' rights advocates, and the coal mining industry, and the small town of Whitesburg in the next county was the home of Harry Caudill, *The Mountain Eagle* newspaper, and Appalshop, a nonprofit group of young filmmakers and other artists. I worked as an editor of *Mountain Review*, a literary quarterly published at Appalshop at the time, but when I could no longer afford to buy gas or pay the baby-sitter, I took a job teaching GED students at Hazard Community College. From there I decided to go to graduate school in English at the University of Kentucky.

In all the jobs I had during those years—teaching, typing, technical writing and editing—I experienced a recurring feeling of having wandered into the wrong room and being stuck there. I kept sweating and looking for the nearest exit. I felt as if I were in a play all the time, in a part for which I had been slightly miscast. I could play it but the effort left me exhausted and unsettled. In Lexington, several people and events came together to help me think of myself as a writer.

Gurney Norman (*Kinfolks, Divine Right's Trip*) came to UK about the same time as a creative writing professor, and introduced me to George Ella Lyon (*Borrowed Children, A Hammer for My Heart*). Both Gurney and George Ella have helped many writers get their start, but, to me, even more important than their stimulating company and exemplary work has been the very fact of their existence as writers of my generation from the mountains. Meeting them, several forbidding barriers began to crumble.

During this period the University of Kentucky began hosting an annual Women Writers Conference, where I heard for the first time the work and experiences of many contemporary women writers. One year at the conference the UK Appalachian Center sponsored a reading by Appalachian women writers—George Ella Lyon, Jo Carson, Betsy Sholl, Lee Howard and others. I sat in the audience, still a rather timid and eager-to-please graduate student, and smiled. I had finally stumbled into the right room. Not long after that, I was reading with them.

I had another wonderful friend then, Belinda Mason, whom I had known in Hazard and who had come to UK as a journalism student. We made a pact one night to start writing, regardless of the response we got or did not get from friends, acquaintances, relatives, and potential publishers. For years I'd been reading and analyzing literature, teaching writing, editing other people's writing. The semester in which I happened to be studying both Walt Whitman and Kate Chopin, I decided that I didn't want just to *teach* writing, *talk* about writing, *write* about writing. I wanted to *write* writing. I didn't want to be the preacher's *wife*, I wanted to be the preacher. With one class to go towards the Ph.D., I tore up my registration cards, walked out of the UK registrar's office, and went home to write, poems first, and newspaper columns, then plays, essays, and children's books.

"With my sister, Lynne, at Myrtle Beach," South Carolina, 1955.

That was many years ago, and my job description hasn't changed much. I write. Sometimes it goes well. Often it does not. Sometimes what I write gets published. Often it does not. Sometimes I get paid for my work. Too often I do not. But I know what I am now. I'm a writer. And that old unsettling feeling of being stuck in the wrong room? I don't have that anymore.

George Ella and I visited often during this period, talking about everything and reading our poems to each other. She began publishing children's books and encouraged me to try it, an idea I rejected for some time, but George Ella's work in picture books opened up for me the possibility of working in that form. I remembered how much I'd loved reading to Graham when he was a kid. I moved in part-time at the children's section at the Lexington Public Library and sat, a giant among stuffed animals and toddlers, reading picture books.

One of the first things I tried was an alphabet book, *Potluck*. In addition to loving the alphabet, I am drawn to

"When I was in eighth grade," Burkesville, Kentucky, 1961.

images of people coming together, sharing and cooperating, perhaps because this type of thing eludes me in real life. But mostly I'm crazy for the sounds of language and share with all poets and children the fun of playing with words. I sent the manuscript to Richard Jackson, then an editor at Orchard. He liked it but did not accept it for publication on the grounds that there were too many alphabet books in the world already. This was bad news for me, as I had hoped for a career writing alphabet books. Knowing how to end a piece is one of the hard parts of writing, but with an alphabet book this difficulty is overcome. When you get to Z, you're done.

At this same time I had been writing about the little country store my grandparents ran. I had worked on this material for months and had hundreds of pages, but I still didn't know what it was. I was frustrated, but I knew that lurking in this big shapeless insistent mess were a few strong images and phrases. With a certain degree of resignation, I started pulling those out to make a poem. I don't remember how this happened, but somewhere in the process the point of view shifted from that of an adult remembering to that of a child experiencing. It sounded like a children's book.

When Dick Jackson, in rejecting *Potluck,* asked me if I had anything else, I sent him *We Keep a Store* the next day, reasoning, in an uncharacteristic demonstration of business sense and good timing, that I had better send him something quick before he forgot about me and this small

chance dissolved back into the void of things that almost happened but didn't. He liked the book, took it, and a few months later decided to publish *Potluck,* too, which goes to show you something though I don't know what. The first two children's book manuscripts I sent out were accepted. I have had a number of rejections since then, of course, and as recently as, well, the other day.

Trying to figure out what publishers want and don't want is a big waste of time. By the time you figure it out, they don't want that any more. Besides, they have their own preferences, agendas, fads and fashions which have to do with a lot of things besides the actual writing. I try to do my job—writing—the best I can and trust that, if I keep writing and sending things out, if I keep sprouting those seeds and throwing them on the wind, some of them, some time, will hit good ground and grow. I have to remind myself of this when I feel discouraged, confused, and underpaid.

The main thing I have learned from getting published is that getting published is not the main thing. Oh, it's great, don't get me wrong, and it far surpasses not getting published. I like going into a bookstore and seeing my books, and I like meeting people who say they have read a book of mine, and I like getting checks in the mail which I can exchange for goods and services. But we all know the pleasures of receiving pay and recognition, and we have plumbed the depths of those pleasures and touched bottom. I know that if I depend for my happiness on recognition and checks, that I am going to be happy only a small fraction of the time and hopelessly miserable the rest. The best part of being a writer is writing.

Not that writing is unmitigated joy. Sometimes it almost is, and when it goes well it gives me tremendous energy and satisfaction. But certain projects are more difficult than others and certain stages of the process more painful to go through. With a short piece, a poem or song or picture book, the energy from the original idea will get me started and carry me through. But getting started on a longer project can be pretty awful. I seem to have to go through a long period of anxiety, self-doubt, and procrastination. At this stage I avoid writing like the plague. I'll do anything—clean bathrooms, organize closets, even bake— anything to keep from writing. I send off for brochures with titles like "So You Want to Operate a Small Mail Order Business in Your Own Home." Only when the discomfort of not writing becomes equal to or greater than the discomfort of writing, I begin. I turn off the telephone, turn on the computer and the coffee pot, click in an Elvis CD, and I'm back in business.

When I do, something surprising happens. I find out that I already knew a lot more about the piece than I thought I did, that I have, in fact, been working on it all along. I start writing and revising, and then I don't want to stop. Before, I wouldn't go into my office. Now I won't come out. Before, I cleaned everything in sight. Now I hardly even wash my face. I've been through this a hundred times but that doesn't seem to help. I have to go through all the stages every time—excitement, anxiety, confusion, avoidance, procrastination, resignation, writing, rewriting, editing, relief, celebration. With each new project I step up to the platform, hand the man my ticket, climb into the swinging chair, and I'm off on the wild ride again.

High school graduation picture, London, Kentucky, 1966.

Potluck began with a word game my son and I played one winter afternoon, over a generous and unusually alliterative after-school snack. The foundation of *The Someday House* was the fragment of a dream, a line ringing in my head when I woke up one morning. *What to Do about Pollution* also came—whole, unbidden and nearly intact—in a dream. And as with *We Keep a Store*, I did not have to look far for the inspiration for *Homeplace*.

Down the road from where I live, there's a log cabin my grandfather helped build in the 1930s for a friend, a country doctor who rode his horse up creek beds and mountain trails to treat his patients. When I was a child, Ailie Felty lived in the cabin, a gentle, sweet-smelling old lady who, in the 1950s, still wore a sunbonnet and carried an egg basket to the store. When Ailie died, the cabin changed hands again, and later a man was shot there, victim of a drug deal gone sour. But the playhouse my grandfather built still stands, its tiny stone chimney still intact. Children still wade the creek that runs by the cabin, and though my uncle died an old man years ago, the jonquils he planted as a boy still blossom in March. I had watched the changes in the cabin over the years, and thought I might write about it someday, a sure sign I never would.

Where I come from, the place where your family has lived for a long time is called your "homeplace." It's not a word you hear much anymore, since people move around so much. We moved around when I was a kid, too, but we always came back to visit my grandparents' home, an old farmhouse in the country. Up and down the road, other nineteenth-century dwelling houses have been torn down to make room for trailers or new houses, or left to collapse in a mound of vines and briars. Somebody in my family has lived in the homeplace since my great-grandparents bought it from Old Man Roberts in 1905, a two-room log cabin with a dogtrot. Before the white settlers came, the Cherokee fished and hunted here. We've plowed this ground for more than a hundred springs, and we still turn up arrowheads.

My uncle lived in the old house after my grandparents died, and when my uncle died my husband and I decided to leave the suburban ranch house where we'd been living in Lexington and move to the old homeplace. I set my microwave on my grandmother's wood-burning stove, put my computer on a table my grandfather made, and sat in front of the fireplace in Granddad Combs's wicker rocker. I thought about all the changes in the house over the years, and how those changes reflected the times. I thought about all the people who had lived in the house before me, babies who had been born here, grown up and worked these fields, had children and grandchildren, grown old and died here. For a minute I felt how I was part of all that, and it felt comforting somehow, as if everything was okay just the way it was. One summer afternoon without planning to, I took notebook, pen, quilt, and jug of water to the hill and wrote the first draft of *Homeplace*, sitting on the ground in the family graveyard.

The next part of the story is not as romantic, the part where I came down off the hill and revised for two solid weeks. I sent the manuscript to Dick Jackson, and when I didn't hear from him I figured he didn't like it. Late that fall I got a bad cold. All day I lay in my recliner chair in a nightgown, sneezing and blowing my nose and feeling pitiful, ill, and unpublished. The phone rang and it was Dick Jackson. He was going to publish *Homeplace*. After our conversation I ran round and round the yard, still in my nightgown, yelling "Yippee" and things like that, Kleenex like confetti catching the breeze behind me, my five dogs leaping and barking in celebration, though I am not sure they knew just why. I was happy to have the book published, and happy, too, when I saw the beautiful and detailed artwork by Wendy Anderson Halperin. We never talked about it, but I knew from the pictures that she understood what I was thinking when I wrote the book. I wanted kids who read the book to feel how we are all part of something that goes on, to feel at home in time, as well as in their own "homeplace."

Having the books published has led to other work, and over the years I have taught writing for, among others, the School for Creative and Performing Arts in Lexington, the University of Kentucky Program for Gifted Students, the Appalachian Writers Workshop at Hindman Settlement School, the Kentucky Arts Council's Artist-in-Residence program, and the Kentucky Governors School for the Arts. I travel to schools and libraries as a visiting author, where I usually give a brief presentation and then ask for questions. The question I hear most often is: *Can I go to the*

"With my sister, mother, father, and son, Graham," Lexington, Kentucky, 1989.

bathroom? This is because most of my audiences are four- and five-year-olds. In other settings people often ask about the relationship between the author and the illustrator of a picture book.

John Ward, the artist who did the beautiful acrylic paintings for *We Keep a Store*, called me when he was working on the book and I sent him some pictures of my grandparents' store, which he used in doing the painting for the book's first double-page spread. Seeing that for the first time was such a thrill to me, though it made me cry for some reason.

Most of the time I don't have any contact with the illustrator. The editor hires the artist he or she thinks will do the best job of interpreting a particular text, and the artist sets to work. Conversations about what the writer wants or envisions are not part of the process. And that's okay. I do my job and they do theirs. They don't tell me what to write, I don't tell them what to draw. To me writing is largely oral. I hear voices. I don't see visions. What the artist can produce, with a well-developed visual imagination and the skills to execute those images, is going to be more interesting and effective than what would happen if the artist had to reproduce the writer's visual images. Every

time I look at *Homeplace*, I see something wonderful I hadn't seen before, a wooden crib or gold pocket watch, falling down through time. The rich acrylics and the composition of the figures in *We Keep a Store* radiate a warmth just right for the text. I love the whimsy and movement of Rosanne Litzinger's work in *The Someday House*, the hyperbole and fun in Irene Trivas' pictures for *Potluck*. And in *What to Do about Pollution*, which encourages everyday acts of kindness in the midst of despair, Trivas splashes reds, blues, greens, and yellows against a ground of gray.

Having said that, I must also say that there is a certain somewhat wrenching process that has to take place of letting go. Even though I know the illustrations are not going to be realistic portrayals of my life or dream, still, when I first see a new book, it takes me a while to get used to it, to accept the fact that it isn't just my book anymore, that a lot of other people have worked on it to make it what it is. When I had it, it was just words on a page. Good words, maybe, and they could hardly have done it without me. Still it wasn't a book. All this provides good lessons in letting go. It never is easy, but it's something we need to get good at.

People also ask me about getting published, and I am not as much help as I would like to be. If I had some secret trick or knowledge I would share it, but I don't. Getting published is not about who you know, anyway. It's not even just about doing good work. More important than either of those is sticking with it. A lot of that and a little luck will take you a long way.

I meet many people who want to be writers, so many, in fact, that I've grown skittish of them. I don't mean to sound snotty or cynical, but I am approached by so many people who want to write children's books that I'm grateful and interested when I meet someone who does not have a children's book manuscript and has no intention of writing one. I suspect that some people think they want to be writers when what they really want is something else—acknowledgment, job satisfaction, a creative outlet, genuine communication, or escape from the mundane. Writing can satisfy those needs, but it isn't the only thing that can, and it isn't the way for everyone.

More than anything else, writing is about working with words—thinking them, hearing them, typing them, changing them, adding them, deleting them, moving them around, going over them seventy-five times and then doing it again. To me that is my idea of a good time. If that sounds crazy to you, you may need to find some other way to satisfy your needs. But if that sounds like your idea of a good time, too, then you may be a writer. If you are not a writer, find what you are and do that with all your might. If you are a writer, for God's sake get to work. Stop thinking about it and talking about it and stop putting it off. Just shut up about it and write. That's my advice.

I almost forgot to tell this next part. It happened a number of years ago and doesn't seem very important anymore, but it is part of the story. Drinking coffee in bed one morning in fall, I was surprised to see that the bedroom door frame had developed overnight a large bulge in the middle, as if it were pregnant. This seemed unusual, but not wanting to make a big deal out of it, I got up and dressed for work. Driving downtown, it was hard to ignore the fact that the lines painted on the street rose and fell like roller-coaster tracks.

You'd think that if the world suddenly began to wave this way, you'd report it to a doctor—or somebody—right away. I'd think so, too, but I didn't. Probably things like this happen all the time, I told myself, probably related to stress or excessive use of eye makeup. Things would straighten up. They didn't. Telephone poles curved. Buildings wrinkled. Other surfaces blurred—trees, faces, words on the page. The world was a picture, not quite dry, and somebody had smeared the paint. I called the ophthalmologist, who told me to come in immediately. I lay in a darkened room, pupils dilated, while he bent over me, a solemn lover. "This is very serious," he said.

Ocular histoplasmosis is a disease of the retina, caused by a fungus common in the Ohio River Valley. It can lie dormant for years then suddenly become active, for reasons not understood, allowing fluid to leak through scar tissue. In the lungs, this can be fatal. In the eye, it can cause permanent loss of vision.

Two treatments are available: laser surgery and steroids. They are not very helpful, but they are available. During laser surgery you sit strapped to a large machine, with bands around your head to keep it still. Anesthetic is administered through a series of injections to the eye. A console clicks, whirs, and blinks. There is a burning sensation behind the eyes. Afterwards you wear an eyepatch for a day, and when it comes off there are new spots everywhere, like a swarm of flying bugs you can't swat away. Steroids are uppers. After the first week I couldn't sleep. The second week my face swelled up, so that I looked like somebody else, a second cousin to myself. The third week I sprouted hair on my face and chin. My husband became alarmed. After a month the doctor discontinued the treatments, which he said had no significant effect.

Traditional medicine—the guys with diplomas, pills, needles and machines—had failed. I started taking medical advice from the girl who made tofu shakes at the health food store. "Look at a candle," she instructed, "a beeswax candle. More natural." Every day I stared at a burning beeswax candle, thinking positive thoughts. This was far more pleasant than laser surgery, but had no effect on my vision.

I went to a spiritual healer, a thin intense young man with sunken eyes and long delicate fingers. I sat in a straight-back chair and closed my eyes. New age music tinkled from a cassette player on the floor. The young man moved his hands above my body—back, shoulders, belly, legs. He never touched me, but under his hands my body warmed, and I grew peaceful. I saw myself in a green valley with the people I loved, happy, smiling. I felt better for days after that. I couldn't tell any difference in my eyes.

I don't look for cures anymore, from conventional or non-conventional sources. I've learned to live with the waves and curves, the blurs and bulges and bugs. I've had to make adjustments. I've had to slow down. If I don't I run into things—glass doors, table legs, inconspicuous-looking people. I pour milk till it spills over the rim of the glass,

Shelby with her daughter-in-law, Gabrielle, and son, Graham, Fukushima City, Japan, 1996.

"With my husband, Edmund, at home," 1993.

squeeze the toothpaste onto the wrong side of the brush. Once at a luncheon meeting as I was about to speak, I reached for my crumpled napkin and came up with a handful of whipped cream.

I have to ask questions at movies. If two characters have similar builds and hair styles, I think they're the same person, which complicates the plot. *Was that his brother in the police car? Is that the same woman who was hiding in the foyer?* I have to ask questions in real life, too. *What flavors of frozen yogurt do you have? Does this bus go to the mall? What does this note say? How many fat grams in this granola bar?*

Some people, when asked such questions, just answer them, which I appreciate. Other people answer, but you can tell they think you're a nuisance, a little scary, and possibly insane. Group three runs. They figure something is off here and they want no part of it. They're afraid whatever it is might jump off you and onto them. At K-Mart I approached a woman shopper. I held up a large bra and asked if she would tell me what size it was. She shot me a look of alarm, turned on her heel and bolted, suddenly losing interest in low-cost lingerie.

I miss driving, not the convenience of it so much as the physical sensations—taking a hill or rounding a curve, feeling the steering wheel in your hand, the clutch under your foot. But by walking, taking buses, and bumming rides, I get around. Taking the bus has taught me patience. It gets you there but it takes a while and you have to remember you're not the only one riding. I miss reading, too, but even that is not without its compensations. I kept my head in a book most of the time for thirty years. Now I've had to take it out. I read large print, but mostly I have to learn what I learn in other ways. I listen more, and I watch more movies. *Is that guy in the hat the same one who was playing the piano at the party?*

But what I really miss that I can't find a way to make up for is people's faces. The unique individual face, the expression in the eyes, the smile, these are lost to me, replaced by a fleshy blur. I miss eye contact, the quick furtive glance that says, "Do you believe this clown?" or "I find you very attractive. Would you like to meet somewhere later?" I feel cut off, alone in a blurry place.

But in some ways I see better. Most of us, most of the time, regard aging, accidents, sickness and death, not as universal and indisputable facts but as unfortunate aberrations which occasionally present themselves, usually to other people who are probably asking for it. Along with half my vision, I lost that illusion. Things happen. People get AIDS, Alzheimer's, cancer. Cars wreck, planes crash, houses burn. We do what we can, but we can't always keep these things from happening, and neither can the doctor or the government or the people at the health food store. I see other things differently, too. I do less of what I think I should, more of what I want to. And mostly what I want to do is write.

One thing I appreciate about writing is the limitlessness of it. You can never be bored. You can always get better. You can always try new forms and learn new things. In addition to children's books I work on poems, plays, and essays. I tell stories and study folk tales. In 1996 I traveled to Japan to visit Graham and Gabrielle, my son and daughter-in-law who were working as English teachers there, and to learn more about Japanese folk tales.

In Japan I tasted *sushi* and rice cakes and bathed in the *onsen.* I saw rock gardens where carp swam in deep pools and stone statues rose from the ground like trees. I walked with my Japanese friends to the temple on the first night of *Obon,* carrying candles and small dishes of food to the graves of the ancestors. I danced the dance of *Obon* and watched fireflowers bloom in the night sky. I composed *haiku* under an ancient tree on the mountain above Ishikawa.

Flying home to Kentucky, pleasantly exhausted, hopelessly confused about the time, and with a suitcase full of souvenirs, somewhere out over the Pacific I shed another skin. I knew that with all our interesting differences, people are more alike than different, so that no matter where we go in this world, we are always home.

Writings

FOR CHILDREN; FICTION

We Keep a Store, illustrated by John Ward, Orchard, 1990.
Potluck, illustrated by Irene Trivas, Orchard, 1991.
What to Do about Pollution, illustrated by Irene Trivas, Orchard, 1993.
Homeplace, illustrated by Wendy Anderson Halperin, Orchard, 1995.
The Someday House, illustrated by Rosanne Litzinger, Orchard, 1996.

PLAYS

Passing through the Garden: The Writing of Belinda Mason, premiered at the Kentucky Governor's School for the Arts, July, 1996.
Lessons, a one-woman show based on the writings of Belinda Mason, premiered at Appalshop, October, 1997.

Also author of *Them Days,* a play for voices in *Heartworks: A Collection of Kentucky Writing,* and *Storehouse,* a play for voices, a winner of West Virginia Public Radio playwriting competition.

OTHER

Also contributor of poems to anthologies and periodicals, including *A Gathering at the Forks: Fifty Years of the Hindman Settlement School Appalachian Workshop, Old Wounds, New Words: Poems from the Appalachian Poetry Project, Writing Community: New Work from the Working Class Kitchen, Now and Then, Mountain Review, Appalachian Heritage, Appalachian Journal,* and *Pine Mountain Sand & Gravel.* Has also contributed both fiction and nonfiction to *Appalachian Heritage* and other anthologies and periodicals, as well as writing regular columns for *The Lexington Herald, The Barbourville Mountain Advocate,* and *The Manchester Enterprise.*

SHUSTERMAN, Neal 1962-

Personal

Born November 12, 1962, in New York, NY; son of Milton and Charlotte (Altman) Shusterman; married Elaine Jones (a teacher and photographer), January 31, 1987; children: Brendan, Jarrod, Joelle, Erin. *Education:* University of California, Irvine, B.A. (psychology and drama), 1985. *Politics:* "No." *Religion:* "Yes."

Addresses

Home—7 Columbine, Dove Canyon, CA 92679. *Office*—P.O. Box 18516, Irvine, CA 92623-8516. *E-mail*—Nstoryman@aol.com.

Career

Screenwriter, playwright, and novelist. *Member:* PEN, Society of Children's Book Writers and Illustrators, Writers Guild of America (West).

Awards, Honors

Children's Choice Award, International Reading Association, 1988, and Volunteer State Book Award, Tennessee Library Association, 1990, both for *The Shadow Club;* American Library Association (ALA) Best Book, 1992, Children's Choice Award, International Reading Association, 1992, Outstanding Fiction for Young Adults Award, 1992, Young Adult Choice Award, International Reading Association, 1993, and Oklahoma Sequoyah Award, 1994, all for *What Daddy Did;* C.I.N.E. Golden Eagle Awards, 1992 and 1994, for writing and directing educational films *Heart on a Chain* and *What About the Sisters?;* New York Public Library Best Book for the Teen Age list, 1992, and California Young Reader Medal nomination, 1995-96, both for *Speeding Bullet;* Best Books for Reluctant Readers, ALA, 1993, for *The Eyes of Kid Midas;* ALA Best Book for Young Adults and Quick Pick list nominations, 1996, and New York Public Library Best Book for the Teen Age list, 1997, for *Scorpion Shards;* Best Books for Reluctant Readers, ALA, 1997, for *MindQuakes: Stories to Shatter Your Brain;* ALA Quick Pick Top Ten List and Best Book for Young Adults, both 1998, Outstanding Book of the Year, Southern California Council on Literature for Children and Young People, 1999, and state award lists in California, New York, Maine, South Carolina, Oklahoma, Texas, Utah, Indiana, Illinois, and Nebraska, 2000, all for *The Dark Side of Nowhere; Downsiders* was a Junior Literary Guild selection and a Texas Lone Star Award Book, 2000-01.

Neal Shusterman

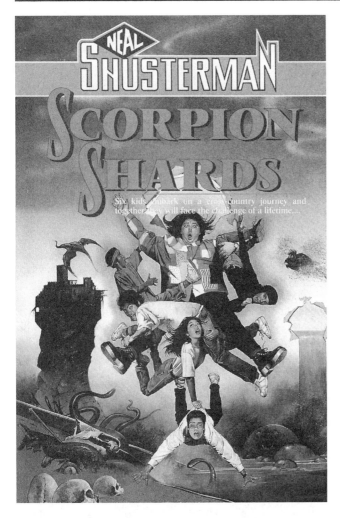

Deriving special powers from their afflictions, such as obesity and acne, six teens face a classic battle between good and evil in this science fiction/fantasy story. (Cover illustration by Gabriel Picart.)

Writings

FOR YOUNG ADULTS

It's Okay to Say No to Cigarettes and Alcohol (nonfiction), TOR Books, 1988.

The Shadow Club (novel), Little, Brown, 1988.

Dissidents (novel), Little, Brown, 1989.

(With Cherie Currie) *Neon Angel: The Cherie Currie Story,* Price, Stern, 1989.

Speeding Bullet (novel), Little, Brown, 1990.

What Daddy Did (novel), Little, Brown, 1990.

Kid Heroes: True Stories of Rescuers, Survivors, and Achievers, TOR Books, 1991.

The Eyes of Kid Midas (fantasy), Little, Brown, 1992.

Darkness Creeping: Tales to Trouble Your Sleep (horror), illustrated by Michael Coy, Lowell House, 1993.

Piggyback Ninja (fiction), illustrated by Joe Boddy, Lowell House, 1994.

Scorpion Shards (fiction), Forge, 1995.

Darkness Creeping II: More Tales to Trouble Your Sleep (horror), Lowell House, 1995.

The Dark Side of Nowhere (novel), Little, Brown, 1996.

MindQuakes: Stories to Shatter Your Brain, TOR Books, 1996.

MindStorms: Stories to Blow Your Mind, TOR Books, 1996.

MindTwisters: Stories to Play with Your Head, TOR Books, 1997.

The Thief of Souls (fiction; sequel to *Scorpion Shards*), TOR Books, 1999.

Downsiders (fiction), Simon & Schuster, 1999.

MindBenders: Stories to Warp Your Brain, TOR Books, 2000.

Also author of novel *Shattered Sky,* St. Martin's, as well as of television adaptations, including *Night of the Living Dummy III* and *The Werewolf of Fever Swamp* for R. L. Stine's "Goosebumps" series; staffwriter for *Animorphs* television series; author of educational films for the Learning Corporation of America, including *Heart on a Chain* and *What About the Sisters?* Creator of "How to Host a Mystery" and "How to Host a Murder" games.

Sidelights

"Writers are a lot like vampires," noted author Neal Shusterman on his Web site. "A vampire will never come into your house, unless invited—and once you invite one in, he'll grab you by the throat, and won't let go. A writer is much the same." Shusterman, an award-winning author of books for young adults, screenplays, stage plays, music, and games, works in genres ranging from biographies and realistic fiction to fantastic mysteries, science fiction, and thrillers. Following the publication of *Dissidents,* Shusterman's third book, *Bulletin of the Center for Children's Books* critic Roger Sutton called the author "a strong storyteller and a significant new voice in YA fiction." Lyle Blake, writing in *School Library Journal,* found *The Eyes of Kid Midas* to be "inspired and hypnotically readable." In his many books for young readers Shusterman acts the part of benevolent vampire, "feeding on your turmoil, as well as feeding on your peace," as he put it on his Web site.

It was this power of books to not only entertain and inform but to totally captivate that Shusterman himself experienced as a young reader. "Books played an important part in my life when I was growing up," Shusterman noted. "I always loved reading. I remember there was this trick I would play for my friends. They'd blind-fold me, then shove a book under my nose, and I could tell them the name of the publisher by the smell of the paper and ink." At age ten, Shusterman, who was born and raised in Brooklyn, went off to summer camp. One particular book, *Jonathan Livingston Seagull* by Richard Bach, which he discovered in the rafters of one of the cabins, swept him away in time and place, as did Roald Dahl's *Charlie and the Chocolate Factory* not long after. "I remember wishing that I could create something as imaginative as *Charlie and the Chocolate Factory,* and as meaningful as *Jonathan Livingston Seagull,*" Shusterman said. Writing his own stories came soon thereafter; inspired by the movie *Jaws,* he wrote the scenario of a similarly beleaguered small town, substituting giant sand worms for the shark.

Shusterman moved with his family to Mexico City, where he finished high school, and then went on to the University of California, Irvine, where he earned degrees in drama and psychology and set out to write his own novels. Returning to the same summer camp he had attended as a boy—now as a counselor—he tried out his stories on youthful ears and left another copy of *Jonathan Livingston Seagull* in the rafters for some other imaginative youth to discover. At age twenty-two he became the youngest syndicated columnist in the country when his humor column was picked up by Syndicated Writer's Group.

Shusterman first gained larger recognition for his first novel *The Shadow Club,* published in 1988. It tells the story of seven junior high school friends who grow tired of living in the shadows of their rivals. Each one is second-best at something, and they form a secret club in order to get back at the students who are number one. At first they restrict their activities to harmless practical jokes like putting a snake in an actress's thermos or filling a trumpet player's horn with green slime. Before long, however, their pranks become more destructive and violent. The mystery involves whether the members of the club have unleashed "a power that feeds on a previously hidden cruel or evil side of their personalities," as David Gale wrote in *School Library Journal,* or whether another student has been responsible for the more dangerous actions. In *Voice of Youth Advocates,* Lesa M. Holstine predicted that the book would be popular with young adults, since it would likely resemble their own experience with "rivalries and constantly changing friendships."

Dissidents, Shusterman's next novel, tells the story of Derek, a rebellious fifteen-year-old who is shipped off to Moscow to live with his disinterested mother, who is the U.S. ambassador to Russia, after his father dies in a car accident. Derek misses his father, hates all the restrictions of his new life, has trouble making friends at school, and acts out his frustrations in wild behavior. He soon becomes fascinated with Anna, the daughter of an exiled Soviet dissident, after he sees her in a television interview. Anna's mother is dying, and Derek comes up with a scheme to reunite her with her father. Although a *Publishers Weekly* contributor found Shusterman's portrayal of U.S.-Soviet relations "simplistic," the reviewer went on to praise the book as "a briskly paced, intriguing" adventure. Kristiana Gregory, writing in the *Los Angeles Times Book Review,* called the novel "an excellent glimpse of life on the other side of the globe."

Horn Book reviewer Ellen Fader called 1990's *Speeding Bullet* a "gritty, fast-paced, and, at times, funny novel." Nick is an angst-ridden tenth grader who does poorly in school and has no luck with girls. His life changes dramatically one day when, without thinking, he puts himself in danger to rescue a little girl who is about to be hit by a subway train. He becomes a hero and is thanked personally by the mayor of New York City. Nick then

decides to make saving people his mission in life, and before long he also rescues an old man from a burning building. His newfound celebrity status gets the attention of Linda, the beautiful but deceitful daughter of a wealthy developer, and the two begin dating. Nick continues rescuing people, but he soon discovers that Linda has set up the situations and paid actors to portray people in distress. His next real rescue attempt results in Nick being shot, but he recovers and ends up with a better outlook on life. In *School Library Journal,* Lucinda Snyder Whitehurst called Shusterman's book "a complex, multilayered novel" that would provide young adults with "much material for contemplation," while a writer for *Publishers Weekly* found it to be "a fast-paced modern parable with compelling characters and true-to-life dialogue." Shusterman followed this fictional story with a 1991 book about real heroes called *Kid Heroes: True Stories of Rescuers, Survivors, and Achievers.*

Shusterman's next novel, *What Daddy Did,* is based on a true story. It is presented as the diary of fourteen-year-old

Jason discovers that he is the son of aliens from a failed invasion. (Cover illustration by David Gaadt.)

Preston, whose father killed his mother during a heated argument. It details Preston's complex emotions as he deals with the tragedy, learns to live without his parents, and then struggles with his father's release from prison. Preston finally comes to forgive his father, and even serves as best man when his father remarries. Dorothy M. Broderick, writing in *Voice of Youth Advocates,* called *What Daddy Did* "a compelling, spellbinding story of a family gone wrong," adding that it might inspire young adults to "actually stop and think about their own relationship with their parents." Though Gerry Larson commented in *School Library Journal* that "too many issues are not sufficiently resolved" in the book, Rita M. Fontinha wrote in *Kliatt* that it "is an important book for many reasons: violence, love, faith, growth, denial, forgiveness are all explored and resolved."

In *The Eyes of Kid Midas* Shusterman takes an amusing fantasy situation and shows the frightening consequences as it spins out of control. Kevin Midas, the smallest kid in the seventh grade, is continually picked on by class bullies and annoyed by his family at home. Then he climbs to the top of a mysterious hill on a school trip and finds a magical pair of sunglasses that make all his wishes come true. At first, he uses the sunglasses for simple things such as making an ice cream cone appear in his hand or making a bully jump into a lake. Over time he becomes addicted to the power, even though he realizes that his wishes can be dangerous and irreversible. When even his dreams start turning into reality and no one seems to notice that anything is out of the ordinary besides him, Kevin must find a way to return things to normal before it is too late. *Voice of Youth Advocates* contributor Judith A. Sheriff stated that events in the novel "provide much for thought and discussion, yet do not get in the way of a well-told and intriguing story." Writing in *Wilson Library Bulletin,* Frances Bradburn noted that "Shusterman has written a powerful fantasy based on every adolescent's desire to control his or her life," while a contributor for *Publishers Weekly* called "this fable for the 90s" both "imaginative and witty," and one that "convincingly proves the dangers of the narcissistic ethos of having it all."

For his next novel, *Scorpion Shards,* Shusterman took special powers once step beyond, enlisting the science-fiction/fantasy genre and the realms of the supernatural for a projected three-part series. A *Publishers Weekly* reviewer writer noted that in this novel "Shusterman takes on an outlandish comic-book concept and, through the sheer audacity and breadth if his imagination, makes it stunningly believable." Six teenagers are outcasts because of the usual afflictions of the age, such as acne, obesity, and the fear of being different. But the exaggerated sense of their problems is also accompanied by something special: supernatural powers. Tory's acne makes/enables her to taint everything she touches; Travis likes to break things and subsequently destroys several homes in a landslide. Soon these six divide into those who want to get rid of such powers and those who wish to cultivate them. "This is a classic story about the battle between [good] and evil made especially gripping as the teenagers struggle with opposing forces literally

Downside dweller Talon goes Topside and meets Lindsay, who discovers that the secret civilization living in the New York subway and sewers is not all it appears to be in Shusterman's "parable about cultural identity," by the author's own admission his best book. (Cover illustration by Greg Harlin.)

within themselves," wrote *Kliatt* reviewer Donna L. Scanlon. *Booklist* critic Bill Ott felt that "[w]ith all the symbols, metaphors, archetypes—so much meaning—clanging around in this book, it's hard for the characters to draw a breath." However, Ott went on to note that "the horror story is suspenseful and compelling."

The second novel in the proposed trilogy, *Thief of Souls,* appeared in 1999. It follows five of the teenagers who have discovered the origins of their superhuman powers yet attempt to live normal lives. Now, drawn to San Simeon, California, by the sixth, Dillon, they are enlisted to become "misguided miracle workers," according to a reviewer for *Publishers Weekly,* by the mysterious and "Mephistophelean" Okoya. "Echoes of classical and Christian mythology reverberate throughout this tale of fallible messiahs and fallen creatures," noted the reviewer, "giving it an uncommonly solid subtext." Jackie Cassada, reviewing the novel in *Library Journal,* commented, "The author's economy of style and bare-bones characterization propel his tale to its climax with few distractions."

Shusterman further explored the supernatural with the short stories in the "MindQuakes" series, including *MindQuakes, Mind Twisters, MindStorms,* and *Mind-Benders,* stories guaranteed to "snare even reluctant readers," according to a contributor for *Publishers Weekly.* Reviewing the second installment in the series, *MindStorms,* Scanlon noted that "these stories range from humorous to poignant and capture the reader's imagination," while in their "quirky, off-the-wall" style they resemble the *Twilight Zone* in "tone." A contributor to *Voice of Youth Advocates,* writing about *MindTwisters,* warned readers to "prepare to have your mind twisted and your reality warped by this exciting collection of weird tales."

The Dark Side of Nowhere is a science fiction thriller in which teenager Jason feels trapped in his small town until he discovers an awful secret about himself. He undergoes an identity crisis and a crucial choice after discovering that he is the son of aliens who stayed on earth following an unsuccessful invasion. *Booklist* critic Carolyn Phelan noted that "Shusterman tells a fast-paced story, giving Jason many vivid, original turns of phrase, letting the plot get weird enough to keep readers enthralled, then coming back to the human emotions at the heart of it all." A writer for *Kirkus Reviews* felt that "Shusterman delivers a tense thriller that doesn't duck larger issues," and "seamlessly combines gritty, heart-stopping plotting with a wealth of complex issues." *School Library Journal* contributor Bruce Anne Shook concluded, "This is great science fiction."

With his 1999 title *Downsiders,* Shusterman built another tale skirting the boundaries between reality and science-fiction/fantasy. Talon is a young New Yorker—with a difference. His people live underground—the "Downsiders" of the title—in the sewers and subways beneath the city. His people never mix with "Topsiders" until Talon falls for Lindsay. But their fragile romance is threatened when Lindsay's father, a city engineer, is working on an underground aqueduct and one of Talon's friends denounces him for his collaboration with the Topsiders. "Facts ... are blended with fantasy until it is difficult to tell where truth stops and fiction begins," wrote Shook in a *School Library Journal* review of the book. Shook went on to note, "Overall ... this is an exciting and entertaining story that will please fans of adventure, science fiction, and fantasy." Janice M. Del Negro, reviewing the same title for *Bulletin of the Center for Children's Books,* commented specifically on the "quick and suspenseful" pace of the novel and on the "believable underground culture" that Shusterman created. "Shusterman twines suspense and satire through this ingenious tale of a secret community living deep beneath the streets of New York," wrote a contributor for *Kirkus Reviews.* The same reviewer concluded, "Urban readers, at least, will be checking the storm drains for peering faces in the wake of this cleverly envisioned romp."

Shusterman has also written for television and film, as well as directed educational short films. In all of his ventures, he takes the creative process and its responsibilities to heart. "I often think about the power of the written word," he explained on his Web site. "Being a writer is like being entrusted with ... or, more accurately stealing the power of flames, and then slingshotting it into the air to see who catches fire. I think writers have a responsibility not to launch those fireballs indiscriminately, although occasionally we do. Still, what a power to find yourself responsible for, because words can change the world. I've always felt that stories aimed at adolescents and teens are the most important stories that can be written, because it is adolescence that defines who we are going to be."

Biographical and Critical Sources

PERIODICALS

Booklist, March 15, 1993, p. 1346; February 1, 1996, Bill Ott, review of *Scorpion Shards,* p. 926; April 1, 1997, Carolyn Phelan, review of *The Dark Side of Nowhere,* p. 1322; March 15, 1998, pp. 1218, 1226; March 15, 1999, p. 1293.

Bulletin of the Center for Children's Books, May, 1988, p. 188; June, 1989, Roger Sutton, review of *Dissidents,* p. 264; May, 1991, p. 227; January, 1993, p. 157; September, 1999, Janice M. Del Negro, review of *Downsiders,* p. 31.

Children's Book Review Service, July, 1999, p. 155.

Horn Book, May-June, 1991, Ellen Fader, review of *Speeding Bullet,* p. 340; July/August, 1997, p. 463.

Kirkus Reviews, December 1, 1992, p. 1508; March 15, 1997, review of *The Dark Side of Nowhere,* p. 468; June 1, 1999, review of *Downsiders,* p. 889.

Kliatt, May, 1993, Rita M. Fontinha, review of *What Daddy Did,* p. 10; July, 1994, p. 18; January, 1997, Donna L. Scanlon, review of *Scorpion Shards,* pp. 10-11, and *MindStorms,* p. 16; May, 1999, p. 13.

Library Journal, March 15, 1999, Jackie Cassada, review of *Thief of Souls,* p. 113.

Los Angeles Times Book Review, July 23, 1989, Kristiana Gregory, review of *Dissidents,* p. 11.

Publishers Weekly, May 12, 1989, review of *Dissidents,* p. 296; December 14, 1990, review of *Speeding Bullet,* p. 67; November 16, 1992, review of *The Eyes of Kid Midas,* p. 65; March 28, 1994, p. 98; December 4, 1995, review of *Scorpion Shards,* p. 63; May 27, 1996, review of *MindQuakes,* p. 79; November 18, 1996, p. 78; February 8, 1999, review of *Thief of Souls,* p. 199; June 28, 1999, p. 80.

School Library Journal, May, 1988, David Gale, review of *The Shadow Club,* p. 113; October, 1989, p. 137; February, 1991, Lucinda Snyder Whitehurst, review of *Speeding Bullet,* p. 94; June, 1991, Gerry Larson, review of *What Daddy Did,* p. 128; December, 1992, Lyle Blake, review of *The Eyes of Kid Midas,* p. 133; March, 1996, p. 221; July, 1997, Bruce Anne Shook, review of *The Dark Side of Nowhere,* p. 9; November, 1997, p. 123; May, 1998, p. 51; July, 1999, Bruce Anne Shook, review of *Downsiders,* p. 100.

Voice of Youth Advocates, June, 1988, Lesa M. Holstine, review of *The Shadow Club,* p. 90; February, 1991, p. 358; June, 1991, Dorothy M. Broderick, review of *What Daddy Did,* p. 103; February, 1993, Judith A. Sheriff, review of *The Eyes of Kid Midas,* p. 358; April, 1998, review of *MindTwisters,* p. 14; July-August, 1997, p. 463; October, 1997, p. 254; December, 1997, p. 328; June, 1998, p. 103; August, 1999, p. 196.

Wilson Library Bulletin, March, 1993, Frances Bradburn, review of *The Eyes of Kid Midas,* p. 85.

ON-LINE

Neal Shusterman Homepage, http://www.storyman.com/ (October 26, 2000).

—*Sketch by J. Sydney Jones*

* * *

SIBURT, Ruth 1951-

Personal

Born August 13, 1951; daughter of Earl E. (a factory worker and carpenter) and Beulah V. (a homemaker; maiden name, Claytor) Traughber; married Michael E.

Ruth Siburt

Siburt (a carpenter), May 9, 1970; children: Matthew E. *Education:* Richland Community College, A.A.; University of Illinois at Springfield, B.A. (English). *Politics:* Independent. *Religion:* Christian. *Hobbies and other interests:* Oral history, birds, music, reading.

Addresses

Home—3850 East Cerro Gordo St., Decatur, IL 62521-1171. *Office*—Washington Elementary School, 400 South Maffit, Decatur, IL 62521. *E-mail*—msiburt@ aol.com.

Career

Richland Community College Library, Richland, IL, circulations manager, 1991-95; Decatur Public Schools, Decatur, IL, elementary technology assistant, 1996—. Founder, Decatur Area Writers' Fair. *Member:* Society of Children's Book Writers and Illustrators (network co-representative), Illinois Reading Council, Federation of Teaching Assistants.

Awards, Honors

Named outstanding alumni, Richland Community College, 1996; Lincoln Library Writer of the Year, 1999-2000.

Writings

(With Carol Rippey Massat) *My Mommys,* American Foster Care Resources, 1984, revised edition, 1989.
(With Massat) *No Angel,* American Foster Care Resources, 1984, revised edition, 1989.
(With Massat) *Earth to Amy,* American Foster Care Resources, 1984, revised edition, 1989.
(With Massat) *Just like You,* American Foster Care Resources, 1984, revised edition, 1989.
Dragon Charmer (juvenile novel), Royal Fireworks (Unionville, NY), 1996.
The Trouble with Alex (juvenile novel), Royal Fireworks, 1998.

Contributor of short stories "Tough Times" to *Cicada* magazine, "Story Fortune" to *Spider* magazine, and "Dinah's Halloween Mystery" to *Short Stories to Be Read Aloud,* Education Center, 2001.

Work in Progress

Kaloni and the Dreamer, a fantasy novel for middle grades; *A Shepherd's Story,* a novella for middle grades; *Grumpy Gus,* a picture book co-authored Larry Jenkins; *Spit,* a middle-grade historical novel. Research on influenza epidemic of 1918.

Sidelights

Ruth Siburt told *SATA:* "I learned to love stories at the dinner table. As the youngest of seven children, born late in my parents' lives, I had the advantage of having my mother almost to myself during most of my growing-up years. Momma had an interesting childhood. She'd traveled to New Mexico by horse-drawn wagon with her parents about the year 1910 in order to work a claim at a place called Elephant Butte.

"After her mother's death four years later, her father brought Momma and her three sisters back to Illinois where the children were split up and lived with a variety of family members. Momma loved to tell stories about the time in New Mexico and about her stays at various relatives' homes. Some of Momma's childhood stories made me laugh. Others broke my heart. Whether I laughed or cried, I did not leave the table until Momma had run out of stories. Her stories gave me a sense of the significance of personal history. They also demonstrated a belief in the indomitable nature of the human spirit. These two things are what I hope my written stories convey to their readers.

"There are three authors in particular whose work I admire and whose words have given me guidance in my journey thus far. The first two of whom I have had the pleasure of meeting in person and the third I've met only in print. Madeleine L'Engle was the featured author at the first writers conference to be held at Illinois Wesleyan University. She was generous with her time, and her passion for writing was contagious. She told us many things, but the comment that proved most enduring for me was that to write about the 'particular' was to touch the 'universal'. I took this to mean that while the basic human emotions—acceptance, love, fear, joy, grief, longing, etc.—are overwhelming concepts to write about in broad terms, they can be understood or at least touched upon through the thoughtful relating of individual stories.

"Richard Peck who, I am honored to say, hails from my town, has been a continuing source of encouragement to me and has also provided a guideline for writing that has proved both valid and valuable. His observation is that readers look not necessarily for the 'happy' ending but for the 'hopeful' ending. This idea and the permission it brings not to wrap stories up with a bright bow at the end helps to keep the characters honest and the stories true to themselves.

"Anne Lamott is the third author who has helped me. I've only met Ms. Lamott through print, but I count her a friend nonetheless. Her book *Bird by Bird* allows me to feel less alone and peculiar. The piece of Lamott wisdom I return to most often is this: It really is okay to write crummy first drafts. There's no saying how freeing it is to realize this is true. No piece of writing needs to be perfect the first time around. The words need only to be gotten down, initially. Shining them up comes later."

Biographical and Critical Sources

PERIODICALS

Children's Bookwatch, September, 1998, review of *The Dragon Charmer,* p. 6.

SINCLAIR, Olga 1923-
(Ellen Clare, Olga Daniels)

Personal

Born January 23, 1923, in Watton, England; daughter of Daniel Robert and Betty (Sapey) Waters; married Stanley George Sinclair (a headmaster), April 1, 1945; children: Michael, Alistair, Jeremy. *Education:* Educated in Norfolk, England. *Religion:* Church of England.

Addresses

Home and Office—Edenhurst, Ludham Rd., Potter Heigham, Norfolk NR29 5HZ, England.

Career

Writer. Justice of the peace in county of Norfolk, England, 1966-93. Auxiliary Territorial Service, pay-clerk, 1942-45. *Member:* Society of Authors, Society of Women Writers and Journalists, Romantic Novelists

Olga Sinclair

Association, Romance Writers of America, Norwich Writers' Circle (president).

Awards, Honors

Margaret Rhonda Award, Society of Authors, 1972, for research on Lithuanian immigrants.

Writings

FOR CHILDREN

Children's Games (nonfiction), Basil Blackwell (Oxford, England), 1966.

Gypsies (nonfiction), Basil Blackwell (Oxford, England), 1967.

Dancing in Britain, Basil Blackwell (Oxford, England), 1970.

Toys and Toymaking (nonfiction), Basil Blackwell (Oxford, England), 1975.

Gypsy Girl, Collins (London, England), 1981.

NOVELS

Night of the Black Tower, Lancer Books, 1968.
Man of the River, R. Hale (London, England), 1968.
The Man at the Manor, Dell (New York City), 1972.
Bitter Sweet Summer, Simon & Schuster (New York City), 1972.
Wild Dream, R. Hale (London, England), 1973.
Tenant of Binningham Hall, Woman's Weekly Library (London, England), 1975.
My Dear Fugitive, R. Hale (London, England), 1976.
Where the Cigale Sings, Woman's Weekly Library (London, England), 1976.
Never Fall in Love, R. Hale (London, England), 1977.
Gypsy Julie, Woman's Weekly Library (London, England), 1979.
Master of Melthorpe, R. Hale (London, England), 1979.
Orchids from the Orient, R. Hale (London, England), 1986.
The Family Feud ("Penrose Chronicle" series), International Masters, 2001.

UNDER PSEUDONYM OLGA DANIELS

Lord of Leet Castle, Mills & Boon (London, England), 1984.
The Gretna Bride, Mills & Boon (London, England), 1985.
The Bride from Far Away, Mills & Boon (London, England), 1987.
The Untamed Bride, Mills & Boon (London, England), 1988.
The Arrogant Cavalier, Mills & Boon (London, England), 1991.
A Royal Engagement, Mills & Boon (London, England), 1999.

UNDER PSEUDONYM ELLEN CLARE

Ripening Vine Mills, Mills & Boon (London, England), 1981.

NONFICTION

When Wherries Sailed By, Poppyland (Norfolk, England), 1987.
Gretna Green: A Romantic History, Unwin Hyman, 1989.

Potter Heigham: The Heart of the Broadland, Poppyland (Norfolk, England), 1989.

Sidelights

English novelist Olga Sinclair, who has penned a number of romantic and historical novels, some under the pseudonyms Olga Daniels and Ellen Clare, has also written several books for children—including her nonfiction debut works, *Children's Games* and *Gypsies.* Her adult novels are usually set in the small villages of rural Norfolk, England. Sinclair has, however, depicted other locations in her works, including Czechoslovakia, Austria, and Germany.

In her novels, Sinclair often features young heroines who are torn between their affections for two men, one of whom is generally less charming, but more worthy, than the other. The author also uses elements of suspense in many of her stories, often in the form of a mysterious young man. Commenting on Sinclair's use of cryptic story lines, *Twentieth-Century Romance and Historical Writers* essayist P. R. Meldrum observed that the author's plots "depend heavily on the 'mystery' as a central feature."

Sinclair once commented: "My nonfiction book *Gretna Green: A Romantic History* ... is the only book to cover the history of this extraordinary little village—Scotland's gift to lovers—[and its] 250 years of runaway marriages. There sixteen was old enough for a lad and his lassie to know their own minds and wed if they so wished—whereas almost all the Western world said not until they were twenty-one unless their parents consented.

"I have a continuing urge to write and cannot now imagine being without it. Although I have had a very happy life, my writing still has an element of escapism in it—and I hope it also takes my readers away to a land where dreams can come true.

"Most of my books have been translated into foreign languages, I have been published in fifteen different countries, and I have five recorded on cassette and many in large print. Editors are as unpredictable now as they were when I sent out my first pieces thirty years ago. The main thing I have learned is that rejections need not be final. You have to keep on and on. Writing is a constant challenge."

Biographical and Critical Sources

BOOKS

Meldrum, P. R., "Olga Sinclair," in *Twentieth-Century Romance and Historical Writers,* third edition, St. James Press, 1994.

PERIODICALS

Books for Keeps, July, 1986, pp. 6, 7.

STEWART, Chantal 1945-

Personal

Born January 16, 1945, in Paris, France; daughter of Georges Henry (a chandelier maker) and Madeleine Simonet-Henry; married; first husband's name, Constantine (divorced); married Peter Stewart, June 9, 1979 (deceased); children: Vanessa (first marriage), Laurence, Claire. *Education:* Attended Ecole des arts appliques, Paris, France. *Hobbies and other interests:* Drawing, children and pets, gardening (especially weeding), buying and reading children's books, listening to classical and ethnic music, yoga, walking.

Addresses

Home and office—29 Moola Place, Eltham, Victoria 3095, Australia.

Career

Freelance illustrator. *Member:* Australian Society of Authors, Illustrator Association of Australia.

Awards, Honors

Crichton Award shortlist, Children's Book Council of Australia, for *Percy;* Young Australians Best Book Award shortlist, 1997, 1998, 1999, all for *Smelly Chantelly;* honor book designation, Children's Book Council of Australia, 1999, for *A Ghost of a Chance;* Best Cookbook for Children in English designation, World Cookbook Awards, Michelin Australia Best Food Book finalist, Jacob's Creek World Food Media Awards, both 1999, and Young Australians Best Book award shortlist, 2000, all for *Anyone Can Cook.*

Writings

ILLUSTRATOR

Roger Dunn, *Percy,* Ghost Gum Press, 1988.
Stephen Ray and Kathleen Murdoch, *The Ant Nest,* SRA/McGraw-Hill (Santa Rosa, CA), 1993.
David Drew, *How Many Legs?,* SRA/McGraw-Hill (Santa Rosa, CA), 1993.
Mary Roberts, *The Creeper,* SRA/McGraw-Hill (Santa Rosa, CA), 1994.
Joan Van Loon, *Smelly Chantelly,* Reed Books, 1996.
Nette Hilton, *A Ghost of a Chance,* Puffin (Ringwood, Australia), 1998.
Van Loon and Gabriel Gate, *Anyone Can Cook,* Five Mile Press, 1999.

Also contributor of illustrations to educational publishers, including Pearson, Rigby-Heinemann, Nelson, and Macmillan.

Work in Progress

An Anglican Missel for young children and another cookbook with Joan Van Loon and Gabriel Gate.

Chantal Stewart

Sidelights

"I loved drawing from a very young age, and find myself very lucky to have made my hobby my job," Australian illustrator Chantal Stewart explained to *SATA.* Among Stewart's illustration projects are the award-winning *A Ghost of a Chance,* winner of the Australian Children's Book Council's Honor Book designation.

"Born Chantal Henry in Paris, I have devoted my life to art, whilst raising two families and traveling to broaden my horizons and influences. Considering my family background, it is not surprising. My father was an arts graduate and maker of chandeliers prior to [World War II]. With the invention of Plexiglass, he set up a factory designing and making ultra-modern lights. In addition, both parents were very musical—Papa on the piano and Maman on the violin. They were creative in many ways, including gardening, which has become one of my great loves. Sadly Maman died when I was just seven, but Claudine, my eldest sister, came home, and together with her new husband, they raised the younger family members.

"Like most artists, I have always loved drawing and creating, but after school and studying at the Paris School of Applied Arts, I commenced my career as a graphic designer/art director. I married Constantine, a Greek, and we traveled to Canada, where our daughter

Vanessa was born. I studied etching at Ottawa University during my pregnancy. Unfortunately, this marriage disintegrated and on returning to Paris, I successfully worked as a graphic designer in various advertising agencies. In 1980, with my new Australian husband, Peter, I traveled through India, Sri Lanka, and Bali studying religions and lifestyles. I also collected a substantial body of paintings by top Balinese artists. In search of a purer, more alternative lifestyle, we bought a small holding in Bellingen, an exquisitely beautiful and lush area of northern New South Wales, Australia, with the idea of raising a family tree away from the stresses and poisons of modern life. Two children arrived—Laurence and Claire—but the idyllic life was interrupted when crop dusting and other agricultural methods wrecked the pure environment. Achieving a reasonable standard of living proved elusive, although I had two very successful exhibitions in Sydney and Bellingen at this time. Also in Bellingen, I illustrated my first book—a black and white *recueil* (anthology) of poems. This exercise gave me the confidence to switch from graphic design to book illustration.

"After seven years, the family packed up, moved, and settled into suburban Melbourne, where my professional life blossomed again. After some years, we moved to the outskirts of Melbourne into a rural area called Eltham. This area has been the home to many of Melbourne's artists through our short history, so it really is a prefect venue for a successful book illustrator.

"With three children, a grandchild, three cats, and a dog, life is very fulfilling," Stewart added on a personal note. "Recently widowed, I am once again commencing a new phase of life with many professional and personal challenges facing me."

V

VINCENT, Gabrielle
[A pseudonym]

Personal

Born in Brussels, Belgium.

Addresses

Home—Brussels, Belgium.

Career

Illustrator and author of children's books, 1980—.

Awards, Honors

Notable Book designation, American Library Association, 1982, for *Ernest and Celestine, Ernest and Celestine's Picnic,* and *Smile, Ernest and Celestine;* Best Illustrated Children's Book of the Year designation, *New York Times,* 1982, for *Smile, Ernest and Celestine;* Children's Books of the Year selections, Child Study Association, 1986, for *Breakfast Time, Ernest and Celestine* and *Ernest and Celestine's Patchwork Quilt.*

Writings

FOR CHILDREN; SELF-ILLUSTRATED

Ernest and Celestine, Greenwillow (New York City), 1982.
Bravo, Ernest and Celestine!, Greenwillow (New York City), 1982.
Ernest and Celestine's Picnic, Greenwillow (New York City), 1982.
Smile, Ernest and Celestine, Greenwillow (New York City), 1982, published as *Smile Please, Ernest and Celestine,* Picture Lions (London, England), 1986.
Merry Christmas, Ernest and Celestine, Greenwillow (New York City), 1984.
Ernest and Celestine's Patchwork Quilt, Greenwillow (New York City), 1985.
Breakfast Time, Ernest and Celestine, Greenwillow (New York City), 1985.

Where Are You, Ernest and Celestine?, Greenwillow (New York City), 1986.
Mimi und Brumm in museum, Sauerlaunder, 1986.
Feel Better, Ernest!, Greenwillow (New York City), 1988, published as *Get Better, Ernest,* Julia MacRae (London, England), 1988.
Ernest and Celestine at the Circus, Greenwillow (New York City), 1989.
Mr. Bingley's Bears, Hutchinson (London, England), 1993.
a day, a dog, Front Street (Asheville, NC), 2000.

ILLUSTRATOR

Christophe Gallaz, *Threadbear,* translated by Martin Sokolinsky, Creative Education (Mankato, MN), 1993.
Charlotte Pomerantz, *Halfway to Your House* (poems), Greenwillow (New York City), 1993.

Adaptations

Ernest and Celestine's Picnic was adapted into a filmstrip with cassette by Weston Woods, 1984; *Ernest and Celestine* was adapted into a filmstrip by Weston Woods and is available in a Braille edition.

Sidelights

Painter, illustrator, and author Gabrielle Vincent is the creator of the popular children's book characters Ernest and Celestine, a stalwart bear and young mouse, respectively. In a series of warmhearted adventures, the two friends celebrate holidays, travel together, and serve as close companions in times of trouble. With their simple texts originally written in French, Vincent's stories have proved universal, appealing to children around the world as much for their text as for the author's gentle sepia ink and watercolor artistry. Commenting on the illustrations for *Breakfast Time, Ernest and Celestine, School Library Journal* contributor Susan McCord noted that Vincent's "soft pastel watercolors shine with a joy of simple life" while "wonderful expression in the simple faces make up for the lack of words." Linda Boyles echoed such praise by noting in her *School Library Journal* review that the series'

Gabrielle Vincent's black-and-white line drawings document, without words, the poignant story of a dog's abandonment on a highway and new friendship with a young boy in **a day, a dog.**

popularity is based on "the display of gentleness and warmth between Ernest, the grown-up; and Celestine, the child." In *Junior Bookshelf* a critic hailed Vincent's text in *Get Better, Ernest!* (published in the United States as *Feel Better, Ernest!*) as "a model of its kind, not a word too many and all to the point."

Born and raised in Belgium, Vincent made the decision to become an artist when she was a child. Unfortunately, as often happens, life got in the way and it wasn't until 1980 that she was able to fully devote herself to drawing, painting, and writing. In 1981, Vincent's popular Ernest and Celestine characters first appeared, presented at the Bologna Book Fair shortly before making their way to bookstore shelves. The bear and mouse have continued to be popular throughout Europe as well as in the United States, and Vincent's books have been translated into several other languages.

In *Ernest and Celestine,* readers meet the bear and mouse for the first time as tiny Celestine is in a tizzy over the loss of her toy duck. With only a few days to go before the Christmas holidays, she can count on reliable Ernest to help her in her hour of need in a story that a *Publishers Weekly* contributor dubbed effective at illustrating a "loving relationship." *Merry Christmas, Ernest and Celestine* finds the friends throwing a holiday party in a book that *New York Times Book Review* contributor

Molly Ivins hailed as "world-class adorable." In a *Kirkus Reviews* article, a critic found *Merry Christmas, Ernest and Celestine* "buoyant and poignant ... with the perennial appeal of Christmas from scraps."

In *Ernest and Celestine at the Circus,* readers follow the pair under the Big Top, Ernest donning the clown outfit he once wore in his younger days and Celestine embarrassed at the way her companion is attracting attention. After Ernest wins a round of applause in center ring, the young mouse's embarrassment changes to pride in her friend. *School Library Journal* contributor Linda Boyles called the story "a warm and gentle vignette from the daily life of two caring friends." On the move again in *Where Are You, Ernest and Celestine?,* the bear and mouse travel to the Louvre in Paris, where Ernest wants to find a job. While he is turned down because of his condition that he be allowed to bring young Celestine with him to work everyday, Ernest nonetheless enjoys the museum with his tiny companion, although at one point she fears she has lost her guide. The two are once again close to home in *Feel Better, Ernest!,* as Celestine becomes caretaker of her older companion. While finding this installment in the series less effective than other books, Denise Wilms maintained in a *Booklist* critique that *Feel Better, Ernest!* shows Vincent's writing to be "as fluid as ever, and the sketches ... very apt."

Biographical and Critical Sources

BOOKS

Children's Literature Review, Volume 13, Gale (Detroit, MI), 1987.

St. James Guide to Children's Writers, fifth edition, St. James (Detroit, MI), 1999.

PERIODICALS

Booklist, January 1, 1985, Denise Wilms, review of *Merry Christmas, Ernest and Celestine,* p. 644; September 15, 1985, Denise Wilms, review of *Breakfast Time, Ernest and Celestine* and *Ernest and Celestine's Patchwork Quilt,* p. 141; November 15, 1988, Denise Wilms, review of *Feel Better Ernest!,* p. 588; August, 1989, Denise Wilms, review of *Ernest and Celestine at the Circus,* p. 1982.

Books for Keeps, May, 1986, Jill Bennett, review of *Smile Please, Ernest and Celestine,* p. 19.

Bulletin of the Center for Children's Books, January, 1986, Zena Sutherland, review of *Breakfast Time, Ernest and Celestine,* p. 98; February, 1986, Zena Sutherland, review of *Ernest and Celestine's Patchwork Quilt,* p. 119.

Horn Book, November, 1987, review of *Merry Christmas, Ernest and Celestine,* p. 763.

Junior Bookshelf, October, 1988, review of *Get Better, Ernest!,* p. 230; April, 1994, review of *Mr. Bingley's Bears,* p. 52.

Kirkus Reviews, November 1, 1984, review of *Merry Christmas, Ernest and Celestine,* p. 92; July 1, 1989, review of *Ernest and Celestine at the Circus,* p. 998.

New York Times Book Review, November 11, 1984, Molly Ivins, review of *Merry Christmas, Ernest and Celestine,* p. 58; October 6, 1985, review of *Breakfast Time, Ernest and Celestine,* p. 41; March 30, 1986, Arthur Yorinks, review of *Where Are You, Ernest and Celestine?,* p. 23; February 12, 1989, review of *Feel Better, Ernest!,* p. 25; April 10, 1994, Cynthia Zarin, review of *Halfway to Your House,* p. 35.

Publishers Weekly, October 31, 1986, review of *Ernest and Celestine,* p. 74.

School Librarian, November, 1988, Maisie Roberts, review of *Get Better, Ernest!,* p. 133; May, 1994, Janet Sims, review of *Mr. Bingley's Bears,* p. 56.

School Library Journal, May, 1985, Susan McCord, review of *Breakfast Time, Ernest and Celestine,* p. 78; November, 1985, Susan McCord, review of *Ernest and Celestine's Patchwork Quilt,* p. 78; May, 1986, Cathy Woodward, review of *Where Are You, Ernest and Celestine?,* p. 85; December, 1988, Gratia Banta, review of *Feel Better, Ernest!,* p. 94; October, 1989, Linda Boyles, review of *Ernest and Celestine at the Circus,* p. 97.*

*　　*　　*

VOLLSTADT, Elizabeth Weiss 1942-

Personal

Born December 28, 1942, in New York, NY; daughter of Alexander (a civil engineer) and Therese (a home-maker; maiden name, Moncsko) Weiss; married Peter J. Vollstadt (a visual communications manager), August 14, 1965; children: Christopher E., Heidi Marie. *Education:* Adelphi University, B.A. (cum laude), 1964; graduate study at Cleveland State University, Northeastern University, and Queens College of the City University of New York; John Carroll University, M.A., 1981. *Religion:* Roman Catholic. *Hobbies and other interests:* Reading, boating, travel.

Addresses

Home—1416 Whispering Woods Way, DeLand, FL 32724. *E-mail*—lizvolls@totcon.com.

Career

Junior high school English teacher in Herricks school district (NY), 1966-68; Lakeland Community College, Kirtland, OH, adjunct instructor in English, 1982-85; Rainbow Babies and Childrens Hospital, Cleveland, OH, manager of publications, 1986-92; Lakeland Community College, adjunct instructor, 1992-95; freelance writer, 1995—. *Member:* Society of Children's Book Writers and Illustrators.

Awards, Honors

Awards from International Association of Business Communicators, including feature writing awards, 1987, for the article "Treating the Whole Child;" 1991, for the article "A Day in the Pediatric Intensive Care Unit: High Tech, High Stress, High Reward;" and 1994, for the

Elizabeth Weiss Vollstadt

article "CT: Not Just for People Anymore;" and a regional award in special publications category, 1988, for *Rainbow Babies and Childrens Hospital: Celebrating 100 Years of Caring.*

Writings

Teen Eating Disorders, Lucent Books (San Diego, CA), 1999.
Teen Dropouts, Lucent Books (San Diego, CA), 2000.

Other writings include *Rainbow Babies and Childrens Hospital.* Work represented in anthologies, including *The Christian Family Christmas Book,* Augsburg (Minneapolis, MN), 1988; *Emergency Pilot: Adventure Stories from Highlights,* 1995; *Laughing on Butterfly Wings: Long-Ago Stories from Highlights,* 1995; and *Reflections from a Mud Puddle: Helping Children Cope and Grow,* compiled by Marcella Fisher Anderson, Boyds Mill Press (Honesdale, PA), 1998. Contributor of articles and fiction to periodicals, including *Rainbow Magazine, Jack and Jill, Children's Digest, The Church Herald, Highlights for Children,* and *My Friend.*

Work in Progress

A book for teenagers about the historical novel *Johnny Tremain,* by Esther Forbes, for Lucent Books; research for an anthology of true and fictional stories from the American Revolution, with Anderson.

Sidelights

Elizabeth Weiss Vollstadt told *SATA:* "I decided early on that I liked writing for children because they still have a sense of wonder about the world, and they get excited when they discover something new. I still love discovering new things, too. I especially enjoy exploring new places and learning about their history. Then I like to imagine how ordinary people must have felt, especially children, as events swirled around them.

"Many of my published stories are historical. One is about the Boston Tea Party, another the underground railroad, another the whaling days in Nantucket. I learned to enjoy history through novels (*Johnny Tremain* for the American Revolution and *Gone with the Wind* for the Civil War, for example) and hope to pass on some of that excitement to children. I especially wanted to show that girls could do brave and exciting things, too. Some of my favorite authors of historical fiction are Ann Rinaldi, Patricia Gauch, Avi, and Katharine Paterson.

"When I turned to nonfiction, I selected eating disorders for my first book because I felt for a long time that we over-emphasize thinness in our culture. I was glad to be able to show young people how they are being pushed to accept artificial standards of beauty—and was pleased to find there are many groups now working to encourage healthy eating habits."

Biographical and Critical Sources

PERIODICALS

Booklist, July, 1999, Debbie Carton, review of *Teen Eating Disorders,* p. 1938.
School Library Journal, August, 1999, Joyce Adams Burner, review of *Teen Eating Disorders,* p. 180.

ON-LINE

Amazon.com, www.amazon.com/ (August 26, 2000).

*   *   *

VONDRA, J. Gert
See VONDRA, Josef (Gert)

*   *   *

VONDRA, Josef (Gert) 1941-
(J. Gert Vondra)

Personal

Born June 11, 1941, in Vienna, Austria; son of Josef Vondra (an architect) and Theresa Knoll Horvath (an actress); married Janet (a journalist), August 18, 1975 (divorced); children: Alexandra (Ally). *Education:* Attended De La Salle College, 1952-59; attended University of Melbourne, 1960-63. *Religion:* Pantheist. *Hobbies and other interests:* Swimming.

Addresses

Home and office—27 Waverley Ave., Lorne, Victoria 3232 Australia. *E-mail*—jvondra@crimus.com.au.

Career

Sun-New Pictorial, Melbourne, Australia, cadet journalist, 1960-63; Radio Australia, reporter, 1964-67; freelance writer, 1967—.

Awards, Honors

Senior Writer's fellowship, Australian government, 1974.

Writings

(Under name J. Gert Vondra) *Timor Journey,* Lansdowne (Melbourne, Australia), 1968.
The Other China, Lansdowne (Melbourne, Australia), 1968.
(Under name J. Gert Vondra) *Hong Kong: City without a Country,* Lansdowne (Melbourne, Australia), 1970.
A Guide to Australian Cheese, Lansdowne (Melbourne, Australia), 1971, 4th edition published as *A Guide to Australian Cheese: A Complete Guide,* Cavalier Press (South Yarra, Australia), 1992.
Paul Zwilling (novel), Wren (Melbourne, Australia), 1974, published as *For the Prime Minister: The Paul*

Josef Vondra

Zwilling Papers, David & Charles (London, England), 1975.

Hellas Australia/Ellada Australia, Greek translation by George Psaros, Widescope (Melbourne, Australia), 1979.

German-speaking Settlers in Australia, Cavalier (South Yarra, Australia), 1981.

No-Name Bird (young adult), Puffin (Ringwood, Australia), 2000.

Work in Progress

A novel on the Lorne, Australia Blue Water Swim Classic "Pier-to-Pub" race, and a young adult novel about dolphins. Researching a young adult novel on Guillet-Barre Syndrome.

Sidelights

Journalist Josef Vondra told *SATA:* "Coming from an Australian mainstream journalistic professional background, I have always tried to write about what I know, rather than what I have made up. In writing fiction, however, the straight putting down of facts is often not suitable and therefore I try to separate the emotion from the fact. A story can be pure fiction, though the thoughts and feelings expressed are personal. This is especially helpful in writing for children as they have keen senses on what is real and what is not.

"I started off writing for adults—travel books, a biographical novel, two historical works and a guide to cheese—but since the publication of my novel, *No-Name Bird,* I have been drawn to writing more for young adults. There is a strong link between the very young and the mature—a child is the most truthful of human beings. As you grow, you learn to lie, cheat, and to acquire all the other characteristics that make up an adult. With age, however, you tend to know who and what you are and life does become simpler and more truthful, certainly more honest.

"I live in Lorne, a seaside resort town on the southwestern coast of Victoria and the place does inspire me to write. Not so much the peace and quiet, but rather the companionship of a small community. It's hard to be lonely (and writing is a lonely occupation) in a place like this. Most of my work is done in the morning, from 6:30 a.m. to about 2 p.m. Often, I work the day through. Lorne has inspired at least one work—a novel about the town's "Pier-to-Pub" swim over a 1.2 km distance. About 3,500 swimmers aged between fourteen and eighty swim the distance each year. It is the biggest "Blue Water Classic" in the world.

"For recreation, I swim at a pool at least twice a week at Colac, a country town about a forty minutes' drive from Lorne. I used to swim competitively and swimming still gives me enormous joy."

*   *   *

VOS, Ida 1931-

Personal

Born December 13, 1931, in Groningen, Netherlands; daughter of Joseph (a commercial agent) and Bertha (Blok) Gudema; married Henk Vos (an insurance broker), April 3, 1956; children: Josephine, Karel, Bert. *Education:* Kweekschool Voorbereidend Ondervijs Training College, teaching certificates, 1950, 1952.

Addresses

Home—Dr. Wibautlaan 6G, Rijswijk, Holland 2285XY, Netherlands; c/o Terese Edelstein, 1342 Devonshire, Grosse Pointe Park, MI 48230.

Career

Writer. Teacher in Den Haag, Rijswijk, Holland, Netherlands. *Member:* Dutch Writers Association, Women's Club.

Awards, Honors

Has received numerous Dutch awards for writing.

Writings

Vijvendertig tranen (poetry; title means "Thirty-five Tears"), [Holland], 1975.

Schiereiland (poetry; title means "Peninsula"), Nijgh & van Ditmar (Netherlands), 1979.

Miniaturen (poetry; title means "Miniature"), Nijgh & van Ditmar (Netherlands), 1980.

Hide and Seek, translated by Terese Edelstein and Inez Smidt, Houghton (Boston), 1991 (published in the

Netherlands as *Wie niet weg is wordt Gezien,* Leopold, 1981).

Anna Is Still There, translated by Terese Edelstein and Inez Smidt, Houghton (Boston), 1993 (published in the Netherlands as *Anna is er nog,* Leopold, 1986).

Dancing on the Bridge at Avignon, translated by Terese Edelstein and Inez Smidt, Houghton (Boston), 1995 (published in the Netherlands as *Dansen op de brig van Avignon,* Leopold, 1989).

The Key Is Lost, translated by Terese Edelstein, Morrow (New York City), 2000.

Also author of *Witte zwanen zwarte zwanen,* 1992. Author of radio play *De bevrijding van Rosa Davidson* (title means "The Liberation of Rosa Davidson"), first broadcast, 1984. Contributor of articles and short fiction to periodicals.

Sidelights

In her homeland of the Netherlands, Ida Vos is well known as the author of several books, numerous short stories and poems, and many articles focusing on her experiences growing up during World War II. Four of Vos's book-length works have been translated into English, allowing readers and critics in the United States to appreciate the author. Her most widely read work, the 1981 novel translated in 1991 as *Hide and Seek,* has become one of the classic works of fiction relating to the Holocaust. Praising Vos's novel *Dancing on the Bridge at Avignon, School Library Journal* contributor Ann W. Moore commented that Vos's "short, episodic chapters are well crafted; her writing is poignant in its understatement."

Born in Groningen, Netherlands, in 1931 and raised in a traditional Jewish family, Vos and her family moved to Rotterdam when she was five years old. "In 1940, Germany started the war with Holland and my life changed totally," Vos once recalled to *SATA.* "The big bombardment of Rotterdam on May 14, 1940, made a deep impression on me. Seeing the Germans enter our city shocked me terribly. All my books are connected with World War II."

Vos was a novice reader by the time she was four years old and spent much of her time trying to make sense of the books and newspapers she discovered in her home. "My parents felt unhappy about my reading habits," she recalled. "I could read for hours. They thought that a child of my age should play outside instead of reading all the time. My books brought me to places I never visited. By reading I could fly from reality and forget the terrible world around me." Writing quickly followed, and by the age of eight Vos was composing poems, letters, and short stories. "Unfortunately nothing has been kept," she explained. "The Nazis stole everything from our home."

Following the bombing of Rotterdam in 1940, Vos, her sister, Esther, and the girls' parents relocated to Rijswijk, a small city near the Hague. Although she was immediately enrolled at the local elementary school, Vos was soon forced to change schools due to increasing measures taken against Jews. "We were forbidden a lot of things," the author recalled: "Entering a park, visiting a cinema, library, or swimming pool. We were not allowed to travel by train, enter restaurants, etc." Like the character in *Hide and Seek,* Vos had to wear a large yellow star of David inscribed with the word "Jew" on her clothing.

Gradually the Voses became aware of friends and family members being gathered up and sent to German concentration camps; they decided it was time for the family to go into hiding. With help from friends in the Dutch resistance movement, they went underground, hiding with first one family, then another, to avoid capture. "We had to move so many times that I really don't remember all the people that helped us," Vos commented. "I owe a lot to all of them. They risked their lives and that of their families in order to save us." At first the family managed to stay together, but eventually Vos and her sister were separated from their parents. "As a child of eleven, I had to play the role of older and wiser sister," Vos recalled, remembering her efforts to calm her younger sister through stories and games while never revealing her own fear. In 1945, when Europe was liberated from German control, Vos and her family were reunited. "But I couldn't feel happiness," Vos explained. "The counting had started—counting all our relatives and friends who didn't come back from the concentration camps, being murdered—gassed—by the invading Nazis."

The following year Vos returned to school, a thirteen-year-old enrolling in the fifth grade. "I had forgotten many of the things I learned before the war," Vos admitted. "I felt stupid sitting between younger children." She quickly got up to speed with her studies, and moved to the appropriate grade in high school. After graduation, Vos entered a teacher's training college, where she earned teaching certifications in 1950 and 1952. By 1956 she had married Henk Vos, with whom she would have three children. Vos suffered an emotional breakdown in the early 1970s. "All the grief of the war came back to me," she explained. "I wanted to stay in bed all the time. I wept the whole day and didn't see any future." She eventually checked into a psychiatric clinic for war victims, where she underwent therapy for three months. "I was never fully cured but I could endure life again," she admitted to *SATA.*

It was during her stay at the psychiatric clinic that Vos began putting her memories and feelings about the war down on paper. "Poems flew out of my pen and I couldn't stop. The poems were printed and I got enthusiastic reviews. Now the author Ida Vos was born.... I also wrote several short stories.... An editor, reading some of them, asked me to write a book about my life during World War II. First I refused, thinking that I was not able to stand it, being also afraid that I would again break down mentally." It was an article she discovered in a local newspaper—an article explaining that there were people claiming that the Holocaust never really happened; that it was an invention of the Jewish people—that inspired her to put pen to paper. "I was terribly shocked and it made me change my mind. Now I wanted to tell the truth. People should know what really happened." Vos's contribution to telling the truth began with *Hide and Seek.*

Reviewers have praised *Hide and Seek* for its compelling portrayal of the experiences of a young Jewish girl during the Nazi invasion of Holland. In Vos's novel, eight-year-old Rachel Hartog's life is suddenly turned upside down during World War II. The invading Nazis force Rachel to wear a yellow star to indicate her Jewish heritage and to attend a school for Jewish children only, and they forbid Rachel to enter the local parks or use the neighborhood swimming pool. Rachel cannot understand these injustices and wrestles with the many intense emotions she feels as she and her family struggle to survive. A reviewer for *Publishers Weekly* remarked of *Hide and Seek* that Vos "fills the narrative with understated but painfully realistic moments ... [Her] novel deserves special attention for its sensitive and deeply affecting consideration of life after liberation." Equally laudatory, *Booklist* contributor Hazel Rochman added that "any number of the vignettes—wearing the star for the first time, hiding with the Dutch underground, Rachel's parting from her parents ...—would make a gripping book-talk/read-aloud that will move children to imagine 'What if it happened to me?'"

Vos followed *Hide and Seek* with several other books. The next to appear in U.S. bookstores was a 1986 novel translated in 1993 as *Anna Is Still Here.* In this story, which serves as a sequel to *Hide and Seek* in that it continues to parallel the author's own experiences, Anna survives the war by hiding with her family, but must learn to readjust to a normal life. Forced to attend school with younger children because her education has lapsed, and reacquainting herself with her parents and other family members, thirteen-year-old Anna begins to learn about the horror of the concentration camps—a horror that had taken the life of at least one of her former friends. "Vos conveys Anna's heartbreaking and heroic efforts with exemplary economy," noted a *Publishers Weekly* contributor, adding that the author's answers to the questions her novel raises are "hard-won and profoundly stirring." Praising the simplicity of the "terse" translation by Terese Edelstein and Inez Smidt, *School Library Journal* contributor Susan Kaminow added that *Anna Is Still Here* "is a stark reminder that the effects of the Holocaust did not end with the end of the war."

Dancing on the Bridge at Avignon, published in English translation in 1995, breaks even more into fictional territory than Vos's earlier works. In this story ten-year-old Rosa de Jong and her little sister, Sylvie, try to escape from the fear and tension caused by the Nazi occupation of their home town by keeping to their normal routines, which include playing the violin, getting into trouble, starting up an informal school, and making the Nazi edicts into quiz games; all the while the girls' parents live in quiet fear and plan for an escape that, tragically, does not happen in time. Noting the novel's "dark lyricism," a *Publishers Weekly* critic maintained that *Dancing on the Bridge at Avignon* contains a message likely to be "haunting and inescapable" to both adult and teen readers. Similar praise was given *The Key Is Lost,* which describes life for two Jewish sisters as they are moved from house to house while in hiding from the Nazis. "The precariousness of the hiding places, the dangers of moving from one to another and the girls' unnatural existence within them are thrown into sharp relief as Vos distills each scene to its most telling moments," noted a *Publishers Weekly* contributor.

In addition to writing, Vos speaks at libraries, schools, and other gatherings around the world, describing her memories of being a Jew in Holland in World War II. "Children are very interested," she explained. "I have received many letters and paintings from them. I am very happy about my contacts with youth. Through my lectures I am able to warn them against war, discrimination, and fascism."

Biographical and Critical Sources

PERIODICALS

Booklist, March 15, 1991, Hazel Rochman, review of *Hide and Seek,* p. 1504; April 15, 1993, Hazel Rochman, review of *Anna Is Still Here,* p. 1513; October 15, 1995, Hazel Rochman, review of *Dancing on the Bridge at Avignon,* p. 405; April 1, 2000, Hazel Rochman, review of *The Key Is Lost,* p. 1478.

Horn Book, January-February, 1996, Hanna B. Zeiger, review of *Dancing on the Bridge at Avignon,* p. 75.

Publishers Weekly, February 15, 1991, review of *Hide and Seek,* p. 90; April 19, 1993, review of *Anna Is Still Here,* p. 62; November 13, 1995, review of *Dancing on the Bridge at Avignon,* p. 62; June 5, 2000, review of *The Key Is Lost,* p. 95.

School Library Journal, May, 1993, Susan Kaminow, review of *Anna Is Still Here,* p. 110; October, 1995, Ann W. Moore, review of *Dancing on the Bridge at Avignon,* p. 141; July, 2000, Jack Forman, review of *The Key Is Lost,* p. 112.*

W

WATT-EVANS, Lawrence 1954-

Personal

Born July 26, 1954, in Arlington, MA; son of Gordon Goodwin (a professor of chemistry) and Doletha (a secretary; maiden name, Watt) Evans; married Julie Frances McKenna (a chemist), August 30, 1977; children: Kyrith Amanda, Julian Samuel Goodwin. *Education:* Attended Princeton University, 1972-74, 1975-77. *Hobbies and other interests:* Comic book collecting.

Addresses

Agent—Russell Galen, Scoville Chichak Galen, 381 Park Ave. S., 11th Floor, New York, NY 10016.

Career

Novelist. Purty Save-Mor supermarket, Bedford, MA, sacker, 1971; Griffith Ladder, Bedford, worker, 1973; Arby's, Pittsburgh, PA, counterman and cook, 1974; Student Hoagie Agency, Princeton, NJ, occasional salesman, 1974-76; Mellon Institute of Science, Pittsburgh, bottle washer, 1976; freelance writer, 1977—. *Member:* Science Fiction and Fantasy Writers of America, Horror Writers of America.

Awards, Honors

Hugo Award, World Science Fiction Society, Nebula Award nomination, Science Fiction Writers of America, and reader's poll award, *Isaac Asimov's Science Fiction Magazine,* all 1988, all for short story "Why I Left Harry's All-Night Hamburgers"; reader's poll award, *Isaac Asimov's Science Fiction Magazine,* 1990, for "Windwagon Smith and the Martians."

Writings

"THE LORDS OF DUS" SERIES; FANTASY

The Lure of the Basilisk, Del Rey (New York City), 1980.

Mother of triplets, a sign of adultery, Queen Artemisia of Hydrangea sends her servant to hide the girl and younger boy, leaving the older boy as heir; instead, the girl is left behind in Lawrence Watt-Evans's and Esther M. Friesner's humorous fantasy. (Cover illustration by Walter Velez.)

Malledd disbelieves the prophecy that he is the Champion of the Domdur Empire and struggles to lead his normal life rather than lead his empire in war, as the gods have decreed. (Cover illustration by Tristan Elwell.)

The Seven Altars of Dusarra, Del Rey (New York City), 1981.
The Sword of Bheleu, Del Rey (New York City), 1983.
The Book of Silence, Del Rey (New York City), 1984.

"WAR SURPLUS" SERIES; SCIENCE FICTION

The Cyborg and the Sorcerer, Del Rey (New York City), 1982.
The Wizard and the War Machine, Del Rey (New York City), 1987.

"LEGENDS OF ETHSHAR" SERIES; FANTASY

The Misenchanted Sword, Del Rey (New York City), 1985.
With a Single Spell, Del Rey (New York City), 1987.
The Unwilling Warlord, Del Rey (New York City), 1989.
The Blood of a Dragon, Del Rey (New York City), 1991.
Taking Flight, Del Rey (New York City), 1993.
The Spell of the Black Dagger, Del Rey (New York City), 1993.

"THREE WORLDS" TRILOGY; FANTASY

Out of This World, Del Rey (New York City), 1993.
In the Empire of Shadow, Del Rey (New York City), 1995.
The Reign of the Brown Magician, Del Rey (New York City), 1996.

FANTASY NOVELS

(With Esther M. Friesner) *Split Heirs* (humorous fantasy), Tor (New York City), 1993.
Touched by the Gods, Tor (New York City), 1997.
Dragon Weather, Tor (New York City), 1999.
Night of Madness, Tor (New York City), 2000.

OTHER

The Chromosomal Code, Avon (New York City), 1984.
Shining Steel, Avon (New York City), 1986.
Denner's Wreck, Avon (New York City), 1988.
Nightside City, Del Rey (New York City), 1989.
The Nightmare People, New American Library (New York City), 1990.
(Editor and contributor) *Newer York,* New American Library (New York City), 1990.
The Rebirth of Wonder, Wildside Press, 1992, bound with *The Final Folly of Captain Dancy,* Tor (New York City), 1992.
Crosstime Traffic (short stories), Del Rey (New York City), 1992.

Author of e-books, published by Alexandria Digital Entertainment, including *The Final Challenge, Foxy Lady, The Murderer,* and *Spirit Dump,* all 1998, and *Efficiency,* 1999. Work represented in anthologies, including *One Hundred Great Fantasy Short Short Stories,* edited by Isaac Asimov, Terry Carr, and Martin H. Greenberg, Doubleday, 1984; *"Why I Left Harry's All-Night Hamburgers" and Other Stories from Isaac Asimov's Science Fiction Magazine,* edited by Dehlia Williams and Charles Ardai, Delacorte, 1990; *Dead End,* edited by Paul F. Olson and David B. Silva, St. Martin's, 1991; and *Prom Night,* edited by Nancy Springer, DAW, 1999. Contributor to game *Tales of Talislanta,* Wizards of the Coast, 1992.

Also author of column "Rayguns, Elves, and Skin-tight Suits" for *Comics Buyers Guide,* 1983-87, and of comic book scripts and stories for Marvel Comics and Eclipse Comics. Contributor of short stories, articles, poems, and reviews to periodicals, including *Amazing,* Louisville *Courier-Journal, Bedford Patriot, Dragon, Late Knocking, Movie Collector's World, Sagebrush Journal, Space Gamer,* and *Starlog.*

Sidelights

Working primarily in the fantasy and science-fiction genres, Lawrence Watt-Evans has produced a number of novels, poems, and short stories that feature both intricate plots and a sense of fun. Watt-Evans once told *SATA:* "My parents both read science fiction—and lots of other things—so I grew up in a house filled with books and magazines, many of them with bright, splashy covers showing spaceships and monsters and people firing rayguns. I loved it all." School seemed dull by comparison, and as Watt-Evans admitted, "I would sneak in books and comic books and read them in class; fortunately, I had tolerant teachers, and as long as I kept up with the class work they didn't object."

"I wasn't clear on the distinction between children's books and grown-up books (I'm still not always)," the author admitted, "so at age seven I started borrowing my mother's books as soon as she was done reading them— I figured if she liked them, I would too. So in second grade, while the other kids read 'Dick and Jane,' I read Ray Bradbury, and fell in love with words and stories. And I never got over it."

After graduating from high school, Watt-Evans enrolled at Princeton University in 1972, but eventually ended his college studies to devote his time to writing. His first novel, *The Lure of the Basilisk,* was published in 1980; it would be the first in a four-part series called "The Lords of Dus." Other novels and other series have followed, among them the "War Surplus" series of science-fiction novels, the "Legends of Ethshar" fantasy series, and the "Three Worlds" trilogy, which Watt-Evans published between 1993 and 1996.

Beginning with *Out of This World,* the "Three Worlds" trilogy introduces readers to life in the parallel universes of the raygun-toting Galactic Empire and Faery. Maryland lawyer Pel Brown and his client, Amy Jewell, have their everyday lives disrupted by elves and robed medieval-looking figures, as well as futuristic forces drawn right from 1950s pulp sci-fi, all claiming to be from other worlds and engaged in a classic battle of good against evil. Calling the first installment in the "Three Worlds" trilogy "well-told" but not altogether "believable," *Voice of Youth Advocates* contributor Larry Condit praised the work as being of interest to "fantasy and imaginative fiction readers." Sally Estes dubbed the novel a "playful spoof" of the science fiction and fantasy genres in her *Booklist* review, while a *Publishers Weekly* critic noted that Watt-Evans "initially displays a fine wit and intelligence" despite the novel's somewhat disjointed cast of characters. *Out of This World* was followed in 1995 by *In the Empire of Shadow.* In this book Pel and friends continue their battle against the evil "Shadow" in an unfamiliar, war-torn land. "Lighthearted moments contrast with dark undertones" to create an "uncomfortable ambiance," noted a critic for *Library Journal,* who nonetheless recommended the series. In *Booklist* Carl Hays commended Watt-Evans for "blend[ing] just the right touch of whimsy into his well-told action adventure." The battle concludes with *The Reign of the Brown Magician,* which was published in 1996.

In addition to book series, Watt-Evans has authored numerous stand-alone volumes, many of them in the fantasy genre. *Dragon Weather* finds an eleven-year-old boy named Arlian trapped in his basement after his home is destroyed by a dragon attack. During his imprisonment Arlian is transformed into a "dragonheart" by an accidental infusion of dragon blood. After being rescued, he eventually becomes a slave of the dragon overlord and is forced to work in the mines for many years. This treatment does not endear Arlian to dragons. Ultimately he frees himself, determined to avenge the death of his grandfather as well as the loss of his village. "Remarkably inventive" was the description given the novel by a *Kirkus Reviews* writer, who went on to call the plot of *Dragon Weather* "commendably well organized."

In the 1997 novel *Touched by the Gods,* Watt-Evans also focuses his story on a young boy. Malledd, a blacksmith's son living in the Domdur empire, is proclaimed to be the champion of the gods of his world at his birth, but he has tried long and hard to ignore his fate and lead a normal life. Unfortunately, an evil magician puts his world into peril, causing Malledd's abilities to be put to the test in a novel that a *Library Journal* contributor deemed "gracefully present[ed] by its author." On a more humorous note, Watt-Evans teamed up with co-author Esther M. Friesner to write *Split Heirs,* the story of a twisted family tree, mistaken identities, secret multiple births, painful puns, and muddled magic. A *Publishers Weekly* reviewer praised it as an "often funny, frequently precious" fantasy. And the author's

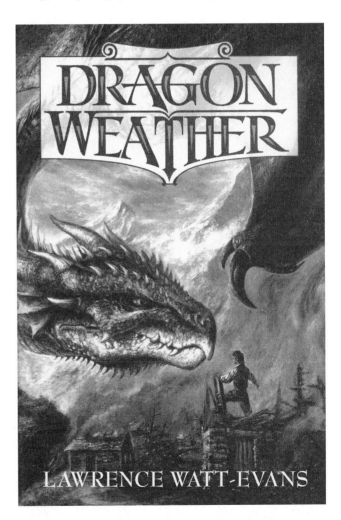

Orphaned and sold into slavery after dragons destroy his village, Arlian becomes obsessed with justice in his quest to destroy those who wronged him. (Cover illustration by Bob Eggleton.)

1992 book *Crosstime Traffic* collects nineteen short stories that feature parallel worlds, resulting in a work of "great entertainment with an occasional jolt into serious thought," according to *Kliatt* reviewer Sister Avila Lamb.

Biographical and Critical Sources

PERIODICALS

Booklist, July, 1993, review of *Split Heirs,* p. 1953; February 1, 1994, Sally Estes, review of *Out of This World,* p. 1000; February, 1995, Carl Hays, review of *In the Empire of Shadow,* p. 993.

Kirkus Reviews, September 1, 1999, review of *Dragon Weather,* p. 1355.

Kliatt, January, 1993, Sister Avila Lamb, review of *Crosstime Traffic,* p. 20.

Library Journal, February 15, 1995, review of *In the Empire of Shadow,* p. 186; November 15, 1997, review of *Touched by the Gods,* p. 79.

Publishers Weekly, June 21, 1993, review of *Split Heirs,* p. 90; December 20, 1993, review of *Out of This World,* p. 54; September 27, 1999, review of *Dragon Weather,* p. 79.

Voice of Youth Advocates, April, 1994, review of *Split Heirs,* p. 8; August, 1994, Larry Condit, review of *Out of This World,* p. 161.*

*   *   *

WATTS, Nigel 1957-

Personal

Born June 24, 1957, in Winchester, England; son of John (a journalist) and Joane (Martin) Watts; married Sahera Chohan (a broadcaster), August, 1991. *Education:* University of West of England (formerly Bristol Polytechnic), B.A. (with honors), 1979; University of Nottingham, Post-Graduate Certificate of Education, 1981; University of East Anglia, Ph.D. (creative and critical writing), 1994.

Addresses

Agent—David Higham Associates, 5-8 Lower John St., London W1R 4HA, England.

Career

English teacher in Japan, 1982-84; writer, 1984—; founder of The Writing Room, 1990; teacher of creative writing, 1990-98.

Awards, Honors

Betty Trask Award, Society of Authors, 1989, for *The Life Game;* shortlisted for Mail on Sunday award, 1990, for *Billy Bayswater;* Arts Council Award, 1990; Oppenheim-John Davies Memorial Trust Award; Mary Trevellyan Award, for travel writing; British Library/Penguin Writers fellowship, 1995.

Writings

FOR CHILDREN

The Penknife, Collins Educational (London, England), 1995.

Professor Blabbermouth on the Moon, illustrated by Jamie Smith, Hippo (Leamington Spa, England), 1996.

NOVELS

The Life Game, Hodder & Stoughton (London, England), 1989.

Billy Bayswater, Hodder & Stoughton (London, England), 1990.

We All Live in a House Called Innocence, Hodder & Stoughton (London, England), 1992.

Twenty Twenty, Sceptre (London, England), 1995.

The Way of Love, Thorsons (Wellingborough, England), 1999.

OTHER

Writing a Novel and Getting Published (nonfiction), Teach Yourself, 1996.

(Editor) *Most This Amazing Day—An Anthology of Spiritual Verse,* HarperCollins (New York City), 1998.

Work in Progress

An "as yet untitled novel about the journey of the Zen monk Bodhidharma, from India to China in the 6th century."

Sidelights

English novelist and educator Nigel Watts has also written two books for children, *The Penknife* and *Professor Blabbermouth on the Moon.* The latter, targeted to reluctant readers, tells of a professor and her assistant—a rat—who hope to capture the prize in a scientific competition by building a rocket that will transport them to the moon, where they will gather evidence to support their theory that earth's primary nighttime luminary is in fact made of cheese. *School Librarian* contributor Irene Babsky offered a favorable assessment of *Professor Blabbermouth,* maintaining: "The book is well crafted and well paced, and there is plenty of direct speech and pithy description to keep the reader involved."

Of his work as a novelist, Watts once commented: "Language is a faulted medium, and yet it is the best I have at my disposal to communicate and explore what is important to me: the heart of what it is to be human. What is the essence of being a human? Some call it self-expression, or self-fulfillment or self-actualization: I call it spirit. Spirit is the essence behind and within everything; the manifest universe is the expression of that spirit. There is nothing more important than the continuation and fulfillment of that spirit. That *is* the function and purpose of life. It is my conviction and, increasingly, my experience that the natural unfolding of the spirit in the material form is beautiful and a cause for celebration and worship. Human unfolding of spirit manifests in its most unsullied form as health, love, joy, compassion, devotion.

"I write because I can think aloud that way, exploring and trying out ideas which relate to my personal unfolding. In this way, I suppose my writing is narcissistic in origin: I want to understand myself and the chains which confine the expression of my spirit so I can free myself. However, communication [of] my insights are an essential part of why I write: I want to contribute to the liberation of us all. Cloaking these ideas in fiction means I can humanize them, bringing them from the abstract into the concrete, seeing how these things: God, meaninglessness, the religious impulse, existential dilemmas, impact on my life, our lives. I also write because I feel impelled to.

"My writing process evolves and changes with every novel; however, they mostly begin with a vague sense of the area I want to explore (for instance: the self-imposed restraints we adopt *(The Life Game)*; vulnerability *(Billy Bayswater)*; sex and disability *(We All Live in a House Called Innocence)*; the nature of separate identity *(Twenty Twenty)*; the journey of the lover of God *(The Way of Love)*. Once I have the itch, I look for something to scratch it with, an image which somehow represents or can manifest that idea. Then I usually read about that subject, sketch ideas, let the plot simmer for anything up to two years (while I'm finishing another project). By the time I am ready to begin writing I usually have the core characters and the basic plot mapped out. I then plunge into the book, starting with the first line and moving ahead as swiftly and as unselfconciously as I can. I find it helpful to never read back what I'm writing until I can reach the end—this means leaving gaps in the narrative, and also not worrying about thin characterization, short scenes, undeveloped ideas, too-brief dialogue. Building the momentum is essential for me: if I am enthusiastic about the writing, the book almost writes itself; however, if I take breaks, or lose my rhythm, I can stagger along for weeks achieving almost nothing. Once the first draft is complete, it is usually half the length I want it to be, and so I immediately begin on the second draft, which usually takes as long as the initial write-through. By the end of the second draft (by which time I have been writing between six months and a year or so), the book is in presentable enough form for me to show it to my wife, who reads it and gives me her feedback. I am either elated or depressed, according to what she says, and thus I begin the third draft, where I can change emphasis in order to steer the narrative through the rocks I have unwittingly sailed into. This takes a couple of months, and then it is time for the book to try itself out in the real world: I send it to my agent, and then to my editor, [by] which time I have probably lost interest in it, and have trouble taking it too seriously, and so hope no further work is needed on it, because by then I [am] already researching the next book.

"I read very little fiction when I am writing, finding that it can interfere with my artistic judgements (are all artists hopelessly insecure, thinking others have got 'it' while you wander in the darkness?). My influences are most often from non-fiction and history, and I find current news items which somehow signify an issue sometimes creep into the narrative."

Biographical and Critical Sources

PERIODICALS

School Librarian, August, 1997, Irene Babsky, review of *Professor Blabbermouth on the Moon,* p. 148.*

*　　　*　　　*

WESTAWAY, Jane 1948-

Personal

Born February 22, 1948, in Watford, England; daughter of James Frederick (a manager) and Mollie Eileen (a homemaker) Westaway; companion of Norman Bilbrough (a writer); children: Sarah Tomlin, Jonathan Tomlin. *Education:* Victoria University of Wellington, B.A. (with honors); University of Canterbury, diploma in journalism.

Addresses

Home—Wellington, New Zealand. *E-mail*—jane_westaway@xtra.co.nz.

Career

Freelance writer and reviewer, 1989—. Copyright Licensing Ltd., member of board of directors; Peppercorn Press, member of board of directors. Also worked as a speechwriter; worked in offices, factories, canteens, and

Jane Westaway

shearing sheds; worked as a domestic servant. *Member:* New Zealand Society of Authors (PEN NZ Inc.) (vice-president, 1995-98), New Zealand Book Council, Wellington Children's Book Association.

Awards, Honors

Health Journalism Award, Pharmaceutical Association, 1985; Reader's Digest-PEN-Stout Research Centre fellowship, *Reader's Digest,* 1993; grant from Arts Council of New Zealand, 1994; award for best first book, Children's Book Awards, *New Zealand Post,* 1997, for *Reliable Friendly Girls.*

Writings

(With Judith Davey) *Where to Now? New Zealand in the 1990s,* New Zealand Planning Council, 1990.
Reliable Friendly Girls (young adult stories), Longacre Press (Dunedin, New Zealand), 1996.
Love and Other Excuses (young adult novel), Longacre Press (Dunedin, New Zealand), 1999.
Good at Geography (adult novel), Penguin, 2000.

Contributor of articles, stories, and reviews to periodicals, including *New Zealand Listener, More,* and *Consumer.*

Work in Progress

An adult novel.

Biographical and Critical Sources

ON-LINE

Amazon.com, www.amazon.com/ (August 26, 2000).
FlyingPig.co.nz, www.flyingpig.co.nz.
New Zealand Book Council, www.vuw.ac.nz/book council/ (January 15, 2000).

*   *   *

WILSON, Barbara Ker
See KER WILSON, Barbara

*   *   *

WILSON, J(erry) M. 1964-

Personal

Born January 21, 1964, in Newport News, VA; son of James (a tax consultant) and Anne (Golden) Wilson; married Cathy Zolkowski (a writer and gymnastics choreographer), May 15, 1994; children: Symone. *Education:* University of Minnesota—Twin Cities, B.A., 1987; University of St. Thomas, M.A., 1999. *Religion:* Nondenominational.

Addresses

Home—4509 West 36th St., St. Louis Park, MN 55416.

Career

Servant Alpha Janitorial, Inc., operations manager, 1987-92; Steven/Scott Management, Inc., apartment manager, 1993-95; Wilson Consultants, Inc., manager of research and analysis in Tax Division, 1995-98; writer, 1998—.

Writings

(With wife, Cathy Zolkowski) *Breathless: The Adventures of a Gymnast* (novel), Verona Publishing (Edina, MN), 1999.
(With Zolkowski) *Treasure Hunt 2000* (novel), Verona Publishing (Edina, MN), 2000.

Work in Progress

The third book in a gymnastic adventure series, tentatively about the lost city of Atlantis, with Zolkowski.

*   *   *

WOOD, Nuria
See NOBISSO, Josephine

*   *   *

WRIGHT, Judith Arundell 1915-2000

OBITUARY NOTICE—See index for *SATA* sketch: Born May 31, 1915, in Armidale, New South Wales, Australia; died June 25, 2000. Editor, author, and poet. Judith Wright wrote prolifically and was one of Australia's best-known poets, though she remained rather obscure on other continents. Active in ecological, gender, aboriginal, and social justice issues, Wright touched on these motifs in her work in stirring ways. Her first volume of poetry, *The Moving Image,* was published in 1946, and her *Woman to Man* followed in 1949; these two works are thought to contain Wright's finest writing. Wright published *Kings of the Dingoes,* the first of her five books for children, in 1959. Her other titles for young people include *The Day the Mountains Played,* which is based on an aboriginal legend, *The River and the Road,* and a book of verse. Her writing career spanned nearly fifty years, and some of her later works include her 1985 *Phantom Dwellings* and her 1994 *Collected Poems.* Wright was showered with accolades throughout her life, and some of her more notable awards include the 1987 Premier's Prize of New South Wales and the 1992 Queen's Prize for Poetry.

OBITUARIES AND OTHER SOURCES:

BOOKS

Writers Directory, 14th edition, St. James Press, 1999.

PERIODICALS

Arena Magazine, October, 2000, Val Plumwood, "Remembering Judith Wright," p. 44.

Southerly, autumn, 2000, p. 78.
Times (London), June 27, 2000.

*   *   *

WYLER, Rose 1909-2000

OBITUARY NOTICE—See index for *SATA* sketch: Born October 29, 1909, in New York, NY; died June 27, 2000. Educator and author. Rose Wyler was a prolific writer of several children's books. From 1934 to 1941 she taught science at Columbia University, and during the late 1940s served as a scriptwriter for Encyclopedia Britannica Films. Wyler was most known for the 1968 Halloween book she wrote with her husband Gerald Ames called *Spooky Tricks.* Her writing career was focused on her lifelong interest in science and nature, which came to her at a very early age. Some of her works include her *Planet Earth,* which was published in 1952, her 1958 *Exploring Space,* and her 1979 *It's All Done With Numbers.* During the mid-1970s, Wyler traveled to Cuba and the former Soviet Union with a host of other children's book authors in order to study the use of science-oriented reading materials in such rapidly developing countries.

OBITUARIES AND OTHER SOURCES:

BOOKS

Authors of Books for Young People, 2nd edition, Scarecrow Press, Incorporated (New Jersey), 1971, p. 566.

PERIODICALS

New York Times, June 6, 2000, p. A23.

Z

ZOLKOWSKI, Cathy (A.) 1969-

Personal

Born March 9, 1969, in Neenah, WI; daughter of Jack (in sales) and Nancy (in electronics assembly) Zolkowski; married Jerry M. Wilson (a writer and tax researcher), May 15, 1994; children: Symone. *Education:* University of Minnesota—Twin Cities, B.A. *Religion:* Nondenominational.

Addresses

Home—4509 West 36th St., St. Louis Park, MN 55416.

Career

Writer. Former competitive gymnast.

Awards, Honors

Inducted into University of Minnesota Women's Gymnastics Hall of Fame, 2000.

Writings

(With husband, J. M. Wilson) *Breathless: The Adventures of a Gymnast* (novel), Verona Publishing (Edina, MN), 1999.
(With Wilson) *Treasure Hunt 2000* (novel), Verona Publishing, 2000.

Work in Progress

The third book in a gymnastic adventure series, tentatively about the lost city of Atlantis, with Wilson.

ZYMET, Cathy Alter 1965-

Personal

Born December 25, 1965, in Hartford, CT; daughter of Elliott (an optometrist) and Susan (a retailer; maiden name, Kane) Alter; married Matthew Zymet (a producer), September 14, 1997. *Education:* Attended Franklin and Marshall College, 1983-85; Colgate University, B.A., 1987; Johns Hopkins University, M.A., 2000.

Cathy Alter Zymet

Addresses

Home—2511 Q St. N.W., Washington, DC 20007. *Office*—Bureau of National Affairs, 1250 23rd St. N.W., Washington, DC.

Career

Bureau of National Affairs, Washington, DC, senior copywriter.

Writings

LeAnn Rimes, Chelsea House (Philadelphia, PA), 1999. *Backstreet Boys,* Chelsea House (Philadelphia, PA), 2000. *Ricky Martin,* Chelsea House (Philadelphia, PA), 2000.

Sidelights

Cathy Alter Zymet told *SATA:* "I have a weak chin. I do poorly at sports. I cling to my husband because I am afraid he will wander away. I should be attached to an analyst's couch. I can't do so many things, but I know I can write.

"Being able to write is not the same as being a writer. I hope that, with each chance that I get to tell a story, to expand my own or someone else's world, I get still another chance to improve as a writer. Developing my voice, engaging an audience, learning rules and then breaking them, making sense—these are the skills that constant writing encourages.

"I don't write books to impress my friends, to bandy the books around at swishy cocktail parties, or to stand in front of an Ivy League classroom. It is my intent to write simply because writing will help me become a better writer."

Biographical and Critical Sources

PERIODICALS

Booklist, April 15, 1999, "Series Roundup," p. 1538.

ON-LINE

Amazon.com, http://www.amazon.com/ (August 26, 2000).

Cumulative Indexes

Illustrations Index

(In the following index, the number of the *volume* in which an illustrator's work appears is given *before* the colon, and the *page number* on which it appears is given *after* the colon. For example, a drawing by Adams, Adrienne appears in Volume 2 on page 6, another drawing by her appears in Volume 3 on page 80, another drawing in Volume 8 on page 1, and so on and so on . . . .)

YABC

Index references to *YABC* refer to listings appearing in the two-volume *Yesterday's Authors of Books for Children,* also published by The Gale Group. *YABC* covers prominent authors and illustrators who died prior to 1960.

C

X

Y

Author Index

The following index gives the number of the volume in which an author's biographical sketch, Autobiography Feature, Brief Entry, or Obituary appears.

This index includes references to all entries in the following series, which are also published by The Gale Group.

YABC—*Yesterday's Authors of Books for Children: Facts and Pictures about Authors and Illustrators of Books for Young People from Early Times to 1960*

CLR—*Children's Literature Review: Excerpts from Reviews, Criticism, and Commentary on Books for Children*

SAAS—*Something about the Author Autobiography Series*

C